THE CONTEMPORARY
MIDDLE EAST

THE CONTEMPORARY MIDDLE EAST

with special contributions by

ARTHUR GOLDSCHMIDT JR.

and

SHIBLEY TELHAMI

A WESTVIEW READER

edited by

KARL YAMBERT

Senior Editor, Westview Press

A Member of the Perseus Books Group

Copyright © 2006 by Westview Press, a Member of the Perseus Books Group.

Published in the United States of America by Westview Press, A Member of the Perseus Books Group, 5500 Central Avenue, Boulder, Colorado 80301-2877, and in the United Kingdom by Westview Press, 12 Hid's Copse Road, Cumnor Hill, Oxford OX2 9JJ.

Find us on the world wide web at www.westviewpress.com

Westview Press books are available at special discounts for bulk purchases in the United States by corporations, institutions, and other organizations. For more information, please contact the Special Markets Department at the Perseus Books Group, 11 Cambridge Center, Cambridge, MA 02142, or call (617) 252-5298, (800) 255-1514 or email special.markets@perseusbooks.com.

Library of Congress Cataloging-in-Publication Data
The contemporary Middle East / edited by Karl Yambert; with special contributions by Arthur Goldschmidt, Jr. and Shibley Telhami.
p. cm.
Includes bibliographical references (p.) and index.
ISBN-13: 978-0-8133-4339-6 (pbk. : alk. paper)
ISBN-10: 0-8133-4339-9 (pbk. : alk. paper) 1. Middle East. I. Yambert, Karl.
DS44.C575 2005
956.05—dc22
2005027281

The paper used in this publication meets the requirements of the American National Standard for Permanence of Paper for Printed Library Materials Z39.48–1984.

06 07 08 / 10 9 8 7 6 5 4

For Hallie

CONTENTS

HISTORY AND BACKGROUND

Situated at the hub of Europe, Asia, and Africa, the Middle East is a crossroads of great strategic significance, both historically and looking forward into the future.

Within its regional unity, the Middle East possesses great cultural diversity. Differences of language, religion, and ethnicity create a complex mosaic of peoples.

Varieties of Arab nationalism—the belief that all Arabs do (or should) constitute a single political community—share a consistent distrust of the West, based on bitter historical experience.

ISRAEL AND PALESTINE

The year 1979 is significant in recent Middle East history for several events that continue to have repercussions today, including the Egyptian-Israeli peace treaty.

IRAQ AND IRAN

Among many other significant events, the year 1979 is important for the Iranian Revolution. The perceived threat of a new Shiite theocracy next door inspired Saddam Hussein of Iraq to invade Iran and begin the 8-year-long Iran-Iraq war.

Revolution has demonstrated that faith alone cannot solve the economic, social, and political problems of a modern society. A new generation of Iranians seeks to shape an Islamic society tolerant of democracy and human rights.

The US occupation of Iraq was predicated on unrealistic expectations about the ease and speed of the transition to democracy, and has been marked by infighting between the Department of State and the Pentagon.

To safeguard its strategic interests in the oil-rich Persian Gulf, the United States has pursued a policy of "dual containment," playing Iraq against Iran so that neither could dominate the bulk of the world's known oil reserves.

SAUDI ARABIA AND EGYPT

Saudi Arabia is ethnocentric and even xenophobic, but, paradoxically, it maintains close relations with the West, which in turn makes it a target for Islamist attacks.

The aftermath of the bombing of the World Trade Center on 11 September 2001 has caused both Americans and Saudis to reevaluate the long-standing relationship between their two countries.

PERSPECTIVES ON THE UNITED STATES AND THE MIDDLE EAST

PREFACE

THE MIDDLE EAST AFFECTS US ALL, oftentimes in ways that many of us are just beginning to appreciate. In just the past month (August 2005), the following stories from the Middle East have been featured prominently in world news reports:

- After 38 years of occupation, Israel withdraws from the Gaza Strip, razing 21 Israeli settlements in Gaza and another 4 in the West Bank. The question remains whether the Israeli disengagement will prove to be a step toward establishing a true Palestinian state that will also include the West Bank, or whether it will only help Israel consolidate its occupation of the West Bank.
- To prepare for a new constitutional government by year's end (2005), Iraqis struggle to draft a new constitution amid Sunni Arab protests that Shiite- and Kurdish-dominated regions might too easily split off from Iraq under the proposed plan for a federated state. Still to be seen is if Shiites will succeed in defining Iraq as an Islamic republic, with legislation based on Islamic law.
- Led by its newly elected president, Mahmoud Ahmadinejad, Iran defiantly confronts the West by refusing to halt its nuclear program, even as it faces the possibility of economic sanctions imposed by the Security Council of the United Nations. President Bush hints that military action against Iranian nuclear facilities might have to be considered.
- After a reign of 23 years, Saudi Arabia's 82-year-old King Fahd dies and is succeeded by his 81-year-old half-brother, Abdullah. The issue of succession after Abdullah remains open, as the kingdom grapples with the contradictory pressures of (on the one hand) modernization and cautious democratic reforms and (on the other hand) religious conservatism and domestic Islamic terrorism, aimed at undermining the House of Saud.

- Egypt prepares for its first-ever election with more than one presidential candidate. Despite widespread concerns about possible voting fraud, a top aide to President Hosni Mubarak insists that international monitors will not be allowed to observe the polling. Mubarak has ruled Egypt since 1981, making him the longest-tenured leader in the Middle East.

As a collection of sometimes provocative but always authoritative contributions by an impressive array of leading Middle East observers, *The Contemporary Middle East* provides students and instructors with an integrated and accessible introduction to selected topical issues of the Middle East. Even those readers with no previous background in the Middle East will find the volume an invaluable catalyst to their fundamental understanding of the current events in the region.

In order to illuminate basic topics in current Middle East affairs and in the relations between the Middle East and the United States, *The Contemporary Middle East* draws upon the work of a number of distinguished writers who have published with Westview Press. Incisive essays by noted scholars William Cleveland, Lawrence Davidson, Samih Farsoun, Calvin Goldscheider, Yvonne Haddad, Colbert Held, David Lesch, Ann Mosely Lesch, David Long, Phebe Marr, and Bernard Reich are complemented by the keen insights of former State Department adviser David Phillips, senior journalists Mark Huband and Thomas Lippman, and Pulitzer Prize–winning reporter Anthony Shadid. In addition, honored scholar, author, and teacher Arthur Goldschmidt Jr. provides an integrative opening essay, specially written for this volume; likewise, a new concluding chapter by a prominent commentator on Middle East matters, Shibley Telhami, candidly addresses commonly asked questions about the Middle East and United States today.

Instructors and students will also find the following attributes of the book especially appealing:

- ***Strategic Pairing of Topics***. The book is organized around related pairs of topics (Israel and Palestine, Iran and Iraq, Saudi Arabia and Egypt) in order to enhance student comprehension through comparison and contrast.
- ***Reiterative Pedagogy***. Key issues and events are addressed in varying contexts by the several chapters of *The Contemporary Middle East*, ensuring that students repeatedly reencounter those topics from a variety of perspectives. The result is that students gain an added appreciation of the interconnectedness of recent events around the Middle East.

- ***Additional Features***. Students and instructors alike will find the Select Bibliography by William Cleveland useful, as well as the reference materials in the Glossary, Brief Biographical Register, and Chronology. A concise summary opens each chapter, and the volume's several maps provide an essential sense of place.

The staff at Westview Press would like to thank all of the contributors to this volume. We acknowledge with especial gratitude the contributions and encouragement of Shibley Telhami and particularly, Arthur Goldschmidt Jr., whose active support exceeded our hopes and made this a better book than it would otherwise have been.

Karl Yambert
Westview Press

A Note on
Editorial Matters

Two chapters—the Introduction by Arthur Goldschmidt Jr. and Chapter 21 by Shibley Telhami—were specially commissioned for this volume. The remaining chapters, including the Select Bibliography by William Cleveland, have been condensed from materials appearing in a number of volumes recently published by Westview Press. The surprisingly few and minor editorial revisions necessary to preserve grammar and continuity in those shortened chapters have been made silently; other, possibly more significant, interpolations by the editor are acknowledged within square brackets.

The attentive reader will soon discern that certain Arab words are transliterated differently in different chapters. The spellings are original to each chapter; no attempt has been made to standardize spellings across chapters. Thus "Saddam Hussein" in one chapter may appear as "Saddam Husayn" in another, and "Gamal Abd al-Nasir" and "Gamal Abdel Nasser" are to be recognized as references to the same person. Likewise, "Shia," "Shi'a," "*shi'a*," and "Shiite" all denote the second-largest denomination of Islam, just as the code of Islamic ritual and law is variously labeled as "*Shari'a*," "Shari'ah," "*shari'a*," or "*sharia*." The Glossary, Brief Biographical Register, and Index attempt to take some of the alternative possibilities into account.

INTRODUCTION

Arthur Goldschmidt Jr.

HAVE YOU EVER GONE TO A MIDDLE EASTERN RESTAURANT—Arab, Turkish, Greek, Syrian, or Lebanese? If not, a real treat awaits you. If you have eaten in one you may have seen the word *meze* on the menu, probably under "Appetizers," and wondered what it meant. In Turkish the word corresponds roughly to what we call *hors d'oeuvres*. It is very common in Middle Eastern restaurants—and homes—to start a meal with an assortment of little dishes that may include *hummos* (chick peas mixed with sesame oil), *tabbouleh* (mint and parsley salad), pickled vegetables, stuffed grape leaves, hard-boiled eggs, and possibly pieces of *kebab* (grilled lamb or beef). These make up *meze* (or, in Arabic, *mazza*), which stimulates your appetite and often tells you what treats lie ahead in the feast to come. Middle Eastern Christians or Jews often wash down their *meze* with an alcoholic beverage like *arak* or *ouzo*. Everyone eats *meze* with pancake-shaped loaves of bread called *pita* in Hebrew and *khubz* in Arabic.

This book is *meze* in literary form. It introduces you to the endlessly fascinating study of the contemporary Middle East—with all its problems and promises—by exposing you to selected chapters of books that have been written for Westview Press by authors who are authorities in their specialized fields of Middle Eastern studies. Once you have read *The Contemporary Middle East* I hope that you will want to read some of these books in their entirety. When you have done so you will be on your way to becoming an authority on an area of the world that looms large in today's news, and it will be time to learn one or more of the languages and to spend time in some of the countries of the Middle East.

I am going to tell you a secret that probably most of the authors—and maybe even our Westview editor—do not know. The Press's founder, Frederick A. Praeger, one of the giants of twentieth-century American publishing, once told my wife and me that he planned to turn out a series of introductions to various aspects of the Middle East, including its history, geography, politics, and economics, and, lo, Westview Press did just that. Many of the authors whose works are excerpted on these pages, including myself, contributed to this effort. I hope that we—and others—will carry on his mission during the twenty-first century, which Praeger did not live to see.

David Long and Bernard Reich have been among the most prolific writers on the Middle East during the past three decades. Valuing Long's lucid descriptions of Saudi Arabia and Reich's cogent treatment of Israel, I have assigned *The Government and Politics of the Middle East and North Africa* in some of my classes. In a few pages they manage to encapsulate the basic facts about the main religions and ethnic groups that make up this diverse region, its resources, and its relationship to other countries and regions of the world. Much of what they write will be repeated in other parts of this reader. Chapter 1, taken from their book, gives you a good starting point and it will not overwhelm you with statistics or unfamiliar names.

Chapter 2, written by a retired diplomat and teacher, Colbert C. Held, expands on this theme of the Middle East's linguistic, religious, and ethnic diversity. Is Arabic the main language? Well, twelve of the sixteen countries covered in this reader speak and write mainly Arabic, and even in Iran, Israel, and Turkey, where other languages prevail, you can hear Arabic spoken in some places. On the other hand you can find people speaking Kurdish in parts of Iraq and Syria, Azeri Turkish in northwestern Iran, Nubian dialects in Upper Egypt, Armenian in a number of cities, and French in some Beirut neighborhoods. When as a teenager I accompanied my parents on a car trip to Iran, I studied in the backseat to learn some basic words and expressions for the countries that we visited. I assumed that I should consult the Turkish phrasebook in Turkey and the Persian one in Iran. Only much later did I realize that I should have kept on using that Turkish phrasebook in northwestern Iran! A visitor to Israel needs to learn Hebrew for the streets in Haifa and Tel Aviv but also Arabic for the market in Jerusalem's old city. And when we learn Arabic we must differentiate among its spoken dialects that vary from one region to the next, modern standard Arabic used in writing and lecturing, and the classical language of the Quran and the finest works of Arabic literature, also used by Muslims in ritual prayer.

While most Middle Eastern peoples are Muslims, Egypt, Lebanon, and Syria contain substantial Christian minorities having significant sectarian differences. As you probably know, most Muslims are either Sunni or Shi'ite (it would be more correct to write Shi'i, but the press prefers Shiite or Shi'ite; the word *Shi'a* is the name of the sect). Although Sunnis predominate, Iran, Iraq, and Bahrain are all preponderantly Shi'ite. Although the Jews, almost all of whom are now gathered in Israel, have fewer sectarian differences, they often divide on ethnic and political issues, as Colbert explains. Political differences *within* Islam, Christianity, and Judaism contribute to Middle Eastern tensions today.

You will also come to know some of the Middle East's main ethnic groups, which do not coincide with nationalities. Maps in classrooms and on television tend to be political and show national boundaries (which in the Middle East may be fictitious); we need more maps showing mountains, valleys, rivers, and deserts. We must also be able to locate Kurds, Armenians, and Palestinians. Political maps do not help us.

The disconnect between nationalism and nationality helped to inspire my chapter, "The Roots of Arab Bitterness," but I must admit that when I first wrote it in 1977 most scholars expected Arab nationalism to keep on gaining popular support among Middle Eastern Arabs, but this has in fact not happened. Arabs may still argue that they should constitute one political community (or nation) and ought to share a common government—the main goals of Arab nationalism. However, as Lawrence Davidson and I wrote in our latest edition of *A Concise History of the Middle East*, they are divided. We ascribe this division to various factors: alienation of citizens from their rulers; manipulation, control, or military occupation by foreigners; and the growing appeal of Islamism. Arab nationalism crossed religious boundaries; its pioneers and proponents included Christians as well as Muslims. They fought first to cast off Ottoman Turkish rule; later, the Arabs opposed French and British mandates in Southwest Asia and colonialism in North Africa and Egypt. They also struggled against Zionism, the movement to create a Jewish state in Palestine, most of whose inhabitants up until 1948 were Arabs. Our chapter shows you how the British made conflicting promises to the Arabs, the French, and the Zionists during World War I and how the postwar peace settlement divided the Arabs and left them feeling betrayed by the West. The Arabs of Iraq responded with a massive anti-British revolt that was suppressed with more severity than our chapter admits. Iraq long aspired to be to the Arabs what Prussia had been to the Germans; this attitude inspired Saddam Hussein's policies, as well as the current insurgency against the US occupation and the Iraqi government that it has established in Baghdad. You will learn more about the Iraq war in later chapters of this reader.

We often talk about a year, such as "1492" or "1776," as verbal shorthand for an important event that occurred during that time. David Lesch, who teaches at Trinity University in San Antonio, sees 1979 as such a year in Middle Eastern history and has written a book showing how it marked the turning point in various trends and issues. Called *1979: The Year that Shaped the Modern Middle East*, the book shows how three events of that year—the signing of the Egyptian-Israeli Treaty, the displacement of Iran's shah by the Ayatollah Khomeini, and the Soviet invasion of Afghanistan—had momentous consequences for the next quarter century in the Middle East. This excerpt is limited to the treaty, which ended Egypt's role as leader of the Arab fight against Israel, emboldened Israel to annex the Golan Heights and invade Lebanon, and inspired Iraq and Syria to compete for the leadership of Arab nationalism. The treaty's failure to promote meaningful Arab-Israeli negotiations over the Palestinian question eventually inspired the Palestinians living under Israel's occupation to rebel (the Intifada of 1987–1993). This led to the secret Oslo negotiations between Israel and the Palestine Liberation Organization and thus to their signing of the Declaration of Principles on the White House lawn in 1993, not far from the site of the 1979 treaty signing that set this course of events in motion. The same author has books coming out on Bashar al-Asad in fall 2005 and on the Arab-Israeli conflict in 2006.

The next chapter homes in on the Palestinians and their political development, complementing the treatment by David Lesch. Ann Mosely Lesch (no relation) had extensive field experience with Arab Palestinians while writing her Ph.D. dissertation and also as a field worker for the American Friends Service Committee. She later became professor of Political Science at Villanova University, president of the Middle East Studies Association, and in 2004 accepted the position of Dean of Humanities and Social Sciences at the American University in Cairo. The excerpt used here comes from her chapter in the textbook, cited earlier, that was edited by David Long and Bernard Reich. She has also written *Arab Politics in Palestine, 1919–1939* (Cornell University Press, 1979).

You may find it hard to study the Palestinians. "Palestine" as a political entity did not exist before it was created by the British after World War I; it was mainly a name used by Protestants for what other Christians called "the Holy Land" and Jews termed "the Land of Israel." Its people, whose numbers were difficult to count before 1918, would have seen themselves as Ottoman subjects, southern Syrians, Arabs (if they were among the few bedouins), or simply Muslims and Christians who happened to speak Arabic. Once they recognized the possible threat of Zionism to their livelihoods and political rights, they began to develop a political consciousness of themselves as Palestinians, but many espoused Arab nationalism and actively sought the support of neighboring Arab countries against the Jewish settlers or, after 1948, the State of Israel. Only in 1964 did they form the Palestine Liberation Organization (PLO), but the initiative came from a summit meeting of kings and presidents of the Arab states, and it was only after the Arab armies were defeated in June 1967 that the Palestinians emerged as a major force fighting against Israel. It took the Intifada of 1987–1993 to make the Israelis undertake secret talks with the PLO, or for this organization to recognize and deal with Israel for that matter. The Palestinians were not inherently anti-Jewish; their opposition to Jewish settlement and statehood grew out of their desire to preserve their control of the land and their own national rights.

Israel became an independent Jewish state in May 1948, but its existence was threatened by its Arab neighbors and it needed outside military and diplomatic support. As Bernard Reich, who teaches political science at George Washington University, explains, the US government has become Israel's main backer. From the 1960s to the 1980s, Washington's policies reflected the exigencies of the Cold War, in which it had to counter Soviet military and diplomatic support to Egypt, Syria, Iraq, and other Arab governments. More recently, it has vacillated between backing Israel as a bulwark against terrorism and purportig to be the honest broker in peace talks between Israel and the Palestinians. As Reich's chapter shows, Israel and the US have no formal alliance treaty but have often signed memoranda of understanding in order to coordinate their goals and their means of attaining them. At times, however, they have differed sharply because of policy differences or personality clashes between their leaders, many of which Reich describes in Chapter 6.

Understandably, some of the issues between Washington and Jerusalem relate to the Palestinians. In his authoritative textbook, *The History of the Modern Middle East*, William Cleveland relates the complicated story of how relations between Israelis and Palestinians deteriorated after their leaders signed that Declaration of Principles on the White House lawn in September 1993. Many reasons can be given for this gradual abandonment of the US-sponsored "peace process" by both sides. Cleveland, a Canadian historian who has also written intellectual biographies of several early Arab nationalist leaders, manages to show how the agreements signed by Israel and the PLO showed the weakness of the latter group, which was gradually losing its legitimacy in the eyes of most Palestinians. The unsuccessful July 2000 Camp David Summit of US President Bill Clinton, Israeli Prime Minister Ehud Barak, and PLO Chairman Yasir Arafat, followed by the controversial visit of Ariel Sharon to Jerusalem's Temple Mount, led to a renewed Palestinian Intifada, in which both Israel's soldiers and the Palestinian fighters used deadlier weapons and tactics than ever before. Israel's invasion of West Bank cities and accelerated buildup of Jewish settlements in the occupied territories highlighted Palestinian weakness and raised fears that continuing the "peace process" would ensure ongoing dominance by the settlers and lead at best to a truncated Palestinian state reminiscent of the South African "Bantustans" during the Apartheid Era. The Islamic militant group, Hamas, gained the popular support that Chairman Arafat was losing, in part because of its "suicide bombings" that so horrified Israel and its backers. The Israelis, increasingly anxious about their own security, elected Ariel Sharon as their prime minister and supported his hard-nosed policies against the Palestinians. Cleveland's chapter ends before the construction of Israel's "Security Fence" (which Palestinians call the "Apartheid Wall") that separated Israel's populated areas and some of the Jewish West Bank settlements from the Palestinians. The death of Arafat and the election of Mahmud Abbas as the new president of the Palestinian Authority have also occurred since this chapter was written, but the problems between the two sides remain and the fighting goes on.

Calvin Goldscheider, a sociologist who has written several books about ethnicity, immigration, and population, treats in Chapter 8 two cogent identity issues: the ties between Israel and the American Jewish community and the relationship between Israeli Arabs and other Palestinians and the Arab world in general. American Jews increasingly identify with Israel and its policies; Zionism (or what Goldscheider calls "pro-Israelism") seems to have eclipsed traditional religious observance. The growing assimilation of Jews into American society has been accompanied by rising rates of marriage between Jews and non-Jews. Jews used to assume that any coreligionist who married a Gentile ceased to be Jewish, but in recent years the non-Jewish partner has often converted to Judaism and the children have been reared as Jews (although Goldscheider provides no supporting statistics on this trend). Israeli Jews are much less likely to marry non-Jews and they tolerate more political control over Judaism than would be accepted by their American counterparts. Israeli Arabs suffer some forms of social and economic discrimination as non-Jewish citizens in a Jewish state, and some of them now tend to identify with the Palestinians under Israeli occupation. They also compete with them for the same jobs and admit that they enjoy some advantages as voting citizens that their Palestinian cousins lack. Understandably, Israel's Arab population, now close to 20 percent, would like the Israeli government to be less Jewish and more supportive of Palestinian political ambitions.

In Chapter 9 Samih Farsoun, the late professor of sociology at American University and founding dean of the American University of Sharjah's College of Arts and Science (he died suddenly in June 2005), brings us back to the Palestinians of the West Bank and the Gaza Strip. He recently published *Cul-*

ture and Customs of the Palestinians (Greenwood Publishing Group, 2004). In *Palestine and the Palestinians* he recounts the history of the Palestinian people from the beginning of the modern Zionist colonization of Palestine up to what he views as the failure of the Oslo-inspired "peace process" of the 1990s. In the chapter chosen for this reader, he reviews the Palestinian response to the evolution of Israel's policies and focuses on the reaction to Yasir Arafat's signing the Declaration of Principles in September 1993 and subsequent developments in the Palestinian-Israeli conflict. To Americans who get their news from US newspapers and electronic media, which stress Israel's concern for security from terrorism, it may seem surprising that the Palestinians care equally about their security from Israeli military incursions, loss of jobs in Israel due to border closures, and failure of the Palestinian Authority to protect them. Although this work takes you only to 1997, it is clear that already the Palestinian people were disillusioned with the "peace process" and very skeptical about the American role as a broker between them and the government of Israel. These perceptions help you to understand why Arafat and the Palestinians would later reject what the Western press regarded as the generous peace offers of Israel's Prime Minister Barak at the July 2000 Camp David Summit, an issue you have already read about in Chapter 7.

At this point, the reader shifts eastward to Iraq and Iran, two countries whose names sound alike in English and whose fates have at times been intertwined, but that are in fact quite different from each other. Phebe Marr has worked in the oil industry, for the US government, and academe. She now serves on the editorial board of the *Middle East Journal,* belongs to the Council on Foreign Relations, and writes and speaks frequently about Iraq. The selection from *The Modern History of Iraq* stresses the Iraqis' religious and linguistic diversity and the persistent influence of tribalism on a people who have, in fact, become mainly urban. This diversity, combined with the fact that Iraq belonged to outside empires until it was set up as a British mandate after World War I, has made it hard to build a nation without frequently resorting to dictatorial rule from Baghdad. Chapter 10 serves, therefore, as an introductory overview of a very troubled country.

Iran, although diverse linguistically and heavily tribal socially, has at least the advantages of traditional political unity and a strong identification with Shi'ite Islam. David Lesch, whose book *1979* has already been excerpted once in Chapter 4, "The Egyptian-Israeli Peace Treaty," also discusses the Islamic Revolution that brought the Ayatollah Khomeini to power, leading to the Iranian Hostage Crisis later that year and eventually to the Iran-Iraq War, the Iran-Contra Scandal, and Iraq's annexation of Kuwait, which set off the 1991 Gulf War. His concern is less with developments in Iran than with the international repercussions of its Islamic Revolution, especially how it changed the Middle East policies of the United States, which has become much more interventionist in the late twentieth and early twenty-first centuries.

Internal change in Iran since the revolution is the central concern of *Washington Post* correspondent Anthony Shadid in the excerpt taken from his *Legacy of the Prophet: Despots, Democrats, and the New Politics of Islam*. The Islamic Revolution of 1979 promised to create a republic governed by the Shari'a, meaning the rules and laws of Islam. Although this has not been achieved in the way that Khomeini might have hoped, the revolutionaries did succeed in raising the level of education and reducing income inequality. Iranians, increasingly an urban people, now yearn for more freedom and a higher standard of living, and the general feeling that Shadid observed when he lived in Iran was that the concept of an Islamic republic had failed. The population, which has almost doubled since 1979, is relatively young, in part because the revolutionaries tried to make women leave their jobs, marry young, and stay at home, all of which led to a higher birth rate, compensating for the loss of a slightly older generation as the casualties of the Iran-Iraq War. Although many Muslims in other countries backed the revolution, no country has managed to create and sustain a comparable regime, except possibly the Sudan. However, you probably know that the Iranian people elected a fairly conservative president in June 2005 to replace the liberal Khatami. The overall thesis of Shadid's book is that the United States should encourage the growth of democracy in the Middle East, even if popular opinion favors bringing Islamists to power. One of its attractive features, evident in Chapter 12, are his perceptive sketches of some of the Muslims whom he came to know during the years when he was living in the Middle East as an Associated Press correspondent.

Like Shadid, David L. Phillips has had extensive field experience, and in Chapter 13 he paints a devastating picture of the American failure to establish order and win local support following the invasion of Iraq in March 2003. Phillips had spent time in Iraqi Kurdistan and worked with the Iraqi exiles who had drafted a detailed plan for how to govern their country if Saddam Hussein was overthrown, a plan that the White House and Pentagon leadership ignored as it directed the invasion and occupation of Iraq. Ahmad Chalabi had persuaded many of the neoconservatives that the Iraqi people would welcome US troops and that it would be easy to set up a pro-Western government in Baghdad. As Phillips shows, the Americans were ill-prepared to manage Iraq and slighted experts who knew the Arabic language and Iraqi culture.

Shibley Telhami, Anwar Sadat Professor for Peace and Development at the University of Maryland, is also (like Marr) a fellow of the Council on Foreign Relations. In addition to *The Stakes*, from which Chapter 14 is taken, he has written many books and articles on US policy in the Arab-Israeli conflict and toward the Persian Gulf. He argues that the importance of Persian Gulf oil is likely to grow as other sources decline and as China's demand rises (as indeed it has since 2002, when Telhami's book was published). Since Iraq's invasion and occupation of Kuwait in 1990 the US government has spent billions of dollars on stationing troops and military equipment in the Gulf countries, without winning any additional support from their rulers and peoples. Telhami argues that working with those governments to strengthen their overall economies and educational systems would be a more effective way to defend their interests and to blunt the appeal of terrorism.

In Chapter 15 David E. Long, a retired Foreign Service officer who has written a book and several articles about Saudi Arabia in addition to this chapter from the political science textbook that he and Reich edited, argues that the kingdom is, on the whole, ably governed and modernizing. The Saud family, which has ruled parts of Arabia since the eighteenth century and most of it since 1925, is closely allied with the fundamentalist Wahhabi sect of Islam, but its power depends on its revenues from the sale of oil and on close military cooperation with the United States. Since the 9/11/2001 terrorist attacks, many sensational books and articles have appeared attacking Saudi society, education, financial support for terrorism, and Wahhabism; but Americans and Saudis still need each other and should reconcile their differences.

Thomas Lippman, a journalist who has also written books on Islam and on Egypt under Sadat, offers a slightly less optimistic view in Chapter 16, adapted from his conclusion to *Inside the Mirage: America's Fragile Partnership with Saudi Arabia*. This book, which draws on published documents, interviews, books, and articles, as well as Lippman's own experiences and observations, portrays Saudi Arabia's modernization as resulting from the discovery and exploitation of oil. This was achieved mainly under the guidance of Americans, although they were often baffled by Saudi culture and society. The chapter selected for this reader shows how the participation of Saudi nationals in the 9/11 attacks alienated many Americans and led to reprisals against innocent Saudis who sought education or business opportunities in the United States. The Americans who live and work in Saudi

Arabia have also declined in number, and those remaining have become less involved in the country. There are hopeful signs that the Saudis will evolve toward a more open and democratic government, but the influence of the Wahhabi religious leaders limits their room for maneuver, and US support for Israel against the Palestinians angers both the rulers and the people. The death of King Fahd and succession by his half-brother, Crown Prince Abdallah, in August 2005 took place quietly, but some editorialists echoed Lippman's concerns.

Saudi Arabia and Egypt are an interesting pair of countries to compare and to contrast. Both are Arabic speaking, Muslim, and predominantly desert countries. Egypt has westernized extensively during the past two centuries and has often been viewed as the political and cultural leader of the Arabic world, though overpopulation has hobbled its economy. Saudi Arabia used to be desperately poor but has become fabulously rich. Having modernized during the past sixty years, it is now respected—if not well liked—by Egyptians and other Arabs. The concluding chapter of my *Modern Egypt* tried to sum up the major political, economic, and social trends in the country under President Husni Mubarak. His leadership style is less flamboyant than those of Nasser or Sadat, leading to a relatively stable government, but popular anger over the economy, social conditions, the peace treaty with Israel, and dependence on the United States could flare up at any time (indeed, street demonstrations are taking place as I write). I hesitated to predict how long Mubarak or his policies will endure, or whether Egypt's Islamists will seize power. I still hesitate.

Mark Huband, London-based national security correspondent for the *Financial Times*, has written for *The Guardian*, *The Observer*, and *The Times*, and has reported on Africa as well as the Middle East. In *Warriors of the Prophet*, from which Chapter 18 is excerpted, Huband describes the Society of the Muslim Brothers, Egypt's oldest and best known Islamist organization. Before the 1952 revolution that toppled King Farouq and brought Nasser to power, the Brothers appealed to Egyptian Muslims of every class, owing mainly to its trenchant critique of westernization and its affirmation of Islamic values and institutions. Although fiercely suppressed by Nasser, it made a comeback in the 1970s and continues to function as a moderate Islamist movement. Huband interviews one of its senior leaders and describes the teachings of its founder, Hasan al-Banna, and its best known ideologue, Sayyid Qutb. Egyptians have exercised enormous influence over the rest of the Muslim world, and the Society of Muslim Brothers, including its youth movement and its terrorist Secret Apparatus, has been the model for similar groups in other Arab countries, as well as in Iran, Pakistan, Afghanistan, and Indonesia.

Yvonne Yazbeck Haddad is professor of Islam and Muslim-Christian Relations at Georgetown University and has written numerous books, including *Islam and the Challenge of History* (1982), *Islam, Gender, and Social* Change (1998), *Daughters of Abraham: Feminist Thought in Judaism, Christianity, and Islam* (2001), and *Not Quite Americans?* (2004). She has also edited books about Muslims in the United States and the West in general, and contributed to David W. Lesch, ed., *The Middle East and the United States* a chapter on Islamist perceptions of US policy that has become Chapter 19 of this reader. Having surveyed Islamist opinion in 1985 and 1989 and read widely in their writings, she finds that they have grown increasingly hostile to the United States because of its pro-Israel and anti-Palestinian policies. Additional reasons include the rapid and violent US reaction to Iraq's invasion of Kuwait in 1990 as contrasted with American indifference to Israel's occupation of Palestinian lands, the repressive treatment of Muslims in America since 9/11, and statements by leading Americans that demonize Islamism. Seemingly, they argue, it is acceptable for Israel to be a Jewish state, but not for Pakistan to be an Islamic one. Americans justify Israeli control of Jerusalem because the city is sacred to 15 million Jews, but ignore its importance to 1.2 billion Muslims. The Islamists conclude that the US government has declared war, not on terrorism, but on Islam. To protect their religion and way of life they aspire to bring back the caliphate (the Islamic community's early leaders were called "caliphs"), make the Shari'a the primary guide for Muslim behavior, strengthen the political ties among the world's Muslims, and ultimately avenge the injustices that have been wrought by American policy-makers.

The last part of this Westview reader is the concluding chapter of a new book by an author to whom you have already been exposed, Mark Huband. In *Brutal Truths, Fragile Myths: Power Politics and Western Adventurism in the Arab World* (2004) he contrasts what he views as a failing US policy toward the Arab states and peoples with the growing power and influence of al-Qa'ida and related terrorist groups. This chapter draws on the preceding one that depicts what the author views as a one-sided American policy favoring Israel over the Palestinian Arabs. He shows how American actions regarding Israel, Afghanistan, and most notably Iraq have undermined the Palestinian Authority, antagonized Arab public opinion, and failed to promote the security of the United States and other countries against terrorism (as we have seen recently in Spain, England, Israel, and Egypt).

Viewed overall, the readings selected for *The Contemporary Middle East* cover mainly the recent political history, aspirations, and grievances of the

Middle Eastern countries and some Islamist groups. They only tangentially treat economic and social development, cultural and intellectual trends, or the lives of ordinary people living in the Middle East. They do not cover Turkey, Lebanon, Syria, or most of the Persian Gulf states. Although some chapters discuss Israel and its concerns, most of the chapters deal with the hopes and fears of Arabs and other Muslims. Given the biases of the American news media, the major lobbies and pressure groups operating in Washington, and the political posture of the US government generally and the George W. Bush administration in particular, it is good for you to learn how American actions affect Middle Eastern rulers and peoples.

On the other hand, you should also learn some of the motivating factors behind the policies of the US government and Israel, the need to ensure the security of their citizens, the interests of oil companies and consumers, the promotion of democracy throughout the Middle East, and the importance of ending terrorism. For these aspects of your introduction to the Middle East, you can learn more from the speeches of President Bush and his top advisers, the information published by the Pentagon, and news reported by most print media and on most radio stations and television channels.

I believe that as we learn more about Arabs (including Palestinians), Israeli Jews, Iranians, Afghans, Kurds, Turks, Sunnis, Shi'ites, and other actors on the Middle Eastern political scene we will find that no group is totally right or wrong. Both scholars and journalists should observe the Middle East carefully and report what they find without bias or tendentious moralizing, but in reality we often do have biases. A careful reader can spot them best, not by what is written, but by facts or interpretations that an author has omitted. Only by learning as much as you can about the Middle East, and about the policies toward that region pursued by the United States and other interested outside governments, can you spot the omissions and weed out the biases and thus make reasoned judgments about what you hope will happen in the future. And, as Muslims say, *Allahu a'lam* (God knows best).

CHAPTER 1

THE MIDDLE EAST

David E. Long and Bernard Reich

Written shortly before Saddam Hussein of Iraq was removed from power by the US invasion of Iraq in 2003, Long and Reich's brief introduction outlines several of the chief parameters to the study of the Middle East. Among those is the very definition of the Middle East itself. The "core" Middle East includes the Arab nations of the Arabian Peninsula (Saudi Arabia, Yemen, Kuwait, Oman, United Arab Emirates, Bahrain, and Qatar) and the Fertile Crescent (Jordan, Lebanon, Syria, and Iraq), along with the Jewish nation of Israel and the stateless Palestinians. Turkey, which is Muslim but not Arab, is usually included as well. In terms of strict geography, Egypt is in North Africa, but it is an integral constituent of the core Middle East. Libya, Tunisia, Algeria, and Morocco are—like Egypt—also North African, Arab, and Muslim countries. Because of their geographic remove they are sometimes considered separately from the Middle East proper, but because of their ethnicity and their religion they are sometimes included as part of an "extended" definition of the Middle East. Iran is Muslim but not Arab, and its Shiite Muslim majority distinguishes it from most other Muslim states of the Middle East, which are commonly dominated by Sunni Muslims. Though sometimes assigned to "South Asia" or "Southwest Asia," Iran is usually considered part of the Middle East, particularly since it is a major oil-producing power in the Persian Gulf along with Iraq and Saudi Arabia.

David E. Long is retired from the US Foreign Service and has written extensively on Saudi Arabia and terrorism. Bernard Reich is professor of political science and international affairs at George Washington University with an expertise on Israel.

THE MIDDLE EAST as it enters the twenty-first century is a far different place than the one familiar to many students and observers of an earlier generation. The last half of the twentieth century saw monumental and dramatic change in a region beset by wars and revolutions, military coups and turmoil. But the region is also one of great accomplishment. There have been numerous changes of government and regime throughout the region and in many instances there has been a generational change in leadership. In some cases we have seen long-term leaders—King Hussein of Jordan, King Hassan of Morocco, and President Hafez al-Asad of Syria—replaced by members of a younger generation. Other long-term leaders remain with us, such as Muammar Qaddafi of Libya and Saddam Hussein of Iraq. [Saddam Husseim was removed from power as a consequence of the 2003 US invasion and occupation of Iraq. —Ed.]

Developments within the region have gone in several directions since our last edition. The Israeli-Palestinian negotiations that were moving ahead in a limited positive way as we published the last edition are increasingly marked by an Israeli and Palestinian retreat from negotiations to tension and clashes (some would even call it "war"). The diminished centrality of the oil-rich Gulf region has come full circle as the world oil market has finally recovered from a twenty-year glut.

A decade after the implosion of the Soviet Union, Russia continues to play a significant, though diminished, role in the area, primarily with Iran and Iraq. China has become more dependent on the oil of the Middle East, and the European powers have sought to remain engaged in the region's international relations at a level they had not done in decades. The United States continues as a dominant external power with substantial interests and involvement in the region.

Despite these changes, however, the Middle East of the twenty-first century retains many of the attributes that the region possessed throughout most of the previous century. Most, if not all, of its component states have acquired the characteristics that have increasingly become commonplace worldwide. The Middle East and North Africa continue to be a region of great strategic significance owing to their geographic location and their possession of most of the world's identified oil reserves. But it is a region that has also been affected by generational changes in leadership, by the impact of globalization, and by the impact of the Internet. Increasingly developments elsewhere readily crossed national boundaries even as each state retained its individual identity.

The term *Middle East* was coined at the turn of the twentieth century to refer to the Gulf area lying between the Near East and the Far East. Since then, *Middle East* has come to incorporate the older term, *Near East,* and *North Africa* as well. Politics has led to the inclusion and exclusion of various countries over time. Egypt, Israel, the Arab states of the Fertile Crescent (and the Palestinians), and the Arabian Peninsula constitute the core area. The remainder of North Africa, particularly the Magrib (Tunisia, Algeria, and Morocco), is sometimes considered separately. Because of their close Arab ties, however, we have chosen to

Map 1.1 The "core" Middle East (excluding countries in North Africa), showing international boundaries, country names, and capital cities. *Source:* Map 1-2 of Colbert C. Held, *Middle East Patterns: Places, Peoples, and Politics, Fourth Edition* (2006, Westview Press).

include those countries in this volume. Turkey lies in both Europe and Asia, but it is an integral part of the Middle East. For example, it has been a member of the North Atlantic Treaty Organization (NATO) for five decades but also has close ties with neighboring Arab states and shares an ethnic Kurdish problem with Iraq, Iran, and Syria. Similarly, Iran is sometimes grouped with Afghanistan and Pakistan as an extension of South Asia, but its location in the Gulf area and its identity as a major Middle East oil producer dictate its inclusion in the Middle East.

In the recent past, especially since the implosion of the Soviet Union, the region has often been extended to include the states of central Asia and the

Caspian region. We have chosen the more traditional approach, in part to ensure continuity with previous volumes but also because historical and political factors suggest the logic of our approach. We realize that our choice of countries is somewhat arbitrary, but we feel that it best represents the broadest group of countries exhibiting sufficient commonality to constitute a single region.

For centuries the Middle East has fascinated scholars and observers and has been the focal point of great-power attention. The region's strategic significance and the variety and importance of its political, social, and cultural heritage have generated this concern. Through the centuries the Middle East has had intense religious meaning for the peoples of the Western world. Judaism, Christianity, and Islam all originated in the area, and the most sacred holy places of these three monotheistic faiths are located there. In the latter half of the twentieth century occasional wars and superpower rivalry added to the region's strategic dimension. The overall importance of the region, however, is broader; that importance is tied to the region's location and to its primary resource—oil.

Situated at the hub of Europe, Asia, and Africa, the Middle East is a crossroads and a bridge. Historically it linked the trade routes connecting Europe with Asia and Africa. Today its location makes the Middle East a critical link in the communications network joining Western and Eastern Europe with Eastern Africa, the Indian subcontinent, Southeast Asia, the Far East, and Australasia. The Middle East's military importance is a direct result of its location; the region has long fascinated the powers interested in greater control of that portion of the world and the adjacent areas.

Oil is the major resource of the Middle East. It is abundant, of unusually high quality, and exported in huge quantities. It is an essential energy source for the industrialized states and for many of the developing states. The export and sale of Middle Eastern oil, at high prices, has generated a surplus of "petrodollars" in many of the oil-producing states, has contributed to area-wide economic growth, and has provided the leading producers with increased potential in the international financial community. The importance of Middle Eastern oil and the oil-producing countries' economic potential have combined to increase the concern shown for the Middle East by outside commercial and strategic-political interests.

This interest in the Middle East seems unlikely to abate. The ongoing efforts to achieve a settlement of the Arab-Israeli conflict continue to involve the major powers and numerous others in the Middle East. Furthermore, it seems likely that the dependence of both the industrializing and the industrialized world on Middle Eastern oil (and, increasingly, natural gas) will persist for the foreseeable future.

The states of the Middle East have a variety of political systems, each one reflecting its state's historical background, colonial experience (or lack of it), social and economic conditions, religions, geographical setting, climate, and population pressures. There is no single category that includes all these systems, which run the gamut of political structures and dynamics. Personalized one-man authoritarian regimes have coexisted in the region with Marxist regimes, monarchies, religiously oriented systems, and democratic regimes. However, the Middle Eastern governments perform the various functions of the standard political system, albeit with varying degrees of ability or success and in numerous and diverse ways. These differences in background and in existing conditions provide for variations in political life, structure, and style.

The very real differences that exist among the states of the Middle East should not obscure their similarities, such as the heritage of Islam, the presence of foreign influences, the concentration of leadership in the urban upper and middle classes, and the rise of new elites of technocrats and military officers. Throughout the Middle East, political life in the past few decades has been characterized by the shift from traditional to modern activity. The traditional family-based elites are either declining in power or have already been replaced in many of the political units in the area. A new salaried middle class is emerging as the most active political, social, and economic force, and leadership is increasingly passing into its hands. This group is made up of government and private-sector technocrats, university students, and middle-grade military officers. In many of the states the military forms the core of this new politically conscious middle class that is striving to modernize the state. Members of the military have assumed a modernizing role as a result of their training, skills, and motivation. The great majority of the population—the peasants and the workers—are only now beginning to enter the realm of politics.

Pan-Arabism and Islamism (commonly referred to as Islamic fundamentalism and/or political Islam) are integral parts of contemporary activity in the Middle East. In a sense they are complementary movements that have rekindled an Arab and Muslim identity among the diverse peoples of the area, which has affected both the foreign and the domestic policies of the Middle Eastern states. In the post–World War II era, for instance, pan-Arabism helped to determine the Arab response to Israel. It has also led to attempts at federation and economic cooperation among several of the Arab states. The Islamic heritage and revival have acted simultaneously as a revolutionary and a conservative force. In such countries as Saudi Arabia this force has helped to shape the response to modernization and Westernization by advocating an Islamic way of life in the face of change. At the same time, Islam has been a divisive force as differences between and among the various sects and traditions surface and intrude into politics.

CHAPTER 2

PEOPLES AND CULTURES OF THE MIDDLE EAST

Colbert C. Held

It may be tempting to think of the Middle East as uniformly Arab and Muslim, but, as the following essay makes clear, the Middle East comprises a great cultural diversity of ethnic groups, which are further fragmented by differences of language and religion. About half the population of the Middle East is not Arab, including notably the Turks of Turkey, the Jews of Israel, the Persians of Iran, and the Kurds, who have no nation of their own but who live in so-called Kurdistan at the mountainous intersection of Turkey, Iraq, and Iran. Likewise, though over half of the population of the Middle East speaks Arabic, and though Arabic is the national language of most countries in the region, large numbers of Middle Easterners speak Turkish, Farsi, or Kurdish instead of Arabic.

The Middle East is more Muslim than Arab: over 90 percent of Middle Easterners practice Islam. However, a fundamental and often rancorous division between Sunni and Shiite Muslims complicates any apparent unity of the region on the basis of religion. Furthermore, it should not be overlooked that a great many followers of Islam do not reside in the Middle East at all. In fact, the four nations of the world with the largest Muslim populations are (in descending order) Indonesia in Southeast Asia and Pakistan, India, and Bangladesh in South Asia.

Colbert C. Held is a former Foreign Service officer in the Middle East and a retired diplomat-in-residence at Baylor University. He is the author of Middle East Patterns: Places, Peoples, and Politics, *now in its fourth edition.*

IT IS THE CULTURAL DIFFERENTIATION AMONG PEOPLES—variations in language, religion, customs and dress, values, and historical experiences—that creates separate group identities and nations. Thus, examination of the mosaic of peoples, or ethnic groups, is a major component of this analysis of Middle East patterns. Cultural patterns are, in effect, shuffled three times. The two dominant cultural patterns, language and religion, deserve individual attention; sections on those patterns are followed by a survey of ethnic groups. Two salient points about the patterns of peoples in the Middle East are worth noting at the outset: Half of the population of the region is non-Arab, although twelve of sixteen countries are Arab states [Iran, Israel, and Turkey are not Arab, and Held is counting non-Arab Cyprus as well. —Ed.], and within its essential unity, Islam carries ethnic and political imprints and also has a number of sectarian variations. Thus, within its regional unity, the Middle East possesses great cultural diversity. When the extended Middle East states are considered, much greater diversity appears, which is one factor that hinders greater regional unity.

LANGUAGES

Language is the principal criterion for defining ethnic groups. The principal languages of the region are, in order of the number of speakers: Arabic, Turkish, Farsi, Kurdish, Azeri, and Hebrew (Map 2.1).

Arabic

Arabic is the national language of twelve of the sixteen countries of the region and is spoken by more than half the total population of the core countries, about 163.5 million people. It is spoken by an additional 81.2 million North Africans. Three levels of usage have emerged: (1) colloquial, informal spoken Arabic; (2) modern standard Arabic, or "newspaper Arabic," the more formal Arabic used in books and lectures; and (3) classical Arabic, the formal and highly conventionalized style based on the language of pre-Islamic poetry, the Quran, and the writings of the first few centuries of the Islamic era. Educated Arabs understand all three, but uneducated Arabs have difficulty understanding the two more formal levels. In addition, four major dialects of Middle East Arabic are generally distinguished: those of Egypt, Syria (western Arabic), Iraq (eastern Arabic), and the Arabian Peninsula. Significant differences of vocabulary and pronunciation exist among, and even within, these four dialects. One major example is the pronunciation in Egypt of the Arabic "j" *(jiim)* as a hard "g." Thus, *jabal* (mountain) is pronounced *gabal* in Egypt, which creates problems with the transliteration of place-names. Differences are even greater between the Arabic of Morocco and that of Syria.

Speaking Arabic as a mother tongue is the hallmark of being an Arab. Since it is the language of the Quran, the holy book of the Muslims, Arabic has a mystical quality for many Arabs. It has additional emotional overtones as the language

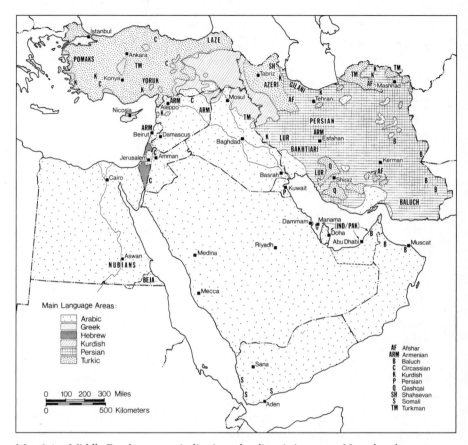

Map 2.1   Middle East languages, indicating ethnolinguistic groups. Note that the complexity of the pattern of languages is greatest in mountain areas, notably in Iran. *Source:* Map 4-3 of Colbert C. Held, *Middle East Patterns: Places, Peoples, and Politics, Fourth Edition* (2006, Westview Press).

in which speeches and documents on Arab nationalism are prepared. The written language even plays a central role in Middle East art, since it is used in traditional decorative motifs in lieu of the sometimes-proscribed human, animal, and vegetal motifs. Calligraphy is one of the highest forms of the fine arts in Islam.

Hebrew

Compared with Arabic, Hebrew is spoken in a relatively limited area by a comparatively small number of people, approximately 4.7 million. It should be noted that not all Jews in the region—not even all Israeli Jews—speak Hebrew. An ancient language, it was a major vernacular for more than 1,000 years in the traditional

Old Testament area of Israel. It ceased to be used as a working language centuries ago, but it was studied by biblical scholars and was used in Jewish communities as a ritual language, much as Latin, Greek, and Syriac are used in Christian church liturgies. It is also a scriptural language and therefore, like Arabic for devout Muslims, has a mystical quality for religious Jews. Ultrareligious Jews consider Hebrew so sacred that they reserve it for ritual use only and refuse to use it as a vernacular, employing Yiddish or other languages for everyday use.

Hebrew was revived in the late nineteenth century under the stimulus of Jewish nationalism, the Zionist movement, and because of the need for a unifying national language for the new Jewish immigrants to Israel in the twentieth century. Contemporary usage has required adaptation of old terms and the coinage of new scientific terms. Because the large number of Israeli scholarly and scientific writings would have such a limited readership in Hebrew, many are published in English.

Turkish

The best known of the Turkic languages, Turkish is spoken by the largest number of Turkic-language speakers. The national language of the Republic of Turkey, it was brought into the Middle East by Turkish tribes migrating from Central Asia in the tenth to thirteenth centuries. As Turkish speakers adopted Islam and settled Asia Minor, the language absorbed loanwords from Arabic and literary Persian.

Lacking a standard alphabet of its own, for 800–900 years Turkish was written in the Arabic alphabet of the Quran. In 1928, the Latin alphabet, with a number of diacritical marks borrowed from German and French, officially replaced the Arabic alphabet, and the language was "purified" of Arabic and Persian terms. In the Middle East, it is spoken throughout the Republic of Turkey and by the 207,000 Turkish Cypriots in northern Cyprus; otherwise, it is spoken by only small, scattered, family-sized groups in the Fertile Crescent area.

Azeri

Azeri (or Azerbaijani) is the second major Turkic language spoken in the Middle East, centered in northwestern Iran and adjacent areas in Iraq and the Republic of Azerbaijan. Regional variations of Azeri appear in the western Elburz and the southern Caspian littoral among the Afshar, Shahsavan (now called Ilsavan), and Qajar ethnic groups. Like Turkish, Azeri was carried by migrating Turkic tribes during the Abbasid Empire.

Other Turkic languages, spoken by several hundred thousand people each in Iran and Turkey, include Qashqai (spoken by Turkic tribes in the southern Zagros

Mountains of Iran) and various Turkmen dialects spoken by scattered peoples in the Anatolian-Iranian mountains and basins and in small areas in northeastern Iraq. Still other Turkic languages are the national speech of peripheral states: Azeri in Azerbaijan, Turkmen in Turkmenistan and extreme northern Afghanistan, Uzbek in Uzbekistan and northern Afghanistan, Kazakh in Kazakhstan, and Kirghiz in Kyrgyzstan.

Farsi (Persian)

The primary Indo-Iranian language of the Middle East is Farsi, a name taken from the ancient Iranian province of Fars. After Arabic and Turkish, Farsi is spoken by the third-largest language group in the region. The Persian languages were brought to the Iranian Plateau more than 1,500 years before Turkic languages were heard in the area. After the Muslim conquest of Iran in the seventh century, Persian, like Turkish, incorporated hundreds of Arabic loanwords and adopted a slightly modified Arabic script.

Farsi is the primary language of Iran, although nearly half of the Iranians speak a mother tongue other than Persian—Azeri, Kurdish, Gilaki, Luri, Baluchi, Arabic, and others. However, as the official language and the language used by the mass media, government, educational institutions, and most Iranian writers, Farsi is increasingly used as a second language by minority groups. Persian literature has a rich history dating from the Zoroastrian scriptures, the Avesta, written before 500 BCE.

Kurdish

The Indo-Iranian language spoken by the second-largest number of people in the core Middle East, Kurdish is used across a geographical range extending from the streets of Beirut eastward, through its main concentration of more than 20 million speakers in the mountains of Kurdistan, and into the remote valleys of Afghanistan. The pattern of Kurdish speakers exploded into a major factor in the Iraq crisis after mid-2003. The language is grammatically and lexically distinct from Persian. Reflecting the extension of Kurdistan into several hegemonies, Kurdish is written with the Arabic alphabet in Iraq, the adapted Arabic alphabet in Iran, and the Latin alphabet in Turkey.

RELIGIONS

At first glance, the pattern of religions appears simple: Islam embraces all but about 8 percent of the people of the core Middle East. This pattern, however, is complicated by the interwoven and disunited segments of Islam, by the basic divisions within Islam between Sunni and Shii Muslims, and by the splintering of Shii sects.

Divisions within the general Christian religion, which developed its early structure in the Middle East, are even more numerous. Differing theological interpretations resulted in major schisms, which were later only partly mended by the church in Rome, until more than a dozen sects claimed sole possession of Christian truth.

Several million Jews are now concentrated in Israel, where ethnic and sectarian subdivisions periodically dispute such issues as conversion and observation of the Sabbath. Ancient or syncretic religions—Zoroastrian, Yazidi, Mandaean, Bahai—constitute small Middle Eastern minorities.

Religious divisions have long played, and at the present time increasingly play, significant cultural-political-geographical roles in the Middle East. In recent decades, political instability and social violence have increasingly devolved from intensification of religious and ethnic consciousness. In turn, political polarization resulting from religious fervor has inflamed communal feelings and weakened national bonds. The increasing linkages between politics and religion have been a cause of growing apprehension since the 1970s, and especially after 9/11.

A familiar and significant aspect of the Middle East is that it is the birthplace of the world's three major monotheistic religions, all three of which worship the same God, whether called Yahweh, God, or Allah: Judaism, Christianity, and Islam (Map 2.2). Judaism and Christianity both originated in the hill area between the Mediterranean coastal plain and the Jordan Valley, and Islam originated 700 miles/1,125 km to the southeast in hills that lie inland from the Red Sea coast. As Judaism borrowed from Mesopotamian and Canaanite traditions, so Christianity evolved from Judaic traditions and others of the region, and Islam borrowed heavily from Judaism, Christianity, and local traditions in the Hijaz. In the Middle East in 2003, Muslims numbered about 297 million, about 92 percent of the population of the region. Christianity was the second-largest religion, with approximately 13 million adherents, and Judaism third with approximately 5 million.

Islam

The name *Islam* is Arabic for "submission," that is, submission to God's will, and a Muslim is "one who submits." The term "Muhammadan," sometimes used instead of "Muslim," may be misleading, since it may suggest a parallel with

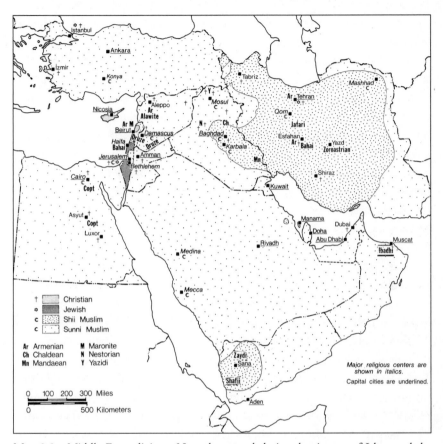

Map 2.2   Middle East religions. Note the overwhelming dominance of Islam and the concentration of Shiism in Iran and southern Iraq. *Source:* Map 4-4 of Colbert C. Held, *Middle East Patterns: Places, Peoples, and Politics, Fourth Edition* (2006, Westview Press).

"Christian" in the sense of worship of Christ, whereas Muslims do not worship Muhammad. They do revere his teachings and consider him the Seal of the Prophets; that is, the last and greatest of the prophets.

The origins of Islam reflect a regional character. Mecca, the Arabian town in which Islam first evolved, was an important midway caravan post between Yemen and Syria. The importance of Mecca was enhanced by the presence of the Well of Zamzam, since water was scarce along Tihamah, the barren Red Sea coastal plain followed by the caravans. The town was also the site of an ancient shrine, the Kaabah, which contained an array of idols and also housed the revered Black Stone of Mecca (a meteorite). Mecca's rapid development in the sixth century stimulated intellectual exchange, as townspeople and Bedouins from the Hijaz mingled with the caravan travelers from Syria, Yemen, and other trade areas.

One Mecca merchant who was inspired by the ideas being discussed was Muhammad ibn Abdullah, a member of the Hashim clan of the Quraysh tribe. While meditating in a cave near Mecca, he received what he later explained were dictations from the Angel Gabriel of the Holy Word of the one God. Preaching his revelations, Muhammad denounced the idols in the Kaabah shrine and thereby reduced Mecca's tourist trade. Harassed by Mecca merchants, Muhammad and his followers—the original Muslims—emigrated to Yathrib, 210 miles/340 km north of Mecca. Yathrib later became known as al-Madinat al-Nabi (the City of the Prophet), or simply al-Madina (the City), and today is commonly known as Medina. The year 622 CE, when the migration to Medina occurred, became the first year of the Islamic calendar. Muslim years, reckoned on the lunar system (which makes them eleven days shorter than Gregorian calendar years), are designated as *anno Hegirae* (AH), year of the *Hegira* (Arabic *hijrah* = flight).

In Medina, the Prophet recited dictations from the Angel Gabriel to his followers until his death in 632. These recitations were assembled in 651 into the Muslim scriptures, the Quran (Koran), meaning "recitation," which plays a central role in Islam. Accepted by Muslims as the precise Word of God that links God and believers, the Quran uses poetic language that reflects the Hijaz desert region and village and Bedouin traditions, just as the Old and New Testaments refer to the desert and nomadic traditions of Sinai and the Syro-Palestinian area.

Translation of the Quran from Arabic was long forbidden, since that would mean altering the direct Word of God, and converts to Islam perforce had to learn the Arabic language in order to understand the scriptures. As Islam spread throughout the Middle East and North Africa to Spain and into Central Asia (Map 2.3), the Arabic language also spread, with crucial historical and political-geographical consequences.

The Muslim place of worship is the mosque (a corruption of the Arabic *masjid,* "place of worship"). Each mosque has an exterior minaret and interior *mihrab,* which indicates the direction worshippers should face to pray, toward Mecca. Over the centuries, thousands of Muslim shrines have also been built by local groups; they are interesting and moving features in many otherwise-barren landscapes.

Although, like all religions, Islam has been elaborated into a complex and subtle body of theology, both its essential message and practice are simple and straightforward. This basic simplicity is one of the religion's appeals to its rapidly growing adherents. Its one fundamental essential is that a new convert express

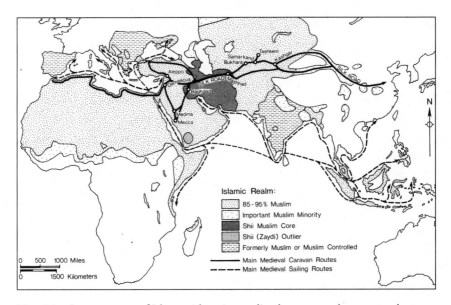

Map 2.3   Present extent of Islam, with major medieval caravan and sea routes that contributed to the spread and persistence of Islam. *Source:* Map 4-5 of Colbert C. Held, *Middle East Patterns: Places, Peoples, and Politics, Fourth Edition* (2006, Westview Press).

and believe the *shahadah,* or profession of faith: "There is no god but God; Muhammad is the messenger of God," a translation of the euphonious Arabic *La ilaha illa Allah; Muhammadun rasulu Allah.* The *shahadah* and four additional primary obligations constitute the five pillars of Islam, which have profoundly affected regional character in the Islamic world: *salah,* devotional worship or prayer five times a day while facing toward the Kaabah, the House of God, in Mecca; *zakah,* religious tax (and *sadaqah,* voluntary almsgiving, as additionally meritorious); *sawm,* fasting during the holy month of Ramadan, ninth month of the Muslim year; and the *hajj,* the pilgrimage to Mecca.

The Quran also underlies the *Sharia,* the sacred law of Islam, which covers all aspects of the lives of Muslims—not only religious and private but also political and public, social and economic. Sharia still plays an important role in the law of several Middle East countries—notably Saudi Arabia, Qatar, and Iran—and complements the more Westernized legal codes of countries such as Egypt, Syria, and Iraq. Resurgent Islamic fundamentalism, which has received so much attention since 9/11, has brought a renewed interest in Sharia law, especially since it has at various times been in conflict with modern secular trends in the region.

Islam was for many centuries both religion and government, and when the Sharia was compiled, it combined religious and civil matters. The caliph (Arabic *khalifah* = successor) thus led both the community of believers (the *ummah*) and the Islamic state. Although subsequent schisms within Islam placed severe strains on this unity of religion and state, resurgent Islamic fundamentalism—Islamism—has revived ferment for Islamized control in several states, from Morocco to Afghanistan and Pakistan.

The most momentous schismatic dispute within Islam occurred with the seventh-century division between Sunni and Shii. This split has precipitated wars, assassinations, civil conflict, and rancor in the Middle East, North Africa, and Central Asia for more than 1,300 years and is having intensified repercussions in the area today. The Sunnis (or Sunnites) consider themselves the original, Orthodox Muslims and have always been in the overwhelming majority. They believe that caliphs could be chosen by leaders of the *ummah* and were secular leaders only. The Shii (or Shiites or Shiah)—*shiat* Ali, "partisans of Ali"—evolved as a separate sect beginning in 657. They believe that only descendants of Muhammad, through his daughter Fatima and his son-in-law Ali, were legitimate successors to the Prophet. To Shii, these successors are divinely guided, sinless, infallible religious leaders (*imams*) with authority to interpret the Prophet's spiritual knowledge. This fundamental theological schism has accentuated political, social, and cultural divisions not only historically but also currently—perhaps as bitterly today as at any time in the past—in Iraq particularly, but also in Lebanon, Yemen, Saudi Arabia, and Bahrain as well as in the peripheral state of Pakistan.

Christianity

Middle East Christianity embraces more than a dozen sects centered on the spiritual and ethical teachings of Jesus of Nazareth, who is believed to have lived and taught in Palestine 2,000 years ago. In the Occidental world, calendar years are designated, with an inadvertent error of about four years, as *anno Domini* (AD), indicating years that have elapsed since the birth of Jesus. This term is often replaced by CE (Common Era).

Although other religions believe in the messianic concept, the Christian religion preaches, as a central belief, that Jesus was the long-awaited Messiah (Greek *Christos* = "the anointed," anglicized to "Christ"). The early apostles compiled his teachings in the Gospels (good tidings) and added their own preachings and letters. Assembled, these writings form the New Testament (New Covenant), the main scriptures of the Christian religion, which is coupled with the Old Testament to constitute the Holy Bible of Christianity. Even in its early years, Christianity incorporated influences from the region's several cultures—Jewish, Greek (Hellenistic), Roman, and Aramaic.

By New Testament accounts, Jesus was acclaimed during his three-year ministry in the area of Judea, Galilee, and neighboring places. However, only a few of his followers, mainly converted Jews, remained faithful after his crucifixion by the Roman authorities. In 66 CE, when the Christian Jews of Jerusalem refused to support the Jewish revolt, Jewish leaders rejected the Christians and their concepts.

After this breach between Christians and Jews, the apostle-missionaries decided to preach to the Gentiles (Greeks) in Asia Minor and Syria. Antioch became the first Christian center, soon followed by Edessa farther east. Suppressed for 200 years by Roman authorities as inimical to their own religion and positions, Christianity was officially permitted by the Edict of Milan (313), was accepted by Emperor Constantine after he moved his imperial capital from Rome to Constantinople in 330, and was made the state religion of the Roman Empire in 380. A series of ecumenical councils, convened in or near the eastern imperial capital of Constantinople, debated heresies and sought unity but engendered fragmentation. Christianity was the dominant religion of the Middle East outside Iran and the Arabian Peninsula between the fourth and the sixth centuries, but today it is a minority faith in an overwhelmingly Muslim area.

The approximately 13 million Christians in the Middle East are divided among more than a dozen Orthodox and Catholic sects, with a minority divided among a number of Protestant churches. Although exact figures are unknown, it is possible to estimate the number of Christians in the main groups. Coptic Christians, about 10 percent of the population of Egypt, form the largest group. The Maronites, concentrated in Lebanon, make up the second-largest group, and a variety of Christian groups constitute approximately 38 percent of the Lebanese population. In Syria, Christians constitute about 6 percent of the population to form the third-largest Christian group of the Middle East. The fourth-largest group is found among a variety of sects in northern and northeastern Iraq, where mountains shelter numerous relict groups—non-Christian as well as Christian. The fifth-largest group of Christians, and the greatest concentration of Greek Orthodox in the region, is in Cyprus, where they constitute about three-fourths of the island's population, and nearly 100 percent of the population of south Cyprus. Finally, Turkey, Iran, and Jordan each have Christian minorities (more than 400,000 in Turkey and Iran, and 210,000 in Jordan).

Judaism

The oldest of the three great monotheistic religions, Judaism evolved over a period of more than 1,500 years, a development that is the theme of the Old

Testament. It takes its name from Judah, the southern kingdom at the time of the northern kingdom of Israel, from which the term "Jew" is also derived. The patriarch Jacob, through his religious name, Israel, became the traditional eponymous ancestor of the *Bnai Yisrael,* or Children (literally, "Sons") of Israel.

Judaism's roots lie in the traditions of a seminomadic Aramaean tribe that is personified in the patriarch Abraham. In the Old Testament narrative, the original group migrated from southern Mesopotamia, Ur of the Chaldees, up the Euphrates Valley to the Harran and then, traditionally in about 1700 BCE, southwestward to the southern hills of Canaan. Abraham's grandson Jacob (Israel) migrated to Egypt, where his descendants multiplied; later, traditionally in the thirteenth century BCE, they made their "Exodus" from Egypt to claim Canaan. In the biblical account, it was out of the tribal growth and development of the *Bnai Yisrael* during the Exodus that evolved the elements of the monotheistic religion that came to be known as Judaism. It revolved around the one God (Yahweh), the covenant between God and the people of Israel, the comprehensive law, and for many Jews, the land.

Missionary activity among the Hebrews (referred to as Jews after the fifty-year Babylonian Exile) following the return of many exiles in 538 BCE reflected the belief in Israel's election by God to mediate divine blessings to all nations. By the time of the birth of Jesus, Judaism was winning many converts in the Roman Empire. However, after the Romans destroyed the temple in Jerusalem in 70 CE and dispersed the Jews from Palestine, Jewish missionary activity almost ceased. Particularism and separatism, as opposed to universalism, increasingly characterized Judaism, which became a token religion in its original territory for more than eighteen centuries.

Different interpretations of the Torah (the Law, the first five books of the Old Testament, also called the Pentateuch) and the Talmud (a body of commentary and guidance) have led to various groupings within Judaism. In modern times, Judaism embraces such groups as the ultra-Orthodox Hasidim (which means "those who are pious"), Orthodox Judaism, Conservative Judaism, Reform Judaism, and the Reconstructionists. Neither Reform Judaism, which seeks to liberalize Orthodoxy and bring Judaism into modern Western life, nor Conservative Judaism, seeking a middle position, achieved recognition in Israel until the 1970s. Bitter debate continued in the early 2000s, both in Israel and among Israeli religious authorities and American Jewish leaders, regarding the status of Conservative and Reform Jews.

The debate is especially relevant to the "right of return" of liberal Jews and of Jews converted by liberal rabbis. Nevertheless, Judaism has not experienced the degree of institutionalized sectarian fragmentation suffered by Christianity and Islam. Reimplanted in its native locale in the mid–twentieth century, Judaism has become for many of its adherents a belief system that is quite different from its original theology. Surveys have shown that only a minority of Israeli Jews actually practice Judaism, and distinctions must be drawn among Jews, practitioners of Judaism, Zionists, and Israelis.

Ethnic Groups

Aspects of Middle East language and religion patterns may now be merged in a survey of ethnic groups of the region. This survey of peoples examines four major ethnic aggregates—Arabs, Turks, Persians, and Jews—and briefly discusses related smaller groups associated with each major group.

Arabs

Even with the diversity of traits and the distribution over vast distances of this largest Middle East group, the ethnic identity of the Arabs is one of the basic realities of the pattern of peoples in the region. Numbering about 159 million, not only are Arabs the overwhelmingly dominant ethnolinguistic group in the twelve Arab countries of the sixteen core states, they also include at least 1 million nationals in each of three more of the countries—Israel, Turkey, and Iran—and are numerically negligible only in Cyprus. And in the five Arab countries in the extended region of North Africa, they number an additional 81.2 million.

All Arabs share two cultural elements, and most share a third. First, the Arabic language provides an element common to all Arabs, despite variations in dialect. As the language of the Quran, it has deep religious and cultural significance for most Arabs. Second, the Islamic cultural heritage embodied in architecture, design, calligraphy, and art provides a common history for Arabs—Muslim and Christian, orthodox and heterodox, Bedouin and city-dweller, Syrian and Qatari, Moroccan and Egyptian. The region's Islamic heritage underlies modern Arab political identity, a relevant factor in many modern problems and conflicts. Third, since more than 92 percent of Middle East Arabs are Muslim, Islam as a religion links the majority of them.

Copts

Coptic ethnic identity derives primarily from the Coptic religion. Numbering about 10 percent of the population of Egypt, Copts are the largest non-Muslim ethnic group in the Middle East, a remnant of the ancient Hamitic Egyptians who converted to Christianity. Practicing endogamy and segregation from other Egyptians and from invaders, they have preserved their Monophysite Christianity as well as a sometimes-disputed genetic physical kinship with the early Egyptians. The Coptic language survived as the vernacular until supplanted by Arabic 1,000 years after the Islamic conquest. Outside the urban centers of Cairo and Alexandria, the Copts are concentrated in Upper Egypt, in Asyut and Luxor.

Maronites

Like the Copts, Maronites are differentiated primarily on the basis of their religion. However, their geographical isolation in the Lebanon Mountains has encouraged independence and endogamy, producing cultural differentiation and substantial political autonomy. Arabic supplanted Syriac during the eighteenth century as a working language, and ties with the French (Franks) during the Crusades and the mandate years (1920–1943) promoted the use of French as a second language. The determined separatism of the Maronites has been a compelling dynamic in Lebanese political-geographical events.

Oppressed for their adherence to a Christian heresy, the Maronites left Syria in the tenth century and concentrated in the Lebanon Mountains around Qadisha Gorge. Their cooperation with the Crusader invaders alienated them from the Muslim population, and a small group of Maronites left with the retreating Crusaders to settle in Cyprus, where a small community remains. Thousands of Maronites emigrated from Mount Lebanon around 1900, and emigration increased after the 1950s because of the civil conflict in Lebanon. An estimated 700,000 Maronites remain in the Levant, the overwhelming majority of them in Lebanon but a few in Cyprus and Syria.

Druzes

Druze identity also originated in religion, with cultural and physical differentiations developing over the centuries. Although originating in Egypt, the Druzes won adherents in the Mount Hermon area, where they are still centered. Additional contemporary concentrations are in the Shuf area in central Mount Lebanon and in the Jabal al-Druze (officially now Jabal al-Arab) of southern Syria.

As heretics, the Druzes were alienated from other Shii Muslims, as well as from their Sunni Muslim neighbors, and clashed with the Maronite Christians as both groups migrated into central Mount Lebanon 1,000 years ago. Rejected by their neighbors, the Druzes separated themselves through endogamy. On one hand, their fierce sense of independence and separatism contributed to their military orientation, which was exhibited against the Crusaders, against the Maronites in the 1840s–1850s and 1958, and in the 1975–1991 civil conflict in Lebanon. On the other hand, Druzes in Israel generally accepted the new Jewish government in 1948–1949, and they have been the only Arabs permitted to serve in the Israeli army. Even so, Druze-Israeli relations deteriorated as a result of Israel's annexation of the Golan Heights in 1981 and the Israeli army's occupation of southern Lebanon in 1978–2000.

Alawis

The Alawis are also primarily distinguished by their religion, and they too have developed distinct cultural attributes through segregation and endogamy. They are concentrated in and around the Jabal al-Sahiliyah in northwestern Syria and constitute about 11 percent of the population of that country.

The Alawis have preserved no ancient language and use Arabic regularly. Although criticized by other Syrians for their cooperation with French-mandate authorities between the two world wars, after World War II the Alawis were trusted in the army and in government because of their minority status. A climax of the group's role came in 1969, when Syrian Air Force General Hafiz al-Asad, an Alawi, seized power in Damascus. He held the presidency from 1971 until his death in June 2000, when he was succeeded by his Alawi son. In religion, but not necessarily in other characteristics, the Alawis are similar to the Alevis in Turkey.

Turks

The second-largest ethnolinguistic group in the core Middle East (after the Arabs), ethnic Turks number about 62 million, somewhat more than one-third of the total number of Turkic-speaking peoples of the world. Generally, Turks speak Turkish as a primary language, are Muslims (90 percent are Sunni), claim a Turkish heritage, and are patriotic about the Republic of Turkey. Culturally, they combined Persian, Arab, Byzantine, and Anatolian cultural elements with their former nomadic Central Asian culture. Turks, Tatars, and Turkmen are difficult to differentiate, despite distinctive characteristics, partly because of intermarriage and cultural assimilation.

Four groups of Turks in the Middle East can be identified on the basis of cultural and geographical differences. First, the Anatolian Turks in Asia Minor are a thorough biological mixture of earlier Anatolian peoples. Second, the Rumelian Turks (from Rum, meaning "Roman," or European) are European

Turks who remained in Europe after Ottoman days but later returned to Turkey. More than 400,000 were expelled from Greece in exchange for a similar number of Greeks from Turkey after World War I, and many other scores of thousands later arrived in Turkey from Bulgaria, Romania, and Yugoslavia. Along with ethnic Turks from Bulgaria came about 150,000 Pomaks, most of whom were Bulgars who converted to Islam during Ottoman control of the Balkans. Now highly Turkified, they live in western Anatolia. Third are descendants of the Ottoman Turks who remained in various areas of the Middle East that were detached from the Ottoman Empire after World War I. They are steadily becoming Arabized. Fourth is a similar group, the 207,000 Turkish Cypriots, who live in northern Cyprus, most of whom are descendants of Ottoman Turks who moved to the island after the Ottoman conquest in the early sixteenth century. However, Cypriot Turks have been joined by more than 50,000 Turks from mainland Turkey since 1974, along with 35,000–40,000 Turkish troops.

Persians

Persians are numerically the third-largest ethnolinguistic group in the Middle East, after Arabs and Turks. Indo-Iranians immigrated into the mountains and basins south and southwest of the Caspian Sea during the second millennium BCE. One branch migrated southeastward into the Indus Valley and evolved into the Hindus, and other groups halted in the rugged folds of the Zagros Mountains and settled in western Iran. Those south of the Caspian evolved as Medes (or Medians), and those in the southern Zagros became Persians. They called themselves Aryans (nobles) and named their new mountain and basin homeland after themselves—Iran.

Evolving for a thousand years in the folds of the Zagros, the Persians emerged as a unified sedentary people in the sixth century BCE and built an unprecedented empire. Although they were later defeated by Alexander the Great and then overwhelmed by Arab Muslims in the seventh century, the Persians repeatedly restored a power base on the intermontane Iranian Plateau. Since World War I, the Persians have become the leading ethnic group in Iran and fill most government, industrial, professional, and cultural positions. By the 1970s, most educated Persians spoke French or English in addition to Farsi, and many have been educated in the United States or France; however, after the Islamic Revolution, the authorities discouraged Westernization and forced a return to Islamic fundamentalism.

More than 95 percent of Persians adhere to Shii Islam, for nationalistic as much as for theological reasons. A small but significant number of Persians are

Zoroastrians and Bahais. Persians live throughout Iran. They make up the majority of the population in many of the foothills, valleys, basins, and plateaus, and they predominate in the cities of Hamadan, Qom, Tehran, Shiraz, and Kerman.

In addition to the approximately 34 million Persians in Iran (about half the population), another million live on the west side of the Gulf, in the Qatif and al-Hasa oases in the Eastern Province of Saudi Arabia (where they are Arabized), and around the Shii shrines in Iraq. Wherever they live, but especially in Iran itself, Persians proudly differentiate themselves by their language, Shii religion, history, 2,000 years of literature, and distinctive arts. The cleavage between Persians and Arabs along the Zagros piedmont has periodically been reignited over the centuries, most recently in the bloody 1980–1988 Iran-Iraq War.

Kurds

The fourth-largest ethnolinguistic group in the Middle East, the Kurds occupy a centuries-old mountain homeland, the politically fragmented Kurdistan, which embraces an irregular area at the junction of and comprising parts of Turkey, Iraq, and Iran (see Map 2.1). The Kurds not only predominate in Kurdistan but also intermingle with neighboring Azeris and Armenians and with Turks, Turkmen, Arabs, and others. Both the total Kurdish population and its distribution among the three countries that share most of Kurdistan can only be estimated and are debatable. Kurdish leaders claim much higher numbers than are accepted by officials and scholars. Reasonable figures as of 2004 suggest a total of 24 million Kurds in "Kurdistan"—11.5 million in Turkey, 5 million in Iraq, and 6 million in Iran—plus another 1.5 million Kurds who live in northern Syria, Armenia, Lebanon, central Anatolia, the central Zagros Mountains, and the Elburz and Kopet mountains.

Language, heritage, culture, and a fierce sense of independence combine to define Kurdishness, along with physical derivation; many Kurds consider themselves descendants of the Medes, while others believe they were formerly part of the Lur. Most Kurds are Sunni Muslims, which separates them from the Shii Persians, but some Kurds in Iran and parts of Iraq have become Shii. Retaining a tribal structure, the Kurds are settled farmers, herdsmen, and townsmen, becoming increasingly urbanized. Especially in their core mountain home area, the Kurds have traditionally resisted outside authority. Those in upper Mesopotamia have notably battled for self-government, especially in 1974–1975, during the 1980s Iran-Iraq War, during and after the 1991 Gulf War, and during the 2003 war in Iraq. Similarly, Kurds in Turkey engaged in a decade-long fight for recognition in which 30,000 died during the 1980s and 1990s. Both the historical and contemporary plights of the Kurds became the focus of intensive media coverage after the Gulf War of 1990–1991, and again during the 2003 war.

Jews

Following their early history narrated in the Old Testament, Jews were deported in the first century CE from most of Palestine by the Romans. In this second phase of the Jewish Diaspora (the first was the Babylonian Exile), Jews settled around the shores of the Mediterranean Basin. Sizable communities developed in several major Mediterranean coastal cities, including Alexandria, Egypt, which had a major Jewish community for more than 2,000 years until after World War II. Under the Ottoman Empire, Jews (like Christians) constituted a *millet,* and Jewish minority rights were sufficiently protected so that after 1492, tens of thousands of Sephardic (Spanish) Jews who fled the Spanish Inquisition settled in the Ottoman Empire. They thus became citizens of successor Arab states after 1918 and continued to receive the rights of *ahl al-kitab.*

Ashkenazi (German) Jews from Central and Eastern Europe have migrated to the Middle East comparatively recently, in the late nineteenth and twentieth centuries, especially in waves of immigration *(aliyah)* after World War II. After the establishment of Israel in 1948, most of the Jews in Middle East Arab countries also emigrated to Israel, and an estimated 300,000 Jews had left Egypt, Lebanon, Syria, Iraq, and Yemen by the early 1990s.

In spite of generally endogamous traditions, Jews arriving in Israel have exhibited physical differences related to their countries of origin in addition to variations in linguistic, political-geographical (or national), and ideological backgrounds. Subethnic divisions have emerged between Ashkenazi Jews and Oriental or Eastern Jews, including Sephardim. The *Sabras,* or native-born Israelis, form another subgroup. The continuing question, Who is a Jew? and the distinctions among observant Jews, nonobservant (or nonpracticing) Jews, *Halakic* Jews (strictly adherent to religious law), assimilated Jews, and even Christian Jews complicate problems of Israeli citizenship, especially in connection with the Israeli Law of Return. Of a world total of about 14.5 million Jews, about 5.4 million lived in Israel in 2004. About 35,000 more lived in the rest of the Middle East (out of a pre–World War II 1 million), mainly in Iran and Turkey.

Armenians

The Armenian people date back more than 3,000 years, to about the time the Hittites disappeared from Anatolia. Prior to World War I, they were centered in the Lake Van area and surrounding eastern Anatolian mountains, long referred to as Armenia. The ancient kingdom of Armenia, located in the same area, was the first state to adopt Christianity as its official religion.

Although Armenians constituted an influential *millet* during the Ottoman Empire, relations between Armenians and Turks became hostile after 1878, and there were battles in 1895–1896, 1909, 1915–1917, and 1920–1921. In a confused, complex, and disputed series of circumstances (including Kurdish-Armenian-Turkish-Russian relations), hundreds of thousands of Armenians in central and eastern Asia Minor were persecuted, massacred, and deported; thousands more fled into adjacent lands for safety. A post–World War I Armenian republic was proposed by the Allies at the Paris Peace Conference, but a sustained independent Armenian Republic materialized only in 1991.

Although the Armenians have survived in their traditional homeland only under Ottoman and Russian overlords, they have maintained a strong separate ethnic identity, language, and religion, partly through a tradition of endogamy. They center on the church (usually Armenian Orthodox), school, newspaper, and businesses and have a cultural emphasis on education and achievement. Armenians in the core Middle East total about 900,000 and are distributed among Syria (more than 2 percent of the population, and found especially in Aleppo and Damascus), Lebanon, Jordan, Iran, Turkey, and Iraq. The Armenian Republic, successor after 1991 to the former Soviet Armenian SSR, has a population of more than 3 million, and thousands of Middle East Armenians have emigrated there as well as to the West since World War II.

CHAPTER 3

THE ROOTS OF ARAB BITTERNESS

Arthur Goldschmidt Jr. and Lawrence Davidson

Arab nationalism—the belief that Arab states should unite under a common government, particularly to resist non-Arab control—is a strong sentiment in the Middle East. Till the aftermath of World War I, many Arabs were under the rule of the Ottoman Empire, a situation causing some ambivalence for the Arabs, since their overlords in most cases were Turks or other non-Arabs, but they were also the Islamic coreligionists of their Arab subjects. Even though Arab nationalists strove to liberate themselves from Ottoman rule, there is detectable even today in Arab nationalist thought a strain of nostalgia for the lost days of a united and powerful Islamic empire that subsumed what are now separate, weak, and often bickering Arab nation-states. There is also some uncertainty about whether Arabs who seek a greater unity ought to consider themselves Arabs first, or Muslims.

The Arab experience with the West has, unfortunately, been less ambiguous. As summarized in the following essay, Arabs repeatedly dealt with Western powers that promised them independence from the Ottomans but that then established for themselves spheres of influence in the Middle East, formalized soon after World War I as mandates, which were little more than colonies in disguise. Even after their eventual independence, Arab states still remain sensitive to perceived instances of Western meddling and power-mongering in the Middle East. To many Arabs, the establishment of the state of Israel in Palestine in 1948 is a highly charged emblem of Western intrusion and duplicity, in that it violated previous Western assurances and displaced a great many Arab Palestinians, leaving them without homes, property, or a country of their own.

Arthur Goldschmidt Jr. is professor emeritus of Middle East history at the Pennsylvania State University and the author of Modern Egypt, Second Edition. *Lawrence Davidson is professor of history at West Chester University and the author of* America's Palestine *and* Islamic Fundamentalism. *Goldschmidt and Davidson are coauthors of* A Concise History of the Middle East, *from which this essay is taken.*

FEW TOPICS IN MIDDLE EAST HISTORY have generated as much heat—and as little light—as Arab nationalism. Few people are as poorly understood as today's Arabs. Even deciding who is an Arab or defining what is meant by Arab nationalism can easily get scholars and students into trouble, with both the Arabs and their detractors. Nevertheless, Arabs are becoming more politically active in the twenty-first century. In our analysis we may find that what is called Arab nationalism is now dissolving into many different movements, whose common feature is that they pertain to various Arabic-speaking peoples who seek to control their own political destinies. We must study these various manifestations of Arab feeling. And let us not fool ourselves: Arab feeling is strong and is likely to get stronger. It is also sometimes bitter, owing to some of the Arabs' unhappy experiences in the early twentieth century. Let us see what happened, and why.

ARAB NATIONALISM

What is Arab nationalism? Simply put, it is the belief that the Arabs constitute a single political community (or nation) and should have a common government. Right away we can see problems. There is no general agreement on who is an Arab. The current definition is that an Arab is anyone who speaks Arabic as his or her native language. This is not enough. Many speakers of Arabic do not think of themselves as Arabs, nor do other Arabs so regard them: Take, for example, the Lebanese Maronites, the Egyptian Copts, and of course the Jews born in Arab countries who went to live in Israel. A more eloquent definition is one adopted by a conference of Arab leaders years ago: "Whoever lives in our country, speaks our language, is reared in our culture, and takes pride in our glory is one of us."

Historical Background

As we review the history of the Arabic-speaking peoples, we must remember that they have not been united since the era of the High Caliphate, if indeed then. Moreover, except for the bedouin, they did not rule themselves from the time the Turks came in until quite recently. The very idea of people ruling themselves would not have made sense to Middle Easterners before the rise of nationalism. Settled peoples cared that a Muslim government rule over them, defend them from nomads and other invaders, preserve order, and promote peace in accordance with the Shari'a. It did not matter whether the head of that Muslim government was an Arab like the Umayyad caliphs, a Persian like the Buyid amirs, a Turk like the Seljuk and Ottoman sultans, or a Kurd like Salah al-Din and his Ayyubid heirs. Almost all rulers succeeded by either heredity or nomination; no one thought of letting the people elect them.

The Arabs Under Ottoman Rule. From the sixteenth to the twentieth centuries, most Arabs—all of them, really, except in parts of Arabia and Morocco— belonged to the Ottoman Empire. Even in periods of Ottoman weakness, the local officials and landlords were apt to be Turks, Circassians, or other non-Arabs. Since World War I, the Arab nationalists and their sympathizers have denounced the horrors of Ottoman rule, blaming the Turks for the Arabs' back-wardness, political ineptitude, disunity, or whatever else was amiss in their society. What went wrong? Were the Arabs under Ottoman rule better or worse off than they had been earlier? In fact, the Arabs' decline cannot be blamed on Istanbul. You can even argue that early Ottoman rule had benefited the Arabs by promoting local security and trade between their merchants and those of Anatolia and the Balkans. If the eighteenth-century Ottoman decline and overly zealous nineteenth-century reforms hurt the Arabs, the Turks within the empire suffered too.

In weighing these facts, historians have concluded that Arab identity played no great part in Middle East politics up to the twentieth century. Muslim Arabs felt that any attempt to weaken the Ottoman Empire was apt to harm Islam. Even under Sultan Abdulhamid, despite his faults, most Arabs went on upholding the status quo. Many served in the army or civil administration. A few were prominent advisers. They might have been proud of belonging to the same "race" as Muhammad, but this did not inspire them to rebel against the Turks, who were Muslims too.

Christian Arab Nationalists. Not all Arabs are Muslim. In the nineteenth century, as many as one-fourth of the Arabs under Ottoman rule belonged to protected minorities. Most of these were Christians, who were less likely than the Muslims to feel a strong loyalty to the empire. But we must pin down the time, the place, and the sect before we can discuss the politics of the Arabic-speaking Christians. The ones whose role mattered most in the birth of Arab nationalism lived in Syria, which then included most of what we now call Israel, Jordan, Lebanon, the Republic of Syria, and even parts of southern Turkey. From the 1820s on, American and French missionaries founded schools in Syria, as did the British, Russians, and other Westerners, though to a lesser extent. Inasmuch as Syrian Christians naturally sent their children to mission schools closest to their own religious affiliation, Maronites and Uniate Catholics tended to go to French Catholic schools and to identify with France. How could the Orthodox Christians compete? Distressed by the low educational level of their own clergy, some were converting to Catholicism or Protestantism and sending their children to the relevant mission schools.

The Americans helped solve their problem, but quite by accident they aided the rise of Arab nationalism. US mission schools, especially their crowning institution, the Syrian Protestant College (now the American University of Beirut), tried to serve students of every religion. But most of them hoped also to convert young people to Protestant Christianity. Because Protestantism has traditionally stressed the reading and understanding of its sacred scriptures, the Bible was soon translated into Arabic for local converts. Many of the early American missionaries learned the language well enough to teach in it and even to translate English-language textbooks into Arabic. Given this relative acceptance of their culture, many Arabs sent their children to American schools despite their Protestant orientation. The Orthodox Christians were especially apt to do so. This led to a higher standard of Arabic reading and writing among Syrian Orthodox youth, many of whom went into journalism, law, or teaching. Some became scholars and writers. Before long they were leading the Arabic literary revival, which turned into a nationalist movement, just as happened to literary movements in some European nations. The growth of nationalism was also fostered by such American ideas as using the schools to develop moral character, promoting benevolent activities, and teaching students to create new institutions to fit changing conditions. The commitment of students and alumni of the American University of Beirut, in both the nineteenth and the twentieth centuries, has nurtured the ideas of Arab nationalism and spread them among both Muslim and Christian speakers of Arabic.

Muslim Arab Nationalists. But Arab nationalism could not have won Muslim acceptance if all its advocates had been westernized Christians. The first breakthrough for Arab nationalism was the 1908 Young Turk revolution, which restored the long-suspended Ottoman constitution. Suddenly, men living in Beirut and Damascus, Baghdad and Aleppo, Jaffa and Jerusalem, were choosing representatives to an assembly in Istanbul. Hopes were raised for Arab-Turkish friendship and for progress toward liberal democracy in the Ottoman state. Arab hopes soon faded, though. Representation in Parliament favored Turks against the empire's many ethnic, linguistic, and religious minorities. The Young Turk regime resumed the centralizing policies of earlier Ottoman reformers. Consequently, the Arabs began to fear that their liberties, preserved by the weakness or indifference of earlier governments, would now be in danger. The imposition of Turkish as the language of administration and education especially angered the Arabs.

But how could they react? Not since Muhammad's day had large numbers of Arabic-speaking peoples mobilized politically to gain unity and freedom. What good would it do Syria's Arabs to overthrow Turkish rule, only to become, like Egypt, a dependency of a Christian power? Few Syrians (other than some Maronites) sought French rule. Nor did Iraqi Arabs want Basra [an Iraqi port city] to become (like Suez) a link in Britain's imperial transport and communications.

The result of these deliberations was a low-profile movement of a few educated Arabs aimed not at separation but at greater local autonomy. It included three different groups: (1) the Ottoman Decentralization Party, founded in 1912 by Syrians living in Cairo and seeking Arab support for more local autonomy instead of strong central control by the Ottoman government; (2) *al-Fatat* (Youth), a secret society of young Arabs who were students in European universities and who convoked an Arab Congress, held in Paris in 1913, to demand equal rights and cultural autonomy for Arabs within the Ottoman Empire; and (3) *al-Ahd* (Covenant), a secret society of Arab officers in the Ottoman army, who proposed turning the Ottoman Empire into a Turco-Arab dual monarchy on the pattern of Austria-Hungary. Each of these groups found backers among educated Arabs living in Istanbul, other Ottoman cities (notably Damascus), and abroad.

But do not overestimate the strength of Arab nationalism before World War I. Most Arabs were not yet Arab nationalists; they remained loyal to the Ottoman constitution that gave them parliamentary representation, and a government in which some Arabs served as ministers, ambassadors, officials, or army officers.

WORLD WAR I

The next turning point in the rise of Arab nationalism occurred when the Ottoman Empire decided in August 1914 to enter World War I on the German side. The CUP [Committee of Union and Progress, a Turkish nationalist party] may have been influenced by their exposure to German military advisers, but their main motives were to regain Egypt from the British and the Caucasus

Mountains from Russia. So strongly did the Ottoman government and people support the German cause that the sultan officially proclaimed a *jihad* against Britain, France, and Russia. All three had millions of Muslim subjects who, if they had heeded the message, would have had to rebel on behalf of their Ottoman sultan-caliph.

Britain and the Arabs

The British, especially those serving in Egypt and the Sudan, wanted to counter this pan-Islamic proclamation. Britain declared its official protectorate over Egypt. Some Ottoman army units reached the Suez Canal in February 1915, and one even crossed to the western side under cover of darkness. For three years, Britain had to station more than 100,000 imperial troops in Egypt—partly to intimidate the Egyptian nationalists, but mainly to stop any new Ottoman effort to take the canal, which the British now viewed as their imperial lifeline.

Britain responded by contacting an Arab leader in the Hijaz—namely, Husayn, the sharif and amir of Mecca. Let us explain these titles. A sharif is a descendant of Muhammad, of which there were many in the Hijaz, especially in the Muslim holy cities. Being protectors of Mecca and Medina conferred prestige on the Ottoman sultans; they lavished honors on the sharifs but also exploited their rivalries to control them. The various clans of sharifs competed for the position of amir (prince), which carried some temporal authority. During the nineteenth century, however, the Ottoman government had tried to strengthen its direct rule over the Hijaz, using an appointed local governor. Sharif Husayn, the leader of one of the contending clans (which he called the Hashimites, the clan of the Prophet himself), had long struggled with the Ottoman sultan and his governors.

The Husayn-McMahon Correspondence

In Cairo, Britain's new high commissioner, Sir Henry McMahon, wrote to the sharif of Mecca. Britain wanted him to rebel against Ottoman rule in the Hijaz. Husayn in turn asked for a pledge that the British would support the rebellion financially and politically against his Arab rivals as well as against the Ottoman Empire. If he called for an Arab revolt, it was not for the sake of changing masters. The British in Egypt and the Sudan knew from talking with Arab nationalists living there that the Hashimites could not rally other Arabs to their cause—given the power and prestige of rival families living elsewhere in Arabia—unless the Arabs were assured that they would gain their independence in the lands in which they predominated: Arabia, Iraq, and Syria, including Palestine and Lebanon.

Keeping these considerations in mind, the amir of Mecca and the British high commissioner for Egypt and the Sudan exchanged some letters in 1915–1916 that have since become famous and highly controversial. In the course of what we now call the Husayn-McMahon Correspondence, Britain pledged that, if Husayn proclaimed an Arab revolt against Ottoman rule, it would provide military and financial aid during the war and would then help to create independent Arab governments in the Arabian Peninsula and most parts of the Fertile Crescent.

Britain did, however, exclude some parts, such as the port areas of Mersin and Alexandretta (which now belong to Turkey), Basra (now in Iraq), and "portions of Syria lying to the west of the areas [districts] of Damascus, Homs, Hama, and Aleppo." One of the toughest issues in modern Middle East history is to figure out whether McMahon meant to exclude only what is now Lebanon, a partly Christian region coveted by France, or also Palestine, in which some Jews hoped to rebuild their ancient homeland. Lebanon was clearly west of Damascus and those other Syrian cities, whereas the area that we now call Israel was significantly less so. The Arabs argue, therefore, that Britain promised Palestine to them. But if the letter referred to the province of Syria (of which Damascus was the capital), what is now Israel and was then partly under a governor in Jerusalem may have been what McMahon meant to exclude from Arab rule. Not only the Zionists but also the British government after 1918, even McMahon himself, believed that he had never promised Palestine to the Arabs. However, since Britain cared more in 1915 about its French alliance than about reserving Palestine for the Jews, we think that Lebanon was the area excluded from Arab rule in the negotiations. Only later would Jewish claims to Palestine become the main issue.

The exclusion of these ambiguously described lands angered Husayn; he refused to accept the deal, and his correspondence with the British in Cairo ended inconclusively in early 1916. The Ottomans could have prevented any major Arab revolt, but for its authoritarian governor in Syria, Jemal, who needlessly antagonized the Arabs there. As a former naval minister and one of the three Young Turks who ruled the Ottoman Empire when it entered World War I, Jemal had led the Turkish expedition to seize the Suez Canal and free Egypt from British rule. Although his first attempt failed, Jemal planned to try again. He settled down as governor of Syria while he rebuilt his forces, but he did little for the province. Many areas were struck by famine, locusts, or labor shortages caused by the conscription of local peasant youths into the Ottoman army. Fuel shortages led to the cutting down of olive trees and also hindered the transport of food to the stricken areas. Meanwhile, the Arab nationalist societies met and pondered which side to take in the war. One of Husayn's sons, Faysal, came to Syria to parley with both the Arab nationalists and Jemal in 1915, but he accomplished nothing. Then in April and May 1916, Jemal's police seized some Arabs, including scholars who were not nationalists, arrested them for treason, and had twenty-two of them publicly hanged in Beirut and Damascus. The executions aroused so much anger in Syria—and among Arabs in general—that Faysal returned to Mecca, a convert to Arab nationalism, and convinced his father that the time for revolt had come.

The Arab Revolt

On 5 June 1916 Husayn declared the Arabs independent and unfurled the standard of their revolt against Turkish rule. The Ottoman Empire did not fall at once, but large numbers of Arabs in the Hijaz, plus some in Palestine and Syria, began to fight the Turks. But were the Arabs in these areas truly nationalists? Most probably did not care whether they were ruled from Istanbul or Mecca, so long as the outcome of the war was in doubt.

The Arab Revolt raged for the next two years. Guided by European advisers, notably T. E. Lawrence [perhaps better known as Lawrence of Arabia —Ed.], the Arab supporters of Amir Husayn fought on the Allied side against the Ottoman Empire. Working in tandem with the Egyptian Expeditionary Force (the British Empire troops advancing from the Suez Canal), they moved north into Palestine. While the British took Jaffa and Jerusalem, the Arabs were blowing up railways and capturing Aqaba and Amman. When Britain's forces drew near Damascus in late September 1918, they waited to let Lawrence and the Arabs occupy the city, which then became the seat of a provisional Arab government headed by Faysal. Meanwhile, the Ottoman army, now led by Mustafa Kemal (later Ataturk), withdrew from Syria. The Turks were also retreating in Iraq before an Anglo-Indian army. Late in October the Ottoman Empire signed an armistice with the Allies at Mudros. The Arabs, promised the right of self-determination by the British and the French, were jubilant. Surely their independence was at hand.

The Sykes-Picot Agreement

But this was not to be. The British government during the war had promised Ottoman-ruled Arab lands to other interested parties. Britain, France, and Russia drew up a secret pact called the Sykes-Picot Agreement (see Map 3.1). Signed in May 1916, it provided for direct French rule in much of northern and western Syria, plus a sphere of influence in the Syrian hinterland, including Damascus,

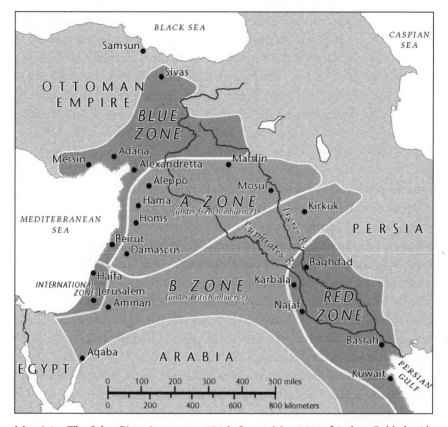

Map 3.1   The Sykes-Picot Agreement, 1916. *Source:* Map 13.1 of Arthur Goldschmidt Jr. and Lawrence Davidson, *A Concise History of the Middle East, Eighth Edition* (2005, Westview Press).

Aleppo, and Mosul. Britain would rule lower Iraq directly. It would also advise an Arab government to be given lands between the Egyptian border and eastern Arabia, thus ensuring indirect British control from the Mediterranean to the Persian Gulf. An enclave around Jaffa and Jerusalem would be under international rule because Russia wanted a part in administering the Christian holy places. The only area left for the Arabs to govern without foreign rulers or advisers was the Arabian desert.

Arab apologists claim that Amir Husayn knew nothing about the Sykes-Picot Agreement until after World War I. T. E. Lawrence was wracked by guilt because he had encouraged the Arabs on Britain's behalf, thinking that they would get their independence after the war, when in fact they were being manipulated by British diplomacy, if not duplicity. Lawrence's *Seven Pillars of Wisdom* is a readable book, and *Lawrence of Arabia* is a great film, but neither one is history. Amir Husayn did know about the Sykes-Picot Agreement. Not only had the Allied secret treaties been published by the communists after they had seized control of Russia in 1917, but Husayn learned about the agreement from Turkish agents trying to draw him out of the war and, indeed, from the British and French themselves. To Husayn, the advantages of directing an Arab revolt against the Turks, who had interned him for so long, outweighed the perils of Sykes-Picot, which the British claimed would not involve the lands he hoped to rule. To other Arab nationalists, this Anglo-French agreement betrayed their cause; worse, it was kept secret until after the war.

The Balfour Declaration

More public was a decision by the British cabinet to help establish a Jewish national home in Palestine, formally announced on 2 November 1917. This was the famous Balfour Declaration, so called because it appeared as a letter from the foreign secretary, Lord Balfour, to Lord Rothschild, titular president of Britain's Zionist Federation. We note here its salient points: (1) The British government would help set up a national home in Palestine for the Jews; (2) it would not undermine the rights or status of Jews choosing not to live there; and (3) it would not harm the civil or religious rights of Palestine's "existing non-Jewish communities." The Arabs' main objection to the Balfour Declaration was that they made up over nine-tenths of the population of what would later become Palestine. How could anyone create a home for one group of people in a land inhabited by another? Worse still, the inhabitants had never been asked if they wanted their land to become the national home for a people who would be coming from far away. Moreover, the Balfour Declaration never mentioned the political rights of non-Jewish Palestinians, a point that still stirs deep Arab resentment. If Britain tried to realize the Zionist dream of a Jewish state, what would be the political status of Palestine's Arabic-speaking Christians and Muslims? Did this document not contradict the Husayn-McMahon correspondence and other statements meant to reassure Arabs who had thrown themselves into the revolt against the Turks?

THE POSTWAR PEACE SETTLEMENT

How would these conflicting commitments be reconciled, once the war was over? In November 1918 the guns in Europe fell silent. Everyone hoped the diplomats would make a lasting peace. During the war, President Woodrow Wilson, the greatest statesman of the day, had proposed a set of principles called the Fourteen Points, upon which he wanted the Allies to build the peace once the war was won. He denounced secret treaties, urged self-determination for all peoples (specifically including those who had been under Ottoman rule), and proposed creating a League of Nations to avert future wars. When he came to Europe to represent the United States at the Paris Peace Conference, Wilson was hailed everywhere as a hero and savior.

But Britain and France, the Allies that had borne the brunt of the fighting and the casualties, were determined to dictate the peace. The defeated powers, Germany, Austria-Hungary, and the Ottoman Empire, could not attend the peace conference until it was time to sign the treaties. Russia (now a communist state that had signed a separate peace with Germany) was also excluded. Georges Clemenceau, who headed France's delegation, expressed a popular mood when he demanded that Germany be punished and that France receive control over all of geographical Syria. David Lloyd George, heading the British delegation, agreed that Germany should be punished, but he also sought a formula to bring peace to the Middle East without harming the British Empire. The Zionist (or Jewish nationalist) movement was ably represented by Chaim Weizmann. The Arabs had Faysal, assisted by Lawrence.

The King-Crane Commission

No one could reconcile the Middle Eastern claims of the Arabs, the Zionists, the British, and the French, but the conferees did try. Wilson wanted to send a commission of inquiry to Syria and Palestine to find out what their people wanted. Lloyd George accepted Wilson's idea, until the French said that unless the commission also went to Iraq (where Britain's military occupation was unpopular), they would boycott it. The British then lost interest, so the US team, called the King-Crane Commission, went alone. It found that the local people wanted complete independence under Faysal, who had already set up a provisional Arab government in Damascus. If they had to accept foreign tutelage, they would choose the Americans, who had no history of imperialism in the Middle East, or at least the British, whose army was already there, but never the French.

The King-Crane Commission also examined the Zionist claims, which its members had initially favored, and concluded that their realization would provoke serious Jewish-Arab conflict. Its report proposed to scale back the Zionist program, limit Jewish immigration into Palestine, and end any plan to turn the country into a Jewish national home. Faysal and his backers hoped that the

King-Crane Commission would persuade Wilson to favor the Arabs. Instead, Wilson suffered a paralytic stroke before he could read the commissioners' report, which was not even published for several years.

Allied Arrangements: San Remo and Sèvres

Contrary to Arab hopes, Britain and France agreed to settle their differences. France gave up its claims to Mosul and Palestine in exchange for a free hand in the rest of Syria. As a sop to Wilson's idealism, the Allies set up a mandate system, under which Asian and African lands taken from Turkey and Germany were put in a tutelary relationship to a Great Power (called the mandatory), which would teach the people how to govern themselves. Each mandatory power had to report periodically to a League of Nations body called the Permanent Mandates Commission, to prevent any exploitation. Meeting in San Remo in 1920, British and French representatives agreed to divide the Middle Eastern mandates: Syria (and Lebanon) to France, and Iraq and Palestine (including what is now Jordan) to Britain. The Hijaz would be independent. The Ottoman government had to accept these arrangements when it signed the Treaty of Sèvres in August 1920. By then the French army had already marched eastward from Beirut, crushed the Arabs, and driven Faysal's provisional government out of Damascus. The Arab dream had been shattered.

The Result: Four Mandates and an Emirate

What happened then to the Arabs of the Fertile Crescent? The French had absolutely no sympathy for Arab nationalism and ruled their Syrian mandate as if it were a colony. Hoping to weaken the nationalists, the French split Syria into smaller units, including what would eventually become Lebanon, plus Alexandretta (which would be given to Turkey in 1939), states for the Alawis in the north and the Druze in the south, and even Aleppo and Damascus as city-states. Lebanon's separation from Syria lasted because it had a Christian majority (as of 1921) that was determined to keep its dominant position. The other divisions of Syria soon ended, but the Syrians rebelled often against French rule, which in the 1920s and 1930s seemed likely to last (see Map 3.2).

The British were inconsistent backers of Arab nationalism, working with the Hashimite family. Husayn still ruled in the Hijaz, but the prestige he had gained from the Arab Revolt made him a troublesome ally for the British. He refused to sign the Versailles and Sèvres treaties, proclaimed himself "king of the Arabs," and later claimed to be the caliph of Islam. These actions so offended the British that, as the Saud family rose to power in eastern Arabia,

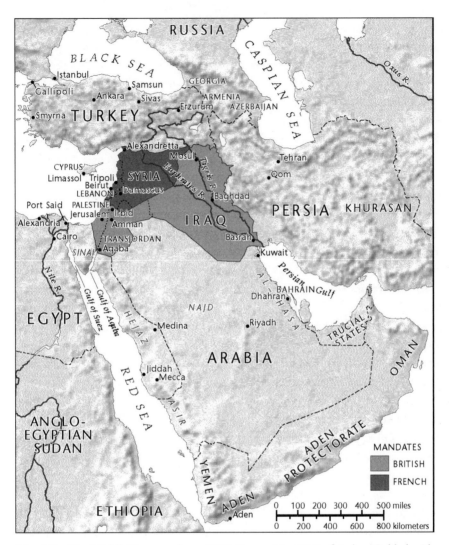

Map 3.2   The Middle East mandates, 1922. *Source:* Map 13.2 of Arthur Goldschmidt Jr. and Lawrence Davidson, *A Concise History of the Middle East, Eighth Edition* (2005, Westview Press).

they did nothing to stop the Saudis from marching into the Hijaz and toppling his regime in 1924. As for Iraq, British control led to a general Arab insurrection in 1920. Needing a strong man to pacify the Iraqis, the British brought in Faysal, who was approved in a rigged plebiscite as their king. Soon peace was restored. The British cooperated with Faysal's government and the local tribal shaykhs to speed Iraq toward independence. Ironically, Iraq, once among the poorest areas of the Ottoman Empire, became in 1932 the first state to graduate from its mandate status.

After Faysal was ousted from Damascus in 1920, Abdallah (another son of Sharif Husayn) gathered about 500 tribal Arabs, occupied Amman, and threatened to raid the French in Syria. Although he could not have expelled them, the British wanted to keep him quiet. Colonial Secretary Winston Churchill met Abdallah in Jerusalem and persuaded him to accept—temporarily—the part of Palestine that lay east of the Jordan River, until the French should leave Syria. This provisional deal was opposed by the Zionists, who wanted all of Palestine as defined by the 1920 peace treaties to be open to Jewish settlement and eventual statehood. France feared that Abdallah's new principality would become a staging area for Hashimite raids on Syria. No one expected this Emirate of Transjordan to last long, but it did. While the western part of the Palestine mandate seethed with Jewish-Arab strife, Transjordan became an oasis of tranquil politics and economic development.

CONCLUSION AND SUMMARY

The Arabs had been roused from centuries of political lethargy, first by American teachers and missionaries, then by the revolution of the Young Turks, and finally by the blandishments of Britain and France during World War I. They recalled their ancient greatness and longed to recover it. From the West they learned about rights and freedoms, democratic governments, and national self-determination. Led by descendants of the Prophet Muhammad, a few Arabs had dared to rebel against the greatest Muslim state left in the world, the Ottoman Empire. In its place they hoped to set up one or more states that would have the same sovereign rights as all other independent countries. They helped the British and French defeat the Ottoman Turks in World War I, but later on the Allies failed to keep the pledges they had made to the Arabs. In the lands of the Fertile Crescent, where Arabs were clearly in the majority, where they hoped to form independent states, where someday the Arab nation might revive its former power and glory, the victorious Allies set up mandates that were mere colonies in disguise. Even if Britain and France governed their mandates well, promoting education and economic development, the Arabs wanted to rule themselves. Instead of coming together, the Arabs found themselves being pulled farther apart. One area, Palestine, was even declared to be the Jewish national home, leaving in doubt the future of its Arab inhabitants. These were the roots of Arab bitterness, put down almost a century ago.

CHAPTER 4

THE EGYPTIAN-ISRAELI PEACE TREATY

David W. Lesch

Egypt has long played a leading role in Arab politics in the Middle East. The 1979 peace treaty between Egypt and Israel was therefore momentous in several respects. It established a precedent for the recognition of Israel and its right to exist by an Arab state. It estranged Egypt from other Arab nations and removed it from the possibility of Arab military alliances against Israel, as had occurred in the 1948–1949, 1967, and 1973 Arab-Israeli wars. And, with Egypt now on the sidelines in Arab confrontations with Israel, it created a power vacuum that Iraq in particular sought to exploit with regard to both the Arab-Israeli issue and the Persian Gulf, where Iraq uneasily neighbored a newly established radical Islamic regime of non-Arab, Shiite Muslims in Iran. The Iran-Iraq war of 1980–1988 can be considered one of the consequences of the Egypt-Israel peace treaty.

Likewise, with the removal of Egypt from any Arab battle plan, Israel became more aggressive in pursuing its interests, as evidenced by the 1981 bombing of a nuclear reactor in Iraq and the 1982 invasion of Lebanon to root out the Palestine Liberation Organization (PLO) guerrillas that operated from bases there.

Nevertheless, the Egyptian-Israeli peace treaty has endured and has reshaped the Arab-Israeli dynamic in the entire region. The 1993 Oslo accords between the PLO and Israel, and Jordan's peace treaty with Israel in 1994, have since followed Egypt's precedent and lessened Egypt's isolation in the Arab world.

David W. Lesch is professor of Middle East history at Trinity University in San Antonio. His several books include The New Lion of Damascus: Bashar al-Asad and Modern Syria, The Arab-Israeli Conflict: A History with Documents *(forthcoming), and* 1979: The Year That Shaped the Modern Middle East, *from which this essay is taken.*

A SINE QUA NON OF ARAB STRATEGY and hope for successfully confronting Israel for three decades prior to 1979 was the active leadership of Egypt, traditionally the most populous and militarily the strongest state in the Arab world. Without Egypt, the Arab states could not hope to defeat Israel in battle.

In essence, the 1979 Egyptian-Israeli peace treaty ended the Arab-Israeli conflict in its original form; that is, there would be no more coalitions of Arab states attempting to defeat Israel. An all-out regional conflict characteristic of the 1967 and 1973 Arab-Israeli wars was a moot point in the foreseeable future—or as long as Israel and Egypt remained on relatively good terms. From the Arab perspective, achieving the full and just rights of the Palestinians became infinitely more difficult the moment Anwar Sadat signed along the dotted line—the Arab world had just lost most of its leverage.

With Egypt on the sidelines after abandoning its traditional leadership role, both Syria and Iraq would desperately try to fill its shoes—and this could not be done together. The rivalry between Damascus and Baghdad would come out into the open after the peace treaty, affecting inter-Arab relationships and alliances to the present day and shaping the tremendously important decisions by Syrian President Hafiz al-'Asad to support Iran against Iraq in the Iran-Iraq war and to support the UN coalition against Iraq in 1990–1991. In fact, with Iraq's understandable preoccupation with matters to its east, Egypt's isolation within the Arab world, brought about by the peace treaty, immediately thrust Syria into the limelight in the confrontation with Israel.

Saudi Arabia took the lead in forming the GCC [Gulf Cooperation Council] not only because of the Iranian revolution and subsequent Iran-Iraq war but also because Egypt was no longer there as a partner, protector, or patron in the inter-Arab arena. The GCC could better represent Saudi and Gulf Arab interests than an Arab League bereft of the moderating and unifying influence of Egypt. Syria, with its self-anointed role as the last stand against Israeli expansionism and hegemony, began its trek to dominate the politics of the Levant, including Lebanon, Jordan, and the PLO [Palestine Liberation Organization].

Two countries seemed to be emboldened by Egypt's departure from the active playing field in the Middle East: Iraq and Israel. Subsequent actions by each, unfortunately, would have devastating results.

Iraq's situation in the wake of the Egyptian-Israeli peace treaty has largely been discussed earlier in this chapter [see Chapter 11 in this volume —Ed.]. Two emergency Arab League summit meetings convened in reaction to both the Camp David accords in September 1978 and the signing of the treaty in March 1979 were held in Baghdad, symbolizing the new inter-Arab future Saddam

Hussein hoped to mold. His pan-Arab charter enunciated in early 1980 supplied further evidence of his self-anointed leadership role within the Arab world. With the effective removal of Egypt from the Arab equation, there was no brake on Iraq's attempts to achieve its dual ambitions of obtaining a hegemonic position in both the Arab-Israeli and Persian Gulf arenas. Even if Egypt had not signed the treaty with Israel and had remained an active player in inter-Arab politics and diplomacy, Saddam Hussein's quest for power may still have gone unchecked. But without Cairo's moderating influence.

Predictions of doom and gloom by the many critics of the Egyptian-Israeli peace treaty were, at least in their eyes, proven true: Israel became much more aggressive. In 1981 Israel bombed a suspected nuclear reactor in Iraq, extended Israeli law over (de facto annexing) the Golan Heights, and accelerated the building of Jewish settlements in the remaining occupied territories, primarily in the West Bank. But it was the 1982 Israeli invasion of Lebanon that clinched the case. Critics of Israeli policy contend that the removal of Egypt from the Arab battle plan allowed Israel to pursue its interests vis-à-vis its northern neighbors, since the southern flank had been secured through peace. Whether this was a specific intention of the Egyptian-Israeli peace treaty is another matter. But surely the Israelis knew the isolation of Egypt would significantly weaken the Arab world as a whole. The PLO, now operating out of Lebanon and feeling left out in the cold by Sadat's separate peace, intensified their guerrilla operations against Israel— operations that were supported vigorously by countries such as Syria and Iraq.

To say that there was no provocation from Lebanese soil would misrepresent the situation. The Israelis had invaded southern Lebanon in 1978 in an attempt to clear out PLO positions that had been threatening northern Israeli settlements. However, what was anticipated as a sweep of PLO positions in south Lebanon, à la 1978, soon devolved into the Israeli government's ultimate goal: the removal of the PLO (and hopefully Syria) entirely from Lebanon and the placement of a Lebanese Maronite Christian ally as president who would sign a peace treaty with Israel—a purely offensive role that was uncharacteristic of the Israelis. That is, the major wars involving Israel up to that point, while taking preemptive action on a number of occasions, were all logically rationalized as necessary for the survival of the state. This was different, and most Israelis, especially as the Lebanese quagmire became evident, vehemently opposed this type of great power imperialism. Soon enough Lebanon became a proxy for almost every conceivable dispute in the area. The Iran-Iraq war, the Arab-Israeli conflict, and to a lesser extent, the superpower cold war would all be fought simultaneously in Lebanon. Implosion and destruction would be the natural results.

Some of the more infamous repercussions of the Israeli invasion have already been discussed, such as the Iran-Contra affair, the radicalization of the Shiite community in Lebanon that created an opening for the entrance of Iranian influence and the creation of Hizbullah [a militant Shiite party founded in Lebanon in 1982 to fight Israel — Ed.], and the subordination of the country to Syria, which after all was said and done, emerged as the victor and power broker. This was in no small part due to the decision by the Gulf war allies to essentially "give" Lebanon to Damascus as the quid pro quo for the latter's participation in the coalition against Iraq.

There has been a great deal of criticism aimed at the Egyptian-Israeli peace treaty over the years, much of which has revolved around the disruptive after-effects just discussed: the 1982 Israeli invasion of Lebanon and the Iran-Iraq war. But it has also been criticized—or more to the point, Anwar Sadat has been vilified in the Arab world—for essentially abandoning the Palestinian cause. The Camp David accords were composed of two frameworks for peace, one of which dealt with Egyptian-Israeli bilateral issues such as the return of the Sinai Peninsula, security measures, and normalization, and the other of which dealt with progress toward a comprehensive agreement, including the Palestinian issue. The major flaw in the accords was the fact that the two frameworks were not linked; that is, progress on the Egyptian-Israeli framework did not necessarily have to be matched by progress on the Palestinian issue. So while Begin and Sadat hurried to consummate the one, the other tended to languish and/or be ignored. So although the chances of a regional conflagration lessened as a result of the treaty, Palestinian frustration increased, combining with the PLO's predicament in Lebanon to produce the fury of the *intifada* by the late 1980s.

On the other hand, the Egyptian-Israeli peace treaty has lasted, despite many serious bumps on the road, particularly the Israeli invasion of Lebanon, which almost ruptured the relationship. Normalization of relations between the two countries has not occurred, certainly not anywhere near the extent many had hoped for when the treaty was signed. At times it seems the only element maintaining the peace is the close (some would say bounded) relationship each country has with the United States. The fact that Jordan signed a peace treaty with Israel in 1994, only a year after the Israeli-PLO accords, along with a plethora of other Arab nations that have de facto, if not de jure, established relations with Israel at a variety of levels, lessened the perceived isolation within the Arab world that many Egyptians felt in being the only Arab nation to make peace with Israel for fifteen years. Indeed, Egypt became a major partner of the United States in Washington's quest to broker peace agreements between Israel and the remainder of its Arab neighbors; in a sense,

Cairo was assuming its traditional leadership position in the Arab world, although this time around in a much different fashion than in the Nasserist era. But tension between Egypt and Israel has remained, and to some degree it has even grown in recent years as frustration over lack of progress on the Palestinian and Syrian peace fronts has led to further disillusionment in Arab quarters and as Cairo and Tel Aviv increasingly see each other, politically and economically, as regional rivals.

However, the peace treaty has somehow survived. And by doing so, it has, despite its acknowledged flaws, provided something of a template for succeeding Arab-Israeli agreements and destroyed psychological barriers. This last point may be the most important long-term development. As Saad Eddin Ibrahim states:

> Most Egyptians may be disenchanted, disillusioned, or outraged at Israeli behavior. Some organized political forces have continuously called for the abrogation of Camp David and the treaty, and several have called for the severing of relations and an end to normalization. But none has . . . suggested a declaration of war or a return to the state of war with the Jewish state. Camp David "normalized the feelings" of most Egyptians toward Israel across the spectrum—hate, anger, disapproval, acceptance, accommodation, and even disposition for cooperation—but no negation.[1]

In addition, the role of the United States in Middle East peace negotiations was inestimably enhanced. It became clear that Washington was the only power able to extract even the tiniest of concessions from Israel. Its role as a broker at some level in future Arab-Israeli negotiations, which today is somewhat taken for granted, became formalized with the treaty. As Quandt writes,

> Whatever one thought of the contents of the Camp David Accords, all saw that the United States had played an essential part. On his own, Sadat would probably have gotten far less from Israel, and indeed it is questionable whether a deal could have been struck at all. This realization raised the question of whether or not the United States could be brought back into the game to do for the Palestinians—and perhaps the Syrians as well—what it had done for Sadat.[2]

CHAPTER 5

THE PALESTINIANS

Ann Mosely Lesch

On 14 May 1948, following the United Nations approval of a plan to end the British mandate and partition Palestine into separate Arab and Jewish states, Israel declared its independence. The next day, armies from Egypt, Syria, Lebanon, Jordan, and Iraq invaded Israel in a struggle that resulted in the thorough defeat of the Arab forces. The result was the expansion of Israeli territory beyond its UN-sanctioned boundaries, the collapse of the United Nations plan for an Arab Palestinian state, and the creation of a population of over 700,000 Palestinian refugees who had fled their homes in the fighting.

The unresolved issue of a Palestinian homeland in the nearly 60 years since 1948 remains a sore problem in Arab-Israeli politics today. As the following essay points out, the creation of a Jewish state at the expense of an Arab majority, the failure to establish a state of their own for Arab Palestinians, and the denial of homes and other property to Palestinian refugees continue to be seen as grave injustices not just by the Palestinians themselves but by Arabs and Muslims throughout the Middle East. The Oslo Accords—the agreement between Israel and the Palestine Liberation Organization (PLO) in 1993—provided for a certain amount of Palestinian self-administration in Jericho, the Gaza Strip, and the West Bank, marking the first time that Israel has recognized Palestinian rights, at least in principle. Likewise, the PLO had also recognized in 1988 the right of Israel to exist. These are positive achievements even as many obstacles to a full and lasting peace remain.

The author of Origins and Development of the Arab-Israeli Conflict *(with Dan Tschirgi) among several other books,* **Ann Mosely Lesch** *is Dean of Humanities and Social Sciences, American University in Cairo and a past president of the Middle East Studies Assoc.*

THE PALESTINIANS ARE CENTRAL PLAYERS in the Arab-Israeli drama. The core issue involves the conflicting claims to the same piece of land made by Israeli Jews and Palestinian Arabs. Palestinians believe that the creation of a separate state for the

Jewish minority at the expense of the Arab majority, the denial of Palestinians' right of self-determination, and the inability of Palestinian refugees to return to their homes or regain their personal assets following their vain attempt to recover their homeland in 1948 all constitute a grave injustice that must be assuaged for the conflict to be resolved.

The terms of assuagement have evolved since 1948 when Palestinians sought the restoration of all their land and properties. After the Israelis occupied the rest of Palestine in 1967, the consensus evolved that any restoration must at least include a sovereign Palestinian state on the West Bank and Gaza, and that Israel must at least recognize its responsibilities toward the refugees in a satisfactory way.

A second major factor in the Palestinian quest for statehood is its ambiguous relationship with neighboring Arab states. From the outset, the Palestinian cause has been espoused as a pan-Arab cause. Nevertheless, each Arab government necessarily gives priority to its own foreign policy interests in how it approaches the Arab-Israeli conflict. Arab states have collectively given political, economic, and military support to the Palestinians, but when Palestinian priorities clash with their own interests, Palestinian interests perforce suffer.

THE OTTOMAN PERIOD

The contest for control over the land of Palestine can be traced to the late nineteenth century, when the area was part of the Ottoman Empire. At that time, the concept of Zionism began to gain support among European Jews, who suffered from discrimination. Some Jews concluded that the only way to end this discrimination would be to establish an independent Jewish state in their ancestral homeland. These Zionists organized the World Zionist Organization (formed in 1897), the Jewish National Fund, and offices in Jaffa and Jerusalem that aided immigrants.

As early as 1891, a group of Muslim and Christian notables in Palestine cabled Istanbul to urge the government to prohibit immigration and land purchases by European Jews, since the petitioners feared that large-scale immigration would displace the Arab residents. By the time that World War I broke out in 1914, the Jewish community in Palestine (Yishuv) comprised 11 percent of the total inhabitants (about 75,000 out of 690,000). That was a visible change since 1880, when the Yishuv was 6 percent of the population (35,000 out of 485,000). Nonetheless, the community's political influence inside Palestine was limited.

THE MANDATE PERIOD

The situation was transformed when the war ended. The British army and allied Arab forces defeated and dismantled the Ottoman Empire; the British army occupied Palestine. Arab leaders thought that Palestine would be included in the area promised independence by Sir Henry McMahon, the British high commissioner for Egypt, in letters he wrote during 1915–1916 to Sharif Hussein of Makkah. Hussein and McMahon had agreed that Arab independence would be recognized by the British if the Arabs launched a revolt against the Ottoman Empire. Indeed, young Palestinian men volunteered for the British and Arab forces on the assumption that this would hasten their liberation. The British, however, promised France that Palestine would come under international (European) rule and, in the Balfour Declaration, offered to support "the establishment in Palestine of a national home for the Jewish people." The declaration gave the Zionist movement its long-sought legal status. Even though the declaration included the qualification that "nothing shall be done which may prejudice the civil and religious rights of the existing non-Jewish communities in Palestine," it was clearly incompatible with the McMahon correspondence.

The Arab politicians in Palestine had assumed that they would gain independence when Ottoman rule disintegrated, either by establishing a separate state or by merging with neighboring Arab lands. They felt betrayed when Britain imposed the mandate and they immediately objected to the Zionist organization's privileged status as well as to the alienation of the land. In the 1930s, with thousands of Jews fleeing Nazi Germany, their fear of Jewish immigration deepened. The Jewish population grew from 11 percent of the population in 1914 to 28 percent in 1936. Immigration reached a high in 1935, when 60,000 Jews came to Palestine.

During the 1920s, the nationalist movement was led by Palestinian elites who, for the most part, employed nonviolent tactics. During the 1930s, however, radicalized youth and labor activists goaded the leadership to use strikes and violence to confront the British and the Zionists. Palestinians launched a general strike in 1936 that they sustained for an unprecedented six months. The strike was followed by a widespread rural revolt that lasted nearly two years.

After the British decapitated the Palestinian national movement and forcibly suppressed the revolt, Palestinians had no coherent organizations or skilled leaders with which to press for self-determination, and Arab states, for the most part still in the last stages of gaining their own independence, were too involved in domestic issues to be of much support. Jewish violence against the British and Arabs, on the other hand, increased. Finally, in 1947, the British, forsaking any hope of a peaceful settlement, announced that they were ending the mandate and turning Palestine over to the United Nations.

In November 1947, the United Nations passed a partition plan of its own that created a Jewish state on 55 percent of Palestine, even though Jewish land holdings comprised less than 7 percent of the total land surface or 12 percent of arable land. The Jewish state would have nearly as many Arab as Jewish residents. The Arab state would control only about 40 percent of Palestine; deprived of the best agricultural land and seaports, it would retain only Galilee, the central mountains, and the Gaza coast. The United Nations would administer Jerusalem, set aside as an international zone.

The Palestinians rejected the partition plan and tried to defend their homeland, but their village-based militias could not stand up to Jewish forces, who seized control of nearly all the areas assigned to the Jewish state during a five-week campaign in April and May, 1948. That campaign forced 300,000 Palestinians to flee from their homes in villages and cities such as Tiberias, Haifa, and Jaffa.

Following the British withdrawal on May 14 and the unilateral declaration of independence by Israel, Arab states sent in troops, and full-scale fighting erupted. They were no match for the better trained and better equipped Israeli forces, and when an armistice was signed ending the fighting in 1949, only 23 percent of Palestine remained in Arab hands, and an additional 400,000 had become refugees. The Egyptian army held the Gaza Strip, and Transjordanian forces held the West Bank, including East Jerusalem. Nazareth was the only important city in which the Israeli government let Arabs remain, due to its significance to European and American Christians.

From a humanitarian perspective, the worst result of the fighting was the uprooting of three quarters of a million Palestinians from the territory that became Israel. The Israelis refused to allow them to return to their homes, to offer any reparation for their belongings, or to accept any responsibility for their plight, thereby creating the Palestinian refugee problem that continues to be a major impediment to peace.

FRAGMENTATION IN EXILE

At first Palestinians were determined to regain all of their country, but starting in the 1970s an increasing number conceded that territorial partition—the establishment of a Palestinian state alongside Israel—was the most that could be achieved. The concept of partition remains controversial, but for many it seemed the only way to ensure their national survival.

The Palestinian community was shattered by the fighting and flight in 1948–1949, which they called *al-nakba* (the disaster). At least 750,000 Arabs fled from the area that became Israel. Fewer than half of the 1.2 million Palestinians remained in their own homes: 150,000 inside Israel and the rest on the West Bank (annexed by Jordan) and in the Gaza Strip (administered by Egypt). The situation facing the Palestinians in the countries to which they fled varied considerably. In Israel, Arabs gained citizenship but lived under strict military administration until 1966. The movement of Arab residents was closely regulated, access to education and employment was restricted, and political activities were curtailed. In the Gaza Strip, the Egyptian military government maintained tight control over the restive Palestinians, of whom 80 percent lived in refugee camps. Egypt did establish a largely elected national assembly in Gaza in the late 1950s as a political safety valve. Palestinians living in Syria had the same access to jobs and schools as Syrian citizens, but their ability to travel abroad was curtailed. The Lebanese authorities were especially restrictive, denying Palestinians the right to study in public schools or obtain permanent employment. Friction developed between the Palestinians, who were largely Sunni Muslim by religion, and those Lebanese politicians who sought to retain the special status of the Maronite Christian minority.

Life was least disrupted on the West Bank, where most people remained in their original homes and the residents gained Jordanian citizenship. Palestinians staffed the administrative and educational systems in Jordan and developed many of its commercial enterprises. But the regime never trusted them with senior posts in sensitive ministries and in the armed forces, and their loyalty to the monarchy remained tenuous. Moreover, the West Bank faced economic hardship as trade with Europe through Mediterranean ports was blocked, villages lost valuable agricultural land to Israel, and the Jordanian government favored the East Bank for industrial and agricultural development.

During the 1950s, Palestinians were attracted to the various forms of pan-Arabism that asserted that Palestine could only be regained if the Arab world were united politically. The idea of Arab unity received a blow in 1961 when the union between Egypt and Syria dissolved after less than three years. Moreover, the belief in Arab military strength was destroyed in June 1967 when the Israeli army defeated the combined Arab forces in a lightning strike and seized the Golan Heights from Syria, the West Bank from Jordan, and the Gaza Strip and Sinai peninsula from Egypt.

That disillusionment accelerated processes that were already under way among Palestinians. Their feeling that they were discriminated against by fellow

Arabs and their disappointment with the rhetoric of Arab regimes led many Palestinians to set aside their own passivity and reject their dependence on Arab states. They sought to transform their situation through their own actions rather than wait for Arab governments to rescue them. Small underground guerrilla cells sprang up in the early 1960s. Al-Fatah, founded in Kuwait in 1959 by the prosperous engineer Yasir Arafat and several professional colleagues who had been student activists in Egypt in the early 1950s, launched its first raid into Israel on New Year's Eve 1965. The fedayeen (guerrillas) sought to catalyze popular mobilization that would shame the Arab rulers into fighting Israel.

EVOLUTION OF THE PLO

Arab governments, aware of the renewed discontent among Palestinians, tried to channel that discontent by forming the Palestine Liberation Organization (PLO) in 1964. Although its leadership was middle and upper class and closely circumscribed by Egypt and other Arab governments, the PLO nevertheless represented a critical step in the process of reestablishing the Palestinians' political center. The first Palestinian National Council (PNC), a kind of parliament in exile that convened in Jerusalem in May 1964, adopted an uncompromising political charter. Just as the Palestinians before 1948 had rejected partition, so too the Palestinians refused in 1964 to acknowledge the right of the state of Israel to exist. The charter called for a return to the status quo that existed before 1948 so that the refugees could reclaim their homes and knit back together the threads of their lives torn in *al-nakba*.

The June 1967 war, which pitted Israel against Egypt, Syria, and Jordan, once more transformed the Palestinians' situation. Israel gained control over all of pre-1948 Palestine and almost half of all the Palestinians when its armed forces seized the West Bank (including East Jerusalem) and the Gaza Strip. The occupation severed ties between the West Bank and Jordan, although limited trade and travel continued. Gaza became isolated from Egypt but was suddenly linked to the West Bank. The residents of those occupied territories could communicate with Palestinian citizens in Israel, enabling families to rediscover each other after nearly twenty years' separation.

The war discredited the Arab states and their armed forces. When guerrilla warfare escalated in its wake, Palestinians felt that the fedayeen defied Israeli power more bravely than the Arab states' heavily armed troops. During 1968–1969 the guerrilla organizations gained control over the PLO. Amendments to the PLO charter at the fourth PNC (1968) reflected the shift: They emphasized popular armed struggle, rejected Zionism and the partition of Palestine, termed Judaism "a religion . . . not an independent nationality" (Article 20), and called for "the total liberation of Palestine" (Article 21).

At the fifth PNC in February 1969, the guerrilla groups ousted the old-guard politicians and selected Arafat to chair the PLO Executive Committee, since Fatah was the largest and politically most active guerrilla organization. Fatah called for the establishment of a "democratic, non-sectarian Palestine state in which all groups will have equal rights and obligations irrespective of race, color, and creed."

Immediately after the 1967 war, Arab regimes felt compelled to support the rapidly growing Palestinian guerrilla movement. The Palestinian cause retained so much popular support that criticism was unthinkable. Nonetheless, Egypt and Jordan accepted UN Security Council Resolution 242 of November 1967, which accorded Israel the right to live in peace and security behind essentially its prewar borders. This appeared the only way to regain control over the territories they had lost in the June war. That resolution mentioned the Palestinians only as refugees, not as a people with political rights.

The contradiction between PLO aims and Arab governments' policies became clear in 1970. Washington proposed a negotiated settlement in which Jordan and Egypt would regain substantial land that was taken by Israel in 1967; once again, the Palestinians were ignored. When the PLO denounced the plan, it collided with the two Arab regimes on which Palestinians relied most heavily.

The PLO had become a state-within-a-state in Jordan and used its territory as the base from which to attack Israel. Its presence challenged the authority of King Hussein, particularly when radical Palestinian movements called for the overthrow of the monarchy. The Jordanian armed forces forced the king to crush the Palestinian movement militarily. The Jordanian army defeated the PLO in a bloody showdown in September 1970, seized control over the refugee camps, and forced the guerrillas to flee to Lebanon in July 1971.

The civil war in Jordan revealed the fragility of the PLO's military structure and the incoherence of its political strategy. The PLO could not find a secure base from which to strike Israel. It could not stand up to the Arab regimes when their interests clashed. Its maximalist goals could not be sustained by its actual power.

Nonetheless, in the 1970s, the fedayeen reemerged in Lebanon. Palestinian despair was signaled by terrorism launched by Black September commandos—their name drawn from Jordan's September 1970 attack on the PLO. Operations included the assassination of the Jordanian prime minister in Cairo in November 1971 and the kidnapping and murder of eleven Israeli athletes at the Olympic games in Munich in September 1972. Guerrillas raided northern Israel from strongholds in south Lebanon, against which Israel retaliated with aerial and artillery bombardments of refugee camps and Lebanese villages.

In the wake of Black September, Palestinians living under Israeli occupation were severely demoralized; political leaders began to reassess their political strategy and consider accepting a Palestinian state in the West Bank, Gaza, and East Jerusalem. A few were attracted by King Hussein's proposal to form a federation between the East and West Banks, which would accord the West Bank Palestinians a higher political status within Jordan than they had held before 1967.

The PLO responded by revising its goals. The eleventh PNC (January 1973) resolved in secret to form an umbrella political structure in the occupied territories, called the Palestine National Front (PNF), which would use political rather than military means to end the Israeli occupation. The PNF sought to help residents overcome their demoralization and build a cohesive national political movement. The PNF encompassed all the political groups that opposed a return to Jordanian rule and that accepted the concept of a separate state alongside Israel.

The Arab-Israeli war in October 1973 led to further shifts in Palestinian attitudes. Whereas the 1967 war altered the territorial map, the 1973 war began to alter the psychological map. Moreover, PLO leaders feared that Egypt and Syria might sign peace accords with Israel that would ignore Palestinian rights, especially if the PLO failed to articulate a realistic program. In June 1974 the twelfth PNC advocated the establishment of an "independent combatant national authority for the people over every part of Palestinian territory that is liberated." This somewhat bellicose language in fact represented a major shift toward accepting Israel's right to exist in return for statehood.

CAMP DAVID

After the 1973 war, Palestinians hoped that multilateral negotiations under UN auspices would not only enable Egypt and Syria to regain land but also facilitate their own effort to achieve statehood. That hope was dashed by the Egyptian-Israeli peace treaty in March 1979. Egypt removed itself from the military arena and regained Sinai in return for establishing diplomatic relations with Israel. Syria, Jordan, and the PLO were left isolated, their strategic posture severely compromised.

The Egyptian-Israeli treaty called for negotiations to establish a five-year transitional period of Palestinian self-rule in the territories. However, the Israelis subsequently undercut the idea of self-rule by accelerating construction of Jewish settlements in the territories, declaring a unified Jerusalem to be Israel's eternal capital, annexing the Golan Heights, and launching an air raid that destroyed a partly built Iraqi nuclear reactor in June 1981.

On October 6, 1981, Anwar Sadat was assassinated. Israel and Egypt retained diplomatic relations, however, and in April 1982, Israel withdrew from Sinai, gaining a virtually demilitarized buffer zone while enabling Egypt to regain political sovereignty over the peninsula.

THE EXPULSION FROM BEIRUT

No longer feeling vulnerable to Arab counterattack, Israel invaded Lebanon in June 1982. The backdrop of the invasion was the protracted Lebanese civil war, which erupted in 1975, and threatened to undermine the territorial base that the PLO had established there after its expulsion from Jordan. The PLO tried to avoid taking sides in the internal strife, but quickly found itself the target of the Phalange, a Maronite militia controlled by the Gemayel family. The Phalange argued that Lebanese independence was compromised by the PLO's state-within-a-state and charged the PLO with aiding radical, secular groups based in Muslim and Druze communities.

By 1982, Israel had already intervened directly in south Lebanon, where it had established a security zone jointly controlled by its army and the South Lebanese Army (SLA), a Lebanese militia that Israel fully funded and equipped. It had also provided arms and funds to the Phalange. The June invasion was partly designed to bring Israel's Phalange ally, Bashir Gemayel, to power as president of Lebanon. The principal aim of the invasion, however, was to destroy the PLO's military and political infrastructure.

During the sixty-seven-day Israeli siege of Beirut, Arafat negotiated the withdrawal of PLO forces from the Lebanese capital. In August, he transferred the PLO headquarters to Tunis; PLO troops were evacuated to several distant Arab countries. Some PLO forces remained in east and north Lebanon, but Palestinians living in refugee camps near Beirut were no longer guarded by the PLO. Phalangists, monitored by Israeli troops, attacked the defenseless refugees soon after, killing hundreds in the houses and streets of Sabra and Shatila refugee camps.

THE INTIFADA

The Arab summit meeting in Amman in November 1987 focused on reinforcing Arab support for Iraq in the protracted Iran-Iraq war. King Hussein feared that Iran might overwhelm Iraq and sought to rally Arab support, including persuading several countries to restore relations with Cairo despite its peace treaty with Israel.

Palestinians were shocked at the summit's apparent lack of urgency toward the Palestinian cause. Their internal cohesion and feeling of external isolation combined to produce the explosion known as the intifada (literally, "shaking off") that began in December 1987. Initiated spontaneously by young people who were born after 1967 and who had faced the Israeli armed forces all their lives, the uprising surmounted the barrier of fear that paralyzed their parents.

The intifada's goals evolved rapidly during the first year. Initially, activists talked about ameliorating the conditions under occupation, but they soon shifted to call for the end to the occupation and the creation of an independent state alongside Israel. That shift reflected the growing confidence that residents felt in their ability to sustain the intifada and to transform it into a strategic victory. Activists realized that the uprising had compelled Washington to turn its attention to the Middle East; they hoped to capitalize on that attention. They emphasized that the United States must not let King Hussein play the leading role in negotiations and they supported convening an international conference in which the PLO would represent Palestinian interests.

The PLO leadership sensed the shift in morale and strategy by the Palestinians on the West Bank and Gaza and sought to capitalize diplomatically on the intifada. A special meeting of the Arab League in June 1988 voiced support for the uprising and called for renewed diplomatic efforts. Local leaders on the West Bank formulated their own peace proposal that summer and issued a draft declaration of independence. The West Bank leaders called for a Palestinian state alongside Israel, not replacing the Jewish state. In November 1988, the PNC endorsed the establishment of an independent state on the West Bank and Gaza, with its capital in East Jerusalem. UN Resolutions 181 and 242 would be the state's legal underpinning. The PNC also renounced the use of terror. Moreover, in a press conference in December, Arafat explicitly affirmed the right of Israel to exist as a Jewish state. It took the intifada for the PLO to gain the confidence necessary to make that historic move.

THE GULF CRISIS

The hard-line Israeli government that came to power on June 8, 1990, placed onerous conditions on negotiations and accelerated the construction of settlements. Some cabinet members advocated expelling Palestinians en masse from the territories. In desperation, Palestinians turned to Iraqi President Saddam Hussein for strategic support. In April 1990 he had hinted that he would attack Israel with long-range chemical weapons if Israel attacked Jordan or deported Palestinians from the West Bank. Palestinians hoped that his threatened balance of terror would prevent Israel from expelling them.

Iraq's seizure of Kuwait on August 2, 1990, however, posed a dilemma for the PLO. Arafat could not condone that occupation without seeming to justify Israel's occupation of the West Bank and Gaza. Arafat stressed that Iraq and Kuwait should negotiate; he strongly opposed the presence of US military forces in Saudi Arabia. When Saddam Hussein claimed on August 12 that Israel must withdraw from the occupied territories before he would consider leaving Kuwait, many Palestinians welcomed that linkage. Palestinian support for Iraq reached fever pitch in January 1991, when Iraq hit Israel with SCUD missiles during the UN-sanctioned war that forced Iraq out of Kuwait.

In the aftermath of Iraq's defeat, Palestinians were traumatized and the PLO was isolated. Saudi Arabia and Kuwait cut off all financial aid to the PLO, Syria continued to disarm Palestinian enclaves in Lebanon, and the disintegration of the Soviet Union removed a diplomatic counterweight to the United States. Kuwaitis wreaked vengeance on Palestinians who had remained in Kuwait during the Iraqi occupation, arguing that they had collaborated with Iraq: Within a year, only 25,000 of the previously nearly 400,000 Palestinian residents remained in Kuwait. Most fled to Jordan, which was already suffering heavy unemployment as a result of the trade dislocations caused by the Gulf crisis. In addition, Israel placed the Palestinians under total curfew during the war, followed by tight restrictions on their movement within the territories. Remittances from Palestinians living in the Gulf dried up and unemployment soared.

The level of violence had already increased significantly during and after the Gulf crisis. Palestinian militants attacked Israeli soldiers and settlers in the territories and also targeted other Israeli civilians. The killing of alleged collaborators by Palestinian groups intensified, despite efforts by Palestinian politicians to stem internecine bloodshed. Moreover, during the summer of 1992, the increasingly strong Islamist movement, led by Hamas, attacked Fatah supporters in the Gaza Strip. Hamas called for an Islamic state in all of Palestine and denounced the PLO for seeking to negotiate with Israel. Israel tolerated Hamas attacks on Fatah activists, but cracked down when Hamas began to kill Israelis.

THE OSLO ACCORDS

Just as negotiations were grinding to a halt, a secret track of PLO-Israeli talks reached a dramatic conclusion. Meeting under the auspices of the Norwegian foreign minister, the two sides hammered out a Declaration of Principles (DOP), which was signed in a formal ceremony in Washington, D.C., on September 13, 1993. Both parties realized that the failure to conclude an accord was rapidly undermining their own internal power and legitimacy. If Rabin could not build a more secure and prosperous Israel through negotiations, public support was likely to shift back to the Likud annexationists. If Arafat could not gain self-rule and recognition of the PLO, the uncompromising Islamists could overwhelm his movement. Moreover, Israeli politicians finally realized that excluding the PLO from negotiations meant that negotiations would fail; only the PLO could deliver.

The impetus was not merely negative. Both sides perceived the need to overcome animosity and mistrust and to place the relationship on a new basis. Israeli Foreign Minister Shimon Peres, in his speech on the White House lawn, called for a fundamental "reconciliation" and "healing" between the two peoples, with their "two parallel tragedies." Arafat stated that his people hope "that this agreement . . . marks the beginning of the end of a chapter of pain and suffering . . . [and ushers] in an age of peace, coexistence, and equal rights." Indeed, the preamble of the accord stressed the importance of this "historic reconciliation."

The agreement provided for Palestinian self-rule in the Gaza Strip and Jericho, followed by Palestinian civil administration over the rest of the West Bank for a five-year interim period. The Palestinian Authority (PA) would control the police to maintain internal security, operate the educational, health, social welfare, and tax systems, and have considerable authority over the economy. Negotiations on final-status issues, including Jerusalem, settlements, statehood, and refugees were supposed to begin in December 1995.

An accord signed in May 1994 enabled Arafat and PLO officials to establish the PA and rule the town of Jericho and most of the Gaza Strip. But the PA did not gain control over other towns on the West Bank until another agreement signed in September 1995 (dubbed Oslo II). Oslo II also enabled the PA to hold elections in January 1996 for an eighty-eight-seat legislative council and for the presidency, which Arafat won handily.

Despite their general enthusiasm for the elections, Palestinians were disappointed that Arafat subsequently concentrated power in his hands and ignored the efforts by the legislative council to finalize a constitution and hold the executive accountable. In addition, Israel's redeployment remained limited under the terms of Oslo II. The area of the West Bank under exclusive Palestinian control totaled only 3 percent. Militant Israelis challenged even these limited changes; the religious Jew who assassinated Rabin in November 1995 denounced the prime minister as a traitor for signing the Oslo accords.

Arafat's authority was challenged by Hamas, which decried the meager results of negotiations. In the summer of 1995 and spring of 1996 Hamas and Islamic Jihad militants bombed buses and markets in Jerusalem and Tel Aviv; more than sixty Israeli civilians died in the bombings that spring. Arafat was unable to stem this violence, particularly as the perpetrators came from areas that were still under Israeli security control. But the violence undermined the Labor government and propelled the Likud back into power in May 1996.

Ehud Barak's election as prime minister in May 1999 on a platform that called for accelerated peace talks offered some hope for an accord. However, serious negotiations did not occur until July 2000 when President Clinton hosted two weeks of intensive talks with Barak and Arafat at Camp David. Although the leaders addressed previously taboo subjects, they could not bridge all the gaps. They came close to agreeing to a Palestinian state on most of the West Bank and Gaza and all of the Gaza Strip, but Israel insisted on controlling the borders, air space, and water resources as well as annexing the areas with 80 percent of the West Bank settlers and all the settlements in East Jerusalem. Barak agreed to accept a token number of Palestinian refugees into Israel on humanitarian grounds but not on the right of return.

In retrospect, the talks were too ambitious and too pressured by President Clinton's overriding desire to reach a settlement before his term of office expired the following January. The talks ended with both sides blaming the other for the failure to reach agreement. Israelis criticized Barak for conceding too much whereas Palestinians praised Arafat for not yielding to US and Israeli pressure.

In the tense atmosphere that followed, Likud leader Ariel Sharon marched onto al-Haram al-Sharif (the site of the Temple Mount) on September 28, in a manner that clearly asserted Israel's claim to political sovereignty. His deliberately provocative action catalyzed months of spontaneous violence that swept across the West Bank and Gaza. This renewed intifada was fueled by rage and frustration over the failure of the Oslo accords to improve Palestinians' lives as well as fear that the terms proposed at Camp David would leave them far short of their goal of sovereignty and independence.

The Israeli government held Arafat responsible for this violence and retaliated by launching mortar barrages and systematic helicopter rocket attacks against alleged terrorist leaders in residential areas. The result was an increasing cycle of violence that made further negotiations futile. The resounding electoral defeat of Prime Minister Barak by Sharon on February 6, 2001, put an end to the Oslo peace process, at least for the near term.

Conclusion: The Past Is Prologue

For the Palestinians, independence has always been a question of when, not whether. Despite the return of violence following the collapse of the peace process in 2000, more progress has been made toward their goal of self-determination than one might think. Despite the fever pitch of mutual animosity engendered in the wake of the collapse of the Oslo peace process, five wars (1948, 1956, 1967, 1973, and 1982) still seem to have taught both sides that achievement of their national goals cannot be attained by force of arms.

The first breakthrough was the Oslo Declaration of Principles in 1993, negotiated directly between the PLO and the Israelis without US participation. While avoiding issues such as Jerusalem and the refugees that appeared still irreconcilable, the declaration marked the first time that Israel recognized Palestinian rights, at least in principle.

Now that the Palestinians have in fact recognized the right of Israel to exist, the harder task rests with the Israelis to accord the same right to the Palestinians in return for the security they seek. Even here, there is a chance for guarded optimism amid the gloom. The proposals put forward by President Clinton before he left office posited an independent Palestinian state, something Israelis have never had the will nor the Americans the courage to admit is a sine qua non to peace. But for the first time, at least, the idea has been placed on the negotiating table.

CHAPTER 6

THE UNITED STATES AND ISRAEL

Bernard Reich

Israel has historically enjoyed the backing of the United States—so much so that Arabs of the Middle East commonly perceive that Israel is in effect a Western proxy state in their midst and, conversely, that Israel wields undue influence over US foreign policy toward the Middle East.

While not denying that a "special relationship" exists between the United States and Israel, particularly with regard to the US commitment to Israel's continuing security, Bernard Reich demonstrates that the two countries are hardly in lockstep agreement over issues. Though they might be in broad concord, the United States and Israel have frequently clashed over specifics and on the means to achieve goals—a situation shaped by differences between the global interests of the United States as the world's lone superpower and Israel's narrower and more regional interests. Tensions have waxed and waned between the governments over pushing for progress on peace talks with the Palestinians, and over linking any such progress to alteration of Israel's policies toward Jewish settlements in the West Bank and the Gaza Strip. As administrations have changed in both countries, their views have oftentimes diverged on the status of the occupied territories and on the potential creation of a Palestinian state. Nevertheless, US support for Israel remains strong overall.

Bernard Reich is professor of political science and international affairs at George Washington University. He is the author of numerous books on the Middle East, including A Brief History of Israel *and* An Historical Encyclopedia of the Arab-Israeli Conflict, *and is coeditor (with David E. Long) of* The Government and Politics of the Middle East and North Africa, Fourth Edition.

IN A PRESS CONFERENCE ON MAY 12, 1977, US President Jimmy Carter said, "We have a special relationship with Israel. It's absolutely crucial that no one in our country or around the world ever doubt that our number-one commitment in the Middle East is to protect the right of Israel to exist, to exist permanently, and to exist in peace. It's a special relationship." In February 1993, US Secretary of State Warren Christopher observed that the "relationship between the United States and Israel is a special relationship for special reasons. It is based upon shared interests, shared values, and a shared commitment to democracy, pluralism and respect for the individual." In spring 1994 President Bill Clinton suggested that, in working for peace in the Middle East, the United States would fulfill its "ironclad commitment" to ensure that these risks would not endanger the security of Israel. George W. Bush has made similar observations.

This perspective tends to "confirm" the Arab view, in the wake of the 1967 Arab-Israeli war (also known as the Six Day War), that there existed a special and exclusive US-Israeli relationship. Nevertheless, there is much that the statements do not say, and though there is a broad-scale commitment on the part of the United States at a very significant level, as in any relationship of this sort there are also areas of discord.

The US-Israeli relationship is not the exclusive one that is often portrayed by Arab spokesmen and others advocating a different Israeli orientation in US policy. Although there was a period of exclusivity favoring Israel following the events of the Six Day War, this lack of a dual relationship began to change after the Arab-Israeli war of 1973 (also known as the Yom Kippur War). By 1977 and the inauguration of Jimmy Carter into office, there had begun a period in which Arab (especially Egyptian) views were factored into the process and affected US policy. Some of the Arab states (but not yet the Palestinians and the Palestine Liberation Organization [PLO]) became increasingly more important from a foreign policy perspective because they were seen as moving in a general direction toward peace. Thus, there was a change from exclusivity to dual-track diplomacy.

The framework within which the United States and Israel have interacted with each other has changed over time, and policies perforce have changed to reflect the altered environment. The US-Israeli relationship had its origins during the time that the United States and Soviet Union—the new superpowers—competed for control following World War II. Both superpowers courted Israel in their efforts to incorporate new states into their spheres of influence. Israel was seen as a valuable prize in the newly important, oil-rich Middle East. Nevertheless, within the US government there was substantial disagreement concerning the appropriate policy, and US support for the Jewish state was a presidential decision, often opposed by the senior bureaucrats in the Departments of State and Defense. Today, the US-Israeli relationship operates within the confines of a new world order in which there is no alternative superpower or US-Soviet competition to curry the favor of states or regional groupings.

A second difference is to be found in the perspectives of a small country confronting a large country (that is, the United States today, the only superpower), which sees the world through a different lens. The United States is a global power with global interests, affected by the residue of the cold war; Israeli interests are more narrow and regional and there are more "life-and-death" issues.

The United States and Israel have been linked in a complex and multifaceted special relationship that had its origins prior to the establishment of the Jewish state in 1948 and has focused on continuing US support for the survival, security, and well-being of Israel. But its content has varied over time. During the first decades after Israel's independence the relationship was grounded primarily in humanitarian concerns, in religious and historical links, and in a moral-emotional-political arena. The United States remained very much aloof from Israel in the strategic-military sector. The United States and Israel developed a diplomatic-political relationship that focused on the need to resolve the Arab-Israeli conflict, but though they agreed on the general concept, they often differed on the precise means for achieving that end. Despite a growing positive connection between the two states, especially after the 1967 Six Day War, appreciation of the linkage, especially in the strategic sphere, remained limited.

RELATIONS BETWEEN
THE CARTER ADMINISTRATION AND ISRAEL

The accession of both Jimmy Carter and Menachem Begin to office in 1977 inaugurated a new period in the relationship, characterized often by increased public tension and recrimination. Egyptian President Anwar Sadat's initiative also reduced the exclusivity of the US-Israeli relationship that had been established after 1967 as a consequence of Soviet policy and the ruptures of relations between some Arab states and the United States.

The Carter and Begin administrations became divided over many issues that directly impacted the health of the US-Israeli relationship. They were in accord in some aspects, however, as on the need to achieve peace and foster the security of Israel. Yet they would often disagree on the methods and mechanisms best suited to achieving those goals, the preferred end results, and the modalities that best served national interests. There were questions regarding the poor personal chemistry between policymakers on either side as well. Mutual dislike and mistrust extended beyond Carter and Begin into the Reagan administration; the

United States was unhappy with Begin and his successor, Ariel Sharon, and Israel had strong anxieties about Caspar Weinberger and his policies. There were disagreements concerning the nature of the situation in the region, often focusing on alternative intelligence estimates of the threat to Israel's national security. These differences involved data, analyses, and policy results. The consensus on major issues did not ensure agreement on all aspects or specifics of each problem. As the dialogue increasingly dealt with details rather than broad areas of agreement, there were disturbances in the relationship.

The Carter administration had its most noteworthy success in effecting change in the Israeli position at Camp David and in the Egyptian-Israeli peace treaty. The main techniques included high risk/high visibility presidential involvement and Carter's suggestion that Israel could not allow the failure of this president, who might then transfer the blame to Israel in Congress and public opinion. Israel was also influenced by the administration's articulated reassurances for continuing economic and military assistance and by their tangible manifestation in the form of such assistance.

THE REAGAN TENURE

Ronald Reagan came to office with a very different perception of Israel and its importance. His campaign rhetoric concerning Israel went beyond the customary pledges of friendship, suggesting strong and consistent support for Israel and its perspective regarding the Arab-Israeli conflict. He saw Israel as an important ally and an asset in the struggle against the Soviet Union. He was opposed to dealing with the PLO until that organization dramatically changed its policies by renouncing terrorism, accepting United Nations (UN) Security Council Resolution 242, and acknowledging Israel's right to exist (which it eventually did in 1988). This pro-Israel perspective was retained and reiterated after he took office.

The US-Israeli relationship during the eight years Reagan held office was generally characterized by close positive ties, but there were also specific, divergent interpretations regarding the regional situation, the peace process, and Israel's security needs. Israel bombed an Iraqi nuclear reactor near Baghdad and PLO positions in Beirut during the summer of 1981, and it took action on other issues when it believed its national interest was at stake—even when it understood this would lead to clashes with the United States. The United States strongly opposed the raid on the Iraqi reactor, questioned the Beirut bombings, and postponed the delivery of previously contracted F–16 aircraft to Israel.

Other issues emerged, including disputes about settlements in the Occupied Territories and Israel's concern about a perceived pro-Saudi tendency in US policy manifested, in part, by arms supplied to Saudi Arabia, including F–15 enhancements and AWACS (airborne warning and control system aircraft).

Reagan sought to reassure Israel that the United States remained committed in helping it to retain its military and technological advantages over the Arab states. In fact, on November 30, 1981, the United States and Israel signed a Memorandum of Understanding on Strategic Cooperation (the MOU) in which the parties recognized the need to enhance strategic cooperation to deter threats to the region from the Soviet Union. For the Begin government it represented an important achievement, suggesting an improved relationship with the United States, and some mitigation of the negative effects of US sales of AWACS and other advanced weapons systems to Saudi Arabia. But this positive aura soon dissipated when Israel decided in December 1981 to alter the status of the Golan Heights by extending the law, jurisdiction, and administration of Israel to that area. The action generated swift negative reactions in Washington, including US support for a UN resolution of condemnation and the suspension of the MOU. Israel was stunned by the extent of the US reaction.

Although Israel's Golan decision exacerbated tensions, the turning point was Israel's 1982 invasion of Lebanon, which called into question the links between the United States and Israel and led to clashes over the nature and extent of Israel's military actions and the US effort to ensure the PLO's evacuation from Beirut. US forces, which had been withdrawn from Beirut following the PLO's evacuation, returned there after the massacres of Palestinians by Lebanese Phalangists at the Shatila and Sabra refugee camps in September 1982, leading to the burdensome involvement of US marines in the turmoil of Lebanon.

Reagan faced other difficult times. US efforts to secure the release of its hostages in Lebanon through arms sales to Iran erupted, in November 1986, into a public scandal that became known as the Iran-Contra affair. This infamous chapter in US history, among other matters, involved active Israeli participation in the planning and execution of some operations of the US National Security Council and demonstrates the high level of strategic cooperation between the two governments during the Reagan administration.

The onset of the *intifada* in December 1987 led to public disagreement over the methods employed by Israel to contain the violence and restore law and order. Israel's use of live ammunition provoked protests by the State Department as early as January 1988. Israel's deportation of Palestinian civilians charged with inciting the demonstrations led the United States to vote in favor of a UN resolution calling on Israel to refrain from "such harsh measures [which] are unnecessary to maintain order." This was the first time since 1981 that the United States had voted for a resolution critical of Israel.

The relationship between the United States and Israel underwent substantial, though incremental, change during the Reagan administration. Ronald Reagan saw Israel as a strategic asset. US economic and military assistance reached $3 billion per annum in essentially all-grant aid. Strategic cooperation between the United States and Israel reached new levels during this period, and on April 21, 1988 (in the Jewish calendar, the fortieth anniversary of Israel's independence), the two states signed a memorandum of agreement that institutionalized the emerging strategic relationship. Growing links in the military sphere involved joint military exercises, sales and purchases of equipment, training, and related activities. Israel had also gained status as a Major Non-NATO Ally.

On December 14, 1988, in a press conference in Geneva, PLO leader Yasser Arafat read the script articulating a change in PLO views toward Israel and the Arab-Israeli conflict, renouncing terrorism, recognizing the state of Israel, and accepting UN Resolutions 242 and 338. Arafat thereby met the conditions for beginning a dialogue between the United States and the PLO that had first been enunciated in 1975 by then Secretary of State Henry Kissinger. The same day as the Algiers statement, Secretary of State George Shultz formally announced: "The Palestine Liberation Organization today issued a statement in which it accepted UN Security Council Resolutions 242 and 338, recognized Israel's right to exist in peace and security, and renounced terrorism. As a result, the United States is prepared for a substantive dialogue with PLO representatives." The administration sought to reassure Israel that "those who believe that American policy is about to undergo a basic shift merely because we have begun to talk with the PLO are completely mistaken."

THE BUSH TENURE

President George Bush took office in January 1989 with no long-range strategic plan or specific policies for the Arab-Israeli issue or the Gulf region of the Middle East. The end of the cold war, the implosion of the Soviet Union, the collapse of the Warsaw Pact, and the emerging new democracies in eastern Europe preoccupied the administration and Congress and entranced the media and public. The Iran-Iraq war had given way to a cease-fire, the departure of Soviet troops altered the hostilities in Afghanistan, and a dialogue with the

PLO, established in the last days of the Reagan administration, continued. Within the context of a changing international system the Middle East was not a high national priority.

During the first year and a half of the Bush administration, Israel and the United States were preoccupied with the effort to begin a negotiating process between Israel and the Palestinians. Bush administration frustration with the Shamir government was obvious in its preference for a Peres-led government after a successful vote of no-confidence terminated the tenure of the Israeli government in the spring of 1990 and in its voiced concerns about the prospects for peace after Shamir succeeded in constructing a new government in June 1990. The peace process was moribund when the Iraqis invaded Kuwait in August 1990, attributable, in large measure, to the policies of the Shamir government in Israel (at least in the eyes of the Bush administration).

During the Gulf crisis and the war against Iraq, Israel was relegated to a marginal role. Israel did not serve as a staging area for forces or as a storage depot for military materiel, nor was it utilized for medical emergencies. There was a conscious US effort to build a broad-based international force with an Arab component to oppose Saddam Hussein and to distance Israel from any such activity. Israel was determined not to be used as a tool to break the coalition, although the Israelis did endorse the firm and rapid US reaction to Iraq.

The inauguration of the Arab-Israeli peace process in the aftermath of the Gulf war revived traditional Israeli concerns about the United States as something less than a wholly supportive and reliable ally. Within several months of the Gulf war cease-fire, the US-Israeli relationship was again characterized by discord. Tensions developed as the Bush administration appeared to link proposed housing loan guarantees, essential to the settling of Soviet Jews in Israel, to Israel's actions on settlements in the West Bank and Gaza Strip and its responsiveness to the peace process. Secretary of State James Baker observed, "I don't think that there is any bigger obstacle to peace than the settlement activity that continues not only unabated but at an enhanced pace." In the autumn of 1991 tensions became public when Bush asked Congress to postpone consideration of Israel's request for US guarantees of $10 billion in loans.

Despite numerous denials and claims to the contrary, the Bush administration and the Shamir government were not harmonious on many of the issues central to peace in the Middle East. The outcome of the June 1992 elections in Israel, with Yitzhak Rabin replacing Shamir as prime minister, was welcomed by the Bush administration as a significant and positive factor that would alter the regional situation, the prospects for progress in the Arab-Israeli peace process, and the nature of the US-Israeli relationship. In late June 1992 Secretary of State Baker called for a quick resumption of Middle East peace talks, reflecting the administration's view that the elections had resulted in the demise of a hard-line Likud government and thereby facilitated the prospects for success in the peace negotiations. They saw the onus now falling upon the Palestinians and other Arabs to make serious compromises and proposals for peace.

Bush and Arab-Israeli Peace

US determination to see the peace process through was stressed by Bush in a speech to a joint session of Congress on March 6, 1991: "A comprehensive peace must be grounded in United Nations Security Council Resolutions 242 and 338 and the principle of territory for peace. This must provide for Israel's security and recognition, and at the same time for legitimate Palestinian political rights. Anything else would fail the twin tests of fairness and security."

Eventually, Baker convened the Madrid peace conference at the end of October 1991. The Madrid conference was attended reluctantly by the parties, who retained substantial concerns about the nature of the conference. The conference did not achieve a substantive breakthrough, although it eliminated the procedural barriers to direct bilateral negotiations between Israel and its immediate neighbors when the Israeli and the Syrian, Egyptian, Lebanese, and Jordanian-Palestinian delegations met at an opening public session and an official plenary session and delivered speeches and responses. Bilateral negotiations between Israel and each of the Arab delegations followed.

The Madrid conference was followed by bilateral talks in Washington later in 1991, talks that directly or indirectly contributed to the September 1993 Israel-PLO Declaration of Principles, the October 1994 Israeli-Jordanian peace, and Israeli-Syrian talks focusing on the Golan Heights. The first rounds achieved accord on nonsubstantive matters. Progress was measured primarily by the continuation of the process rather than by significant achievements on the substantive issues in dispute. The wide gap between the Israeli and Arab positions was not narrowed in these initial encounters. The United States adhered to its role as facilitator and sought not to intervene on substantive matters. It was not a party to the bilateral talks and its representatives were not in the room or at the negotiating table, although it did meet separately with the parties and heard their views and perspectives.

In the bilateral negotiations the Israeli-Palestinian and Israeli-Syrian negotiations were the most central and most difficult. In the case of both Jordan and Lebanon the general perception at the time was that agreements would be relatively easy to achieve, although these would have to await the resolution of the Syrian and Palestinian talks. In the case of Syria the central issue was peace and the future of the Golan Heights, with little likelihood of compromise in the short term. In the Israeli-Palestinian discussions the disagreement centered on the Palestinian desire for self-government and the Israeli opposition to that goal. Compromise was elusive, as the positions were mutually exclusive. However, Israeli proposals for elections in the territories and the reality of the situation in the region suggested areas for continued negotiation, ultimately leading to the "Oslo Channel" bilateral negotiations outside of the Madrid process that resulted in the September 1993 signing of the Israel-PLO Declaration of Principles on the White House lawn.

Despite the achievements symbolized by the Madrid conference and the subsequent bilateral and multilateral discussions, by the time of the Israeli and US elections in 1992 no substantive breakthrough had occurred and no specific achievement (beyond continuation of the process) had been recorded. Nevertheless, the Baker team seemed optimistic in the spring of 1992: Although the differences between the parties were still wide, they would eventually narrow and then it would be possible to bridge the gaps. US policy under the Clinton administration continued to emphasize the US role of facilitator.

THE CLINTON TENURE

The accession of the Clinton administration to office in 1993 and of the Rabin government in 1992 provided the basis for a continuation of the relationship, but in a more positive mode, with strong and improving personal and country-to-country relations focusing on the Madrid-inaugurated Arab-Israeli peace process. The United States reassured Israel that the US commitment to its security would be sustained. And a strong positive personal relationship seemed to develop between the American president and his Israeli prime minister counterpart.

The relationship between Clinton and Rabin continued to grow closer and became more intimate as the peace process, begun at Madrid and amplified by Oslo, continued to make progress. Each achievement seemed to be marked by an added positive glow to both the personal chemistry and the political accord between the two partners. This, of course, was demonstrated and exemplified by the assassination of Rabin in November 1995. Clinton appeared to be personally moved by the death of his peace partner and issued the famous statement "Shalom, chaver" (goodbye, friend) that struck close to the heart of their dealings.

The success of Benjamin Netanyahu in his race against Shimon Peres (Rabin's foreign minister and alter ego in the peace process) in the first-ever popular election of the prime minister in Israel in the spring of 1996 illustrated again the unusual nature of the connection. The Clinton administration, seeking continuity in the peace process, clearly preferred that Shimon Peres succeed. Nevertheless, despite the outcome, the relationship endured and the United States continued to support Israel's security and quest for peace. Even though there was a lack of personal chemistry between Clinton and Netanyahu, many in the Republican-dominated US Congress saw the latter's victory as a positive accomplishment and endorsed his approach.

The Clinton administration continued to press for progress on the peace process begun at Madrid and expanded in Oslo and by subsequent Israeli accords with the Palestinians and with Jordan. The prime minister of Israel, reflecting a skepticism of the Palestinian position and a deep-seated concern for an arrangement that would ensure Israel's security as well as a personal goal of ensuring the stability of his governing coalition, acted with considerable deliberation and pursued a pace seen by the Clinton administration as far too slow. By the middle of 1998 the Clinton administration presented an "ultimatum" to Israel that was ignored and then faded from public view. The two states pursued the peace process and clashed with each other. But, as before, the administration often was not backed by the Congress, which seemed more sympathetic to the Netanyahu approach and position and provided public and private positive reinforcement to the Israeli government.

These episodes and others in the Clinton tenure reflected the themes that marked the Carter-Begin relationship and characterized the broader relationship between the United States and Israel, which centered on endurance and continuity in the quest for peace and Israeli security, and on discord concerning the means to best achieve those ends.

The election of Ehud Barak as prime minister of Israel in May 1999 was seen in the Clinton administration, and elsewhere, as an opportunity for peacemaking to resume and make progress; expectations were high that he would be a prime minister in the mold of Rabin, his mentor and friend. Barak set out on an ambitious diplomatic program and, with Yasser Arafat, set February 12, 2000, as the target date for preparing a framework agreement for an Israeli-Palestinian permanent peace settlement, the completion of which was to occur by September 12, 2000. Israelis and Palestinians had a large number of meetings, and there was extensive involvement by the United States.

As the Clinton administration entered its final year in office, accelerated efforts suggested a possible tripartite summit involving Clinton, Barak, and Arafat. But the parties were far apart. The objective of the negotiations in July 2000 at Camp David (generally referred to as Camp David II) was to put together a package that Barak believed would generate acceptance and recognition from the Palestinians, which had eluded Israelis to that point, on the basis of a two-peoples, two-state solution within the region. But this was not to be. Arafat rejected the Barak proposals, left the negotiating table, and thereby provided the basis for the al-Aqsa intifada, which soon brought violence to the area. The Clinton tenure ended without an Israeli-Palestinian peace accord and with the area engulfed in violence.

BUSH AND SHARON

The end of the Clinton administration and the ascension of George W. Bush to the presidency, and the election of Ariel Sharon as prime minister of Israel to replace Ehud Barak, brought to an end the Madrid-Oslo "peace process" in which President Clinton, personally, and his administration had been both central and active. Sharon and Bush would establish their own "special" connection and would be free to develop their own approaches to peace. Significantly, while the Bush administration called for an end to Arab-Israeli violence and initially put the onus on Arafat to call publicly for the termination of violence, it signaled its determination to be less activist and not to be involved in a detailed way on a continuing basis, suggesting it would not emulate the Clinton depth and extent of involvement in the details of the conflict.

As violence continued to mark the Arab-Israeli sector after Sharon's election, efforts to halt it, to restore confidence between the parties, and to resume negotiations became the core of the US efforts to facilitate a "peace process" (by whatever name) between Israel and the Palestinians. The situation was dramatically altered by the September 11, 2001, attacks on the United States. The Bush administration worked to create an international coalition to respond to terrorism, focusing on Osama bin Laden and the al-Qaʿida movement, and sought Arab and Muslim participation in that effort. For his part, bin Laden continued to link the attacks to the plight of the Palestinians and attributed that to unequivocal US support for Israel. Although these comments were widely discounted as efforts to further split the United States and the Muslim states, many in the Palestinian and Arab worlds saw this as an accurate depiction of the situation.

The United States sought to clarify its position. In his press conference on October 11, 2001, President Bush noted that his administration would continue to focus on resolution of the Arab-Israeli conflict within the context of continued US-Israeli friendship. At the same time, he noted: "I believe there ought to be a Palestinian state, the boundaries of which will be negotiated by the parties so long as the Palestinian state recognizes the right of Israel to exist, and will treat Israel with respect, and will be peaceful on her borders." But negotiations for an end to violence and to achieve resolution of the Arab-Israeli conflict were held hostage to the continued violence that erupted in the wake of the failure of the Camp David talks.

A year after the termination of the Middle East peace process launched at Madrid, the new efforts seemed to be moving in the opposite direction. Arafat was unwilling or unable to halt Palestinian terrorism and violence against Israelis, thereby incurring Israeli responses and US concern, frustration, and disappointment. In late January 2002, President George W. Bush publicly expressed his disappointment in Arafat for his involvement in an arms shipment that could escalate Palestinian violence against Israel and for his not preventing terrorism. The United States proved unable to secure the end of violence and terror, and to get the Israelis and Palestinians back to the negotiations.

Endurance and Continuity

Israel's special relationship with the United States has not been enshrined in a legally binding commitment joining the two in a formal alliance. Despite the extensive links that have developed, the widespread belief in the existence of the commitment, and the assurances contained in various specific agreements, the exact nature and extent of the US commitment to Israel remains imprecise. Israel has no mutual security treaty with the United States, nor is it a member of any alliance system requiring the United States to take up arms automatically on its behalf.

It has largely been assumed by both parties that the United States would come to Israel's assistance should it be gravely threatened; this perception has become particularly apparent during times of crisis. Despite this perception and the general feeling in Washington (and elsewhere) that the United States would take action if required, there is no assurance that this would be the case. Israeli leaders continue to be interested in military and economic assistance as the primary tangible expression of the US commitment and have been particularly cautious about potential US participation in a conflict, fearing that combat losses might lead to a situation analogous to that in Vietnam. Thus, the exact role of the United States in support of Israel, beyond diplomatic and political action and military and economic assistance, is unclear.

The United States is today an indispensable if not fully dependable ally. It provides Israel, through one form or another, with economic (governmental and private), technical, military, political, diplomatic, and moral support. It is seen as the ultimate resource against potential enemies, it is the source of Israel's sophisticated military hardware, and its interest in lasting peace is central to the Arab-Israeli peace process. Although there is this positive relationship, there is also an Israeli reluctance, bred of history, to abdicate security to another party's judgment and action. Israel will continue to consider its perceptions of threat and security as decisive.

The two states maintain a remarkable degree of parallelism and congruence on broad policy goals. The policy consensus includes the need to prevent war, at both the regional and international levels, the need to resolve the Arab-Israeli conflict, and the need to maintain Israel's existence and security and to help provide for its economic well-being. At the same time, however, there was, is, and will be a divergence of interests that derives from a difference of perspective and overall policy environment. The United States has broader concerns resulting from its global obligations, whereas Israel's horizon is more narrowly defined and essentially limited to the survival of the state.

Despite the generally positive nature of the relationship since 1948, Israelis tend to recall a series of negative episodes as well. They highlight the 1947 arms embargo and the subsequent refusal to provide military equipment or other assistance during the War of Independence and the period that followed; [Secretary of State John Foster] Dulles's aid suspensions and general unfriendliness; US actions in connection with the Sinai War of 1956 and Israel's subsequent withdrawal from the Sinai and the Gaza Strip; and the disappointing lack of action by the United States just prior to the Six Day War. In 1967—the year of the Six Day War with Egypt—Israel determined its need to act alone and estimated that the United States would not object to or seek to prevent its action and, when Israel decided to go to war, it did not consult or inform the United States.

There has also been a divergence on methods and techniques to be employed, as well as discord on specific issues. During the Six Day War there was a clash over Israel's mistaken attack (and causing of casualties) against the US intelligence ship *Liberty*. They disagreed on the matter of reprisals by Israel in response to Arab fedayeen (literally, "self-sacrificers") actions and on the limits placed on the refugees from the West Bank in the wake of the Six Day War.

There was major disagreement concerning the value of a great power to resolve the Arab-Israeli conflict, Israel's need for military supplies, and the status of the Occupied Territories and Israel's role with respect to them, including the building of settlements. They have argued over Israel's desire for significant changes in the pre–Six Day War armistice lines as contrasted with the US perspective that there be "insubstantial alterations" or "minor modifications." The two states will continue to hold divergent views on the several elements of the Palestinian issue, particularly the West Bank's future, the rights of the Palestinians, and the potential creation of a Palestinian homeland, entity, or state.

In many respects the issue of Jerusalem has highlighted the areas of discord. The United States has supported the Partition Plan designation of Jerusalem as a separate entity and has stressed the international character of the city while refusing to recognize unilateral actions by any state affecting its future. The United States refuses to move its embassy to Jerusalem and maintains it in Tel Aviv, thus illustrating the differing perspectives of the two states. These perspectives have placed the two states in conflicting positions continuously from 1947 to the present, especially since the Israeli declarations of Jerusalem as the capital of the state and the reunification of the city during the Six Day War.

Changing administrations in Washington, and of governments in Jerusalem, have all affected the nature and content of the links between the United States and Israel within the broad parameters of the enduring special relationship. The patterns of agreement and discord established from the outset have manifested themselves subsequently—broad patterns of concord on the more strategic and existential issues, accompanied by disagreement on the specifics of many of the elements of the Arab-Israeli conflict and on the means to achieve congruent objectives.

At Israel's birth the United States seemed to be a dispassionate, almost uninterested, midwife—its role was essential and unconventional but also unpredictable and hotly debated in US policy circles. Today, more than fifty years later, some of the policy debate continues, and there are periods of discord in the relationship. Some of this reflects personality and related differences between US and Israeli leaders. But there is little doubt about the overall nature of US support for its small and still embattled ally.

CHAPTER 7

ISRAELI-PALESTINIAN RELATIONS
SINCE THE GULF WAR

William L. Cleveland

In September 1993, PLO Chairman Yasser Arafat and Israeli Prime Minister Yitzhak Rabin shook hands on the White House lawn, publicly ratifying agreements secretly reached in Oslo earlier that year. The Oslo accords provided for mutual recognition between Israel and the PLO and laid the foundations for Palestinian autonomy in the West Bank and the Gaza Strip. The optimism generated by the agreement contributed to the signing of a separate peace treaty by Israel and Jordan the next year.

However, the momentum of the Oslo agreements has gradually dissipated. Among the Palestinians, Arafat proved to be a less able administrator than a resistance leader. His corrupt and autocratic administration disaffected many Palestinians and turned them against the peace process. Israel, on the other hand, has been sharply divided between those who are intent, often for religious reasons, on retaining the occupied territories as part of a Greater Israel, and those who are more willing to trade at least some land for peace. The election of Ariel Sharon as prime minister in 2001 signaled the divisiveness of Israeli society on the issue, for he became Israel's fifth prime minister in six years.

William L. Cleveland is professor of history at Simon Fraser University, British Columbia. He is the author of A History of the Modern Middle East, *now in its third edition.*

WE ACKNOWLEDGE THAT THE ARAB-ISRAELI CONFLICT was but one of several sources of regional instability during the 1990s and that the launching of the Oslo peace process was far from being the only major development in the Middle East of the 1990s. Nevertheless, the rise and fall of the peace process was a momentous occurrence and deserves the careful attention of historians of the modern Middle East. The first agreement in the process, known as Oslo I, was concluded outside the glare of media scrutiny in secret face-to-face meetings between Palestinian and Israeli officials, and its disclosure took the world by surprise. It set the stage for additional steps toward the normalization of relations between Israel and its Arab neighbors, the most important of which was a full treaty of peace and mutual recognition between Jordan and Israel. It led also to the return of Yasir Arafat to Palestine and his assumption of full authority over a small portion of the West Bank and the Gaza Strip. But Oslo I and the agreements that followed it produced darker moments as well. They contributed to the assassination of an Israeli prime minister by a Jewish Israeli citizen and thus exposed the deep divisions within Israeli society over the future direction of the state and its role in the occupied territories. They revealed similar divisions within Palestinian society as Arafat, a virtual outsider, sought to suppress any local rivals, including the Hamas leadership, for control of the Palestinian ministate in the making by transforming the democratic framework envisaged by the Palestinians into an authoritarian apparatus controlled by his personal security forces. This chapter examines the key developments that opened up the possibilities of a peaceful settlement between Palestinians and Israelis but turned instead into a hostile impasse. In so doing, the chapter attempts to show the linkages between the *intifada*, the Gulf War, and the proposals for peace. The chapter also seeks to identify those currents within Palestinian and Israeli society that generated the early momentum for a peaceful settlement and those that contributed to the breakdown of negotiations.

THE ROAD TO THE OSLO PEACE ACCORDS

The Madrid Conference of 1991

In the aftermath of the Gulf War, the [George H. W.] Bush administration embarked on an extensive effort to achieve a resolution of the Arab-Israeli conflict. The proposed instrument of conflict resolution was an international peace conference jointly sponsored by the United States and the Soviet Union. The historic gathering opened in Madrid on October 30, 1991. In the short term, the Madrid Conference was more about public gestures than substantive discussions, and subsequent events have tended to relegate it to the background. However, the gathering at Madrid should not be overlooked; it was a significant step in bringing Israelis and Palestinians to a new level of contact. It brought together, for the first time, representatives from Israel, the Palestinian community, and the neighboring Arab states that had not yet recognized Israel's right to exist—Jordan, Lebanon, and Syria—to discuss peace. And the negotiating sessions that it set in motion conferred a sense of normalcy to the practice of Israeli and Palestinian spokespersons engaging in face-to-face meetings. The Madrid Conference also focused attention on the Palestinian delegation, which was composed of "insiders"—that is, Palestinians who lived and worked in the occupied territories. They presented their case with clarity and in tones of relative moderation and made the aging PLO exile leadership appear politically stale and out of touch with the realities of life in the occupied territories.

Between December 1991 and spring 1993, the Arab and Israeli delegations met several more times in Moscow and Washington. In these post-Madrid meetings, the sticking point was, as it had been in all discussions since 1967, Israeli settlement policies in the occupied territories. But this time, the US administration adopted a firm stance against continued settlement activity.

In 1990, in the midst of the *intifada* and on the eve of the Gulf War, Israel embarked on the most ambitious program of settlement construction in the occupied territories it had yet undertaken. The settlement program continued during the Madrid conference and the subsequent peace talks. In the opinion of the Bush administration, Israel's provocative actions in the occupied territories constituted the main obstacle to a successful outcome of the peace process. Israel's refusal to heed US requests to freeze the settlements embroiled the two countries in a bitter dispute that finally drove President Bush to take a step that no US president before him had taken: He linked US financial aid to Israel to Israel's willingness to curb the settlements in the West Bank and Gaza Strip. The policy that Bush adopted was not new—every US administration since 1967 had expressed its opposition to Israeli settlements in the occupied territories—but Bush was the first to enforce that policy.

The US-Israeli dispute reached a climax in February 1992, when the United States announced that it would not approve a $10 billion loan guarantee to Israel unless Israel agreed to a freeze on the construction of all settlements in the West Bank and the Gaza Strip. Israel's Prime Minister Shamir was defiant and insisted that his government would never back down in its determination to populate the occupied territories with Jewish settlers. Shamir's uncompromising attitude caused the most serious strain in US-Israeli relations since Israel's formation.

Despite Shamir's defiant rhetoric, Israel badly needed the US loan guarantee so that it could borrow money on the international markets to help defray the costs of absorbing the new wave of Jewish immigration from the former Soviet Union. Israel planned to use the borrowed funds for housing construction and other measures required by the immigrants. Without the loans, Israel could not afford to finance its settlement policies in the occupied territories and at the same time prepare for the influx of Soviet immigrants.

All of the controversies associated with Shamir's government received intense public scrutiny during the buildup to Israel's national elections scheduled for June 1992. The elections pitted Shamir's Likud bloc against a Labor Party led by former Prime Minister Yitzhak Rabin. In a bitterly fought campaign, Shamir stressed Likud's commitment to Greater Israel, whereas Rabin expressed a vague but conciliatory position on the future of the occupied territories and pledged to restore friendly relations with the United States. The Israeli public rejected Shamir's ideological hard line and gave Rabin's Labor Party an overwhelming victory, bringing to office the first Israeli prime minister to be born in Palestine. The election results created an intriguing historical irony: Twenty-five years to the month after Rabin, as chief of staff of the Israeli army, commanded the campaign that captured the West Bank and Gaza Strip, he was given a popular mandate to negotiate a resolution of the problems caused by Israel's continued occupation of those same territories.

Rabin was no dove (as defense minister he had recently been charged with crushing the *intifada*), but he was willing to support measures designed to restore good relations with the United States. Immediately after forming a government, he announced a partial freeze on settlement construction. That was far from the total freeze demanded by Washington, but it was enough to persuade the Bush administration that it should encourage Rabin's moderation. When the new Israeli prime minister made his first state visit to the United States in 1992, President Bush announced the authorization of the contentious $10 billion loan guarantee. In taking this action, the United States surrendered some of its financial leverage over Israel without gaining a complete freeze on Israeli settlements.

Israel and the PLO: The Breakthrough of 1993

In late summer 1993 Arab and Israeli delegates gathered in Washington to attend the eleventh round of the peace talks begun two years earlier in Madrid. The talks had become stalemated, and little was expected of this new session. For that very reason, the sudden disclosure of a secret agreement reached between representatives of the Israeli government and the PLO took the world by surprise. It was an astounding document, stunning both for its unexpectedness and its contents: The agreement provided for mutual recognition between Israel and the PLO and laid the foundations for Palestinian autonomy in the West Bank and Gaza Strip.

The circumstances that brought Israeli and PLO officials together in a series of clandestine meetings outside Oslo, Norway, in the winter and spring of 1993 originated outside normal diplomatic channels. In the course of conducting studies in the occupied territories, the director of a Norwegian research institute discovered that certain well-placed Palestinians and Israeli government officials were receptive to the idea of direct PLO-Israeli negotiations. Following an exchange of information, the Norwegian government volunteered to provide facilities for secret talks, and the two parties agreed to participate. From this uncertain beginning emerged the agreements that had the potential to change the political landscape of the Middle East. The reasons that prompted the two parties to depart so sharply from their established positions rested with a combination of factors.

Following the Gulf War of 1991, the PLO entered a period of political and economic disarray. Yasir Arafat's tilt toward Iraq cost the organization dearly and led to criticism of his leadership. Within the occupied territories, and especially in the Gaza Strip, the PLO's claim to political primacy came under renewed challenge from Hamas. The PLO leaders, fearful of being overtaken by the appeal of Hamas, looked to negotiations with Israel as a way of retaining their dominance. The new administration of President Bill Clinton was preoccupied with domestic affairs and had a distinctly pro-Israeli bias that made it unwilling to push Israel to make concessions as President Bush had done.

Faced with a deteriorating financial base, declining popular support, and an indifferent US administration, the PLO leaders were desperate for a diplomatic triumph that would revive the organization's reputation and solidify their positions. It was evident to them, and most especially to Arafat, that the years of rejectionism and maximalist demands had failed to bring about the creation of a Palestinian state; the Norway meetings presented an opportunity, very possibly the last one their generation would have, to salvage something from their efforts—even if it meant accepting less than they had previously called for.

From the perspective of the new Israeli government, the prospect of endless violence and occupation was unacceptable. The *intifada* had shown the Israeli public the depth of Palestinian nationalism and had served to make many Israelis aware, for the first time, of the oppressive features of the occupation. The growing strength of Hamas, with its ties to other Islamic opposition groups throughout the region, concerned the Israeli leaders and gave them cause to consider negotiations with the PLO as a means of defusing the discontent from which Hamas drew its strength.

The two agreements hammered out in the forests near Oslo were unprecedented. The first was a document of mutual recognition in which Israel recognized the PLO as the legitimate representative of the Palestinian people and, in return, the PLO unequivocally recognized Israel's right to exist in peace and security, renounced the use of terror and violence, and pledged to remove the clauses in the PLO Charter that called for the elimination of the state of Israel.

The second agreement, formally known as the Declaration of Principles on Palestinian Self-Rule but commonly referred to as Oslo I, outlined a five-year program for interim Palestinian autonomy in the occupied territories. Although Israel would retain overall sovereignty throughout the term of the agreement, the period was divided into several stages, each of which granted increasing administrative responsibility to the Palestinians. During the first stage, Israeli troops were to withdraw from the Gaza Strip and the West Bank town of Jericho, and Palestinian authorities were to assume immediate administrative control of the two areas. In the next phase, an elected Palestinian Council was to assume responsibility for education, health, social welfare, tourism, cultural affairs, and direct taxation throughout the entire West Bank and Gaza Strip. At the same time, the Israeli armed forces were to be redeployed outside the populated areas of the West Bank. It needs to be emphasized that Oslo I was not a peace treaty but an interim agreement that was to lead in stages to a final peace settlement. In essence, the PLO accepted the notion of interim phases without any advance agreement on what the features of the permanent settlement would be. Thus, while the creation of an independent Palestinian state was implicit in the entire Oslo process, neither of the two 1993 documents made explicit mention of such a state. Israel simply recognized the PLO as the legitimate representative of the Palestinians and agreed to negotiate with it. The PLO, however, had fully recognized Israel's right to exist.

According to the schedule set forth at the time, the interim negotiations would conclude in 1998 with a permanent agreement based on UN Security Council Resolutions 242 and 338. Like most of the deadlines established in Oslo I, this one was not met.

The declaration postponed a number of crucial issues for the interim discussions, prominent among them the future status of East Jerusalem and the Israeli settlements, the fate of Palestinian refugees living abroad, and, as noted above, the crucial question of Palestinian sovereignty. Yet for all the hard bargaining still to come, it appeared that the Israelis and Palestinians had, through direct negotiations, taken a major step toward peaceful coexistence.

As the two parties to the agreement worked out last-minute details, the rest of the world scrambled to catch up. Arab leaders, though upset at their total exclusion from the Norway talks, cautiously endorsed the proposal. Although the agreement had caught the United States off-guard, President Clinton pledged his country's moral and financial support and agreed to reestablish formal contacts with the PLO.

On September 13, 1993, Israeli and PLO leaders assembled on the White House lawn to participate in a ceremony that would have been unimaginable a few weeks earlier. It began with the signing of the autonomy agreement and then moved to a round of speeches. The speeches were followed by a defining moment when the two former enemies, PLO Chairman Arafat and Israeli Prime Minister Rabin, exchanged a handshake of reconciliation. It seemed at the time to represent one of those instances when historical patterns are overturned and new beginnings made possible.

The Promising Beginnings of the Oslo Peace Process

Despite intense opposition to Oslo I from prominent Israeli and Palestinian figures and despite frustrating delays and frequent setbacks in the negotiating process, the overall momentum toward a negotiated settlement was maintained for two years following the signing ceremony. The challenge facing the two parties centered on the need to add specific details to the general principles and vague guidelines of the 1993 accords. Crucial to the successful implementation of Oslo I was the establishment of a self-governing Palestinian authority. Both sides understood that Arafat and the PLO would constitute the leadership of any such authority. For Israelis, this meant allowing an individual and an organization that they had come to associate with the destruction of their state to return to Palestine. In the optimism of the time, these reservations were put aside, and in July 1994 Yasir Arafat, amid tumultuous rejoicing, established residence in Gaza and began to put in place the rudiments of an administrative and security structure. The broader regional impact of Oslo I was made dramatically evident in fall 1994, when Israel and Jordan signed a treaty of peace and mutual recognition, and President Clinton made an unprecedented visit to Syria in hopes of persuading Hafiz al-Asad to open negotiations with Israel. It appeared that the opportunity for a resolution of the entire Arab-Israeli conflict was tantalizingly near at hand.

The final agreement of the two-year period following Oslo I was signed in September 1995. Although it appeared to represent a logical outcome of the accords that had preceded it, this agreement, in combination with other developments to be discussed below, can be identified as a key factor in solidifying opposition to the peace process. Known formally as the Interim Agreement but commonly referred to as Oslo II, the 1995 document spelled out in excruciating detail (it was more than 350 pages long) the stages of Israeli military redeployment in the West Bank, the process by which power would be transferred to Palestinian civil authority, and several other long- and short-term matters. As shown in Map 7.1, Oslo II divided the West Bank into three zones and specified a phased redeployment of the Israeli Defense Forces (IDF) from each zone. However, the extent of power was to vary from zone to zone. The end result was that the Palestinian authority would have direct control of Area A, 3 percent of the West Bank; it would control some municipal functions and would share control with Israel in Area B, 24 percent of the territory; and Israel would retain total control of Area C, an area that made up 74 percent of the West Bank and included all of the 145 settlements in the territory.

The clauses and maps of Oslo II made it impossible to sustain the pretense that the PLO had done anything other than negotiate from a position of weakness and that it had received anything other than the peace of the weak. To the Palestinians who had applauded Oslo I and the promise it had seemed to hold, Oslo II looked more like a step toward the creation of Palestinian bantustans on the West Bank than the recognition of Palestinian statehood, and increasing numbers of them began to gravitate toward opposition groups.

Problems with the Oslo Process: Two Perspectives

Palestinian. Even as the White House hosted official ceremonies of public self-congratulation for Arab and Israeli leaders at each conclusive stage of their negotiations, Palestinians continued to suffer through the hard realities of Israeli military occupation, land expropriation, and settler violence. The peace process notwithstanding, Rabin had ended the freeze on settlement construction, and Israel confiscated 20,000 acres of Palestinian-owned land on the West Bank between 1993 and 1995.

Even the establishment of a Palestinian self-governing authority brought as much disappointment as it did satisfaction because the qualities that made Yasir Arafat a successful exile resistance leader did not always serve him well as a civil administrator. From the moment he arrived in Gaza in 1994, Arafat endeavored to monopolize the decision-making process in the Palestinian Authority (PA). To limit the potential for the formation of opposition groups,

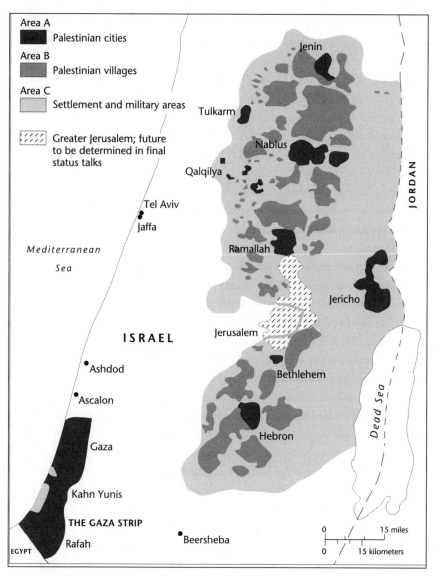

Map 7.1   The territorial provisions of Oslo II, 1995. *Source:* Map 23.1 of William L. Cleveland, *A History of the Modern Middle East, Third Edition* (2004, Westview Press).

Arafat appointed to the top posts in the PA his loyal associates from among the former PLO exiles in Tunis. Those among the local Palestinian elite who had risen to prominence through their role in the *intifada* and who were sensitive to the needs and aspirations of the Palestinian population were largely bypassed in favor of the exile politicians. The result was increased tension between the outsiders, disdainfully referred to as "the Tunisians" by the local Palestinian population, and the resident elite, who were systematically excluded from positions of authority.

This situation did not noticeably change with the election of a Palestinian Council in 1996. Although some local opposition candidates were elected, Arafat's supporters won a comfortable majority, and Arafat himself was chosen president. He then simply ignored the new council and proceeded to set up an authoritarian regime buttressed by an elaborate hierarchy of security forces. As many as seven different security services, numbering upwards of 40,000 men and ranging from uniformed presidential guards to ordinary policemen, were deployed on behalf of the regime. They silenced Arafat's opponents through arbitrary arrests, brutal interrogation methods, and the enforcement of press censorship. Palestinians began to feel that the PA was becoming as oppressive as the Israeli occupation forces had been.

The deteriorating economic situation in the occupied territories after 1993 further alienated the Palestinian community from the peace accords. Palestinian economic conditions were worse than they had been at any time during the Israeli occupation. This was caused in part by Israel's practice of sealing off the territories in response to terrorist activities and thus denying Palestinians access to the Israeli labor market on which they had become dependent. The corruption within Arafat's circle also contributed to the economic malaise. Profiteering and the establishment of monopolies on the sale of basic commodities were common practices among the PLO leaders from Tunis. Arafat himself exercised personal control over the foreign aid donated to the PA, using it to pay his security forces and top-heavy bureaucracy instead of channeling it into infrastructure development. As the oppressive burden of economic hardship spread throughout the occupied territories, increasing numbers of Palestinians became disillusioned with the peace process and with Arafat's one-man rule.

Hamas was the main beneficiary of the growing disenchantment with the PA. The Hamas leadership resented Arafat's takeover of the PA and his promotion of external PLO figures to positions of authority. They felt the outsiders were reaping the benefits of the sacrifices Hamas members had made during the *intifada.* This sentiment was shared in many quarters of Palestinian society and enabled Hamas to consolidate its position as a legitimate home-grown opposition movement to Arafat and "the Tunisians." Hamas was firmly rooted in the shared hardships and poverty that Palestinians had experienced under Israeli occupation and was more directly involved in grassroots social welfare activities than were the PA ministries.

At its most extreme, Hamas's rejection of the entire Oslo peace process was manifested in suicide bombings directed at Israeli civilians in the larger cities. The objective of the bombings was to sabotage the peace negotiations by turning the Israeli public against Rabin and the Labor government that had endorsed Oslo I.

Arafat's regime proved particularly vulnerable in its relationship to Hamas. Israel made it clear that if Arafat failed to rein in Hamas militants, he would prove himself to be an unreliable partner in the peace process, and negotiations would cease. In short, Israel encouraged Arafat to become the authoritarian ruler he was already inclined to be. Yet in complying with Israeli demands and conducting raids against Hamas, Arafat undermined his credibility and turned Palestinians against his administration.

Israeli. In the aftermath of the signing of Oslo I in 1993, the majority of Israelis were prepared to give Rabin's peace initiative a chance to succeed. However, the Hamas bombings and the prospect of the eventual establishment of an independent Palestinian state brought to the forefront of public concerns the sensitive issue of security, an issue that had served to unify the diverse strands of Israeli society since the formation of the state. If the Oslo Accords did not lead to security, then the peace process was not worth pursuing.

Opposition to the Oslo process was increasingly framed in religious terms. Like Hamas's founders, Jewish religious spokesmen presented a vision of the West Bank as sacred land and argued that any Israeli withdrawal would constitute a surrender of the biblical heritage of the Jewish people. To those who shared this vision, the Oslo compromise giving up portions of the West Bank in exchange for peace was more than a security risk; it was a violation of God's covenant and of a divinely presented opportunity to restore the connection between the Jews and the land God had promised them. In 1995 a group of rabbis placed the religious imperative above the laws of the state by issuing a decree instructing soldiers to resist orders to evacuate army bases in the West Bank. With each Hamas bombing, other segments of the population began to question the risks to which Rabin's peace process exposed Israel.

Israeli militants, like their counterparts in Hamas, resorted to violence to express their opposition to the Oslo Accords. In February 1994 Baruch Goldstein, an Israeli settler activist, turned an automatic weapon on a large gathering of Palestinians praying in the Mosque of Abraham near the West Bank city of Hebron, killing twenty-nine of them before he himself was killed. Goldstein's murderous assault brought to the surface a threatening undercurrent of violence that was circulating within Israeli society. On the evening of November 4, 1995, that current manifested itself in a sudden and tragic moment. As Prime Minister Rabin was leaving a large peace rally in Tel Aviv, he was assassinated by Yigal Amir, a young Israeli student at an institute of Jewish religious studies. Subsequent investigations showed that Amir had received a devoutly Jewish religious education and that he acted out of the conviction that Jewish law required the death of any Jew who turned Jewish land over to the enemy. Once again, Israeli society seemed to be torn from within, and the question of which of the competing ideological forces would control the future direction of the country was prominently raised.

The assassination of Rabin left negotiations between Israel and the Palestinians suspended. But developments in the two years following Oslo I had revealed the lack of mutual trust that still divided the two peoples: There existed among Israelis a lingering suspicion that Palestinians were unreliable terrorists, and among Palestinians, a suspicion that the Israelis were determined expansionists.

The Unraveling of the Oslo Peace Process

During the interval between Rabin's assassination and the Israeli elections of May 1996, Hamas carried out another round of suicide bombings in Jerusalem and Tel Aviv that caused public opinion to shift away from support for the peace process. The Israeli government responded with a demonstration of its dominance over the Palestinians, sealing off the occupied territories, placing many West Bank towns under curfew, and causing increased economic distress within the Palestinian community. This crackdown, in turn, fed the atmosphere of hopelessness and despair among the Palestinians and led more and more of them to turn away from Arafat and the unsatisfactory status quo that he represented.

In this atmosphere of heightened tension, Israelis went to the polls and, by the narrowest of margins, chose as their new prime minister Binyamin Netanyahu, the leader of the Likud coalition. Netanyahu had campaigned on a pledge to "slow down" the peace process. Subsequent events showed that what he meant by that phrase was to end the process as it had been defined by the Oslo Accords. Yigal Amir's bullets and the bombs of Hamas had, it seemed, achieved their intended results.

In his need to conciliate the religious and nationalist elements upon which his coalition government depended, Netanyahu adopted hard-line policies toward the occupied territories. He refused to acknowledge any connection between land and peace, assuring Israelis that they could have security, settlements, and peaceful coexistence with the Palestinians. At the same time, he inaugurated a new round of provocative settlement activities—initiating the construction of new settlements and expanding existing ones—that seemed to invite Palestinian retaliation. The most controversial of the several settlement projects was the start of a large settlement project on confiscated Arab land in East Jerusalem that would eventually house 30,000 Israelis. This was a violation of the Oslo Accords, which stated that no change in the status quo of Jerusalem should take place until final negotiations. At the same time that it promoted settlement activities in the occupied territories, Netanyahu's government stalled on carrying out the full range of troop redeployments agreed to in the Oslo Accords.

The intensified Israeli settlement activities exposed the most serious flaw in the entire Oslo process—namely, the imbalance of power between the two parties. The Oslo negotiation process was not carried out between equals. Israel was the occupying power, and Oslo I consigned the Palestinians to the status of the occupied for at least the full five years of the interim agreement. Moreover, because the Oslo agreements were made by the PLO and Israel alone, they fell completely outside the domain of the United Nations and were not subject to any UN resolutions or enforcement mechanisms. Although the United States, as the moral guarantor of the Oslo Accords, could and did raise objections to Israel's land confiscation, increased settlement activities, and refusal to redeploy its troops, Washington showed no inclination to back up its objections with anything more than rhetoric. Thus, Israel could ignore the terms of Oslo I with impunity, whereas the Palestinians had no choice but to bow to superior Israeli power. The continued deterioration of Palestinian-Israeli relations raised the possibility of a major armed confrontation more violent and deadly than the *intifada* had been.

The Wye Accords and the Fall of the Netanyahu Government

As tensions increased, the Clinton administration assumed a more direct role in the stagnant peace process. US pressure finally succeeded in bringing Netanyahu and Arafat together at the Wye River estate in Maryland in autumn 1998. After days of bitter haggling mediated by President Clinton's daily interventions, Arafat and Netanyahu signed a set of agreements known as the Wye Accords. They represented a very minor achievement, merely elaborating on the original Oslo agreement in which Israel had accepted the principle of exchanging occupied land for peace, in this case a withdrawal of its military from an additional 13 percent of the West Bank, and the PLO had renounced the use of terrorism.

The most significant aspect of the Wye Accords was not the agreement itself but, rather, Netanyahu's reluctant acceptance of the principle of exchanging occupied land for peace and security. In accepting this principle, he created deep rifts within the ruling Likud coalition, which had consistently demanded the establishment of Greater Israel and denounced all compromises on withdrawal from West Bank territory. As his government teetered on the brink of collapse, Netanyahu sought to appease his critics on the religious Right with an announcement that Israel would suspend its scheduled withdrawal from an additional 13 percent of the West Bank. This was a violation of the Wye Accords he had signed only a month earlier. Riddled by dissension within and pressured by the United States from without, the Netanyahu government voted in December 1998 to dissolve itself and hold new elections. Netanyahu's attempt to satisfy the United States and the Israeli moderates by signing the Wye Accords and to mollify the religious Right by refusing to carry them out had failed. He now had to submit his government's record to the Israeli electorate.

The election campaign, vituperative even by Israeli standards, pitted Netanyahu and his Likud bloc against Ehud Barak, a former army chief of staff, and his Labor coalition. When Israelis went to the polls on May 17, 1999, they delivered a harsh verdict on Netanyahu's leadership. Barak received 56 percent of the votes for prime minister to Netanyahu's 44 percent. In the context of Israeli politics, this constituted a landslide victory for Barak and showed that Israelis had become disenchanted with Netanyahu's political machinations and his failure to pursue a true peace agreement with the Palestinians.

If Barak's victory represented the desires of the majority of Israelis for a revival of the peace process, the results of elections to the Knesset revealed a society deeply divided on domestic issues. Beginning with the elections of 1996, Israeli voters cast two ballots, one for prime minister and another for the party list. In the 1999 elections, an unprecedented thirty-three parties received official authorization to field candidates, and fifteen of these parties ended up with representation in the Knesset. The two parties that made the biggest gains in the Knesset held firm—and opposing—views on the role of religion in the state. One was a new rigorously secular party, Shinui, and the other was Shas, an ultra-Orthodox religious party of Sephardic Jews that became the third largest party in the Knesset. Shas did not object to the peace process, but it rejected the concept of a secular legal system and insisted instead that Israel should be governed by Jewish law. The growth of these two parties suggested that the issue of peace with the Palestinians was no less divisive than the differences between secular and religious sectors of Israeli society. And Israel's electoral system embedded these differences in day-to-day political life, ensuring further factionalism and stalemate.

Barak's Failed Efforts to Revive the Peace Process

As was becoming the norm in Israeli politics, Ehud Barak held power for only a portion of his four-year mandate—his government fell after only seventeen months in office. It will be remembered for having good intentions, few achievements, and a disastrous ending.

The most decorated soldier in Israeli history, Barak was a dovish hawk in the image of his mentor, the late Yitzhak Rabin. He endorsed the resumption of peace negotiations with the Palestinians and sought to avoid the confrontational posture adopted by Netanyahu. During the election campaign, Barak had pledged to end the eighteen-year Israeli occupation of southern Lebanon, a promise he fulfilled in May 2000.

Nevertheless, his government was brought down by the Right's reaction to the concessions he allegedly offered the PA at a two-week summit conference known as Camp David II, which US President Bill Clinton convened in July 2000. Because written offers were not placed on the table during the conference, reports on the precise nature of the exchanges between Barak and Arafat differ widely. However, to the Israeli Right, the most sensitive of Barak's alleged concessions was an offer to grant the PA partial sovereignty over certain Arab sections of Jerusalem. This was anathema to the Likud opposition and other rightist parties that insisted on the retention of Israeli sovereignty over the entire city. Camp David II ended in an impasse, but Barak's willingness to compromise over Jerusalem prompted several of his cabinet members to resign and left him with a minority government. In December 2000, Barak announced his resignation and called for a special election in which he hoped to receive a popular mandate for his peace initiatives.

The Second Intifada and the Election of Sharon

The election campaign took place against the backdrop of a new Palestinian uprising and harsh Israeli reprisals. The factors that prompted the uprising were firmly rooted in the failure of the Oslo peace process to halt Israeli efforts to colonize the occupied West Bank and Gaza Strip and in the parallel failure of Yasir Arafat and the Palestinian Authority to provide competent governance. At the core of the uprising was the Palestinian reaction to the increasingly oppressive

Israeli occupation of the West Bank and Gaza Strip and the ever-expanding net-work of settlements. The proliferation of Israeli military checkpoints and the ongoing confiscation of land increased Palestinians' feelings of being dispossessed and deprived of a future.

Those sentiments exploded in an outbreak of anger over a provocative gesture undertaken by Ariel Sharon. In September 2000, Sharon, accompanied by a security force 1,000 strong, made a visit to the sacred Islamic shrines of the Haram al-Sharif or, in Jewish terminology, the Temple Mount. Sharon's purpose was to demonstrate that any Jew had the right to visit the Jewish holy site. The Palestinians regarded the visit as an affront to Islam and protested in an outbreak of demonstrations and stone throwing. The Israeli reaction was swift and deadly—during the first two days of protest, Israeli security forces killed eighteen Palestinians, turning a series of demonstrations into a sustained popular uprising that soon spread beyond Arafat's control. For Israelis, the uprising served once again to place the issue of security at the top of the electoral agenda.

In the election campaign of February 2001, Barak argued that there was no alternative to compromise and that efforts to impose a military solution on the Palestinians would fail. His opponent, Ariel Sharon, projected the image of an old warrior who knew how to protect Israel's security but who could, at the same time, pursue a peaceful resolution to the conflict with the Palestinians. In a devastating rebuke to Barak, who had been elected by a large majority only seventeen months earlier, Sharon received 62 percent of the votes to Barak's 37 percent. Another important statistic was one that revealed the divisiveness within Israeli society: When Sharon assumed office he became Israel's fifth prime minister in six years.

As Sharon formed his government, television newscasts, in what looked like a replay of the first *intifada*, showed Palestinian youths throwing stones and Molotov cocktails at Israeli military vehicles while Israeli soldiers responded with live ammunition. Appearances aside, however, this uprising differed in several respects: The goals of the uprising were not clearly stated, popular participation was not as widespread, and no coordinated leadership group emerged. The driving force of the second *intifada* consisted of loosely organized groups of young men affiliated either with one of the militant Islamic groups (Hamas and Islamic Jihad) or with Yasir Arafat's al-Fatah.

Another difference between the two *intifadas* was the relative militarization of the second one. On the Palestinian side, the Islamic groups, joined by elements of the Palestinian security forces, were armed with light automatic weapons; the stones and burning tires that had characterized the first *intifada* were still present, but they no longer symbolized the Palestinian preference for nonviolent protest. On the Israeli side, the use of force was far deadlier and more heavily mechanized than before. The IDF deployed tanks, Apache helicopters, and F–16 fighter jets against what was essentially a civilian population. As the uprising continued into 2002, Israel escalated its military operations and forcibly reoccupied all the territory in the West Bank and Gaza Strip that it had earlier turned over to the Palestinian Authority. At the same time, Israel imposed an internal closure on the West Bank, prohibiting Palestinians from leaving their communities of residence and effectively shutting down all forms of internal commerce. The result was economic disaster for the occupied territories. By summer 2003, the spiraling death toll had reached 2,400 Palestinians and 780 Israelis.

The perpetual cycle of violence suggested that neither Israeli Prime Minister Sharon nor PA President Arafat had a vision for conflict resolution that extended beyond the deployment of brute force. Sharon believed that Israel could crush the rebellion with superior firepower. Arafat, confined by the IDF to his isolated and battered headquarters in the West Bank city of Ramallah, suffered an erosion of his authority during the years of the second *intifada*. He took no public role as leader of the uprising, but did nothing to discourage the militants. His continued presence in his half-ruined compound as an ineffectual but disruptive leader was a reminder of both his material weakness and his residual power as a humbled but defiant symbol of Palestinian resistance.

CONCLUSION

The divergent domestic objectives of the parties within Israel's governing coalitions during the 1990s and early 2000s were representative of the larger domestic controversy surrounding the direction of Israeli society and the meaning of a Jewish state. One component of this controversy, the hard-edged religious nationalist current, was represented by the settler groups who demonstrated against any redeployment of Israeli forces in the West Bank by waving placards that read "All of Israel is ours." A much different current existed at the opposite end of the social and cultural spectrum. It was represented in part by the activists in the Peace Now movement and other organizations that called for a return of at least a large part of the occupied territories in exchange for peace. This current also included those who frequented the beaches and nightclubs of Tel Aviv, who were more interested in consumerism than in colonizing the West Bank, who held a more secular view of the application of religious law in public life, and who yearned for Israel to become what they thought of as a normal nation. The struggle for the soul of Israel continues, and in its outcome rests the future of the peace process and thus of Palestinians as well as Israelis.

CHAPTER 8

ETHNICITY AND NATION-BUILDING IN THE STATE OF ISRAEL

Calvin Goldscheider

In this essay, Calvin Goldscheider examines Israel's connection to Jewish communities outside of Israel and calls into question the role that ethnically Arab citizens of Israel (Arab-Israelis) might play in Israel's future.

The two largest Jewish communities in the world are those of Israel and the United States. American Jewish identity over time has become defined less by religious ritual and belief and more by "ethnic" Jewishness, and particularly by support for the state of Israel. Yet, the two communities are diverging. The American commitment to the separation of church and state is at odds with Israel's religiously infused politics, and the American tolerance of Jewish diversity contrasts sharply with Orthodox Judaism's intolerance of religious diversity in Israel.

Arab-Palestinians in the occupied West Bank and Gaza have not been officially integrated into Israel as citizens. In contrast, Arab-Israelis are caught in the middle because, while they are Arabs, they are also Israeli citizens, albeit citizens who rank below Jewish Israelis in the social hierarchy of Israel. So long as being Israeli involves a dominant component of Jewish history and culture, Arab-Israelis can never be fully Israeli. Barring fundamental changes in the Jewish state of Israel, Arab-Israelis will remain socially and economically disadvantaged, and the nature of their links to the Palestinians and to Arab states will therefore remain an open question.

Calvin Goldscheider is professor of sociology and Judaic studies at Brown University. His many books include Studying the Jewish Future, The Arab-Israeli Conflict, *and* Israel's Changing Society, *from which this essay is selected.*

MY GOAL IN THIS CHAPTER is to focus on three questions. First, what is the relationship between Jewish communities outside of the state of Israel to developments in Israeli society? I shall refer to this as the "Jewish diaspora" question. Second, what has been the relationship of the state of Israel to the territories it administers (referred to as Judea and Samaria, or the West Bank, or Palestine by persons of different political-ideological orientations)? I shall refer to this as the "Palestinian" question. Third, what are the prospects for Jewish ethnic assimilation in Israel, and what is the role of the Arab or Palestinian citizens living in the state in the context of both the Palestinian and Jewish diaspora questions? I shall refer to this as the "ethnic-national" question.

THE JEWISH DIASPORA QUESTION

The links between Israel and the Jewish diaspora, that is, Jewish communities outside the state, are important because these Jewish communities have been sources of immigrants to Israel. Hence, they have had a powerful influence on the changing population growth and ethnic composition of Israel. Moreover, these Jewish communities have been Israel's financial and political backbone, supporting domestic programs and providing important aid for defense purposes and political legitimacy in the international arena. Jews outside of Israel have been partners in formulating the intellectual and ideological basis of Israeli society and have provided the political rationale for its reemergence. What occurs in outside Jewish communities has important consequences for developments in the state; what happens in Israel has implications for Jewish communities outside Israel.

Three brief examples illustrate some of the more obvious interdependencies between Israel and Jewish communities outside of Israel. First, the size of particular Jewish communities and the pool of potential Jewish immigrants have varied since the 1950s, in part in relation to the rate of immigration to Israel. The end of Jewish emigration from Yemen or Iraq can only be understood against the background of the demographic demise of those Jewish communities. The commitment of American Jews to remain in the United States has a major impact on the relationships between Israel and the American Jewish community and the US government. Shifts in the cohesion of the Soviet Union and its breakup, along with implications of these changes for the Jewish population living there, were the most immediate cause of the large-scale immigration of Russian Jews to Israel in the 1990s. The impact of the timing and rate of Jewish immigration from various countries of origin to Israel must be understood in the context of these Jewish communities.

A second example relates to the ways that events in Israel affect Jewish communities in the world. The 1967 Six Day War between Israel and its Arab neighbors had a major impact well beyond the borders of the state, increasing the financial and political support to Israel by Jewish communities around the world and more firmly anchoring their ethnic identities in Israel's development. As the very survival of Israel was perceived to be threatened, the post-Holocaust generation of Jews outside Israel responded in a variety of ways to link itself to the future of the Jewish state. These developments, in turn, led to new and more conspicuous dependencies between Israel and Jewish communities, often involving the exchange of Jewish "ethnic" identity for financial and political support.

A third illustration relates to the continuous terrorist attacks directed at Jews in Israel. These have always generated political responses and concerns among Jews outside Israel; attacks on Jewish communities in North and South America, in Europe, and in Asia and Africa have, in turn, generated responses from the Israeli government. Israel views itself as the guardian of the Jewish people; Jewish communities outside Israel are defined as part of the history and culture of Israeli Jews. An attack on Jews anywhere is treated as an attack on Jews everywhere, promoting a mutual, unwritten pact of normative responsibilities and obligations, reinforcing the bonds between Israel and Jewish communities around the world.

These simple illustrations can be multiplied. My major point is that there are important linkages between internal developments in Israel and Jewish communities outside Israel that require analysis if the goal is to understand the dynamics of Israel's changing society.

Who Is Jewish in Israel and in the Jewish Diaspora?

Since Israel defines itself as the center of the Jewish people, an elementary question about the "ethnic" relationships between Israeli and non-Israeli Jews is, Who is included as a member of the Jewish people? The definitional question of Who is a Jew? in the state of Israel symbolizes the connections, and the gap, between the two largest Jewish communities in the world: that of Israel and the United States.

The issue of defining who is Jewish is not new historically nor is it particular to the state of Israel. All societies struggle with defining membership and citizenship. In Israel, the definition has been decided by Israel's parliament, the Knesset, on "religious" grounds and has been implemented by the Jewish religious authorities of the state, that is, by Orthodox rabbis and their institutions. The paradox is that American Jews are concerned about the legalities of citizenship in a Jewish country thousands of miles away that the majority have not visited and in which most have no intention of applying for such citizenship and are unlikely to test whether they would ever fit those criteria.

To understand this elementary issue from the point of view of Israeli society, we can unravel the Israeli view of the core issue of Jewish life in the aftermath of European modernization: the integration and assimilation of Jews in modern, secular, open pluralistic societies. In its most simple form, the Israeli argument about the assimilation of diaspora Jews is as follows. In modern, open pluralistic societies, for example in America, Jews are assimilating. Assimilation, they argue, means the erosion of Jewish life in the process of becoming like non-Jews. Intermarriage is the most conspicuous indicator of such erosions, because when Jews intermarry with non-Jews, they are distancing themselves from their "traditional" roots, rejecting their Jewishness and their Judaism together with their links to the Jewish people, community, history, and culture. Such inter-marriages are unlikely to occur in Israel (in large part because of the boundaries between Jews and Arabs). Since American Jews are assimilating, the Israelis argue, it is particularly unclear why they should be concerned about the way Jews are being defined in the state of Israel. Assimilating Jews should be partic-ularly indifferent to formal issues about the Judaism of the Jews. Why should American Jews care about the way rabbis, from another culture and with very different values from theirs, jockey for political power and make legal and polit-ical pronouncements that are irrelevant to their lives and their Jewishness? Shouldn't Jewish Americans, who are committed to American political values of separation of church and state (not necessarily Jewish or Israeli political values), be indifferent to religious-political parties in Israel?

The answer to these questions relates to changes in Judaism in the process of modernization. Over the past century, American Jews have become less observant religiously, their institutions have become secular, and their Judaism has been re-formed. At the same time that traditional religious practices and institutions were declining, new ways of expressing Judaism were emerging and new forms of Jew-ishness were substituting for religion. As American Jews became less religiously and ritually observant, moving away from Orthodox toward Conservative and Reform Judaism, the state of Israel became a major basis of communal consensus, reinforcing Jewish continuity as part of ethnic activities, in other words, Jewish peoplehood. Thus, religious changes did not imply the end of their commit-ments as Jews within their families and their communities or as part of the Jew-ish people everywhere and over time. "Ethnic" Jewishness, and especially its Israel-centered component, emerged to replace the Judaisms of ritual and belief.

Most American Jews, then, define Israel as a very important part of their lives and central to the education of their children. Substantial proportions of American Jews have visited Israel, have relatives and friends living in Israel, and financially contribute to Israeli-related projects. Israel's survival is bound up with the ethnic lives of American Jews since they consider themselves part of the Jewish people. The state of Israel has become a psychological anchor for many American Jews and is the sociocultural foundation of their Jewishness and a source of communal cohesion. American Jewish identity is defined by its pro-Israelism.

Although there have been increases in the rates of intermarriage between Jews and non-Jews in the United States, there is no simple association between intermarriage and alienation from the Jewish community. In many intermarriages, the Jewish partner remains attached to the Jewish community through family, friends, and organizational ties; often the non-Jewish-born spouse becomes attached to the Jewish community, as do many of the children of the intermarried. Most of their friends are Jewish, many support Israel, and most identify themselves as Jews. Some proportion formally convert to Judaism; many are converted by religious procedures under the direction of Orthodox and Conservative rabbis, but more are converted to Judaism by Reform rabbis using nontraditional religious criteria.

Taken together, the research evidence shows that the intermarried, certainly the formally converted (by whatever denomination and by whatever criteria) cannot be written off as lost to the Jewish community. Their families, rabbis, and Jewish organizations have not excluded them and they have not excluded themselves. Can a citizenship law in the state of Israel write them off as Jewish people without creating concern among the intermarried, their families, their rabbis, their community, and their institutions?

Even though immigration is not part of the agenda of most American Jews, their identity as Jews is intertwined in complex and profound ways with their associations with Israel. At the same time, about 85 percent of American Jews reject Orthodox Judaism as their form of religious expression, and most have developed religious alternatives; their legitimacy as Jews is unquestioned in America. Although, in large part, they have rejected the version of Zionism that insists on their immigration as the only legitimate solution to the Jewish condition in the diaspora, they have developed alternative versions of Zionism that allow them to have strong bonds to the state of Israel. Pro-Israelism has been their commitment without the ideological imperative of immigration or the rejection of the continuation of American Jewish life.

American Jews are comfortable as Jews where they live and display their Jewishness openly and legitimately. Anchoring their Jewish identity in the Jewish state, which calls into question their legitimacy as Jews, their children's legitimacy, and that of their religious leaders, becomes untenable. For some time, Orthodox rabbis have called into question the Jewishness of those who have become Jews by choice or who practice their Judaism differently from theirs. American Jews have, in large part, ignored these Orthodox rabbis and have been indifferent to their values. Orthodox Judaism in Israel, in its political form, has become more intolerant of Jewish diversity, at the same time that American Jews have embraced pluralism in Judaism.

The United States and Israel represent different strategies of Jewish survival in the modern world. The state of Israel is a major source of Jewish culture, experience, identity, and history for American Jews, since it is their link to Jewish peoplehood, the quintessential form of political ethnicity. Israel is not their "national origin" in the geographic sense. In its constructed ideological form, Israel is no less powerful as a symbol of ethnicity for Jewish communities. For many Israeli Jews, the American Jewish community is the paradigm of erosion and decay and the lack of Jewish viability and continuity, yet a source of potential immigration.

There are increasing indications that Israeli Jews and Jews in communities outside Israel are moving apart from each other. Although the state of Israel has become the center of Jewish peoplehood, large, cohesive, and powerful Jewish communities have emerged in modern pluralistic societies. These are legitimate and accepted ethnic-religious communities, with long-term roots in these societies, as well as strong linkages to Israel. Whereas most of the Jews outside of Israel are committed to the state, in their view and in their behavior they are not in "exile" or in diaspora. Their home is where they live, where they expect to continue living, and where they are raising the next generation to live. Mutual dependencies have developed between Israel and the Jewish communities outside Israel. These dependencies have changed over time as these communities have responded to each other and as technology has brought geographically spread persons into new forms of communication to exchange ideas, cultures, and people. The exchanges have flowed in both directions.

In the past, there were major commonalities of background and experience between Israeli and American Jews. Both groups were heavily influenced by their European origins, and many Jews were raised in families where Yiddish was spoken and were rooted in Yiddish culture. Many struggled with second-generation status; in other words, they were raised by parents who were not native to the country in which they were living. Many shared the cultural and social disruptions of secularization and assimilation; the struggles of economic depression, war, and Holocaust in Europe; and the rebuilding of the lives of Jewish refugees. They shared in the most tangible and dramatic ways the establishment and the rebuilding of the state of Israel. In short, there was a shared sense of origins, experiences, and objectives in the past, although each group was living in a different society and building a new community with an appropriate set of institutions.

New generations have emerged in Israel and in the United States that are more distant from Europe and from the commonalities of language. For them, the European Holocaust is history, and immigration origins are far away, as are the struggles of pioneering in Israel and upward generational mobility in the United States. The different experiences of Israel and the United States as societies have shaped the lives, lifestyles, institutions, and values of the people of these communities. Not only have past commonalities declined but also new gaps have emerged. A key example is the role of women in both societies. American Jewish women have been in the forefront of social changes in their increasing independence from traditional gender roles and family relationships. Their high levels of education, career orientations, small family size, and high aspirations for themselves and their children have been truly revolutionary. Many American men have shared and adjusted to these changes in the workplace and in families. In contrast, Israeli men and women tend to have much more traditional segregated family and social roles. Family relationships are more patriarchal, work patterns for women are less tied to careers, and Israeli women lack the autonomy of American women. So this particular gap, with its implications for work and family, has grown in recent years.

Religion is the most serious manifestation of the gap between Israel and Jewish communities external to Israel. Judaism has been highly politicized in Israel, with control over religious institutions exercised by one segment of Judaism (the Orthodox). Religious leaders of Israel and of communities outside Israel have so little in common that there is virtually no communication between them.

The commitment of American Jews to the separation of religion and politics contrasts sharply with the clear interrelationship of religion and politics in Israel, with the long-standing power of religious-political parties, and with the conspicuous intervention of religious leaders in Israeli politics. Religious pluralism characterizes Jewish communities outside Israel, and multiple expressions of Judaism are normatively accepted and valued; only one Judaism, Orthodoxy, is defined as legitimate in Israeli society. Israel and its leaders are not committed to ethnic or religious pluralism in the same way that is characteristic of American Jewry. The trajectories of changes in these two communities are moving in the direction of straining the relationships between them, not in closing the gap.

THE PALESTINIAN QUESTION

How have the external conflicts with Arab Palestinians reshaped and affected the changes within the state? How have they influenced the way Israeli society relates to its Arab minority and to the broader Arab-Israeli conflict? What is the situation of the Palestinians who are residents of the areas that have been administered and occupied by the state of Israel since the 1967 war? Through the end of the 1970s, these territories were referred to officially as administered territories and incorporated the West Bank and Gaza (the latter and Jericho came under Palestinian administration in mid-1994). They became officially known by their Biblical names, Judea, Samaria, and Gaza—reflecting the ascendancy of the Likud government in 1977 and its more nationalistic policies with regard to these territories. The political symbolism of this name switch is of profound importance in understanding the relationship of the Israeli government to these areas, which encompassed around 180,000 Jewish settlers and over 2 million Arab Palestinians at the end of the twentieth century.

The Israeli government has never officially incorporated into Israel the Arab-Palestinian population living in these territories, except for East Jerusalem in 1967. The political rights of citizenship accorded to Arab Israelis were not extended to those living in the West Bank and Gaza. The incorporation of the large Arab population within "Greater Israel" would have threatened the demographic dominance of the Jewish population. In the 1970s and 1980s, a series of demographic projections showed clearly that the differential growth rates of Israel's population and the Arab-Palestinian population under its administrative control would result in a declining Jewish proportion and would entail the risk of losing a Jewish majority in a little over a generation. Ironically, some of the most nationalistic among the Israeli Jewish population argue for the incorporation of the Palestinian population. If they were successful, the demographic result would be the emergence of an Arab-Palestinian demographic majority. Hence, the more extreme among the Israeli nationalists instead argued for the incorporation of the administered land within the state, without integrating the Palestinian population.

The alternatives to returning control over the administered territories to the Palestinians ranged from the development of a quasi-colonial relationship between Israel and the Palestinian population under its administration (which in part occurred) to the evacuation of the Arab population, to be replaced by Israeli residents (which has occurred only marginally). The notion of a combined Israeli-Palestinian state shared between Jewish and Arab-Palestinian populations was not acceptable to either side of the conflict. Such a state would require a radical transformation of the institutions, values, and symbols that mark Israel as a Jewish state.

The size of the Arab population of these territories is somewhat in dispute, since there are different estimates depending on how Palestinians are defined and by which officials. Over the two decades beginning in 1970, there was a substantial growth in the population of the West Bank and Gaza, increasing to over 1.6 million persons from less than 1 million in 1970, and growing at a rate that would double the population every generation. Although not accurate, comparisons over time reveal a tendency toward very high population growth rates with the attendant consequences. With the return of Gaza and its population to Palestinian control in 1994, over 2 million Palestinians are likely to have remained under Israeli administration (in addition to the Israeli-Arab population). The birth rate remains quite high, as are death rates, and the potential for continuing rapid growth is high as a result.

The administration of these territories by Israel involves political control and the presence or involvement of government agencies such as health, education, agricultural regulation, and administrative justice. This administration implies that economic decisions are more likely to serve the interests of the Israeli economy and that investments in local control are minimal. Local Palestinian residents have not been part of the political process that has shaped these economic policies. Domestic needs and local economic development have been secondary to the needs of the Israeli government, including the recruitment of labor to work in Israel and the flow of Israeli goods into the territories.

The occupational patterns of men in these territories are revealing. There are few persons employed in white-collar jobs (less than 10 percent) and the overwhelming majority (over 7 out of 10 of the employed males) are skilled and unskilled workers in industry. A significant proportion of these people work in the state of Israel, commuting on a daily basis. In 1992, three-fourths of Arab Palestinians commuting to Israel were working in the construction industry.

Looking at the employers, the evidence identifies the Jewish role in construction in particular and in the stratification picture in general. Although the number of Jews in construction declined and the number of Arabs from the territories increased significantly, the proportion of employers remained overwhelmingly Jewish. About 80 percent of the employers in 1975 were Jewish, as were 76 percent in 1987. These patterns of employment changed in the years 2000 and 2001, as less daily commuting to the state of Israel was permitted and violence between Israelis and Palestinians became daily occurrences. The Palestinian workers from the territories were replaced by temporary guest workers from a wide range of countries.

The identity of the Israeli-Arab population has been influenced, sharpened, and challenged in a variety of ways by the links between Israel and the Arab Palestinians in the territories. First and foremost, Arab Israelis became linked to Arab Palestinians in the West Bank and in Gaza in their national aspirations. The links have heightened their sensitivities to the value of ethnic networks and their own national origins and have confronted them with the choice between identifying as Arab Israelis or as displaced Palestinians. Arab Israelis are caught in the middle. They are beneficiaries of the system created to control and protect them as a minority and as citizens of the state of Israel, and yet they are viewed as disloyal Palestinians by their Arab-Palestinian cousins. Although Arab Israelis identify as Palestinians in some contexts, they have been living as citizens in Israel for generations. Lacking the structural opportunities to integrate residentially and regionally with Jewish Israelis, they are a minority with rights and entitlements as citizens of the state. Their identity may be challenged and conflicted, but they do not always identify fully with the aspirations of the Palestinians in the territories.

Since 1967, the Arab-Israeli population has been pushed up in the social and economic hierarchy in Israel, ahead of the noncitizen Palestinians (but remaining below Jewish Israelis). They have relinquished part of the lowest paid positions and unskilled work to Palestinian day workers and have been mobile in the Israeli social class system. Even though Arab Israelis live and work and go to school in Israel and have access to the goods and welfare of Israeli society, they are connected ethnically to Palestinians. The linkages between Israel and the territories since 1967 has reinforced and legitimated the minority status of its Arab-Israeli population.

Land for Peace

Some Israelis view giving up land as a violation of a fundamental ideological principle; others are more willing to consider trading territory for a process that would lead to peace. Palestinian control over land occupied by Israel for a quarter of a century is countered by arguments over who has the "right" to the land (divine or political) and by the Israeli concern that terrorism and uncontrollable conflict, not peaceful neighborly relations, will result from Palestinian autonomy and statehood. Fear and distrust have often been replaced by hatred and by Israeli suppression of Palestinian self-determination. This may be slowly changing, but it is a long process that requires unfolding and has been frozen since the second *intifada*, uprising, of the Palestinian population beginning in 2000.

In the 1990s, the world's international situation had altered, particularly with the collapse of the Soviet regime and its diminished influence in the Middle East, with the changing role of the Persian Gulf states, and with the increasing ethnic-national identity of the Palestinians. Israelis and Palestinians had been talking to one another, yet terrorism continued. It is clear that Israel will give up territory (how much and when is not clear) and that the Palestinians will have increasing control over their own autonomous political unit in the West Bank, parallel to the developing institutions and infrastructure in Gaza. There is likely to be a gradual end to the Israeli military presence in the West Bank and diminished control over local Palestinian institutions (health, education, welfare, and economic). The indicators all point to processes that will result in new relationships between Israelis and Palestinians. But, as in the past, these forward patterns toward peaceful resolution have been placed in serious jeopardy by terrorism and mistrust, by actions and reactions, by armed struggle and resistance.

In the late 1930s and 1940s, when faced with a similar dilemma, the Jewish government in Palestine, under the leadership of Ben-Gurion, opted for people over land and accepted the idea of the partition of the land of Israel. It was a decision reached not without considerable pain and internal conflict. Faced with a similar choice, the leadership in Israel at the end of the twentieth century reached similar conclusions. The costs of continuing with occupation and violence were too high, development and peace were too important for the internal development in Israeli society, and the toll in the quality of life in Israel and in the administered territories was too high to justify the continuation of the status quo. The dependency of both populations on other nations and on outside support is too great for either side to only follow its ideological imperatives.

The Ethnic-National Question

The divisions between Jews and Arabs are different from the internal divisions among Jews, although they share some basic similarities. What can one infer from this understanding of the sources of these differences about the relative permanence of these divisions and whether Jewish and Arab ethnicity in Israel is transitional? If ethnic communities are continuous features of Israel's emerging pluralism, how is national integration affected? In short, does ethnic continuity conflict with national Israeli integration?

It is clear that the earlier entry into Israel's society of European immigrants and their socioeconomic and demographic backgrounds facilitated their relatively successful socioeconomic mobility and their access to power, resources, and opportunity. European immigrants could take advantage of their connections to the European-dominated society and economy that they found established as the state was developing. Burdened by larger families, higher mortality and morbidity, and fewer resources than Jews from Western societies, Asian and African immigrants arrived in Israel later in time, with a higher level of dependency on sociopolitical institutions. They came from less-developed societies, with fewer urban skills and less-powerful economic networks, and they were therefore less able to compete with European-origin groups in Israel. The timing of immigration and the cultural differences between groups reinforced these structural background factors that divided Israeli Jews.

The differential timing of immigration and the changing ethnic composition of immigrant streams created the contexts of residential concentration among Jews. Ethnic residential patterns, more so than the legacy of social and cultural origins, shape what ethnicity continues to mean in the process of nation-building in Israel. Residential concentration forged from political and economic considerations has become the key process marking off Israeli-born Jews from each other as it has been the demographic foundation of the continuing Jewish-Arab distinctiveness.

New Israeli patterns have emerged among Jews that are neither fully "Western" nor "Middle Eastern." Residential segregation and its implication for access to opportunity are critical in retaining ethnic distinctiveness. Ethnic residential concentration is linked to educational opportunities and, in turn, to jobs; it is likely to relate to intra-ethnic marriages and a reinforced sense of ethnic self-identity, pride, and culture, connecting ethnic origins and families into networks of relationships.

Ethnic residential concentration among Jews and between Jews and Arabs reinforces the overlap of ethnicity and socioeconomic factors through the impact of locational factors on access to educational and economic opportunities. Together, residential and socioeconomic concentrations shape the continuing salience of ethnic distinctiveness in Israel. When groups are integrated residentially, ethnic differences become marginal in their social, economic, and political importance; where residential segregation in Israel has persisted, it has become the primary engine of ethnic persistence and inequality. Although ethnic segregation is associated at times with poverty and lower socioeconomic status, it also implies supportive and family networks that shape the lives of many Israelis. Local institutions serve as further bases for ethnic continuity. These include ethnic family networks, economic networks that are ethnically based, and some local institutions—synagogues, community centers, political interests, health clinics, and leisure-time and cultural activities (sports and music, for example)—that are concentrated among particular ethnic groups. Jewish ethnic continuities persist despite government policies and ideological orientations to deny the salience of ethnicity.

The Arab-Jewish distinction is driven by these same processes of economic concentration, residential segregation, and institutional separateness. It also reflects the political legacy of the broader Arab-Israeli conflict, the role of Palestinians in their quest for national identity, and the importance of Jewishness in the political shape of Israeli society and its symbols. The ethnic identity of Arab-Israelis can never be fully Israeli as long as being Israeli involves a clear and unmistakable Jewish cultural component, Jewish historical constructions, and dominant Jewish symbols. The economic integration of Israeli Arabs makes their distinctiveness sharper and their powerlessness obvious and does not increase their social integration. The Arab population of Israel is likely to struggle with the conflicts of their identity for another generation and with their unequal access to opportunities as citizens of the state.

Jewish and Arab residential segregation in Israel and the resultant distinctiveness and disadvantage of Israeli Arabs are unlikely to be resolved without major internal changes in the society, its institutions, values, and political system. Barring such fundamental changes in the Jewish state of Israel, the residential segregation of Arab Israelis will continue, and the consequences for socioeconomic inequalities will persist. Only local control over institutions and the development of local opportunities for socioeconomic mobility in Arab-Israeli communities can reduce their disadvantaged status. How Israeli Arabs will be linked to autonomous Palestinian areas and Arab states remains unclear.

CHAPTER 9

WHITHER PALESTINE AND THE PALESTINIANS?

Samih K. Farsoun

The 1993 agreement between Israel and the PLO, known as the Oslo accords, drew mixed reactions from Palestinians. Though it won enthusiastic support or at least conditional approval from many, it was also rejected outright by others, including the groups Hamas and Islamic Jihad (Al-Jihad al-Islami). These groups believed the agreement as negotiated would not result in Palestinian independence and statehood.

Yasser Arafat and the PLO had been headquartered in Tunis since being expelled from Lebanon by the Israelis in 1982. In the view of Hamas and Islamic Jihad, these "Diaspora Palestinians" had grown out of touch with the realities of Palestinian life in the occupied territories. Hamas and Islamic Jihad resented the PLO's usurpation of negotiations on behalf of Palestinians, and resented as well Arafat's consolidation of control over the Palestinian Authority (PA), the agency of self-rule in the West Bank and the Gaza Strip. With the death of Arafat in 2004, a dilemma now facing the Palestinian people is to separate the administrative functions of the PA from the political functions of the PLO, such that the latter reemerges as the political representative of all Palestinians, not just those in the occupied territories.

*The late **Samih K. Farsoun** was professor emeritus of sociology at American University and the author of* Culture and Customs of the Palestinians *as well as* Palestine and the Palestinians, *from which this chapter is excerpted.*

THE PALESTINIAN-ISRAELI CONFLICT passed through four distinct phases.

1. The first emerged with the process of Zionist settler colonialism, which started in the late nineteenth century but intensified greatly after WWI during the British Mandate (1921-1948). Palestinian resistance to European Jewish colonization, settlement, immigration, and the British Mandate was best symbolized by the great Palestinian revolt of 1936–1939 against British authorities and then again by the internal (Palestinian–Jewish/Israeli) war of 1947–1948. This

phase ended with the destruction and dismemberment of Palestine and the dispossession and dispersal of its people.

2. In the second phase the Palestinian-Israeli conflict was "Arabized" into the Arab-Israeli state conflict, which culminated in the 1967 war in a swift defeat of the armies of the nationalist Arab states that had promised to liberate Palestine. "Arabization" of the Palestinian-Israeli conflict failed to liberate Palestine or resolve the Palestine question. It did, however, lead to the emergence of a radical, Palestinian-controlled PLO. The radical Palestinians promised not only the liberation of Palestine but also social revolution through people's armed struggle. But they were quickly crushed by Jordan in 1970–1971.

In the October 1973 war against Israel, Egypt and Syria fell back on conventional military means in an attempt to correct the strategic imbalance between Israel and the nationalist Arab states. This campaign was only partially successful. Thereafter, the Arab states, with the support of the Soviet Union, became willing to negotiate a political settlement, but Israel and its Western supporters remained intransigent. The latter also rejected the PLO as the representative of the Palestinian people, consistently portraying it as a terrorist organization dedicated to Israel's destruction. During this phase Israel and the West dismissed PLO peace proposals out of hand.

Instead of seeking peace according to the internationally acknowledged formula of land for peace, Israel embarked on a program of colonizing and absorbing the West Bank and Gaza Strip, the remaining parts of historic Arab Palestine. The possibility of a comprehensive political settlement and just peace was effectively ruled out in 1977 with Egypt's separate peace treaty with Israel. The 1979 Egyptian-Israeli peace treaty not only removed Egypt, the strongest Arab country, from the Arab-Israeli conflict but altered significantly the strategic balance between Israel and the other Arab states.

This imbalance invited aggressive Israeli expansionism in the West Bank and Gaza and the Golan Heights and military adventurism focused on Lebanon. Israel not only intervened in internal Lebanese affairs but also sought to destroy the PLO, which was headquartered there. These efforts culminated in the 1982 Israeli invasion of Lebanon, the siege of Beirut, and the negotiated exit of the PLO and its military forces from the city. During this period Israel also formally annexed "greater" Jerusalem (East Jerusalem and an area expanded around the city in the West Bank) and the Golan Heights and significantly intensified its colonization and settlement of the West Bank and Gaza Strip.

Also during the 1980s, the decline in oil revenues; the sharp rise of Arab state indebtedness; the profound economic, social, and political-ideological transformation of the eastern Arab world (especially the surge of political Islam); and the Iraq-Iran war diverted Arab attention from the Palestine question and the Palestinian people and hastened the eclipse of the PLO (which had shifted its base to Tunis). These developments, signaling Arab state disengagement from the Arab-Israeli conflict, reflected the erosion of popular public Arab support for the cause of Palestine. In short, this change in the political culture of the Arab peoples—perhaps commensurate with the demise of Arab nationalism—increasingly isolated the Palestinians and the PLO.

3. In 1987, however, a spectacular intifada marked the third major phase of the Palestinian-Israeli struggle. The intifada allowed the Palestinian people, including the PLO, to regain self-confidence, to galvanize the far-flung diaspora communities into renewed political activism, and to reassert Palestinian rights before a rapt international audience. In a dramatic sense the intifada re-Palestinianized the conflict that had so long been Arabized. As important, it exposed the limits of Israeli power and the arrogance, brutality, and racism of its occupation.

The intifada not only revitalized the Palestinian question on the international and regional levels but also tipped the balance of power locally, inside Israel and the occupied territories. The intifada raised the issue of the political, economic, and social cost of the occupation for Israel. As a result, the Likud government participated in the Madrid peace conference in 1991, and Labor won the 1992 Israeli elections on a peace platform of a negotiated settlement with the Arab states and the Palestinians.

In 1991 Israel unleashed a new type of counterinsurgency, what it called a "security offensive," against the intifada. The intifada began to wane because of the massive and unrelenting measures by Israel, the Israeli and Western financial and economic blockade, and the loss of Arab financial and political support. This increasingly untenable situation for the Palestinians in the occupied territories, in combination with the failure of the PLO to relieve if not end the occupation, led to the rise, especially in Gaza, of Hamas and the more extremist al-Jihad al-Islami, which began to challenge the legitimacy and leadership of the PLO and [PLO Chairman Yasser] 'Arafat.

4. Arab economic and political support of the Palestinians never returned to the level of the 1970s despite the popularity of the intifada and the end of the Iraq-Iran war in 1988. The PLO under 'Arafat's direction established closer relations with militarily strong Iraq. But in the 1991 Gulf War the US-led military alliance destroyed Iraq's forces and the country's infrastructure, devastated its economy, and turned the politically weak oil-exporting states of the Arabian peninsula into US protectorates. The PLO policy of opposition to US military

intervention in the Iraq-Kuwait crisis prompted Arab oil-states to end their support for 'Arafat, the PLO, and Palestinian social service institutions. Arab governments and many of their citizens quickly turned hostile to the Palestinians as individuals and as communities living among them. Indeed the large Palestinian communities in Kuwait (about 350,000–400,000 people) and to a lesser extent in other Gulf states were expelled. Palestinian activism in the post–Gulf War period in the Gulf states was constrained. In Lebanon severe restrictions were imposed on Palestinian residents, the chilly relationship between the Syrian government and 'Arafat's PLO put a freeze on mobilization of the Palestinian community in Syria, and loyalists to King Hussein expressed their suspicion of the Palestinians and the PLO in Jordan. The PLO was thus profoundly isolated and weakened as never before in its history.

THE PALESTINIAN POLITICAL CRISIS

The sudden, unexpected agreement between Israel and the PLO and the signing of the Declaration of Principles by 'Arafat plunged the PLO and the whole Palestinian people into a momentous political crisis. The shock and stunned disbelief that greeted announcement of the Oslo Accords quickly turned into four diversified reactions.

The first reaction was enthusiastic support from those who believed that the agreements were a historic breakthrough that would lead to Israeli military withdrawal from the occupied territories and self-determination by the end of the interim period. Palestinians who reacted in this manner were small in number: those in the PLO bureaucracy; most of the PLO functionaries and diplomats; most of 'Arafat's supporters, allies, clients, and dependents.

The second tendency was conditional approval: Some Palestinians saw in the agreement essential progress, although they viewed it as far from satisfactory. Adherents of this view included wide sectors of the Palestinian people in the West Bank and the Gaza Strip. This group was most interested in ridding the occupied territories of the repressive Israeli troops and finding some socioeconomic relief and normalcy in the promised economic aid.

The third response, by those who long supported peaceful resolution of the Israeli-Palestinian conflict, was to see the accord as thoroughly flawed and potentially fatal for Palestinian national aspirations and survival as a people. The adherents of this view were outraged at the enormous concessions of Palestinian rights that 'Arafat made without consultation, public debate, or legitimate formal approval. 'Arafat's secretive, individualistic, and unconstitutional style of negotiating the accords and securing "official" approval of them from the truncated, 'Arafat-dependent rump PLO bodies—not including the PNC [Palestinian National Council]—of highly questionable legitimacy appalled almost all Palestinians. This group saw the accords as controversial substantive agreements that shattered Palestinian consensus and political unity. Above all, this constituency was afraid that the Declaration of Principles, which disregarded international law and United Nations resolutions on Palestine, undermined the internationally recognized and codified rights of the Palestinian people.

Finally, the "rejectionists" saw the accords as high treason, capitulation to the enemy, a violation of the Palestinian national consensus and principles of the national covenant or PLO charter and PNC resolutions. They believed the agreements would never lead to independence and statehood. This group included those of both the Right and the Left in the Palestinian political spectrum: Hamas and Al-Jihad al-Islami on the right and a score of other parties on the left. This view also had significant support both inside the occupied territories and in the diaspora, especially in the refugee camps. It should be pointed out, however, that they did not reject a negotiated settlement; rather, like the previous group, they were against these particularly flawed and capitulationist agreements.

In 1994 'Arafat returned to Gaza to set up the Palestinian Authority in accordance with the terms of the Oslo Accords. The jubilation of the Gaza people upon his entry was genuine, as they expressed the joy of freedom from harsh Israeli control. Through a large police force (agreed to in the accords), 'Arafat set about imposing order and his authority on a restive population and a chaotic situation and terminating the active resistance to the continuing Israeli occupation. The long grassroots political and armed struggle was not to end but was to be mobilized in support of the emerging Palestinian Authority regime. Against his opponents, especially Hamas, 'Arafat utilized his tried-and-true political tactics of negotiations to build a consensus and failing that, co-optation, infiltration, and force. These tactics failed to resolve the disappointment and discontent of the great majority of the Palestinians with the accords, 'Arafat, and the PLO. The political lines and divisions were drawn, and the crisis persisted.

The only serious opposition to both the Declaration of Principles and 'Arafat's regime is Hamas and Al-Jihad al-Islami, which are principally limited to the Gaza Strip. Their attacks against the occupation troops and Israeli civilians inside Israel have been branded by most of the international media and those controlled by 'Arafat's regime as terrorist actions against peace. Their power base in the Gaza Strip is relatively strong and represents, after the years of PA rule, a continuing albeit attenuated challenge to the regime's authority and legitimacy.

But despite the political and violent confrontations in Gaza, the PA-Hamas conflict has settled into mutual accommodation. Although Hamas is the only serious threat to the PLO-Israeli arrangements, its impact has neither stopped nor modified the march of events.

Popular Disillusionment

The disaffected Palestinian majority has become disillusioned, demoralized, politically paralyzed, and unable to mount any significant action to change conditions on the ground in the occupied territories or internationally. This situation reflects the deepening crisis in the Palestinian national movement. This crisis also produced widespread political cynicism and depoliticization and, among some, desperation and profound hopelessness. In the hapless slums of Gaza, many angry young men have volunteered for suicide missions against the Israelis. Many (including former Fateh militants) rallied to the cause of Hamas not out of religious conviction as true believers but because Hamas emerged as the only group to resist the truly unjust and disappointing turn of events.

And yet in their bleak social, economic, and political situation the Palestinian people have made efforts not only to redefine the nature of Palestinian national identity and consciousness but also to address emergent social issues amid the contemporary Palestinian political terrain monopolized by 'Arafat and his PA on one side and the Islamists on the other. The majority of the Palestinian public—the proverbial silent majority—tends to be secular, democratic, and supportive of the idea of Palestinian sovereignty and unhappy with 'Arafat's unprincipled concessions to Israel and his role as Israel's enforcer. This silent majority, including the multiplicity of NGOs, the intellectuals, unions, women's groups, and other economic and cultural organizations in cities, villages, and refugee camps, may be responsive to the proposed alternative: a broad movement that would break the political monopoly of 'Arafat's regime and the religious opposition.

Most of these social service and cultural organizations were the popular groups that mobilized the Palestinian people against Israeli occupation during the intifada. At that time they were morally, politically, and financially supported by the legitimate PLO and Arab and international donors. Currently, however, they are constrained, undermined, and financially starved by Israel, the PA/PLO, and the formerly generous Arab and international donors.

Among the diaspora Palestinians, little in the form of opposition to 'Arafat's policies exists beyond passive antagonism, disaffection, anger, and rhetoric. Diaspora Palestinians are politically rudderless and isolated in the different and disconnected communities. The demise of the PLO institutions all but eliminated the transnational connectedness of the refugee and other diaspora communities.

THE INSTITUTIONAL CRISIS: THE REPRESENTATION DILEMMA

The accords between the PLO and Israel triggered not only a political crisis but also an institutional one. It raised the question of the representativeness, legitimacy, and credibility of the PLO, its institutions, and its leadership. With the creation of the Palestinian Authority, with limited civil and police powers over the population centers of the West Bank and the Gaza Strip, the relationship between the PLO and the PA became an issue. Just as confounding for all Palestinians was the election of a Legislative Council in the autonomy areas in January 1996, which raised questions of the council's relationship to the existing PNC. The PA and the council, legitimate as they may be in the eyes of the West Bank and Gaza Strip Palestinians (and much of the rest of the world), in no way could speak for or represent the diaspora communities. While the Legislative Council may have become the institution that articulates the will and aspirations of three-quarters of a million voters in the West Bank and the Gaza Strip, who represents the 4.5 million diaspora Palestinians? Compounding this dilemma is the behavior of 'Arafat, who continued to hold onto the supreme official powers of both institutions: the PLO and the PA.

The 1996 PNC meeting in Gaza effectively eliminated the existing but moribund PLO Executive Committee, which was anchored in the long-held national consensus and composed of representatives of the major feda'iyyin groups and political parties and some independents. 'Arafat replaced it with a new Executive Committee made up of his allies and loyalists, a rubber-stamp group. In the context of the disarray of the opposition, 'Arafat reasserted his authority over the long-established and legitimate institution of the Palestinian diaspora. The PLO; its Executive Committee; and its legislative council, the PNC, became controlled institutions of the 'Arafat regime, the PA.

"FINAL STATUS" NEGOTIATIONS AND LIKUD ISRAEL

"Final status" negotiations over the occupied territories between Israel and the PLO/PA formally opened on schedule in early May in the Egyptian resort of Taba and adjourned quickly until after the Israeli elections of May 29, 1996. The pro forma meeting was largely ceremonial and accomplished little beyond holding the meeting on schedule and showing the continuing interest of the two parties to carry on the "peace process" in accordance with the Oslo Accords. This meeting took place in an extremely charged political environment within Israel itself and involving Israel and the PA on one side and Hamas and the Islamic movement on the other.

In Israel a right-wing Jewish religious militant, Yigal Amir, assassinated Prime Minister Yitzhak Rabin on November 4, 1995, and plunged the country into a short-term political crisis. Foreign Minister Peres took over the position of prime minister and promised to continue along the path of Rabin. However, despite the agreements and security cooperation between Israel and the PLO/PA, Israel kept up its underground war against Hamas. Israel's security forces, for example, assassinated the top Hamas political leader in Malta. In the course of such attacks and retaliations, Hamas in February-March 1996 launched a series of suicide bombings inside Israel. The civilian death toll was high (fifty-eight dead and more than 200 wounded), and the political reaction, both in Israel and internationally, was extremely strong. Accordingly, the Peres government called on 'Arafat to "crack down" heavily on Hamas and its supporters and itself initiated measures to prohibit entry of Palestinians from the territories to work in Israel.

'Arafat's PA security forces arrested nearly 1,000 Palestinians suspected of links to Hamas. While 'Arafat received kudos from Peres and US president Clinton for his suppression of the Islamic militants, Israel proceeded to impose the tightest closure of the territories in its twenty-nine years of occupation. Not only were Palestinians prohibited from entering Israel, but the Israeli army imposed what the Israelis called "internal closure" on the autonomous population centers of the West Bank and Gaza Strip: For nearly two weeks following the March 4, 1996, suicide attack in Tel Aviv, the Peres government placed the 1.3 million Palestinians of the West Bank under wholesale curfew, with all movement between the "autonomous" towns and villages completely prohibited.

The swift Israeli military closure and control of the autonomous Palestinian population cantons—an action that would have provoked, at the very least, extensive civil unrest and popular resistance during the intifada—elicited no armed or popular resistance on the part of the Palestinians. But this closure occurred in coordination with the Palestinian security forces who basically stepped aside as the Israelis swept through. The only centers they did not enter, but closed off tightly, were the six "autonomous" cities of the West Bank. There and in the Gaza areas, the PA itself imposed a heavy security mantle. In the wake of these events, Palestinian support for the PA plummeted.

And so has the pendulum of antipathy toward the "peace process" also swung in Israel. After the suicide bombings in early 1996, the public mood increasingly favored the hard-line right-wing political coalition (Likud and religious parties). The pro-peace sentiment that had surged and become politically powerful in Israel after the assassination of Prime Minister Rabin had thus waned and nearly disappeared by the May 29, 1996, elections. As a result, Netanyahu, the rightist leader of the Likud, was elected prime minister over Peres of the Labor Party, the principal architect of the accords with the PLO. The Likud victory that put into power a hard-line Israeli leadership articulating intransigent positions, coupled with an Israel–PLO/PA peace process already viewed as unjust, unfair, and economically devastating by the majority of the Palestinian people, has sharpened further the internal Palestinian political crisis and raised doubts about a just or honorable political solution to the Palestine problem.

PALESTINIAN DESTINY

The Palestinian people now face a number of serious historic challenges whose resolution will determine their destiny as a people and the fate of their country. These challenges are of two types: immediate dilemmas and longer-term predicaments. In the political sphere, the immediate dilemmas include finding a credible, rational, and legitimate political process for decisionmaking that would involve and satisfy most political groups and tendencies, including Hamas and the radicals, and the mass of the "silent majority," both internal to the autonomous areas and in the diaspora. Central to the Palestinian political dilemma is the restructuring of the relationship between the PLO and the PA, whereby the PA exists as the agency of self-rule in the West Bank and Gaza Strip, while a reinvigorated, legitimate, and functioning PLO (or successor organization) and its institutions reemerge as the political framework and representative of *all* Palestinians, not just those in the occupied territories.

As have many other critics before us, we believe a careful reading of the texts of the Declaration of Principles, its annexes, and the derivative Cairo, Paris, and Oslo II Accords indicates clearly that they provide only for a limited Palestinian administration—for a fraction of the Palestinian people on a fraction of its land—and do not envision the building of an independent Palestinian state in the future. And because these agreements envision neither political nor economic independence for the Palestinian territories, such independence is not possible through the current "peace process." We therefore believe that in the context of such an imbalance of power between the politically weak Palestinian Authority and a strong Israel, the Declaration of Principles will *not* lead to Palestinian self-determination and independent statehood or to the restoration of or compensation for the internationally codified rights of the Palestinian diaspora.

What, then, would be the character of the emergent Palestinian entity? In debates taking place inside the occupied territories among some Palestinian intellectuals about the future of the occupied Palestinian territories, two possible scenarios are being proposed. The first scenario is that of two peoples (Israeli and Palestinian) living under *one*—Israeli—sovereignty. Under this plan the Palestinians of the West Bank and the Gaza Strip would—unlike the so-called Israeli Arabs (the Palestinian citizens of Israel)—have only civil autonomy, but like them they would become controlled, economically disadvantaged residents of greater Israel. They could commute to work in the lesser Israeli jobs but return at night to townshiplike communities of their own. Even the right-wing Likud is not antithetical to this possible outcome. In the binational option, Israel/Palestine would presumably become a democratic and not just a Jewish state, where the two ethnic nationalities would retain their cultural identity and eventually coexist in harmony in an integrated economy and single sovereignty. This option seems unlikely to us, much as it may superficially resemble the "secular democratic state" imagined by the Palestinian revolutionaries of the 1960s.

The second scenario being debated is a bit more optimistic. In the longer term, the Palestinian elections may, perhaps after several rounds, produce an increasingly autonomous Palestinian Council—autonomous from both Israel and the 'Arafat-type regime—that will establish a new model of intra-Palestinian politics and will draw the West Bank and the Gaza Strip away from Israel's octopuslike grip toward a confederation with Jordan. Of course this option is the old Jordanian option long preferred by earlier Israeli governments and US administrations. Jordanian dominion over the occupied territories or a Jordanian-Israeli condominium is indeed possible in the medium to long term. Should this happen, the economically subordinated Palestinian territories would likely remain poor and exploitable civil autonomy areas of a confederation.

More likely in our judgment is a Palestinian future of fragmented cantons in parts of the original homeland, the people enjoying fewer political and civil rights than the Palestinians of Israel or those of Jordan. The short and the medium terms are unbelievably bleak for Palestine and the Palestinians.

However, the Palestinians, who have consistently rejected defeat and shown themselves to be resilient, will continue the struggle in other forms in the emergent Middle Eastern realities. In our judgment, it would therefore be a mistake to assume that once established, the new Palestinian order under Israeli dominion would remain unchanged. The region as well as the world is in an era of profound transformation. The global, regional, and local balances of power may well shift to give the Palestinians new and different opportunities to pursue their struggle for an equitable, just, and lasting peace with the Israelis.

CHAPTER 10

THE LAND AND PEOPLE OF MODERN IRAQ

Phebe Marr

The Kingdom of Iraq was created as a British mandate in 1920. In 1932 it became the first mandate to achieve independence. The kingdom was converted to a republic by a military coup in 1958, and a series of succeeding coups culminated in 1968 with the Baath political party in power. Baathist strongman Saddam Hussein became president in 1979 and ruled Iraq till he was displaced in the American invasion of Iraq in 2003.

Iraq had not existed as a unified political entity before 1920. As a result, its borders remain contentious both from within and from without. Though about 75–80% of Iraq's population is Arab, Kurds make up almost all the remainder. The Kurds occupy the mountainous regions of Iraq's north and east, and identify with their fellow Kurds in neighboring Turkey, Iran, and Syria. The Kurds in Iraq have often pressed for greater autonomy within the country, if not for outright independence.

Iraqi Arabs are themselves divided between the ruling Sunni minority and the subordinate Shiite majority. The Sunnis generally occupy the north and west parts of the country, and the urban centers. Their religion tends to ally them with most other (and largely Sunni) Arab countries. The Shiites are strong in the south and maintain connections to Shiite religious leaders in Iran. Anxiety about Iranian influence over a majority of Iraq's population was an enduring issue for Saddam Hussein and remains a concern for the United States and the newly emerging Iraqi democracy even now.

Phebe Marr is a member of the editorial board of the Middle East Journal *and member of the Council on Foreign Relations. She is the author of* Egypt: Domestic Stability and Regional Role *as well as* The Modern History of Iraq, Second Edition, *from which the present chapter derives.*

THE LAND

THE STATE OF IRAQ has existed only since 1920, when it was carved from three former provinces of the Ottoman Empire and waas created under the British aegis as a mandate. With a land area of 168,000 square miles (436,800 square kilometers) and a population of over 23 million in 2003, Iraq is the largest of the Fertile Crescent countries rimming the northern edge of the Arabian peninsula. Lying between the plateau of northern Arabia and the mountain ridge of southwest Iran and eastern Turkey, Iraq forms a lowland corridor between Syria and the Persian/Arabian Gulf. From its earliest history Iraq has been a passageway between East and West. Its borders are for the most part artificial, reflecting the interests of the great powers during the First World War rather than the wishes of the local population. As a result, Iraq's present borders have been continuously challenged by peoples living inside and outside the country. The southern section of the border with Iran, a contributory cause of the Iran-Iraq war of the 1980s, has not been finally settled, while a new, UN-demarcated border with Kuwait, agreed to by Iraq in 1993, under pressure, is still contentious.

The southeastern portion of the country lies at the head of the Gulf. Iraq controls a thirty-six-mile (fifty-eight-kilometer) strip of Gulf territory barely sufficient to provide it with an outlet to the sea. From the Gulf, Iraq's border with Iran follows the Shatt al-Arab north, then skirts the Persian foothills as far north as the valley of the Diyala River, the first major tributary of the Tigris north of Baghdad. From here the frontier thrusts deep into the high Kurdish mountain ranges, following the Diyala River valley. Near Halabja it turns northward along the high mountain watersheds—incorporating within Iraq most of the headwaters of the major Tigris tributaries—until it reaches the Turkish border west of Lake Urmiyya. The mountainous boundary with Turkey ends at the Syrian border just west of Zakhu, Iraq's northernmost town. This northeastern region includes difficult and unmanageable mountain terrain and a substantial Kurdish population. The loss of control by the central government over substantial portions of this region in the 1990s made Iraq's northern borders with Turkey and Iran porous.

In the northwest the frontier separating Iraq from Syria meanders south across the Syrian desert from the Turkish border until it reaches the Euphrates near Qa'im. Here the borders make little pretense of following geography, jutting out into the adjacent desert and incorporating large areas of steppe. At the Euphrates the border turns west until it reaches Jordan, also a former British mandate, and then south a short distance to the Saudi frontier. From this point the border follows a line of water wells separating Iraq from Saudi Arabia until it reaches the Kuwaiti border at Wadi al-Batin, at which point it turns north again, forming a common frontier with Kuwait, until it reaches Umm Qasr on the Khaur Abd Allah channel leading to the Gulf.

The terrain included within these boundaries is remarkably diverse, making Iraq a country of extreme contrasts. The Shatt al-Arab is a broad waterway with villages on its banks, lined with date groves. To the north of the Shatt lies swampland, traditionally inhabited along the Tigris by marsh dwellers living in reed houses built on stilts and raising water buffalo, and along the Euphrates by rice-growing villagers. This natural wetland area, with high reeds and hidden waterways, has often functioned as a refuge for dissidents. A massive drainage system, constructed by the central government in the 1990s, has progressively dried up much of this terrain and is ending a traditional way of life. Between the marshlands and Baghdad is the delta, the most densely populated area of Iraq, once inhabited by the Sumerians and Babylonians of ancient Mesopotamia. It is a dry, flat area consisting almost entirely of irrigated farmland, with large mud-hut villages and regional market towns hugging the river banks. North of Baghdad the two rivers diverge widely to form the Jazira (Island), the territory between the two. Although some irrigation farming is practiced here, it is mainly rain-fed territory—a land of gentle uplands sprinkled with smaller villages and provincial towns. Mosul, near the site of Nineveh, is the Jazira's major city and the center of its commercial life. To the north and east of the Jazira, the plains give way to foothills filled with settled villages and prosperous towns (mainly inhabited by a mixture of Turkish- and Kurdish-speaking people) and then to the high mountains, the home of the Kurds. Iraqi Kurdistan, as this territory has frequently been called, is a remote and inaccessible area of deep gorges and rugged, snow-capped mountains rising to 12,000 feet (over 3,600 meters), broken only by the fertile valleys of the Tigris tributaries.

Within this diversity of territory the unifying feature of Iraq's geography is its twin river system. From the dawn of civilization the rivers have provided the irrigation that made life possible for those inhabiting the flat, dry plains through which they flow, uniting the populations of the north and south and giving them a common interest in controlling the rivers and their tributaries. The rivers have also provided the arteries for trade and communication without which the cities that have made Mesopotamia famous could not have flourished.

The rivers are not an unmixed blessing, however. The Tigris has often delivered torrential floods in the spring, too late for the winter crop and too early for the summer. The south of the country has a poor natural drainage system, causing progressive salinization of the soil if irrigation is not controlled or the soil flushed. Without dams, barrages, and artificial drainage systems, the rivers cannot support continuous agriculture. Whenever such an organized system has existed, the country between the two rivers has flourished; when it has not, decline, unrest, and turmoil have often resulted.

Iraq today is a country rich in resources. With proper management, the river system can provide agricultural production to feed a good portion of the population. Its agricultural potential, declining through overuse and, in recent years, neglect and abuse, is now dwarfed by petroleum. Iraq's proven oil reserves in 2000 were over 112 billion barrels, with another 200 billion of probable or possible reserves in areas not yet extensively explored. These reserves are the world's second largest, exceeded only by Saudi Arabia. With a national income of ID 15.3 ($51 billion) in 1980, before revenues declined owing to wars and sanctions, Iraq has ample sources of capital for development, if properly used and husbanded. After three quarters of a century of modern education, Iraq's population has acquired much of the technical capacity to manage a complex economy. Yet Iraq's problems as it faces the twenty-first century resemble those of its past. The challenge is to organize the political and social environment in a way that will bring Iraq's considerable potential to fruition, give peace and prosperity to its people, and put an end to the repression and mismanagement that have often led to conflict, disunity, and decay.

THE PEOPLE

If one can speak of an Iraqi state, it is not yet possible to speak of an Iraqi nation. Iraq's present borders incorporate a diverse medley of peoples who have not yet been welded into a single political community with a common sense of identity. The search for this identity has been a shared, if elusive, project of all Iraqi governments. Considerable integration and assimilation has taken place since the inception of the mandate, but there have also been setbacks—especially in recent years—to the process of nation building, revealing the fragility of the demographic mosaic and even of the state itself.

The first and most serious demographic division is ethnic, or more properly speaking, linguistic. Arabic speakers constitute 75 to 80 percent of the population; Kurdish speakers, 15 to 20 percent. The Arabs dominate the western steppe and the Tigris and Euphrates Valleys from Basra to the Mosul plain; the Kurds have their stronghold in the rugged mountain terrain of the north and east.

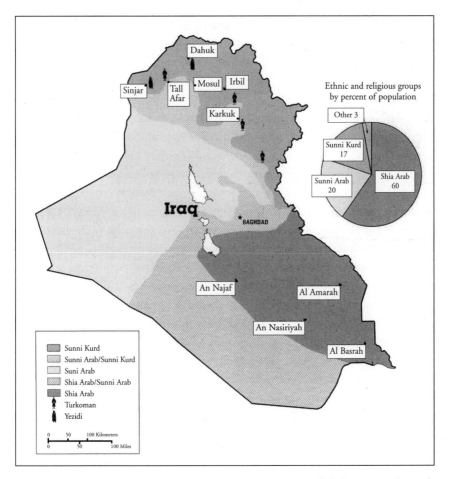

Map 10.1   Ethnoreligious groups in Iraq. *Source:* Figure 1.3 of Phebe Marr, *The Modern History of Iraq, Second Edition* (2004, Westview Press).

However, the Iraqi Kurds are only a portion of a larger Kurdish population with whom they identify on linguistic, cultural, and nationalistic grounds. In 2003 there were a little over 4 million Kurds in Iraq; about 13 million in Turkey (about 23 percent of the population); 5 million to 6 million in Iran (10 to 12 percent of the population), and fewer than 1 million in Syria. There are smaller numbers in Armenia, Azerbaijan, and Europe.

A second major division splits the population along religious lines between the two great sects of Islam, the *shi'a* and the *sunni*. Since the overwhelming majority of the Kurds are *sunni*, this division affects mainly the Arabs, but the outcome has been to segment Iraqi society into three distinct communities: the Arab shi'a, the Arab *sunnis*, and the Kurds.

Arab Shi'a

The division of the Muslim community originated shortly after the Prophet's death in a political dispute over who should be selected caliph, or successor. The *sunnis*, the majority, have accepted all caliphs who have held office regardless of the method of selection, so long as they were able to make their claims effective. The *shi'a*, the minority, took the side of the fourth caliph, Ali, cousin and son-in-law of the Prophet, claiming that the leadership of the community should have been his from the first and that only his heirs were legitimate successors. Eventually the leadership of the *shi'i* community devolved on religious scholars, called *mujtahids*. The fact that each individual *shi'a* is expected to follow a leading *mujtahid* gives the *shi'i* community stronger leadership and a greater sense of cohesion than its *sunni* counterpart. The *shi'a* began as a political party, gradually became an underground opposition movement, and finally evolved into a distinct religious sect.

From the first, southern Iraq has been a stronghold of *shi'i* Islam. Various *shi'i* movements either originated or found a firm reception in southern Iraqi cities, where *shi'i* Islam eventually established a foothold so firm it could not be dislodged by the *sunnis*. As Arab tribes migrated from the Arabian peninsula in the eighteenth and nineteenth centuries and settled in the river valleys, they were converted to *shi'i* Islam by religious scholars and their emissaries. Today the *shi'a* are the largest single religious community in Iraq, outnumbering the Arab *sunnis* three to one and constituting a solid majority of the total population.

Under the *sunni* Ottoman administration of Iraq, which began in the sixteenth century, Iraqi *shi'a* were largely excluded from administrative positions, from the military, and from government-sponsored education institutions that trained for them. Instead, *shi'i mujtahids* in the holy cities, often Persian in origin, were influenced by events in Persia. Not surprisingly, the *shi'a,* so long excluded from government, came to be deeply alienated from it.

Arab Sunnis

In contrast to the *shi'a*, the Arab *sunnis* in Iraq tend to be more secular and, with the exception of some recently settled tribes, more urban in composition. As a result, their communal identity has been less developed. Unlike the *shi'a*, the *sunnis* do not accord special religious authority to their leaders—the scholars, jurists, and judges collectively known as *ulama* who define and uphold the rules that guide the community. Rather they follow the *sunna*, or customs of the Prophet (from which they take their name), and the *shari'a*, the body of Islamic doctrine, law, and ritual derived from the Quran and the *sunna*. It is to the *shari'a*, rather than to any particular leader, that the *sunni* community owes adherence, a factor that has made it far more loosely structured than the *shi'i* community.

Despite their minority status, the Arab *sunnis* have traditionally dominated the political and social life of Iraq, originally due to Ottoman support but later due to the ability of *sunnis* to maintain the command posts of power. Although no census has been taken that distinguishes among various Muslim groups, the Arab *sunnis* probably represent about 15 to 20 percent of the population. Geographically they are concentrated in the northern part of the country, including the Arab tribal groups of the western steppe and the Arab villages of the northern Tigris and Euphrates areas. The remainder of the Arab *sunni* community is almost wholly urban, situated in the cities and towns of the central and northern provinces. Substantial numbers of *sunnis* also live in some cities of the south, especially Basra.

Although the collapse of the Ottoman Empire in the First World War removed Ottoman support for *sunni* supremacy, it did not end *sunni* dominance. Although that dominance has waxed and waned over time, especially socially and intellectually, *sunni* political control was more pronounced at the end of the twentieth century than at any time since the mandate. This political dominance and the resulting enjoyment of most of society's benefits have given the *sunni* community a closer association with—and vested interest in—the emerging Iraqi state. Arab *sunnis* have also had considerable affinity for the secular philosophies of Arab nationalism originating in neighboring (and largely *sunni*) Arab countries.

The Kurds

The third major group, the Kurds, has proved the most difficult to assimilate. Language has been a major stumbling block. The Kurds speak an Indo-European language closely akin to Persian, while Arabic remains the official language of the central government and of the higher educational institutions in Iraq. Even more important has been the sense of ethnic—even national—identity that the Kurds have developed, especially in the twentieth century.

The origin of the Kurds is still a matter of some historical dispute, with most Kurdish scholars claiming descent from the ancient Medes. Whatever their origins, the Kurds were almost completely converted to Islam. They became orthodox *sunnis*, part of a vast Muslim empire and often its staunchest defenders. From time to time, particularly in the seventeenth and eighteenth centuries, Kurdish dynasties arose but lacked cohesion and were unable to maintain their autonomy. In the twentieth century, a sense of Kurdish identity based on language, close tribal ties, customs, and a shared history inspired Kurdish nationalist movements. Like their predecessors, however, these political groups lacked sufficient cohesion and coordination to achieve lasting results.

The majority of Iraq's Kurdish population today is to be found in the mountains of the northeast, with Sulaimaniyya as its intellectual center and stronghold and Arbil its political capital. Until recently most Kurds were rural. However, the destruction of much of the Kurdish countryside, especially adjacent to Iran, and the forced migration of much of this population due to local wars and Iraqi government actions, has resulted in resettlement of large numbers of Kurds in cities and towns.

Of all Iraqi minority groups, the Kurds have been the most difficult to assimilate because of their numbers, geographic concentration, mountain inaccessibility, and cultural and linguistic identity. However, many bilingual Kurds have assimilated into Iraqi society sufficiently to enable them to play an active role in state and society.

Other Minorities

Aside from these three major demographic groups, there are several smaller ethnic and religious communities in Iraq. In northern towns and cities along the old trade route that led from Anatolia along the foothills of the Zagros to Baghdad live members of a Turkish-speaking group known locally as the Turkman. Comprising between 2 and 3 percent of the population and most numerous in the cities of Kirkuk and Arbil, they are probably remnants of migrations of Turkish tribes dating from the Seljuk era in the twelfth century and of the Turkman tribal dynasties of the fourteenth and fifteenth centuries. The Turkman, mainly *sunni* and middle class, have for decades produced a disproportionate number of bureaucrats and have integrated rather well into modern Iraq.

In the south is a group of *shi'i* Persian speakers with strong ties to Persia that have never been severed. Until the 1980s, they constituted 1.5 to 2 percent of the population, but in the wake of the Iran-Iraq war, this community was largely expelled from Iraq. The Iraqi Persian speakers have frequently looked to Persian rulers to support their interests, causing them to be regarded with suspicion by the Ottoman Turks and more recently by Arab nationalist governments. Another

Persian-speaking group distinct from these town dwellers is the Lurs, less than 1 percent of all Iraqis. Often called *faili* or *shi'i* Kurds, they are almost all tribally organized villagers concentrated near the eastern frontiers of Iraq.

Iraq also has a number of non-Muslim minorities—Christians, Jews, and a few other communities that predate Islam. The Jews were the oldest and largest of these communities, tracing their origin to the Babylonian captivity of the sixth century BCE. Overwhelmingly urban, the bulk of the Jewish community lived in Baghdad, where Jews were often prosperous and influential merchants. The position of the community was radically changed by the impact of Zionism. With the establishment of Israel in 1948, the situation of Iraqi Jews became untenable, and their exodus in 1951 left only a handful, whose position today is unenviable.

Various Christian sects comprise a little less than 3 percent of the population. The largest denomination is the Chaldean Church, founded in the fifth century by the followers of the theologian Nestorius. In the sixteenth century they unified with Rome. Centered in Mosul and the surrounding plains, most Chaldeans speak Arabic, although some use a modified version of Syriac as a vernacular.

Second in importance are the Assyrians, those Nestorians who did not unite with Rome. The British settled about 20,000 of them in the northern areas of Iraq around Zakhu and Dahuk following the First World War. The Assyrians, so called because they claim descent from the ancient Assyrians, proved to be one of the most unsettling elements in Iraq's modern history prior to the Second World War. Their uninvited intrusion into the country through the intervention of a foreign power was deeply resented by the Muslims and especially by the Kurds in whose areas they were settled. In recent years, they have become more integrated.

Other Christian groups include the Armenian, Jacobite, Greek Orthodox, Greek Catholic, and Latin Catholic communities, but their numbers are small in comparison to other Christians. A small number of Protestants, almost wholly the result of the nineteenth-century Baptist and Congregational missions, live mainly in Baghdad and Basra.

Two other religious communities of obscure origin deserve mention. One is the Yazidis. Racially and linguistically Kurdish, they are village dwellers located near Mosul. Their religion is a compound of several ancient and living religions, and its most notable element is a dualism most likely derived from Zoroastrianism. They have resisted attempts to integrate them into the larger society. The second group, the Sabians, is a sect of ancient origin and diverse elements inhabiting portions of the southern delta. Their faith stresses baptism and contains elements of Manicheanism, but not Islam.

Town and Tribe

To these ethnic and sectarian divisions, somewhat blurred since mandate days, must be added a third social dichotomy that has played a profound role in Iraq's modern history—the division between town and tribe. Though greatly softened in recent years by the growth of cities and the spread of education to the countryside, the legacy of tribalism is subtle but pervasive in Iraq.

The historical importance of the tribes in Iraq can scarcely be exaggerated. Nomadic, seminomadic, or settled, at the time of the mandate they surrounded the handful of cities and larger towns, controlled the country's communications system, and held nine-tenths of its land. In 1933, a year after Iraqi independence, it was estimated that there were 100,000 rifles in tribal hands and 15,000 in the possession of the government. Although only a few of these tribes were nomadic, the bulk of the settled population of the country, whether Arab or Kurd, was tribally organized and retained tribal mores and customs.

The extension of tribal organization and institutions to rural Iraq has meant that much of the rural population failed to put down deep roots in the soil. The settled village community with its attachment to the land—the backbone of the social structure throughout most of the Middle East—has been a missing link in Iraq's social fabric. Settled agricultural communities completely divorced from tribal structure have emerged in only two areas, the carefully tended date gardens of the Shatt al-Arab and the rain-fed, grain-producing plains of Mosul. Instead of love of the land, loyalty to family and tribe has dominated Iraq's social and political life. Among the legacies of tribalism in Iraq are intense concern with family, clan, and tribe; devotion to personal honor; factionalism; and above all, difficulty in cooperating across kinship lines—the underlying basis of modern civic society.

The only significant counterbalance to tribalism has been the economic and political power of the cities, but until modern times these were few in number and economically and culturally unintegrated with the rural hinterland. Aside from Basra, Baghdad, and Mosul, there were few cities worthy of the name at the end of the Ottoman era. Most were simply caravan stops like Zubair; fueling stations like Kut; or religious shrines like Karbala and Najaf, in which the benefits of law and order, trade and manufacture, were noticeable only against the background of poverty in the countryside.

Rapid urbanization, the spread of education, and the extension of government into the countryside in the last half of the twentieth century have greatly eroded tribalism and decisively shifted the balance of power to the cities. Nevertheless, although tribal organization is rapidly disappearing in the countryside, tribal customs and attitudes have left tangible influences. In political life, family, clan, and local ties often take precedence over national loyalties and broader ideologies.

For centuries this diverse medley of people has lived together in symbiotic proximity within the territory comprising Iraq. Although the population was often difficult to subdue by central governments, real civil conflicts, based on ethnic and sectarian animosities, were rare. But traditional society was a true mosaic, with considerable religious and social autonomy for its various components. The twentieth century, especially its fast-paced second half, with the emergence of new nationalist and religious ideologies and the need for greater interaction and cooperation—even integration—among communities has brought greater social tensions and challenges of organization and leadership not always met by the state.

CHAPTER 11

THE IRANIAN REVOLUTION

David W. Lesch

In his book *1979: The Year That Shaped the Modern Middle East*, David Lesch contends that 1979 was a watershed year in modern Middle East history, particularly notable for the peace treaty between Egypt and Israel (see Chapter 4) and the Soviet invasion of Afghanistan.

But the first major event of the Middle East in 1979 was the culmination of the Iranian revolution, when the Ayatollah Khomeini returned from exile and established Iran as an Islamic republic. Across the Middle East, Iran's Shiite Muslim revolution inspired both Sunni and Shiite Muslims who had become disenchanted with secular Arab nationalism. But it was also a threat to Sunni Muslim regimes, such as Saddam Hussein's neighboring Iraq, that had no wish to see their Shiite populations fanned to religious and political fervor by Iran's clerics. Saddam seized an opportunity to assert Iraq's leadership among Arab nations by claiming to defend the eastern bounds of the Sunni Muslim world against the radical, Shiite extremism ascendant in non-Arab Iran. With those goals in mind, Iraq invaded Iran and began the eight-year Iran-Iraq war.

To prevent either Iran or Iraq from becoming too powerful relative to the other, the United States pursued a policy of "dual containment" by supporting first one side and then the other during the war. It openly armed Saddam Hussein and, in what became known as the Iran-Contra affair, the administration of Ronald Reagan also secretly sold weapons to Iran in violation of its own arms embargo, and, without informing Congress, covertly used the arms-sales revenues to fund a war in Nicaragua. The outcome of the Iran-Iraq war set the stage for the Iraqi invasion of Kuwait in 1990 and the ensuing Gulf War of 1991.

David W. Lesch *is professor of history at Trinity University in San Antonio. He is the author of* The New Lion of Damascus: Bashar as-Asad and Modern Syria *and the editor of* The Middle East and the United States: A Historical and Political Reassessment.

ALTHOUGH SUCH EVENTS SEEM VERY DISTINCT NOW, in five hundred years, if not sooner, historical texts might very well refer to the 1979 Egyptian-Israeli peace treaty, the 1993 Israeli-PLO accords, and the 1994 Israeli-Jordanian treaty (and whatever Arab-Israeli treaties lie ahead) in the same sentence. Similarly, the Iranian revolution, the Iran-Iraq war, and the Persian Gulf crisis and war will most likely be mentioned in the same breath. The links in the chain from important events and situations today can be clearly traced backward in time to their points of origin in the events of 1979—the past as future for the year 1979.

THE IRANIAN REVOLUTION

The culmination of the Iranian revolution occurred in February 1979, when the Ayatollah Khomeini arrived in Teheran after fifteen years of exile and proclaimed the Islamic Republic of Iran, replacing the US-supported monarchy of the Shah of Iran, Muhammad Reza Pahlavi. As events would show, this change severely disrupted the balance of power in and stability of the Persian Gulf region, an area that contains approximately two-thirds of the world's known oil reserves. This fact alone preordained that an event of this magnitude would draw the attention of the international community.

Even though the Iranian revolution was a Shiite Muslim revolution, Muslims across the Middle East, both Sunni and Shiite, who had become disaffected with secular pan-Arab nationalism and state-building since the effectual death of Nasserist pan-Arabism in the 1967 Arab-Israeli war, hailed the event as a true harbinger of things to come. No longer would the Islamic world have to kowtow to the West and accept the inevitability of Israel. Islam's cultural identity and heritage need not be replaced by Western cultural and economic imperialism. The Islamists who survived the secular Arab nationalist era of the 1950s, 1960s, and 1970s could now point with pride to a successful example of religious revolution and Islamic rule in the modern era to combat the internal and external threats to society. If the defeat of Nasserism and secular Arab nationalism in the 1967 Arab-Israeli war created the opening for a resuscitation of Islamism, the Iranian revolution provided the direction and momentum for Islamist groups. Pan-Islamism would replace pan-Arabism, and if successful, a *Pax Islamica* would reign over the region, with Iran showing the way.

With a charismatic and firebrand demagogue such as Khomeini calling on the export of the Islamic revolution, the liberation of Jerusalem, and a confrontation against the Great Satan, the United States, the Middle East would never be the same. In an attempt to portray the revolution as an Islamic rather than simply an Iranian one, the Khomeini regime immediately engaged itself in a variety of issues close to the heart of all Arabs, namely, the Palestinian problem. Symbolically driving this point home was the fact that within about a week after the success of the revolution in February, the Khomeini regime closed down the Israeli embassy in Teheran and gave it to the PLO and Yasir Arafat, who was visiting Iran at the time.

The impact of the revolution was immediately felt in the region. In Iraq, the secular, Sunni, Ba'thist ruling party of Saddam Hussein saw the revolution as both a threat and an opportunity. The revolution created a threat in that the majority of the population in Iraq was Shiite and, therefore, possibly susceptible to Iranian démarches to overthrow a regime that was neither appropriately religious nor adequately representative. It was an opportunity in that Iran was seen as vulnerable due to the domestic turmoil in the aftermath of the revolution as the parties that formed the coalition opposed to the Shah jockeyed for position within the new government.

The rest of the Gulf Arab states—Saudi Arabia, Kuwait, United Arab Emirates, Qatar, Bahrain, and Oman—were equally concerned about this new threat emanating from the east. This was particularly true of states that had substantial Shiite minority populations (Saudi Arabia and Kuwait) and Bahrain, a country that, not unlike Iraq, was (and still is) a majority Shiite state ruled by a Sunni minority regime. It did not take long for this threat to manifest itself in the region. On November 20, 1979, 225 well-armed Islamic militants took control of the Grand Mosque in Mecca, Saudi Arabia, the holiest site in all of Islam. Even though the militants were, by and large, Sunnis, the Iranian revolution had galvanized Islamists throughout the Middle East to take the next step toward action against what they perceived as their combined enemies: the West, Israel, and co-opted and sycophantic Muslims.

This was a very embarrassing episode for the Saudi monarchy, since the Al Saud are officially the Guardians of the Two Holy Places (Mecca and Medina), and a significant part of their legitimacy stems from the family's control and upkeep of the shrines as well as the annual pilgrimage or *hajj*. The apparent inability of the Saudi monarchy to protect the Grand Mosque in the face of continuing accusations of corruption and subservience to the United States amounted to a very serious moment of vulnerability for the Saudi ruling regime. Only after an official religious ruling *(fatwa)* from the Grand Mufti in Riyadh did the regime attempt to retake the shrine through cautious force so as not to damage the structure itself, which only made it that much more difficult to overrun the militants. The resulting blood spilt in Islam's holiest site almost shook the monarchy to the ground.

Only a month later, another disturbance occurred that shook the Saudi regime and indicated to all interested observers that the reverberations from the Iranian revolution would be more than just fitful. The Shiite minority in Saudi Arabia lives, for the most part, in the northeast portion of the country in the al-Hasa region, where most of the active oil reserves in the country are located. The relationship is not coincidental; the Shiite population constitutes the lion's share of oil field laborers. Overworked, underpaid, and underprivileged, the Shiites needed only a spark to cathartically unleash their frustration against the regime. That spark was the annual *ashura* celebration during the Islamic month of Muharram. With the Iranian revolution still burning in the hearts of many Shiites and with the Grand Mosque episode still fresh in their minds, the emotional atmosphere produced by the *ashura* celebration naturally led to riots amid loud support for the Ayatollah Khomeini. Again, the Saudi regime had to use force to put down the disturbances—and Saddam Hussein looked on with increasing consternation.

The Iranian revolution also presented to Saddam Hussein an opportunity. Already claiming a leadership position in the Arab world in the wake of Egypt's peace treaty with Israel, Saddam leveraged this newfound influence into the position of protector of the Arab world against Persian and radical (Shiite) Islamic extremism and expansionism. In one fell swoop, Iraq could fill two vacuums of power in the Middle East—one in the Arab world, and implicitly in the Arab-Israeli arena, created by Egypt's departure and the other in the Persian Gulf arena brought about by the fall of the Shah. As a sign of Saddam's heightened ambitions, he nudged aside President Hasan al-Bakr and assumed the position of president himself on July 16, 1979. Although he had been the strongman behind Hasan for years, Saddam was clearly now coming out of the shadows. He was now in position to implement his agenda.

Iran was, to most observers, vulnerable. Ayatollah Khomeini had not yet solidified his position as supreme ruler, and it was still unclear how Islamic this new republic was going to be. With all the disarray within the regime and at least as much disruption within the Iranian military following the exiles, purges, defections, and executions that came in the wake of the revolution, it seemed that with only a slight push Iran would topple altogether. Paramount in Saddam's calculations on taking advantage of this situation was making sure the United States would not come to Iran's aid.

US isolation from Iran became assured on November 4, 1979, when Revolutionary Guards, the shock troops of Khomeini's revolution, stormed the American embassy in Teheran and took ninety persons, including sixty-three Americans, hostage (fifty-two Americans would be held for 444 days). Washington broke off relations with Iran, froze Iranian assets in the United States, and worked to isolate Iran within the international community, thus inaugurating a period of extreme hostility between the two countries. From Saddam Hussein's perspective, this meant that the mostly American-supplied Iranian military would not be able to easily obtain spare parts, ammunition, or other complementary equipment from American sources. Bereft of these materials and many of the military personnel trained to use the equipment, the multibillion-dollar US-supplied military arsenal the Shah had amassed would be more vestigial than daunting.

All of these new circumstances indicated to Saddam Hussein a unique opportunity with a possible fabulous payoff: the elimination of the threat from Iran and the attainment of personal and national ambitions of leadership in the Middle East. With this in mind, Iraq attacked southwestern Iran in September 1980, and the eight-year Iran-Iraq war was on.

So momentous was the Iranian revolution that even some of its direct repercussions became significant independent variables in and of themselves. The Iranian hostage crisis is a case in point. Although the storming of the American embassy and the taking of hostages was as much a function of internal power-play politics within the faction-ridden Teheran regime as a pure act of anti-Americanism, its repercussions would have at least as much impact on domestic politics in the United States as they did in Iran.

The Carter administration became hostage to the hostage situation. The inability of the Carter administration to either obtain the release of the hostages or rescue them enhanced the appearance of American weakness, a national complex that the country was still trying to shed in the aftermath of Vietnam. When a diplomatic resolution did not materialize, concurrent with the languishing popularity of the administration domestically, President Carter made the fateful decision to attempt a daring rescue in April 1980, while the hostages were reportedly still kept largely together in one location. The disastrous failure of the Desert One action, however, with loss of American lives and the abandoning of several helicopters in the Iranian desert, only added to the appearance of American impotence and to the ineptitude of the administration itself.

To say that the hostage crisis significantly hurt Carter's chances for reelection is quite the understatement. The hostage crisis had significantly helped mold the national psyche into yearning for a strong-willed American patriot who would repair America's image abroad and rebuild the military into a positive instrument of foreign policy. Arch-conservative Ronald Reagan's landslide victory in the 1980 presidential election was the natural response. The crowning blow to Carter delivered by Teheran was the fact that the hostages were released just minutes after Reagan was inaugurated president on January 20, 1981, 444 days after they had been taken.

In Iran, the hostage ordeal helped solidify the power of Ayatollah Khomeini and his radical Islamist faction. His influence over the hostage-taking youths and his manipulation of the diplomatic process clearly popularized his position during this volcanic period of the revolution, cementing the Islamist theocratic nature of the regime and the position of Khomeini as the Supreme Guide.

The success of the Iranian revolution galvanized Islamists the world over. The rise of Khomeini obviously had a direct effect on the takeover of the Grand Mosque in Mecca, the riots by Shiites in the eastern oil fields in Saudi Arabia, and, of course, the hostage crisis. Iran also became the direct sponsor of Hizbullah (the Party of God), a Shiite Muslim group that arose in South Lebanon as a result of the Israeli invasion of Lebanon in 1982. Hizbullah played a prominent role in the hostage-taking and assassinations of Westerners and hijackings in and around Beirut throughout much of the 1980s. The Iranian connection with Hizbullah also led directly to the infamous Iran-Contra affair exposed in late 1986. Hizbullah was, and still is, also supported by Syria. Syria's support of the Shiite group has enhanced its leverage with regard to negotiations dealing with a hoped-for Israeli withdrawal from the Golan Heights.

The Iran-Contra affair was the Reagan administration's attempt to sell arms to the Khomeini regime in Iran (which was obviously desperate for American weaponry and ammunition by that point in its war with Iraq) in return for utilizing its influence with Hizbullah in Lebanon, pressuring it to free American hostages. This was in contravention of Washington's own Operation Staunch, which was (an attempt at) a worldwide arms embargo of Iran. The money paid by the regime in Teheran for the arms was then funneled illegally to the US-supported Contras in Nicaragua to support their attempts to overthrow the Marxist Sandinista regime in Managua. This was in direct violation of legislation passed by Congress that cut off covert assistance to the Contras.

The irony in this whole episode is rampant. First of all, the Reagan administration came to office committed to a policy of not dealing with terrorists and not letting any hostage situation captivate the White House—in direct reaction to the failure of the Carter administration's foibles in Iran. Second, the idea of dealing with so-called moderate elements in Teheran in an arms-for-hostages deal originated with the Israelis. From Israel's perspective, the traditional Arab proverb "the enemy of my enemy is my friend" held true in this instance, as the common foes of Iraq made for strange bedfellows. Yet, it was the Israeli invasion in 1982 that created the environment for the birth of Hizbullah (as well as other anti-American and anti-Israeli groups in Lebanon) and the series of kidnappings and killings. The scandal rocked the Reagan administration and launched a series of investigations and hearings.

The Arab allies of the United States in the Persian Gulf, who had been overtly supporting Iraq to varying degrees in its war with Iran, were obviously shocked and dismayed by the revelations of the arms-for-hostages deal. The United States seemed to be playing both sides of the fence. The Reagan administration's need to regain credibility in the eyes of its Arab friends significantly influenced its decision to begin reflagging Kuwaiti oil tankers under US flags in June 1987, following the initiation of the so-called tanker war by Iraq and the subsequent response by Iran against those tankers, particularly Kuwaiti-registered ones that were carrying Iraqi oil. The United States thus established a direct military presence in the Persian Gulf, which overtly placed Washington on Iraq's side in the Iran-Iraq war, leading to a number of military confrontations with Iranian forces in Gulf waters and solidifying a (hoped-for) strategic partnership with Saddam Hussein. Washington was blinded into thinking Iraq could assume Iran's position under the Shah as America's gendarme of the Gulf. As Gary Sick states, the reflagging operation

> was a fundamental turning point. For the first time since World War II, the United States assumed an operational role in the defense of the Persian Gulf. . . . President Reagan's military intervention thus confirmed President Carter's assertion that the Gulf was of vital interest to the United States and that the United States was prepared to use military force in pursuit of that interest.[1]

All of this stemmed directly from the Iranian revolution. The Islamist drive fueled by Khomeini that led to Hizbullah and ultimately to Iran-Contra and subsequent events also was felt elsewhere in the Middle East. The success of the revolution and the antipathy toward Israel overtly on display in Teheran galvanized growing Islamist opposition in Egypt toward Anwar Sadat's regime, which was seen by Egyptian Islamists as having betrayed Islam by signing a peace treaty with Israel and for embracing the West politically, militarily, economically, and culturally. It is doubtful that the assassination of Sadat by the Islamic Jihad organization on October 6, 1981, the anniversary of the initiation of the 1973 Arab-Israeli war, would have occurred when it did if not for the inspiration from

Teheran. Indeed, there were groups in Egypt that needed no reinforcement from Iran to hate the peace treaty, Sadat, and all he stood for—and attempt to kill him—but the revolution tended to "mainstream" Islamist dissent, popularizing it and generating the buildup of willing recruits, if not martyrs, for the cause in both Sunni and Shiite circles.

The most direct and immediately significant repercussion of the Iranian revolution was, of course, the Iran-Iraq war, which lasted from September 1980, when Iraq invaded Iran, to August 1988, when Iran reluctantly agreed to a UN-brokered cease-fire. The war was less important in and of itself, as it settled down into trench warfare within a year with scant movement on either side of the front for most of the conflict, but more because of its tangential effects.

As previously mentioned, Saddam Hussein ordered the invasion for defensive and offensive reasons. Most of all, he saw an opportunity—Iran was vulnerable and isolated, and the regional and international situation seemed to be in Iraq's favor.

The Arab Gulf countries were not at all unhappy to see Iran and Iraq occupied with each other and weakening over the course of time. Because Iran was more of an immediate threat, the Arab Gulf states were compelled to monetarily support Iraq for most of the war. But they also were cognizant of the ambitions of Saddam Hussein and were fearful of his attempts to translate these ambitions into an attempted hegemonic position in the Gulf, especially if he emerged victorious—a fear that was confirmed when Iraq invaded Kuwait in 1990.

A host of miscalculations on both sides prolonged the conflict. Iraq attacked southwestern Iran not only for geographical and strategic reasons but also because that part of the country was host to the majority of Iran's Arab minority. Indeed, the Arabs living there call it Arabistan, instead of the official name of this province, Khuzistan. Saddam Hussein hoped that the Arabs in Iran would support his invasion, making his putsch that much more effective and depleting Iran's ability to counterattack. Unfortunately for Baghdad, the Arabs in Khuzistan were largely ambivalent to the outcome. Iraq's strategic limitations probably would have forced it to draw back its initial offensive anyhow, but the failure of the Arabs in Iran to come to Iraq's aid at this point made a swift knock-out punch all but impossible. Similarly, when Iran went on the offensive in 1982, it too thought that "fellow travelers" in enemy territory would support its cause, in this case, the Shiite Arab Muslim majority in Iraq, most of whom lived in the southern part of Iraq toward the Iranian border. Again, however, a combatant had badly miscalculated. Although there were certainly some groups of Shiite Arabs that in fact did support Teheran actively, the expected en masse

Shiite uprising never materialized, primarily because of the effective repressive apparatus of the Baghdadi regime and the distaste many, mostly secularized, Iraqi Shiites had for Khomeini's brand of Shiism and theocratic regime.

By 1982, Iran had beaten back Iraq's initial attack and had gone on the offensive. Teheran, trying to take advantage of its superior numbers, established multiple fronts against the Iraqis, hoping to extend Iraqi forces beyond their defensive capacity and to wear down Baghdad through attrition: in the north (with the help of anti-Saddam Iraqi Kurds), in the center toward Baghdad, and in the south toward Basra.

To the extent that Iraq had a strategy after 1982, Baghdad wanted to internationalize the conflict by bringing in the superpowers, especially the United States, so that they could exert pressure on Iran to cease and desist. Other than internationalizing the conflict, Baghdad was simply hoping to hang on as long as possible until the octogenarian Khomeini died, which, unfortunately for the Iraqis, did not come soon enough (the Ayatollah passed away in 1989, almost a year after the war ended).

Indeed, it was the arms provided to Iran in the arms-for-hostages deal that significantly elevated Teheran's ability to launch a major offensive in 1986. Iran took the Fao (Faw) Peninsula, thus cutting Iraq off from the Persian Gulf, and threatened to take Basra, Iraq's second largest city.

With the embarrassing revelation of the Iran-Contra affair and the existing desire not to see Iran victorious in this war, the United States was openly supporting Iraq, most ostentatiously displayed by the reflagging operation. In fact, Washington had reestablished diplomatic relations with Iraq (broken off since 1967) in late 1984, clearly betraying the pro-Iraqi disposition of the Reagan administration. There were some in policy circles who were advocating building up Saddam Hussein as the next "gendarme" of the Gulf—taking the place of the fallen Shah—and continuing the balance of power approach to the region. Furthermore, there were more than a few who suggested that Saddam Hussein could additionally take the place of Anwar Sadat and finish what the Egyptian president was unable to accomplish, that is, lead a moderate Arab consensus into a comprehensive peace with Israel. It seems preposterous now, considering the extremely antagonistic relationship between Iraq and the United States since the Gulf war, but at the time, Khomeinism was the point of focus, and Iran was at least as ostracized and held in as much contempt by Washington as Iraq has been in recent years. The common threat emanating from Iran after 1979 brought Baghdad and Washington closer together, establishing the foundation of the strategic relationship toward the end of the Iran-Iraq war that so colored the environment in which the Iraqi invasion of Kuwait in August 1990 took place.

In a direct reaction to the Iran-Iraq war, the remaining Gulf states—Saudi Arabia, Kuwait, Bahrain, Qatar, the United Arab Emirates, and Oman—agreed in February 1981 to form the Gulf Cooperation Council (GCC). It was the culmination, in the face of the heightened instability in the region brought about by the Iranian revolution and the Iran-Iraq war, of increasing cooperation among these six Arab Gulf states in previous years, particularly in the area of internal security. The GCC, as originally conceived, was supposed to be more of a security and defense organization than anything else. Ironically, the GCC has been most successful in the economic sphere, with the lowering or abolishment of customs duties, the enactment of trade agreements, and the facilitation of freer movement of people and goods within and among the GCC membership. In addition, the GCC has allowed Saudi Arabia to play a dominant role within the organization, cementing its new status as a vital player not only in the Persian Gulf area but also in the entire Middle East equation (and forming the triad of powers in the Gulf: Iran, Iraq, and the Saudi-led GCC).

Most importantly in the long term, what the formation of the GCC indicated was the beginning of subregional organizations in the Arab world. No longer could the Arab League deal with all of the divergent issues in the Middle East. The Arab world had become too divided as a result of the Egyptian-Israeli peace treaty, the Lebanese civil war (and subsequent Israeli invasion in 1982), and of course, the Iran-Iraq war. The "balkanization" of the Middle East had begun in earnest in the wake of the failure of Arab nationalism, resulting in a number of Arab states—Egypt, Syria, and the GCC states the most prominent among them—mapping out their own paths. This did not mean that certain countries and subregions became mutually exclusive of each other. Quite the contrary, this evolved into a more integrated matrix, for no area or grouping could be excluded completely from any equation dealing with any significant issue in the region.

The Iraqi invasion of Kuwait in August 1990 and the ensuing Gulf crisis and war for the remainder of that year and into early 1991 represented the next significant repercussion of the Iranian revolution of 1979—through the intervening prism of the Iran-Iraq war. One of the reasons the Arab Gulf states hesitatingly, and sometimes reluctantly, supported Iraq in its war with Iran was the fact that they understood the ambitions of Saddam Hussein, and if he emerged victorious from the war he might turn his eyes southward toward Kuwait and attempt to dominate the Gulf. It was a prophetic notion.

The Iran-Iraq war set the stage for the Iraqi invasion of Kuwait. Iraq was severely in debt, having gone from a more than $60 billion surplus before the Iran-Iraq war to a $40 billion debt. Saddam Hussein saw the bank to the south called Kuwait and its lucrative oil fields (which would have given Iraq control of 21 percent of the world's known oil reserves) and wanted to initiate his own type of merger and acquisition. A significant portion of that debt was owed to Kuwait, which, unlike the Saudis, was unwilling to erase it.

Perhaps the main reason Saddam Hussein invaded Kuwait is because he thought he could get away with it. In fact, he came very close to it. As mentioned previously, Washington and Baghdad reestablished diplomatic relations in 1984, and the Reagan and Bush administrations believed Iraq could be a very useful surrogate in both the Persian Gulf and Arab-Israeli arenas, filling the empty shoes of both the Shah and Anwar Sadat. Indeed, President Bush and his secretary of state, James Baker, admitted in the aftermath of the Gulf war that they "stayed" with Saddam too long, hoping to moderate his policies and to essentially make him into what they wanted. In doing so, they failed to appreciate signals that in fact indicated that he was an expansionist dictator determined to achieve his national and regional ambitions.

The Iraqi president, on the other hand, in a case of possibly hearing only what he wanted to hear, also failed to read Washington's signals indicating its opposition to his policies. Baghdad apparently concluded that the United States was still hamstrung by the Vietnam syndrome and that with the end of the superpower cold war, Washington had no stomach and little domestic or congressional support for military intervention to protect a nondemocratic regime with which it had not had a particularly close relationship.

Saddam obviously miscalculated. The Bush administration led the charge to liberate Kuwait for a variety of reasons: (1) it did not want Iraq controlling 21 percent of the world's known oil reserves; (2) Iraq had directly threatened Saudi Arabia, an American ally whose borders are the reddest of all red lines in the Middle East—in fact, the decision to move Iraqi troops to the Saudi-Kuwaiti border may have been Saddam Hussein's biggest strategic error; (3) the Bush administration realized as the crisis wore on that it would be a strategic nightmare for the United States to have Iraq's million-man army and weapons-of-mass-destruction capability as a perpetual menace in one of the most vital areas of national interest; (4) unfortunately for Saddam Hussein, President Bush's strategic thinking was not shaped by the Vietnam war syndrome, but by the Munich mentality that emerged out of World War II, in which Bush fought and was decorated. This experience taught Bush and others of this generation not to

appease aggressors, as the Europeans had appeased Hitler following his appropri-
ation of the Sudetenland in Czechoslovakia—aggression of this order must not
be allowed to stand; and (5) President Bush wanted to implement his New
World Order, a new era in the wake of the end of the cold war that would usher
in a cooperative international framework to rein in acts of "naked aggression,"
such as the one perpetrated by Saddam Hussein. Many in the administration
believed that an assertive response in this situation would reinforce the leadership role of the United States.

Operation Desert Storm was launched in January 1991 with an intense aerial bombardment campaign and with the ground war commencing in February,
a 100-hour thrust that successfully expelled the Iraqis from Kuwait. The Gulf
war was over.

The climactic interlude of 1990–1991 spelled the end of balance-of-power
politics; the United States would no longer rely on either Iran or Iraq to be its
gendarme in the Persian Gulf. Instead defense cooperation agreements were con-
summated between Washington and most of the GCC countries and equipment
and materiel were prepositioned just in case military action again became necessary—for although defeated, Saddam remained in power. *munich Ideology but leaves Saddam w power*

The United States adopted a forward policy in the region that required a significant direct presence. The flip side of this new strategic environment was the
"dual containment" of Iraq and Iran. The term "containment" was quite popular in the early 1990s, since the policy it described was deemed successful in winning the cold war with the Soviet Union. Why not apply it at the regional level
in the Persian Gulf against two so-called rogue countries? It was hoped that containment, through economic, political, and military pressure, would compel a
change of regime-type, if not ideology, toward a more compliant, cooperative,
and internationally acceptable status.

Although dual containment has come under intense scrutiny, and even criticism, in recent years, the enhanced American presence in the region has
remained, often producing a negative backlash among the Gulf Arab populations
who had before the Gulf war become accustomed to, at best, a detached relationship with the United States. Even during the Gulf crisis, when the United
Nations coalition was building up its forces in the region, there were rumblings
in the Muslim world regarding the presence of "infidels" in Saudi Arabia, the site
of Islam's two holiest sites—Mecca and Medina. In fact, it was this perceived
affront that initiated Osama bin Laden's quest against the United States.

CHAPTER 12

THE IRANIAN REVOLUTION AND THE REBIRTH OF POLITICAL ISLAM

Anthony Shadid

The Iranian revolution culminated in 1979 when the Shah of Iran was forced to flee the country and Ayatollah Ruhollah Khomeini returned from exile to proclaim the founding of the Islamic Republic. Many Muslims were heartened by the revolution in the belief that Islam would provide a path to a bright future, independent of the Western ideologies of capitalism or communism.

However, many in Iran are discovering that Islam—especially Islam conceived as a complete social, economic, political, and moral system—cannot provide all the answers for a country struggling with development. In the Iranian theocracy, Islam is in the hands of the clergy and the clergy are in control of the government. But then, any failure of the government is potentially regarded as a failure of Islam. To some, the spiritual and sacred qualities of Islam have been sacrificed for an Islam that is rigid government ideology, with little room for pluralism and tolerance. Elected president in 1997 and reelected in 2001, Seyyed Mohammad Khatami, representing moderate and reformist forces in Iran, has sought a less dogmatic reliance on Islam.

(Since the following essay was written, Mahmoud Ahmadinejad, widely considered a religious conservative, was elected president of Iran in 2005.)

Winner of the 2004 Pulitzer Prize for International Reporting, **Anthony Shadid** *is the Islamic affairs correspondent for the* Washington Post. *He is the author of* Night Draws Near: Iraq's People in the Shadow of America's War. *This chapter is from* Legacy of the Prophet: Despots, Democrats, and the New Politics of Islam.

HASAN YUSUFI ESHKEVARI, in so many ways, was the very picture of the glowering Iranian mullah whose brooding, unbending image is seared in the consciousness of the West. Like other devout Muslims, he wore a bushy beard, imitating the style of the Prophet Mohammed in Arabia more than 1,300 years ago. His white turban sat neatly atop his head, and his gray robe draped itself over a body made soft by years of religious study. I had come to interview Eshkevari on the recommendation of several young Iranian intellectuals, visiting him at his modest house in a neighborhood that, like many in Tehran, had been ground down by years of austerity.

Eshkevari, it turns out, was a revolutionary. He languished in jail twice under the despotic rule of the Shah in the 1970s and then took to the streets in heroic protests that captivated a world still oblivious to the horrors that would follow. With the Shah in exile and Ayatollah Ruhollah Khomeini in power, he was elected to the first parliament convened in the Islamic Republic. Its inception was a bold move that many Muslims at the time saw as the initial step on a path that would be distinct from both capitalism and communism, ideologies they associated with the West. More surprising, and unlike many of his fellow citizens in Iran, he withstood the disenchantment and hardships of eight years of war with Iraq or the disgust at hundreds of thousands of young lives lost. Through it all, somehow, he kept his faith in Islam and his belief in justice.

No longer, for Eshkevari was still, in an odd way, a revolutionary, taking part in the far-reaching changes in Iran today that may very well determine the course of Islamic politics in the rest of the Muslim world. As I sat with him, I listened, with growing disbelief, to complaint after complaint of the way things were, a litany recited with barely a show of expression.

"I'm one of the critics of the way of religious thinking in the Islamic Republic," he said to me, with not a hint of fear or irony.

Islam in itself was not meant to rule a country, he said, and its tenets cannot alone solve the economic, social and political problems of a modern society. Like other clergy, he said he feared what the growing disenchantment with the Islamic government would mean for the clergy, who for centuries as guardians of the faith had built a reservoir of support, respect and goodwill among Iranians of all backgrounds, often raising the black banner of rebellion in the face of arbitrary oppression and reckless autocracy. Again and again, he told me that the main threat in Iran today to Islam as a faith is the experience of people under the Islamic government.

"We say under the banner of religion that there will be equality, under the banner of religion, there will be development, under the banner of religion, there will be a successful economy. But if there is not, this failure of the religious state will be a failure of religion," Eshkevari said, leaning back on red pillows against the spartan wall. "The failure of the government, therefore, becomes a failure of the faith."

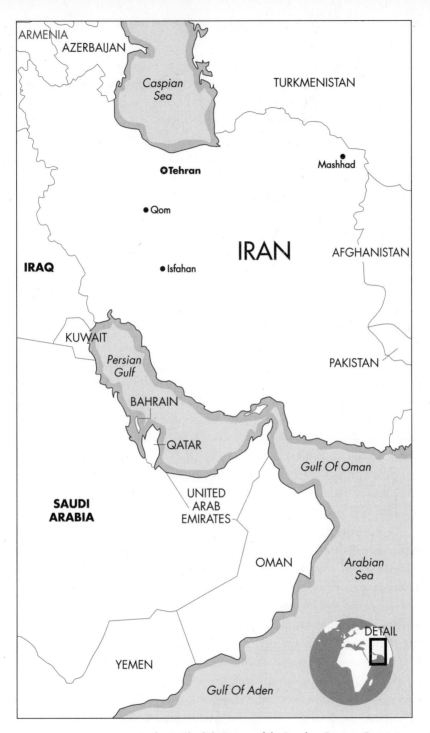

Map 12.1   Iran. *Source:* Anthony Shadid, *Legacy of the Prophet: Despots, Democrats, and the New Politics of Islam* (2002, Westview Press).

In a rapid-fire succession of surprises, he went on to talk about the Arab world and its Islamic movements, groups like the Muslim Brotherhood in Egypt, the Islamic Salvation Front in Algeria or the National Islamic Front in Sudan, all of which have boldly offered to take the religion and create a renaissance in regions that had lost their dynamism, pride and self-confidence centuries ago. Expecting an answer in the abstract, I asked him what message Iran offered these movements.

"Not only does Iran have no message for them," he told me, "the movements themselves in Algeria, Sudan or Egypt have no message either."

So much for abstraction, I thought.

"There is one problem and that is that the governments of these Arab countries cannot solve the problems of the people or the nation. It means that they cannot solve the problem of backwardness and create an independent and modern government and country and not be dependent on the West or others. In any Muslim country, if the government can provide these fundamentals, it will be successful," Eshkevari said.

Iran, today, is a startling place, and its surprises offer the most telling insights into the future of political Islam, a movement in the throes of a transformation in the place, many believe, where it began. I had come to Iran to look for the legacy of the revolution, a movement that had left a decisive impression on me and others of my generation who were raised amid the images of blindfolded hostages in the American Embassy. I hoped to find out what a revolution that promised to create a new society had actually brought about, and what a government's promise to use the faith to solve society's problems had done to Islam itself.

In the early 1980s, Islam was conceived in Iran as a complete social, economic, political and moral system—the almost clichéd reference to "Islam is the solution." That monopoly on truth meant there was no room for competing views or systems. The message that I found in my time in Iran was that Islam was, in fact, not the solution, that the faith by itself could not provide the answers or, perhaps more important, different answers—neither for the economy, nor for spirituality, nor for a morality that would replace the allure of Western materialism and the predominance of Western culture, commerce and politics. The example of the revolution to which Eshkevari dedicated his life had reached a turning point; its symbols, energy, appeal and sources of legitimacy that drew from the climactic days of the Shah's overthrow seemed exhausted.

That was the easy conclusion. Almost always, it seems, failure is far easier to gauge than success. I was in Iran at an opportune time, having the chance to witness the flourishing of a vibrant, skeptical newspaper culture and the breathtaking electoral participation that brought President Mohammad Khatami to power in 1997 and ushered in a parliament of deputies in 2000 who were dedicated to sweeping social and political reform. I found that Iran, despite its failure, could still chart a new style of Islamic politics, one in which dissent, democracy, human rights and even coalitions could take their place in a more wide-open playing field. Here, there seemed to be an attempt to secure greater freedom *and* keep allegiance to God, creating a generation whose commitment to pluralism was matched only by its duty to Islam. I had the sense that people did not want to necessarily overthrow the Islamic Republic or undo the revolution. Rather, they wanted their republic to be more democratic, to reconsider its relationship to religion, to provide security and adhere to the law and to choose an order born of a stable democracy instead of an unsettled revolution. After years of disenchantment and sullen anger, taking shape in Iran was an example of how a government grounded in religious principles could reform along democratic lines.

KHOMEINI'S THEOCRATIC VISION

To many in the West, the Iranian Revolution was Islam incarnate—dramatic evidence that a new force had surged on the world scene, promising to remake politics, alliances and even governments. The Shah's Iran was an oil-rich Western ally, its military the generous recipient of American largesse and its society, from the vantage point of the capital, distinguished by a Western, modern veneer. Foremost, it served US interests, providing oil to Israel, policing the Persian Gulf and Indian Ocean and serving as a bulwark of an American-orchestrated military alliance (and the lucrative arms contracts that entailed). The Shah's unpopularity and repression were less visible abroad. But by early 1979, eighteen months of strikes, bloody clashes and mass protests that brought waves of humanity into the streets had toppled the Shah in a revolution that electrified the Muslim world like no other event this century. The upheaval seemed heroic; the empowerment of a people unprecedented. The arrival of Khomeini, after fifteen years in exile, was greeted by 3 million people in the streets of the Iranian capital and marked the symbolic and decisive end to 2,500 years of Persian monarchy.

Perhaps no Muslim country escaped the rumblings of the upheaval. Here, in its all fervor and excitement, was an example of a Muslim people rising up to take their destiny into their own hands. For the revolutionaries in Iran, many of them hailing from the clergy, Islam would fulfill that destiny, a complete system for a modern society. It was an example in which others found inspiration, if not guidance, and it stands today with Cuba's revolution, Algerian independence and the Vietnam War as one of the Third World's seminal moments.

Iran's revolution was critically guided by one man, Ruhollah Musavi Khomeini, a figure as compelling as any in Islam's history whose life mirrored the intense passion, emotion and sacrifice of the Shiite faith he sought to reshape into a modern ideology of government. He was born in 1902 in Khomein, a provincial town from which he drew his name. After an initial religious education, in which he was said to have memorized the entire Quran by the age of six, he was sent to study with Ayatollah Abdol-Karim Ha'iri, the leading Shiite theologian of the time. He completed his education there, then began teaching Sufi philosophy and Islamic jurisprudence. In general, Khomeini remained aloof from the political struggles of the 1940s and 1950s. His emergence as a leading opposition figure only came during mass protests against the Shah in 1963 that served as a prelude to the revolution. Khomeini was already in his sixties at the time, but endowed with an intuition that would distinguish his activism for the next twenty-five years. He understood mass appeal. Even in 1963, the issues he chose resonated with a people that lived uneasily under the Shah's rule and his modernization program known as the White Revolution, which brought land reform, women's right to vote and a vast expansion of the state throughout Iran. Khomeini, as a populist, railed against corruption, the rigging of elections, violating the constitution, stifling the press and political parties, neglecting the needs of merchants, workers and peasants, undermining the country's Islamic faith, selling oil to Israel, and aping of the West. In his years in opposition and later at the helm of the revolution, he never lost the knack for gauging popular indignation and anger.

In November 1964, after a brief stint in prison, Khomeini was exiled to Turkey and then allowed to go to Najaf in neighboring Iraq, one of Shiite Islam's holiest cities, where he spent the next decade and a half. It was during this time that, as one of the clergy's highest-ranking figures, he delivered lectures on Islamic government that later developed into his idea of *velayat-e faqih*, or "guardianship by the jurist," a formula in which the clergy were not only charged to participate directly in the political process but, in a bold reinterpretation, to actually govern the state. The monarchy, Khomeini argued, was an illegitimate institution that usurped the rightful authority of the supreme religious leader, the *faqih*, who should rule as both spiritual and temporal guardian of the *umma*. The idea would become the framework for the Islamic Republic.

Already by the 1970s, Khomeini had become a lightning rod for militant religious opposition to the Shah. His writings on Islamic government and other speeches circulated clandestinely. As opposition to the Shah grew, Iraq expelled Khomeini in 1978. He was refused entry to nearby Kuwait, then persuaded to locate in Paris. Finally, on February 1, 1979, with the Shah already in exile and his caretaker government under siege, Khomeini returned triumphantly, ready to create what he would describe as a government of God.

In the West, Khomeini was seen as one-dimensional, a revolutionary with a cold but fanatic hatred of the United States and Israel, an almost comic-book figure in his religious zeal. At home, he was far more complex, a man with a mixed relation to his homeland. His weak link to a specifically Iranian nationalism came through in his determined adherence to an Islamic universalism. Iran was where the revolution began, he believed, not where it would end.

He acted as a revolutionary, too, a role he would play with enthusiasm until the end of his life. After eliminating nationalist and leftist forces that might compete with his theocratic vision for the country, and with the religious wing of the revolution firmly in the ascendancy, he proceeded to fashion the *velayate faqih*. He foresaw an ideal polity in which the clergy would be engaged in all aspects of society, acting as guardians of the community. They would interpret and implement law, shepherd the nation and oversee the politicians. Importantly, his vision was not just that of an Islamic government; it was, in fact, a clerical Islamic government, the clergy, in this instance, acting as a vanguard. For Khomeini, to succeed, the clergy had to gain actual control of the state and use its political power to impose Islamic law and create a truly Islamic community. Islam was in the hands of the clergy, and the clergy were in control of the government.

In the heady, ensuing months of the clergy's consolidation of power, ministries and public institutions were purged and staff were replaced by mullahs and their protégés. Across Iran, the government appointed in every city a preacher who led prayers on Friday, the Muslim sabbath, and delivered sermons on behalf of the revolution and its leaders. At the same time, prayers were enforced in the workplace, the veil was made mandatory in the early 1980s and religion—in particular, the symbols of Shiite sacrifice—became the discourse and framework in which politics were played out in daily life.

Khomeini's vision of a theocracy was straightforward enough, but in practice, it had to make compromises and concessions along the way. Always, its survival was paramount, taking precedence even over Islamic law, an idea that many clergy would consider wildly blasphemous. To Khomeini, the revolution's mission was nothing less than the creation of a government and community blessed by God and nothing, not even God's law, could stand in the way of that task.

His government was a theocracy but one with representative institutions, a simmering contradiction between autocracy and democracy. In Khomeini's conception, the government's supreme authority was the guide of the revolution, a position he occupied until his death. (He was replaced by Ali Khamenei, a cleric with substantial revolutionary credentials but who lacked the popular stature and influence of Khomeini and, with a far less rigorous academic and scholarly background, was not generally held in high esteem by the country's clerical elite.) The guide, a position for life, can dismiss the president, acts as commander-in-chief and appoints the heads of the media, revolutionary guards, military, and the judiciary, all among the most important institutions within the government. The president, who is limited to two four-year terms, has the greatest popular mandate. He is popularly elected and appoints a cabinet whose members must be approved by Parliament. The government, though, is designed with the clergy in mind, with all key institutions, including the courts, firmly under the sway of the supreme leader. Yet although the clergy keeps control, there remains room for popular expression and discontent, a feature of the government that has proven responsible for dramatic social and political change and, in the end, may be responsible for its successful reform.

THE LOSS OF THE SACRED

Under the revolutionary government, Iran witnessed sweeping changes in education, political participation, even in the field of women's rights. Higher education, which was a luxury of the rich under the Shah, saw its enrollment rise in the twenty years after the revolution from 175,000 to 1.3 million. On the eve of the Shah's fall, only half of people between the ages of six and twenty-four could read and write. Today, in an achievement that speaks for itself, more than 90 percent of Iranians are literate. Traditional women found the Islamic setting of educational institutions more palatable and hence comprised a larger and larger portion of their ranks. Across society, women continued to participate actively in the workforce and other spheres of public life. Although the economy became lethargic at best, beset by war, isolation and unstable oil prices, income distribution improved: the top fifth of society earned substantially less than it did during the revolution and the bottom fifth earned slightly more.

The popular mobilization of the revolution and war remain, if weathered by middle-aged weariness. Twenty years on, however, the fervor of that revolution was hard to find. Achievements aside, faith in modern Iran more and more resembled a defeated soldier returning from the front—weary of the now-clichéd slogans, blind to the symbols and desperate for an ordered life void of the revolutionary gusto and the tenacious disorder that brings.

Tehran, the capital of the Islamic Republic, is a tantalizing city, full of the contradictions that collide and coexist in Iranian society itself. Oddly, it is not an Islamic symbol—it speaks neither of the faith nor of the revolution. Rather, in many ways, it reminded me of a pleasant European city: sharp confectioneries, clothes and shoe stores advertising in English, the all-too-American hamburger restaurants and canals carrying water along elegant, tree-lined avenues. Its freeways suggested Los Angeles as did its commercial billboards, which seemed irreconcilable with a movement that posed itself as an alternative to Western consumerism. In fact, only the veil, a somber mantle that dates to before the Prophet Mohammed and, its proponents say, is mandated by the Quran, distinguished Tehran as somehow Islamic. To this day, it remains the most visible legacy of the revolution, although the dark, alluring hair that often falls playfully from beneath its sad colors and formless shape signals creeping dissent against even that accomplishment.

I felt those appearances in Tehran suggested a deeper malaise, one that touched the very essence of the republic and its avowed mission. I wondered what the government that Khomeini created and the exhausted revolution he oversaw had done to the faith itself. Did others, in fact, share the fears of Eshkevari, the disenchanted cleric? Those were the questions I took to a friend of a friend, a strikingly beautiful literature professor who like many others in Tehran was reluctant to let her name be published since our visit came during one of the recurring bouts of repression that occasionally gripped the capital. Many Iranians saw the campaigns as an attempt by self-proclaimed defenders of the revolution to keep off balance real and potential opposition in and outside government. I would see that menacing, unpredictable nature of Iranian life played out again and again—on Stalinesque television programs that maligned prominent thinkers as stooges of the West, in death squad–style executions of intellectuals, in arrests and harassment of writers and journalists and in the fear I found so often in interviews. The unease rarely silenced people—Iranians are remarkably forthright—but it was often enough to hang over conversations in Tehran like a sleepy sentry, and no one seemed to know what might bring the guard out of his slumber.

As we sat over small cups of tea sweetened with hard candy, the professor recalled the Islam of her youth, during the Shah's time, when she considered faith sacred, an element of her culture and beliefs that went unquestioned. It was a religion that, reshaped and redefined by the enforced orthodoxy of the revolution and its defenders in government, no longer resonated with her. Islam, she said, had lost its spirituality and its identity.

"It's not sacred anymore," she said firmly, in tones marked more by anger than by regret. "No shah could ever de-Islamize Iran the way the Islamic regime did."

Faezeh, as I will call her, was in every respect a critic of the regime. She was an intellectual and a professor, educated in America and, like most of Iran's intelligentsia, despondent over the limited freedom she found in the country in which she was raised. She was an independent woman with a doctorate from America and a reputation among literary critics in Iran, yet she yearned for the sanctuary and simple solace that Islam had at one time provided. The changes wrought by the revolution had deprived her of that retreat and, with it, the emotional force that Islam in Iran had once meant to her.

In her mind, Islam, particularly Iranian Shiism, had long defined itself as an otherworldly faith that spoke to the people, even at times embodying their opposition to oppression. Across the Muslim world, Shiism is a minority, overshadowed in most countries by the orthodox Sunni sect of Islam. The division between the two major branches dates to a debate over the selection of a successor to the Prophet Mohammed. At the time of his death in 632, the majority believed that the prophet had not designated a successor and accepted the decision of his closest companions to choose a follower as the community's political leader. A minority, however, insisted that Mohammed had chosen his son-in-law and nephew, Ali, to lead the community as a spiritual and political successor. Their name is drawn from that support. *Shi'a* means partisans in Arabic, in their case, partisans of Ali. They believed leadership of the Muslim community stayed in the hands of Ali and his descendants, and their legitimacy as imams, or spiritual leaders, is a central doctrine of the faith.

The legitimacy of the prophet's descendants is what makes so painful to Shiites the martyrdom of Hussein, who was the second son of Ali and the prophet's grandson. He was killed in 680 in a battle at Kerbala near the Euphrates River in modern-day Iraq. Hussein's tragic death gave rise to an elaborate literature of prose, poetry and song that even today brings worshipers to tears and stands as a pervasive element of Iran's rich and enduring culture. It can be read as a revolutionary calling, as well. Within its stories are powerful currents of martyrdom and injustice, a skepticism of temporal authority and an ongoing battle against the illegitimate tyranny embodied by Hussein's killers. The power of that memory and its ability to inspire sorrow and grief struck me almost immediately after my arrival in Tehran, as I watched images on Iranian television of men listening to verse that told of Hussein's death and the legendary sufferings of his family. The force behind the pictures surprised and shocked me. In them, I saw the spirituality, the pain and the personalization of the faith. Men were sobbing, their heads buried in their hands, as they again endured the anguish of his death more than thirteen centuries later.

But to Faezeh, and to many others in Iran today, the faith had lost that mystique, surrendering the majestic for the mundane. She once saw religion as otherworldly, but now she complained that Islam in Iran had been made crass by, for instance, naming streets after imams. Who, she asked, could take seriously a highway named Imam Hussein? In her eyes, the government had brought Islam down to earth, where it could be questioned, doubted, blamed and maligned. No longer could it embody protest or even offer, as it had for centuries, a spiritual refuge for those who were oppressed.

"As soon as the government came to power," she said, her voice heavy with sorrow, "the faith lost that attraction."

What Faezeh alluded to was part of a greater phenomenon that served as a damning verdict of the revolution's legacy. Simply put, many Iranians had lost faith, at least the faith propagated by the Islamic government. In bookstores, in homes and in the streets, I felt people searching for spirituality, seeking a way to fill a void left by Islam's gradual transformation into an ideology. Islam, it seemed, had become shackled by a single interpretation brought to bear on people day after day through laws, edicts, pronouncements and even government policy. The clerical government had become Islam, Islam had become the government, and there was no longer any in between. Its exalted essence had been sacrificed for ideological purity. It was the opposite of what would become the rallying point for the reformers grouped around Khatami: pluralism, tolerance and the range of religious and political views that entails.

KHATAMI'S VISION OF AN ISLAMIC CIVIL SOCIETY

Iran today, in all its complexity, stands on the verge of post-Islam, a condition in which the appeal, energy and symbols of Islam are exhausted. In its place are emerging ideas of democracy, an indigenous conception of human rights and a focus on individual freedom and choice. The ferment itself comes amid a growing perception among Iranians that Islam does not have the answers to all societies' problems, that alone it cannot handle every challenge Iran will confront. That recognition, one only now emerging, will prove crucial to the viability of Islamic movements everywhere. In Iran, it means a search for a new system and a rethinking of the Iranian Revolution are under way, a questioning brought about by the disillusionment and disenchantment that is frank, fresh and invigorating. The force behind that is another cleric who studied in Qom, Seyyed Mohammad Khatami, who was elected in a landslide as Iran's president in 1997.

Khatami's election victory in 1997—he won with a stunning two-thirds of the electorate over a conservative candidate favored by the clerical establishment—was ensured by the votes of women and youth, and the festivities over the outcome reminded many in Iran of the heady days of the revolution itself. Supporters danced in the streets, cars put on their headlights and youths handed out candy, a traditional Iranian gesture of celebration. What they marked was an occasion in which the people did not vote against the revolution but instead— in a remarkably democratic way—decided what direction their government should take. Khatami, who set up a Web site to elaborate on his ideas, promised to answer that call.

Khatami brought intellectual force to his ideas, as well. As a religious thinker, he is fiercely devoted to his faith and Iran, but at the same time, he attempts to realistically appraise both of their places in the modern world. He asks the question posed by so many other Islamic thinkers: How can a society whose identity is religious guarantee freedom, democracy and social justice? To Khatami, the solution is not Islam in itself. Alone, as an ideology of government, it cannot solve the problems of a world that, for better or for worse, is dominated by the West. If the revolution solely sought a return to an earlier Islamic civilization, a golden age, then it failed because that civilization, in Khatami's eyes, is an anachronism. It no longer exists in practical terms and, if it did, it could no longer meet the needs of the modern era. In that argument, he makes a subtle but compelling distinction between Islamic traditionalists who seek a return to what Islam once had and Islamist activists in Iran and elsewhere who seek to progressively reshape the faith into a viable, modern approach to government and society.

The problem then, he argues, is a static society, one that can no longer meet the psychological, material and social needs of the people but, even more dangerous, obstinately refuses to acknowledge its failings. Iran, he suggests, falls into that category, and the dangers posed by it could undo the vision of a religious society. Dynamism must be a goal. "Our society's fabric is strained by vice; economic and political difficulties loom large, and we suffer from the diluted identity of Westoxication—neither ourselves, nor Western," Khatami said. "In practical matters, as we have depended on theology to give order to the individual and social worlds, we face serious inadequacies. This can only mean that our theology must evolve to meet the demands of the revolution and also the practical needs we have today."

Khatami is a skillful politician. He recognizes that he is venturing into uncharted territory, calling for religious reform that could only come from a cleric who speaks the language of the educated clergy. To create the flexibility in theology that Khatami pursues means to break the clergy's monopoly on religious interpretation, a right held by the *ulema* [clergy] in Shiite Iran to a far greater extent than that possessed by their Sunni counterparts elsewhere in the Muslim world. Despite their theological disputes, the Shiite clergy have historically considered themselves the spiritual guardians of the community, and that spiritual prestige was the foundation on which Khomeini built the Islamic state. Khatami, though, sees a danger in that same prestige, the prospect of a single, infallible interpretation, made even more formal when it becomes an ideology of government. In essence, he proposes doing away with the clergy's unique right. In taking that step, he brings the revolution full circle. The fall of the Shah was one incarnation; the fall of an infallible clergy the second.

He urges people not to follow the dictates of the clergy blindly, pointing out that even Khomeini himself is not infallible. Dogma, in particular, worries him. If interpretation remains absolute, Khatami suggests that Iranian society will experience the same dislocation, disruption and strife that came with the fall in the Middle Ages of the Catholic Church's hegemony over western European intellectual and political life. The church sought to maintain a monopoly on thought and to keep the sole right to interpret truth and falsehood; its persistence in defending that eventually obsolete prerogative was its undoing.

Where next, then? Khatami sees religion—in Iran's case, the framework for society and government—as open to an interpretation that changes with time and place. And in today's world, time and place are clearly and overwhelmingly dominated by the West. Although he is critical of the materialism of Western society, its economic and cultural domination and its record of exploitation in colonial and postcolonial times, Khatami nevertheless sees its accomplishments as awesome and urges that it be reckoned with in a balanced, rational way. Muslims, he says, should neither be dogmatically and blindly opposed to it nor captivated by its appeal. Rather, they should draw from it. What the West does offer

Iran, he believes, are some of the institutions that have made it so successful—individual rights, democracy, freedom, plurality of opinion and the rule of law, the very basis of modernity—and Khatami consistently urges the "judicious acquisition" of them.

In his speeches, Khatami, like other Islamic thinkers, draws on Islam's earliest days for inspiration. His Islamic civil society is not a slavish imitation of its Western equivalent. It instead stands as an Islamic alternative, relying as others have on the days of the prophet in the city of Medina, where Islam first held sway—an Islamic Athens of sorts. And in that Athens, Khatami sees a Muslim identity that transcends narrow-minded nationalisms, a community in which the rights of non-Muslims are respected, even guarded, and a society in which its citizens are protected by law, not threatened by the whims of a despotic ruler or the passions of a revolution.

In Khatami's vision, tolerance and plurality—or in another incarnation, faction and division—become the keys to society's survival, as long as they are regulated by the rule of law. At heart, they are signs of a vibrant, rich political life. As Khatami put it, "Destroying the atmosphere of peace in the name of freedom and destroying freedom in the name of religion and national interest represent two sides of the same coin, both symptomatic of the historical ailment that we suffer from due to centuries of despotic rule which has shaped our temperament to become irreconcilable with freedom."

AFTER THE REVOLUTION

The word *after* takes on a new meaning in the Islamic Republic. What comes *after* the revolution? What comes *after* the war with Iraq? What comes *after* Khatami's victory in the election? Iran's recent history is the story of epic conflicts and tragedies, cataclysmic wars and, at times, heroic struggles. A generation after the revolution, nothing was taken for granted in Iran; everything remained in a precarious flux. The question of what comes *after* had to be asked because no one in Iran had experienced what came *before*. The uncertainty colored much of Khatami's presidency.

Yet, as Khatami's presidency went forward, it was an inescapable fact that although the *after* and the *before* seemed so precarious, Iranians were far more aware of their present. Iranian society, in fits and starts, had democratized. Municipal elections in February 1999 increased the number of elected officials from less than 400, concentrated in Tehran, to nearly 200,000 spread out across the country. In elections for Parliament in February 2000, voting lists were

available and information was exchanged about the candidates, through newspapers and even at the voting stations themselves. The political life Khatami
envisioned had begun to take shape, and the questioning it entailed was becoming institutionalized, rather than treated as a luxury.

The vitality seemed fitting to me. The Islamic government in Iran did not
emerge from a strong Islamic movement. Although Islam provided a powerful
means to mobilize, the revolution itself was amorphous and opaque, and in its
early days, many felt a leftist government might even come to power. The idea
of *velayat-e faqih,* rule of the clergy and the constitution were all imposed from
above, in the fashion of a vanguard, once the religious wing of the revolution
won out over its nationalist and leftist rivals. Khatami's liberalization, in effect,
was finishing a discussion cut short by revolutionary necessity and the war with
Iraq. What is an Islamic government? And what are its rights and obligations?

In Iran, two faces of a revolutionary vision still resonate in the lives of its
people. There is the failed revolution, the attempt to transform an insulated
Islam into an ideology that could provide the answers for all matters of life, be
they economic, political, educational, even artistic. As an ideology, it corrupted
itself, repelling the faithful it sought to guide and discrediting the institution that
sought to safeguard it. Islam, in Iran, was not the solution, and Khomeini's rule
by the clergy—and the perpetual revolution to keep it beyond reproach—had
failed.

Yet the other face of Iran's revolution provides a potentially more influential alternative. The generation that emerged toward the end of the 1990s
championed the concept that a religious government could adhere to those
institutions thought to belong to the Western tradition: dissent, democracy,
human rights and basic freedoms. The vision of Khatami and others was not a
crude imitation of Western democracy; it was a society that drew on the still
powerful role of faith and history, but shaped it with the plurality and tolerance of a changing, dynamic polity. They did not seek to disavow the revolution or to bring an end to the Islamic Republic. They sought its maturity. How
that society takes shape is the task that a new generation of thinkers across the
Muslim world is addressing.

CHAPTER 13

THE US OCCUPATION OF IRAQ

David L. Phillips

Citing concerns about reputed weapons of mass destruction (WMD) in the hands of Saddam Hussein, and alluding to possible ties between Iraq and al-Qaeda, the Islamist organization responsible for the 9/11 attacks on the United States, the administration of George W. Bush led an invasion of Iraq in March 2003. No WMD were found, and no credible Iraqi ties to al-Qaeda have been substantiated, but Saddam Hussein was removed from power. The invasion has therefore been both criticized as a needless rush to war and praised as the toppling of a ruthless dictator in order to establish a fledgling democracy (and new US ally) in the Middle East.

In this essay, David Phillips documents some of the chaos of the postwar reconstruction of Iraq, much of it engendered by infighting between the Department of State and the Pentagon. The Bush administration failed to secure true international backing for the war, and badly underestimated the number of troops and the length of time that would be required to secure a peaceful transition to democracy. The failure to prevent extensive looting—including even the ransacking of an Iraqi nuclear complex—crippled Iraq's already overtaxed infrastructure and hopelessly undermined overly optimistic plans to make a revitalized Iraqi oil economy pay for the country's own reconstruction. The banning of Iraqi armed forces left many trained Iraqis sitting at home, unemployed and angry, at just the time the Bush administration was calling on Iraqis to defend their country against a host of jihadists who have flocked to Iraq after Saddam's fall. Of increasing concern to the American public is the absence of a clear exit strategy from Iraq.

David L. Phillips was a senior adviser with the State Department's Future of Iraq Project. He is a senior fellow at the Council on Foreign Relations and a visiting scholar at Harvard's Center for Middle East Studies. This excerpt is from Losing Iraq: Inside the Postwar Reconstruction Fiasco.

ON MARCH 19, 2003, PRESIDENT GEORGE W. BUSH ordered a decapitation strike targeting Saddam Hussein. Two F–117 stealth fighters dropped precision ordnance, US warships in the Persian Gulf and the Red Sea launched Tomahawk cruise missiles, and Special Forces dropped behind enemy lines to secure the Rumaila oil fields as well as other oil fields in the country. On March 20, the ground war of "Operation Iraqi Freedom" began. Despite sandstorms and occasional fierce fighting, US troops took control of the Baghdad airport on April 5. Four days later, they entered Firdos Square and pulled down the statue of Saddam.

[The head of the Office of Reconstruction and Humanitarian Assistance (ORHA)] Jay Garner and his staff were languishing at a five-star hotel in Kuwait and trying to keep a low profile. Garner was itching to receive country clearance and start operations in Iraq. Garner watched with dismay as the basic nihilistic impulse of Iraqis led to chaos and looting across the country. He denied that America was at fault for the situation: "Much of the looting occurred on the streets before the military had taken those streets," he insisted. The Third Infantry Division's "After Action Report" contradicted Garner's claim: "Higher headquarters did not provide the Third Infantry Division (mechanized) with a plan for Phase IV (stability operations). As a result, Third Infantry Division transitioned into Phase IV in the absence of guidance."[1]

[Future of Iraq project director] Tom Warrick had provided ORHA a list of sites to be secured—infrastructure, administrative facilities, financial institutions, religious sites, and cultural monuments, including the Iraqi National Museum. The military went out of its way not to bomb these sites, but Warrick's list was either ignored or never conveyed to field commanders. Lacking instructions and with no one in charge, US troops simply stepped aside when the looting began. Among all of Iraq's government facilities, field commanders protected the oil ministry only, an action which, of course, reinforced perceptions that the United States was after Iraq's oil.

The first days of liberation were an unmitigated disaster. Looting effectively gutted every government institution in Baghdad and in cities across Iraq. Looters dismantled the electricity grid, creating power shortages that shut down refrigeration, lighting, and water systems. Frenzied mobs ransacked hospitals, stealing medicines and even patients' beds. The crowd surged into the universities at Baghdad and Mosul and robbed them of computers and office furniture. The National Library was ransacked; every book ever published in Iraq as well as rare manuscripts and newspapers from the last century were destroyed. Historical records dating from the Ottoman period disappeared. Looters also entered the

National Museum, stealing and destroying 10,000 historical objects, including some of the finest artifacts from the Mesopotamian collection. At the al-Qaqaa weapons-storage facility, looters took tons of high-quality explosives used to detonate nuclear devices. Even the Tuwaitha nuclear complex was left unguarded; looters were able to steal yellowcake and other radiological materials.

It is unclear whether the chaos was random or if Saddam loyalists had orchestrated the events to undermine US efforts. What is clear, however, is that the looting had a devastating effect on the postwar administration of Iraq. The unrest undermined confidence in and respect for the US authorities. In a country where conspiracy theories abound, many Iraqis suspected the United States of orchestrating the mayhem. They could not comprehend how the powerful US military could vanquish Saddam's Republican Guard yet fail to prevent civil unrest.

On April 6, the Pentagon flew Ahmad Chalabi and seven hundred of his Free Iraqi Forces to Iraq. Nobody at the White House or the State Department was notified in advance; [National Security Advisor] Condoleezza Rice was visibly startled by press reports. [Secretary of State] Colin Powell learned about it by reading the newspapers. Upon arriving on Iraqi soil, Chalabi announced that he and his men had come to join the fight with coalition forces.

Garner entered Iraq on April 9, 2003. Though Garner was the official host of a conference involving about eighty Iraqis in Nasariyah on April 15, [US Special Envoy to Iraq] Zalmay Khalilzad ran the meeting. British officials worried that the meeting would founder if Iraqis thought the event was orchestrated by Washington. Sure enough, thousands of Shi'a gathered in peaceful protest of America's role; the Supreme Council for Islamic Revolution in Iraq refused to participate. Chalabi was not asked to attend but announced that he had refused Garner's invitation. Other Iraqi National Congress (INC) representatives were in the tent. ↳ An exiled group

Amid questions about its purpose and place in US postwar plans, Garner called the Nasariyah conference to order; Khalilzad explained that the meeting was the first in a sequence of regional conferences leading up to the establishment of an interim authority. To allay fears of a long-term US military occupation, Khalilzad insisted that "the United States has absolutely no interest in ruling Iraq."

Iraqis were skeptical of US intentions. Iraq's infrastructure was already run down by years of neglect, sanctions, and war. Baghdad's ransacking completely undermined the Bush administration's plan to demonstrate immediate material benefits from liberation.

ORHA had started too late to become fully operational. To make matters worse, ORHA's staff had little on-the-ground knowledge of Iraq. Few spoke Arabic. ORHA staff was sequestered in one of Saddam's huge palaces and had sparse interaction with Iraqis. There was no way to communicate except by using Thuraya satellite phones, which did not work indoors. ORHA needed translators, escorts, and military transport. However, field commanders had scant appreciation for ORHA's efforts and rarely ever showed up at meetings.

In April 2003, the United States had 150,000 troops in Iraq; in addition, 23,000 troops, most of whom were British, came from other countries. The international community was deeply divided over the US-led military action. The Bush administration's effort to secure troops from other countries was hampered by its perceived failure to gain an explicit authorization for military action from the United Nations.

United Nations Security Council resolution 1441 was adopted unanimously on November 8, 2002. It warned of "serious consequences" if Iraq refused to fulfill its disarmament obligations. To accommodate Tony Blair, who was under political pressure in Britain to seek a second resolution mandating the use of force, the United States, Britain, and Spain tabled such a resolution on February 24, 2003. Russia and France threatened a veto, but there was no need. The resolution fell far short of the nine votes necessary for approval. As Powell admitted, "It was a failure."[2] Lacking UN "cover," the failure made it even harder for governments to provide troops to the US-led coalition.

The Bush administration further undermined its efforts to broaden the coalition by announcing that regulations permitted only US companies to bid on reconstruction contracts using US funds. Moreover, only coalition countries were allowed to bid on contracts paid for by the Development Fund for Iraq (DFI), which was capitalized with seized Iraqi assets and money left over in the UN Oil for Food escrow account. More questions about the US-led reconstruction effort arose when the administration awarded [multinational construction and engineering corporations] Halliburton and Bechtel multibillion-dollar deals without going through a competitive bidding process. The need for immediate action and security clearances were among the reasons put forward by the administration, but the explanation did little to quell concerns.

Though the number of countries participating in Bush's "coalition of the willing" exceeded the number of states his father had assembled for the Gulf War, the group was a coalition of convenience rather than of commitment. Few countries rushed to join the coalition; therefore, the US used a combination of perks and punishment to induce countries to participate. Small states, such as Azerbaijan, Macedonia, and Palau, joined the coalition but offered little tangible assistance.

In early April, the leaders of France, Germany, and Russia met in St. Petersburg to discuss Iraq's reconstruction. Arguing that prolonged US military control would be opposed by Iraqis and antagonize the Arab world, they issued a joint statement calling on the United Nations to take the lead in determining Iraq's future.

The following week, UN Secretary General Kofi Annan attended the Athens summit meeting of the European Union (EU). As part of its public diplomacy, the State Department arranged for me to give a series of lectures in Greece on postwar reconstruction plans; I encountered adamant opposition from Greek officials, intellectuals, and think-tank representatives. They complained that unilateral action was in violation of international law and that UN weapons inspectors should have been given more time to do their work. Their objections mirrored concerns that were raised across Europe. It was no surprise when the EU, with Greece occupying its rotating presidency, issued a strong statement calling on the United States to turn over control of Iraq to the United Nations.

Even commonsense initiatives, such as lifting UN sanctions so that Iraq could sell its oil to help pay for reconstruction, ran into problems. Bush declared, "Now that Iraq is liberated, the United Nations should lift economic sanctions on that country,"[3] but the international community responded skeptically; indeed, many countries saw it as a ploy by Iraq's occupying power to dominate the country's oil sales and use the proceeds to enrich US corporations.

After just a few months as ORHA administrator, Jay Garner was replaced. The Bush administration chose Ambassador L. Paul Bremer III for the job and claimed that the change had been planned all along. Garner was replaced because the administration was unhappy about developments and wanted to change course. Ideologues disapproved of Garner's efforts to rehabilitate Ba'ath Party technocrats and reform elements of the Iraqi armed forces. They also disapproved of delays in assigning key posts to Iraqi exiles associated with the INC. After the war, Garner complained bitterly about the Pentagon's failure to appreciate the importance of ORHA's mission and to provide adequate resources to do the job.

ORHA's staff welcomed Bremer's appointment. Despite their loyalties to Garner, they saw it as recognition by the Bush administration that the reconstruction effort needed a more competent and much greater civilian authority. With postwar plans in ruins, Bush appointed Bremer to salvage hopes for a "new Iraq."

Until sovereignty was restored, Bremer envisioned that a US military administration would run Iraq, guarantee security, oversee reconstruction, and organize elections. Bremer had a seven-step plan to hand over sovereignty to Iraqis, starting with the establishment of an advisory council. However, Iraqis reacted angrily when Bremer announced that the transition to self-rule could take several years.

Bremer's decree banning the Iraqi armed forces was a tactical miscalculation with serious strategic consequences. Former members of the armed forces joined the legions of unemployed sitting at home and festering with rage. At the same time, the Bush administration called on Iraqis to defend their country against insurgents, who were increasingly active blowing up water mains, oil pipelines, and electric towers, and attacking military convoys.

With 65 percent of Iraqis unemployed, ample recruits were ready to join the insurgency. Many of the dismissed Ba'athists and senior military officials were Arab Sunnis to whom Saddam had bestowed power and privilege. Suddenly, they were disgraced and destitute. Moreover, their future was uncertain in a country dominated by Arab Shi'a and Kurds.

The initial spasms of violence were concentrated in the Sunni triangle, where many former Ba'athists felt a sense of hopelessness that led them to take up arms against the United States. "Instead of us using these personnel against terrorism, terrorists are using them against us," said Major Mohammed Faour [a former member of Iraq's Special Forces and participant in Future of Iraq project]. "This is a tragedy. We could use these people. They are military people. They are professionals. They are used to obeying orders. They need money. They need the lives they had before."[4]

"Bring 'em On"

The Bush administration had goals for Iraq, but no coherent strategy for accomplishing them. Its policy was based on a combination of naïveté, misjudgment, and wishful thinking. Vengeful insurgents found common cause with al-Qaeda elements, who were able to enter Iraq because the United States did not have enough troops to secure Iraq's borders with Syria and Iran. The chaos was exacerbated by up to 100,000 common criminals that Saddam had let out of jail just before the war. By creating chaos and inflicting casualties, they hoped to break US will and drive the coalition out of the country. That summer, violence started to spiral out of control as the insurgency spread and suicide attacks started.

In response to congressional criticism that the Bush administration did not have a plan to stabilize Iraq, Bremer explained: "My motto is strategic clarity and tactical flexibility. We need to be very clear where we are headed in our strategy on security, on economy, and on political developments. And we are very clear on that. And we need to have a plan, but we need to be tactically flexible as the situation evolves on the ground."⁵

Bremer described the CPA's [Coalition Provisional Authority] agenda. First, the coalition would establish a safe and secure environment. Second, it would expand essential services. Third, it would stimulate the economy to create jobs and economic growth. And fourth, the CPA would steward Iraq's transition to democratic self-rule. Bremer recognized that security, reconstruction, and governance were interconnected. Sabotage worsened electricity problems, electricity shortages enhanced security risks, and reconstruction failures undermined the political transition. "Our task," said Rumsfeld, "is to try and create an environment that is hospitable for the Iraqi people to fashion a new way of governing themselves and be on our way."⁶

Though field commanders had little sense of the insurgency's leadership, organization, or financial sources, they believed that insurgents were organized at the regional level in a cellular structure in what amounted to a classical guerrilla campaign. After drive-by shootings or attacks using rocket propelled grenades, insurgents simply faded into the local population. Attacks were not just hit and run: Explosive devices used in combination with tactical activities implied some level of coordination.

Insurgents attacked pipelines, utility grids and other infrastructure. Convoys were targeted making the drive from the airport to Baghdad a dangerous gauntlet. Soft targets of the international community were also hit. Asked about the escalating violence, Bush replied "Bring 'em on."⁷

The Iraqis themselves were increasingly targeted. Kidnappings and carjackings became common occurrences. Iraqis judged the United States by its ability to deliver security, services, and jobs. They were glad to be rid of Saddam, but they longed for the stability that had existed under the Ba'athist regime. As violence mounted, Iraqi resentment of the United States also increased.

With conditions worsening and Iraqis growing increasingly disaffected, the Pentagon commissioned an independent assessment of conditions in Iraq. The report concluded that "Iraqis uniformly expressed the view that the window of opportunity for the CPA to turn things around in Iraq is closing rapidly. The potential for chaos is becoming more real every day. The next three months are critical."

Support for the Iraq war was also slipping in the United States. The administration cast the Iraq war as part of the broader war on terror. US officials refused to acknowledge that the occupation had inspired the insurgency. Nor did it let on that the US invasion had made Iraq the central front in the war on terror.

Rumsfeld insisted on staying the course:

> Coalition forces will continue to root out, capture, and kill the remnants of the former regime until they no longer pose a threat to the Iraqi people. . . . As we do, it is important not to lose sight of the fundamental fact that our country is still very much engaged in a global war on terrorism. Two terrorist regimes have been removed, but we still have terrorist enemies in Afghanistan and Iraq and across the globe who are seeking to harm our people. We can deal with them in one of two ways: we can find, capture, or kill them in Afghanistan, Iraq, or in other countries; or we can wait and end up having to deal with them here in the United States.[8]

Except for a handful of Arabs who joined Ansar al-Islam, an indigenous terror group encamped on the Iran-Iraq border and composed mostly of radical Kurds, al-Qaeda did not have a presence in Iraq before the war. However, jihadists from Syria, Egypt, Sudan, and other countries flocked to Iraq after Saddam's fall. Abu Musab al-Zarqawi was the most notorious. Zarqawi was an al-Qaeda associate who fought with al-Qaeda in Afghanistan. Previously, he ran a terror group called al-Tawhid, whose goal was to depose Jordan's monarchy. Though former Ba'athists and al-Qaeda are ideologically incompatible, they forged cooperation against their common enemy, the United States. When US forces engaged insurgents at Ar Rutbah in Western Iraq in July 2002, they found passports and identification at the scene, indicating that almost all the eighty fighters killed in the operation were non-Iraqi.

Though it confiscated millions of dollars and large caches of weapons that would otherwise be used to ambush US and British forces, the Defense Department knew that it was impossible to secure every convoy and protect every facility in a country the size of California. Field commanders understood that the best way to achieve a more secure environment was through the active engagement and support of the Iraqi people.

To change the face of occupation, the United States accelerated efforts to set up indigenous security forces. It initiated formation of an Iraqi national army and a civil defense corps in the hope that this would help with border security, site protection, and escorting convoys. Though more than 30,000 Iraqi police were hired, procurement problems delayed provision of their equipment. As insurgents targeted Iraqis cooperating with the US, poorly trained recruits were pushed onto the front lines like cannon fodder.

The Congress wanted details about the Pentagon's plans to rotate forces and bring US troops home. In July, the force level was about 160,000. This included 148,000 Americans and 12,000 troops from nineteen coalition countries. The near total destruction of Iraqi security institutions forced US troops to stay in Iraq for longer than expected. To maintain troop strength, the Defense Department relied on reserves who never imagined they would go overseas for more than a year.

General Abizaid wanted to reduce the US troop presence. He understood that coalition patrols racing around in humvees exacerbated the resentment of Iraqis toward occupation. "There is a downside to having too many troops," Abizaid explained. "I have never been in favor of huge, ponderous forces, but light, agile, mobile forces that not only can deal with the problem in Iraq, but throughout the theater."[9] Abizaid maintained that the number of troops per square inch was not the issue. Capability matched to the mission was much more important; Abizaid took steps to replace heavily armored army units with lighter and more highly mechanized forces. He also expanded the use of private contractors.

Members of Congress started to raise concerns about whether there were enough troops to do the job. They wanted to further internationalize security and give the United Nations a more important role in Iraq's reconstruction and political transition. When [Senator Joseph] Biden inquired about NATO's role, the administration pointed out that Spanish Guardia Civil and Italian Carabinieri had made commitments. US officials suggested that more countries would come in when the security situation improved.

That the United States had failed to secure international backing for waging the war made it even more difficult to arrange international cooperation in winning the peace. [Deputy Defense Secretary Paul] Wolfowitz recognized that "coalition efforts in Iraq must undergo further internationalization to be successful and affordable."[10] However, the Bush administration treated Iraq as though it were a prize to keep. Other than ceremonial roles, it refused to give other countries real decisionmaking authority in Iraq.

Even when it became apparent that it lacked area and language expertise, the Office of the Secretary of Defense still refused to cooperate with the State Department. Whereas Powell recognized the need for UN nation-building expertise after the war, the Pentagon did not appreciate the need for a stronger international civilian component in postwar administration. The United

Nations was no panacea for Iraq's problems. However, its imprimatur would have lent legitimacy to US efforts.

In addition to involving the United Nations in Iraq's transition, other State Department suggestions were also discarded. The Future of Iraq Project had emphasized the importance of cooperation between Iraqi exiles and Iraqis from within Iraq. A State Department official remarked, "When we got to Baghdad the biggest surprise was that divisions between exiles and other Iraqis were much deeper than between Iraq's ethnic or religious groups."[11]

The CPA was discredited by its close association with Ahmad Chalabi. After entering Baghdad, Chalabi called a press conference to announce his arrival. Few reporters showed up. Iraqi bystanders were mostly curious about Chalabi and his entourage of staff and Free Iraqi Forces. As a senior US official noted, "He was jeered more than cheered. Iraqis were shouting him down. It was embarrassing. We had to help bail him out."[12] Surveys of Iraqi public opinion at the time showed that Chalabi enjoyed even less public approval than Saddam. Chalabi's popular standing diminished even further when his militia set up roadblocks and extorted passenger tolls. One of Chalabi's aides declared himself mayor of Baghdad; Iraq National Congress (INC) loyalists sent out the word that Iraqis should report to the INC if they wanted to find jobs.

Despite Chalabi's assurances that the Shi'a would greet US troops "with flowers," Ryan Crocker and other State Department officials knew that unleashing Shi'a passions would have unpredictable consequences. When Saddam's regime crumbled, Shi'a clerics stepped in to fill the void. Wary of exiles who presumed power in the new Iraq, they took over the management of basic services and established their authority over the Shi'a population. Using Ayatollah Khomeini's vitriolic language to describe the United States, Ayatollah al-Haeri, a radical cleric, instructed Iraq's Shi'a clerics to "raise people's awareness of the Great Satan's plans and of the means to abort them." He also called on his Shi'a brethren to "seize as many positions as possible to impose a fait accompli for any coming government."[13]

Meanwhile, conditions in Iraq were going from bad to worse. Bremer's seven-step plan never got off the ground. Because he was unable to establish security, plans for reconstruction and democratization stalled. The lack of progress worsened the disaffection of Iraqis. They, in turn, fueled the insurgency and contributed to heightened violence. Zarqawi's group emerged as the chief organizer of kidnappings, beheadings, and suicide bombings.

On August 7, a car bomb tore apart the Jordanian embassy, killing eleven people and wounding fifty. The UN headquarters was attacked on August 19.

Ten days later, an explosion in Najaf killed scores. Later in the month, nineteen Italian Carabinieri were killed in a bombing. In the fall, violence continued to spread across the country. On October 14, a powerful car bomb blew up outside the Turkish Mission in Baghdad. Two weeks later, on the first day of the Islamic holy month of Ramadan, another car bomb exploded, killing forty people outside the International Committee of the Red Cross headquarters. In addition to the soft targets of the international community, insurgents were successfully killing coalition forces in ambushes and using remote detonation devices. With attacks on coalition forces averaging about thirty a day, postwar US combat deaths in Iraq reached 117 on October 29, more than the number of troops who had died before the war officially ended.[14]

Bush was under fire at home. For the first time since 9/11, his popularity rating fell below 50 percent. Many Americans worried that US policy in Iraq was rudderless. The American public was most concerned about the absence of an exit strategy. Bush insisted, "We've had a strategy from the beginning, Jerry Bremer is running the strategy and we are making very good progress about the establishment of a free Iraq. The definition of when we get out is 'when there is a free and peaceful Iraq based upon a constitution and elections,' and obviously we'd like that to happen as quickly as possible. But we are mindful of rushing the process, which would create the conditions for failure."[15]

CHAPTER 14

THE ROLE OF
THE PERSIAN GULF REGION

Shibley Telhami

Saudi Arabia and Iraq, both bordering the Persian Gulf, have the world's first and second largest oil reserves, respectively. A common theme in American politics is that the United States must reduce its dependence on oil from the Middle East. However, as China and other regions of the world increase their oil consumption, it will be the Middle East (which holds between two-thirds and three-quarters of the world's known oil reserves) that will be most able to respond to the growing global demand for oil. The Middle East will therefore remain an area of vital strategic interest to the United States.

America's interest in the Persian Gulf intensified in the 1960s with a policy of balancing the two dominant regional powers, Iran and Iraq, against each other—a policy that led to sending US military aid to both countries during the Iran-Iraq war of 1980–1988. Iraq's nominal victory in that war emboldened it to invade Kuwait, thus threatening to upset the balance of power in the Persian Gulf. The United States consequently led an international coalition that attacked and defeated Iraq in the Gulf War of 1991. But that very success in turn fueled concerns that the revolutionary regime of Iran might benefit strategically from Iraq's defeat. The United States has since labeled Iran (with Iraq and North Korea) as a member of "the axis of evil," implicitly holding open the possibility of a preemptive strike against Iran in a "war on terror," which would thus prevent a hostile Iranian regime from dominating a significant portion of the world's oil reserves.

Of the nineteen hijackers on 9/11, fifteen were Saudis. Yet, while al-Qaeda has strong roots in Saudi Arabia, the Islamist organization poses an even bigger threat to the Saudi government than to the United States. Saudi authoritarianism has bred radical opposition, but the dilemma that faces the Saudis is that the transition to a more democratic society might itself be unstable. The United States and Saudi Arabia have a mutual interest in implementing incremental change in Saudi politics and economics.

Shibley Telhami *is Anwar Sadat Professor for Peace and Development at the University of Maryland. He is the author of* Reflections of Hearts and Minds: Media, Opinion, and Identity in the Arab World, *and of* The Stakes: America in the Middle East: The Consequences of Power and the Choice for Peace, *from which the present selection is extracted.*

We need to put pressure on Saudi Arabia to change, but we will not have the leverage to do that as long as we have a reliance on them for oil. We have to diminish that reliance.

—Former CIA Director James Woolsey, March 5, 2002

IN THE MONTHS FOLLOWING THE ATTACKS ON US SOIL, many in our national debate have inclined toward arguments of wishful thinking: that the Persian Gulf region is no longer as strategically important as it once was; that Saudi Arabia in particular is less central in the global oil market because of the rise of new energy powers such as Russia; and that the United States can significantly reduce its strategic dilemma in the region simply by importing less oil from the Gulf and more from other sources. These arguments miss the central reasons for the continued importance of the Persian Gulf for world energy supplies and the likelihood that it will become even more important in the future.

The discovery that many of the terrorists responsible for the attacks on the United States, including Usama bin Laden himself, came from Saudi Arabia created unusual tension in one of the longest-standing friendly relationships the United States has had in the Middle East—a relationship born from mutual interests in Saudi Arabia's rich oil fields. Although the United States and the Saudi kingdom have had their disagreements, especially over the Arab-Israeli conflict, both sides have learned to manage the differences for their mutual benefit.

But in the months that followed the attacks on the United States, two things raised the level of tension. First, there was a closer scrutiny of Saudi Arabia's closed political system as people began asking how it could produce the likes of bin Laden. As analysts looked harder, they discovered deep resentment of the United States among Saudis for which their government received a good share of the blame. Many on the American side of the debate believed that the answer was to pressure the Saudi government to confront this anti-American sentiment and, more importantly, to reform and liberalize its political system. Second, as

US support for Israel grew after 9/11 at the same time that the intensity of the Palestinian-Israeli conflict increased, the Arab-Israeli issue became another source of tension.

These tensions ran up against an inescapable reality: that Saudi Arabia remains a central player in the global supply of energy. Hence it was not without leverage in the relationship with the United States. Many US commentators grappled to find ways to reduce this dependence. A favorite idea was to wean America off Middle Eastern energy sources by finding substitutes for Saudi oil, especially in Russia, whose production was rising and whose role as an oil producer was seen by some analysts as rivaling Saudi Arabia's.

THE CONTINUING IMPORTANCE OF GULF OIL

Most scenarios of replacing Middle Eastern oil with other sources are built on wishful thinking. No matter where the United States buys its oil, any reduction in the supply will result in price increases everywhere and will affect the entire global economy. The question is not where one buys oil so much as it is who has the most capacity to supply oil and affect the market. All the scrambling to develop resources elsewhere around the world can only delay the day of reckoning. Although the Middle East produces a quarter of world oil supplies, it holds between two-thirds and three-quarters of all known oil reserves. For this reason, the United States and other Western nations will have to continue to define the region as vitally important.

Barring significant new discoveries of oil, all major increases in oil production from 2010 to 2020 are likely to come from the Persian Gulf as its superior reserves become a central factor in the supply of oil. At the same time, other regions around the world are likely to increase their need for Middle Eastern oil and to compete with the West for these resources. China, for example, now imports 60 percent of the oil it consumes from the Persian Gulf. Forecasts indicate that in the next two decades that figure could increase to 90 percent.

Ultimately, no state around the world has the current impact on and the potential future importance to the oil market of Saudi Arabia—certainly not Russia, whose oil reserves constitute only 5 percent of the global reserves. Saudi Arabia's trump card remains its spare production capacity, which allows it to affect the market significantly by withholding or increasing supply. No other country commands such a capacity, and therefore such power, in the global energy market.

OIL AND MILITARY STRATEGY

That the Middle East is vitally important does not automatically lead to the conclusion that a US military strategy is required there. One central question has been whether the United States needs to have a military presence in the region at all.

It is not entirely clear why oil economics should be mixed with oil politics or why a military strategy is necessary. Many countries that depend heavily on Middle Eastern oil—such as Japan and many European nations—have assumed that they can base their policy entirely on the demands of the market without a need for political and military intervention. This attitude may in part be driven by their taking the United States for granted and assuming that Uncle Sam will do the job to the benefit of all consumers.

But there is more to it than that. Outside the United States, the view is growing that assuring the flow of oil does not require a military approach. This view is bolstered by historical trends. With the exception of the 1973 Arab oil embargo, which was politically motivated and which led to extraordinary increases in oil prices, long-term evidence suggests that the market, more than any other issue, determines trends in oil prices. Historically, political alliances have not greatly altered patterns of trade between the oil-producing countries and the rest of the world. Oil producers sell oil to the countries that need it and that are willing to pay the price. This pattern was true even during the Cold War years, when political relationships were obviously not central to the oil producers' trading behavior. Moderate states in the Middle East did not differ radically from pro-Soviet states in their trading: The oil-exporting nation with the greatest share of trade with the Soviet bloc was the shah's Iran, not Libya, Algeria, or Iraq. The bottom line was that these states did what was in their economic interest, regardless of their political orientation.

Maintaining a US military presence in the Persian Gulf costs American taxpayers billions of dollars each year. Because these forces can be used elsewhere in the world, that sum is not entirely spent on defending the region. Still, one wonders why the United States devotes so much of its resources, energies, and war planning to the Persian Gulf. Would it not be more sensible to leave the oil issue to market forces and to leave politics and the military out of it?

As conventionally understood, the American strategy is based on a resolve to assure the flow of oil to the West at reasonable prices by relying on states, notably Saudi Arabia, that have excess capacity. (This notion alone requires Saudi-US cooperation to assure that the Saudi capacity is used as a moderating force on the oil market.) But for more than half a century, a central drive behind the American military strategy in the oil-rich region—one that has been not fully understood by most analysts—has been not to assure continued oil flow to the United States but to deny control of these vast resources to powerful enemies.

THE OIL-DENIAL POLICY

As the Cold War was moving to center stage in American foreign policy in 1948, a new worry emerged in the White House: that the Soviet Union could control oil supplies in the Middle East. It is no coincidence that much of the early preoccupation with the potential Soviet threat after the end of World War II centered on the remaining Soviet presence in Iran. Unknown to the public until the declassification in recent years of National Security Council documents was the extent of the Truman administration's concern about a possible Soviet takeover of the oil fields. Equally surprising was that the Truman administration built its strategy not so much on the idea of defending the oil fields in the face of a possible invasion as on denying the Soviet Union use of the oil fields if it should invade.

The National Security Council (NSC) quickly developed a detailed plan that was signed by President Truman in 1949 and later supplemented by a series of additional NSC directives. The plan, developed in coordination with the British government and American and British oil companies without the knowledge of Middle Eastern governments, called for storing explosives in the Middle East. In case of a Soviet invasion, as a last resort, the oil installations and refineries would be blown up and oil fields plugged to make it impossible for the Soviet Union to use them.

Even during the Cold War, the "oil denial" policy was expanded beyond the perceived direct threat from the Soviet Union. The Eisenhower administration, which faced upheavals in the Middle East that threatened pro-Western governments in the region, began worrying about the emergence of hostile regimes that would control too much power through oil and thus further undermine Western interests. In 1957, following the Suez crisis and its aftermath, which included the overthrow of a pro-Western government in Iraq, the Eisenhower administration expanded the Truman administration's oil-denial strategy. From that point on, the policy pertained to imminent threats not only from the Soviet Union but also from hostile regional governments.

The logic of denying oil to regional powers became a serious factor in America's policy decisions when Iraq invaded Kuwait in 1990. The thought that a powerful Iraq could dominate the oil-rich region was unacceptable to US strategists. It is thus important to review America's policy toward regional powers in its attempt to protect US interests in the Middle East.

AMERICAN STRATEGY IN THE GULF

America's increased interest in the Persian Gulf began in the late 1960s as the British were finalizing their withdrawal from the Gulf. At the time there were two significant military powers in the Gulf: Iraq and Iran. The former was ruled by an Arab nationalist government that had been at odds with American foreign policy and was supplied with weapons by the Soviet Union. The latter was ruled by the pro-Western shah, Reza Pahlavi, whose throne had been saved by the CIA in the 1950s, when he faced domestic upheavals.

The United States had little chance of deploying major forces in the region to defend Western interests for two reasons: First, the Soviet Union would have resisted such a deployment. Second, and more importantly, the American public was in no mood for such a decision at a time when the United States was trying to disentangle itself from Vietnam. Thus was born the contemporary American approach to Persian Gulf security: balance of power between the two dominant regional powers, Iran and Iraq. Since then no American policy toward one of these states has been contemplated without reassessing the policy toward the other. For the next decade, the United States helped build up Iranian forces, supplying them with modern weapons, especially after Iran benefited financially from the significant increases of oil prices in the mid-1970s. This strategy required little American military presence beyond the reach of US naval forces.

The picture changed dramatically in 1979 when the American-backed Iranian regime was overthrown by a clergy-led popular revolution. Suddenly the two regional powers, Iran and Iraq, were both unfriendly to America, and the one the United States had helped empower was even more unfriendly than the other. Popular anger at America's support of the repressive shah over three decades made Iran a staunchly anti-American country. The hostility was expressed by the taking of American hostages, resulting in a crisis that galvanized the American public for over a year and that contributed to the defeat of President Jimmy Carter in the 1980 presidential elections.

Iraq was at the very same time projecting increasing anti-American sentiment, especially after the United States brokered a separate peace between Egypt and Israel in 1979 that most Arab states rejected. Iraq was a leader of the so-called rejectionist front that refused to accept the bilateral Camp David agreements, which most Arab leaders felt came at the expense of their interests. Iran and Iraq competed during that period to champion the Palestinian cause. Even though Iran is a non-Arab Shiite Muslim state, its spiritual leader, the Ayatullah Ruhollah Khomeini, highlighted the spiritual importance of Jerusalem, and one of his first acts was to close the Israeli embassy and open one for the Palestine Liberation Organization.

The 1979 Soviet invasion of Afghanistan to save the besieged communist government in Kabul made matters seem even more threatening to American interests. This invasion revived US fears dating back to the beginning of the Cold War that the Soviet Union aspired to a foothold in the Gulf. These perceived threats propelled the Carter administration to declare the Gulf region as being "vitally important" to the United States as a way of preempting any Soviet designs to exploit the changed strategic environment.

Many American analysts often lump Arab and Muslim states together. They assume that these states' motivation in regard to America is the single most important issue driving their foreign policies. But the events that transpired immediately after 1979 were a reminder that Iran and Iraq disliked and feared each other even more than they were angry with America. Iran was led by a government of Shiite Islamic clergy who had always opposed the secular Baathist government in Iraq. The Iraqi government's treatment of the marginalized Shiite majority, with whom Iran had religious and cultural ties, was also a point of dispute.

After months of tension over the disputed Shatt-al-Arab waterway that separates the two countries, during which Baghdad accused the Iranian revolutionary government of attempts to sow dissent in Iraq, Saddam Hussein's government launched a war against its neighbor. That war lasted eight years and cost both countries significant losses both in lives and purse. Nonetheless, it was not seen in Washington as especially threatening. Throughout that period, the US outlook was that these two unfriendly states were undermining each other's capabilities to threaten American interests. American policy thus had two primary objectives. First, the war could not spill over to other parts of the Gulf, especially to Saudi Arabia, Kuwait, and the other small Gulf nations, in a way that would undermine the supply of oil. Second, the United States did not want to see a clear winner in the war lest a dominant power emerge with whom the United States would have to contend. Above all, the United States did not want to see an Iranian victory, both because it feared the Islamic revolutionary government in Iran a bit more than Saddam Hussein and because America's Arab friends in the Gulf, including Saudi Arabia, supported Iraq.

When Iraq seemed to gain the upper hand in the war, the Reagan administration, despite its strong public opposition to Iran, secretly began negotiations to supply Iran with weapons in exchange for its cooperation in securing the release of American hostages in Lebanon. Arms transfers in fact took place, beginning in 1985 with the shipment to Iran of American antitank missiles, provided through Israel. Later US officials began worrying about the changing tide of the war, especially in 1986, when the Iranians seemed to overcome their early losses and gain an edge that led some analysts to conclude that time was on Iran's side. After Iranian forces took the Iraqi Faw Peninsula, near Kuwait, in 1986, US analysts feared that the war might expand to affect Kuwait and shipments of oil. In 1987, the United States signaled its commitment to securing the flow of oil by reflagging Kuwaiti ships (with American flags) and providing US Navy protection for them, thus sending a strong message that an attack on these ships would be an attack on America. In addition, the United States began helping Iraq militarily, all in the name of keeping a balance of power in the Gulf. The war ended in 1988 with an Iraqi advantage, though it was a stretch to call it a major military victory for Iraq. However, even without any territorial gains, the appearance of military victory and improvements in Iraq's missile capabilities enabled Saddam Hussein and his government to exploit the end of the war as a major military and political victory.

THE CONSEQUENCES OF THE 1991 GULF WAR

In the months between the end of the Iraq-Iran war and Iraq's invasion of Kuwait in August 1990, the Cold War between the Soviet Union and the United States was coming to an end, and the fear of a Soviet threat in the Gulf had all but disappeared.

Iraq's invasion of Kuwait completely changed the strategic outlook for the United States. If Iraq were allowed to get away with its occupation of Kuwait, it would double its oil capacity overnight and become the most significant power in the Middle East, next to Israel. Even if it did not employ that power to invade Saudi Arabia or the smaller Gulf states, and thus dominate the region, it would be in a position to intimidate them and dictate their policies. The thought that Iraq—whose foreign policy generally was at odds with America's, especially on the issue of Israel—would become such a significant power was probably the primary force behind the American reaction.

The 1991 Gulf War resulted in a significant new development: a large number of American forces in the region and the establishment of new military bases in several Arab states, including Kuwait, Bahrain, Saudi Arabia, the United Arab Emirates, and Qatar. But the United States continued to view Iran and Iraq through the prism of the balance of power between the two countries. The defeat of Iraq in 1991, its reduced power, and the imposition of stringent sanctions that further eroded its power throughout the 1990s raised concerns about Iran. US foreign policy in the past several decades has never envisioned one of the two except in relation to the other. Any new Iraq policy also necessitated change in policy toward Iran. The strategic goal of American policy after 1991 was to preserve the territorial integrity of Iraq lest it be too weakened in relation to Iran while at the same time finding ways to limit Iran's power while Iraq is weak. This logic came to be known as "dual containment," the policy pursued by the Clinton administration. The argument for that policy was that neither Iran nor Iraq was a friendly state, and since Iraq was to be kept under tight sanctions, Iranian power must also be contained. President George W. Bush's policy of including Iran (with Iraq and North Korea) as a member of "the axis of evil," despite Tehran's cooperation with the United States in the first phase of the war on terrorism, was an inevitable outcome of considering a war with Iraq. The short-term consequence of the war was the reduction of Iraq's military power, thus raising the American concern that Iran might benefit strategically.

The central argument made by the Bush administration in defining the "axis of evil" was the notion that states like Iran and Iraq were dangerous because they sought to acquire weapons of mass destruction and because they could provide such weapons to terrorists—thus threatening America and its friends. These arguments assumed that deterrence, which worked against the Stalinist USSR and Maoist China, would not work against these states; that their regimes hated America more than they wished to survive; and that they were connected to the terrorists that attacked the United States. The latter point has been very difficult to support, especially because none of the terrorists involved in the 9/11 attacks came from Iran or Iraq and because al-Qaeda and its backers, the Taliban regime in Afghanistan, were friends of neither state. A better case could be made that these states posed a threat to Israel.

It was hard to imagine circumstances under which Saddam's government in Iraq and the Islamic government in Iran would have been seen by Americans as anything but aggressive, especially since President Bush had declared them part of the "axis of evil," which became a central feature in the war on terrorism, and introduced a policy of "preemption." This outlook made it likely that the United States would continue to prevent these two states from dominating the bulk of the world's known oil reserves.

The Aims of US Policy in Postwar Iraq

It is doubtful that there was unanimity among US policymakers about the aims of US policy in a post–Saddam Hussein Iraq. However, it is clear that the dominant vision was the overt employment of American power to change the strategic picture. The argument was that by winning a war with Iraq, the United States would turn that important country into an American ally, which would automatically change the calculations of all its neighbors. A friendly Iraq bordering three other friendly states, Kuwait, Jordan, and Turkey, would intimidate the other two bordering states, Syria and Iran. The oil potential of Kuwait and Iraq combined with the other smaller oil producers in the Gulf would rival Saudi Arabia's potential. If one adds the enhanced American military presence in the region, the prospect was alluring to many Washington analysts and decision makers.

According to this line of thinking, it was unnecessary to be concerned about international opposition, including in the Middle East, because once the policy was implemented, others would simply have to adapt. There was little doubt that the United States would win any military confrontation with either Iran or Iraq, or, for that matter, any combination of states in the region. Therefore, the assumption was that many states opposing such a scenario would simply jump on the winning bandwagon, and those who didn't would suffer severe consequences.

To add allure to this vision, many advocating it suggested that such a scenario not only would reduce the threat of weapons of mass destruction but also would help transform the region from authoritarian rule to democracy. America would be able to assure the emergence of a democratic Iraq and increase its leverage against states such as Egypt and Saudi Arabia, thus forcing them to change internally—both because their people would see the success of democracy in Iraq and because the United States would be better able to pressure their governments. Such changes would lead to a more stable Middle East and to a reduction of terrorism, since the prevailing assumption was that repression fostered terrorism.

CONCERNS ABOUT
THE WAR'S CONSEQUENCES

The argument that the exercise of military and political power would transform the region from authoritarianism to democracy went counter to the logic of realpolitik both for America and for the regional actors—and it also went against historical evidence. The primary aim was to assure a stable Iraq that is friendly to America and to protect the lives of Americans stationed in the area. This in itself was no small task, given the divisions within Iraq and the influence and interest of some of its neighbors, such as Iran, Turkey, and Syria. Iraq was a devastated country after two full decades of war and economic sanctions and would require considerable reconstruction before it could reap the benefits of its potential. This task, together with the central American priority of preventing terror attacks against the United States, was bound to outweigh all else, including the issue of democracy. Would we allow the long-repressed Shiite majority in Iraq, which has strong religious ties with Iran's Shiite majority, to exercise its democratic power if it turned out that it would be sympathetic to Iran?

The public perception of the United States in much of the Arab and Muslim world was of American imperialism. Increased and visible US military force in the oil-rich regions of the Arab and Muslim world was bound to intensify public resentment of American foreign policy. Governments had two choices: either avoid America's wrath by repressing the public or avoid their public's wrath by annoying America. Either choice was not likely to have a happy outcome for regional politics or for American objectives. In those countries caught in the middle, unable to make up their minds, the resulting instability will be a fertile ground for terrorists. The pervasive psychological humiliation among a new generation of young Arabs and Muslims, connected to America, may in the long term be the most worrisome consequence.

In addition to the issues of repression, public opinion, and resentment of America among a new generation of Arabs and Muslims, there will also be uncertainty about the ability to bring about stability in Iraq and the countries surrounding it. There is little doubt that Iraqis suffered tremendously under the rule of Saddam Hussein, and although most Iraqis were probably happy to be rid of their repressive government and welcomed change, many did not. Moreover, hatred of the Iraqi regime did not by any means translate into a love of the United States or its policies, so the challenge of maintaining a unified, stable, and friendly Iraq should not be underestimated. Was it wise to ignore the fact that our actions would intensify hostility, anger, and a sense of deep humiliation for a new generation of Arabs and Muslims? Was it in our interest to be seen as the new imperialist in a region whose contemporary history is defined by hatred of imperialism?

SAUDI ARABIA AND THE NEED FOR POLITICAL AND ECONOMIC REFORM

It is useful to begin addressing the changing American view of Saudi Arabia with the immediate issue for American foreign policy: the war on terrorism. Much of the official frustration with Saudi Arabia since the 9/11 attacks has been predicated on two assumptions: first, that the Saudis have helped create al-Qaeda by encouraging, or at least not discouraging, anti-American rhetoric in the kingdom; and second, that the closed Saudi monarchic system, which allows little legitimate political dissent and accords religious fundamentalist groups considerable cultural power, radicalizes opposition groups and increases the chance of terrorism. US support for the royal family is seen as a central reason why these groups target America.

Though the Saudis have unwittingly helped create al-Qaeda, and must therefore address the internal causes for its rise, we must put this phenomenon in perspective. Al-Qaeda is a threat not only to the United States but also to the Saudi government; its aim is to overthrow the Saudi regime as much as to hurt America. The Saudis had a role in creating this Frankenstein's monster, but the United States had a significant hand in it too. In fact, America played a greater role than Saudi Arabia in the political origins of Usama bin Laden and his horrible organization. US efforts to mobilize devout Muslim political activists across the globe in the name of jihad against the "infidel" communists in Afghanistan was a central reason for the early success of these groups, which ultimately helped form al-Qaeda. The role that countries such as Saudi Arabia and Egypt played to help recruit such people was in large part in response to US wishes.

Regardless of the roots of al-Qaeda, there is a strong case for the need to reform an authoritarian regional system that has radicalized domestic opposition. Democracy in Saudi Arabia and the rest of the region would be good in itself and would have at least one important stabilizing effect on the political system in the region: bolstering the identity of states at the expense of the pan-Arab and pan-Islamic identities. When the legitimacy of the government is based on elections by its own people, it needs to appeal less to regional causes as proof of its legitimacy.

But if the end result of democracy is desirable, the means of getting there are the subject of continued debate among experts. One conclusion that can be drawn from historical cases is that even if democracy leads to more stability, transitions to democracy are often extremely unstable and, in the end, unpredictable. Rapid radical transitions from authoritarianism to democracy in places such as Saudi Arabia are unlikely, but were they to occur, the resulting instability or unpredictable outcomes, such as the possibility of a militant Islamist regime being democratically elected, may seem even more threatening to American interests than the status quo.

A constructive approach is to seek incremental change. Such change can be achieved only through a mutually beneficial, collaborative effort with others, including willing governments in the region. For many reasons, rulers in the region, whose propensity to keep power remains undiminished, at the same time feel the need to change, especially in the economic arena. The role of the United States should be to increase their incentive to bring about such change.

In the end, the goal of achieving more democracy in the region is complex and challenging. Though the United States can play a role in a process of political reform in the region, no power can bring it about alone. Governments in the region will not happily accommodate plans to undermine their power. A threatening, confrontational strategy creates the dual risk of alienating or destabilizing more states in the region. Neither outcome is a happy one for the war on terrorism: Alienated states are less likely to provide the cooperation the United States needs to battle terrorism, and unstable states may provide fertile grounds for terrorists.

The most promising approach to bringing about gradual political reform in the region, without significantly increasing instability in the process, is to begin by focusing on reform in the economic and educational systems. All states in the region, including the oil-rich ones, are facing serious economic challenges that contribute to the political threats against them. They need to liberalize their centralized economies, attract foreign investment, and create an environment hospitable to international business. The United States can help in these areas, but governments also have their own incentives to pursue these goals, such as the hope of improving their troubled economies. Internal demand for political reform will increase as economic reform takes hold, and the United States could continue to assist the voices of reform in the region.

The states of the Gulf Cooperation Council (GCC)—Saudi Arabia, Kuwait, Bahrain, the United Arab Emirates, Qatar, and Oman—continue to have an interest in maintaining close relations with the United States, especially American military support. That interest gives the United States some leverage, but only up to a point because the GCC states know that the US strategy primarily serves America's own interests. The result is clear mutual incentives to cooperate. When threats to oil are clear, as in the case of the Iraqi invasion of Kuwait in 1990, Saudi Arabia and other GCC states will undoubtedly rally behind the United States to defend the oil fields. Even without an imminent threat, GCC states, especially Kuwait, have an interest in the US presence in the region. US forces are spread throughout much of the Gulf, from prepositioned equipment in Qatar to forces and equipment in Kuwait to naval facilities in Bahrain. Saudi Arabia, which also hosts American troops, has incentives to maintain an American presence in the region because it cannot face Iran or Iraq on its own, even as it seeks to reduce the numbers and the profile of American forces on its soil for fear of public backlash.

Historically, people of the Arabian Peninsula have been fiercely independent— and not just in their relations with the West. In the nineteenth century, they challenged the Ottoman rulers, who controlled much of the Middle East in the name of an Islamic empire dominated by Ottoman Turks. In the early twentieth century, they cooperated with Britain in World War I in order to achieve independence from the Ottomans. They joined the American-led coalition in 1990 because they feared being dominated by Saddam Hussein. Their pursuit of independence was not a function of whether the feared powers or the potential allies were Muslim, Arab, or Western.

Much of the resentment of the United States is based on the Arab-Israeli conflict, which has been a visible sore point in the US-Saudi relationship since the collapse of Arab-Israeli peace negotiations. As recent surveys have indicated, most Saudis, like other Arabs, resent America for its policies, not its values, and they see the Palestinian issue as a central issue of contention.

In the months since September 11, the Saudis have discovered that the popular perception of the illegitimacy of the American presence on their soil is a threat to them as well as to that presence—and the United States is also discovering the depth of public resentment in the region. This problem will necessitate mutual cooperation. The Saudis will continue to need American backing, and the United States will continue to gain more from Saudi cooperation than from confrontation.

CHAPTER 15

THE KINGDOM OF SAUDI ARABIA

David E. Long

The Kingdom of Saudi Arabia was formed in 1932 when King Abd al-Aziz ibn al-Rahman Al Saud united Najd (Central Arabia) with the Hijaz, which contains the two holy cities of Mecca and Medina. A poor kingdom before World War II, Saudi Arabia gained immeasurable wealth from skyrocketing oil revenues in the 1970s.

In the following essay, David Long calls attention to the high degree of ethnocentricity and even xenophobia among the Saudis. They see themselves at the center of both the Arab world and (as guardians of Mecca and Medina) the Islamic world. A puritanical strain of Islam, Wahhabism, provides ideological cohesion for the Saudi state.

Yet, never having experienced a colonial past, the Saudis have been less reluctant than other Arab states to enter into close relations with Western powers. Saudi Arabia has enjoyed a long if sometimes prickly relationship with the United States, given that the Saudis have remained stridently anti-Zionist even as the United States has steadfastly supported Israel. After Egypt signed its 1979 treaty with Israel, Saudi Arabia sought a leadership role in the Arab-Israeli dispute until its proposed "Fahd Plan" of 1981 was spurned by the United States and Israel.

Saudi concerns over both the radical Islamic regime in Iran and the Iraqi invasion of Kuwait in 1990 led to new levels of cooperation with the United States and with the Arab Gulf states of the Gulf Cooperation Council (GCC). The support that Saudi Arabia provided the forces of Desert Storm in the Gulf War of 1991 has made the Saudi government a target of continuing Islamist attacks.

David E. Long *is a consultant on the Middle East and counterterrorism. He is the author of* The Kingdom of Saudi Arabia *and, with Bernard Reich, the editor of* The Government and Politics of the Middle East and North Africa.

THE HISTORY OF SAUDI ARABIA SINCE WORLD WAR II has been one of unprecedented economic and social development. The enabling factor has been oil, first found in commercial quantities in 1938, but not exported in quantity until after the war. King Abd al-Aziz, by the time of his death in 1953, had constructed a firm foundation on which his successors could build a modern oil state.

King Abd al-Aziz was succeeded by his eldest surviving son, Saud. Saud had been groomed for rulership as viceroy of Najd under his father. More at home with tribal politics, however, he lacked the breadth of vision to propel Saudi Arabia from a desert kingdom to a major oil power. His reign was characterized by intrigue and lavish spending. Despite growing oil revenues, the treasury was often virtually empty. In 1962, Saud was obliged to turn government operations over to his half-brother Faysal.

King Faysal was dedicated to the preservation of a conservative Islamic way of life both in Saudi Arabia and throughout the Muslim world, while at the same time encouraging material and technological modernization. The measure of his success in developing the kingdom can be explained in large part by his capacity to be ahead of his people, introducing economic and social development programs, but to never be so far out in front that the essentially conservative, Islamic Saudi public would not follow. By proceeding with care and deliberation, Faysal was able to win over even the most conservative segments of the population to such innovations as public radio and television and education for women. To dispel religious opposition to radio and television, for example, Faysal ordered large portions of programming time be devoted to religious instruction and readings from the Quran.

Faysal's greatest interest, however, was foreign affairs. As foreign minister, he became one of the most widely traveled Saudi officials of his time. For example, he attended the 1945 San Francisco conference that established the United Nations. Faysal's primary focus was on the Muslim world and the preservation of its values. Because of Saudi Arabia's position as a key oil exporter, his ability to act as a moderating force in both the Arab world and the world at large was greatly enhanced by the dramatic increase in oil prices in the 1970s.

King Faysal was assassinated by a deranged nephew on March 25, 1975, and was succeeded by his half-brother Khalid. Another half-brother, Fahd, became heir apparent and attended to much of the day-to-day administration of the government. Khalid died of a heart attack in June 1982 and was succeeded in a smooth transition by Fahd, who also became prime minister. As the twentieth century came to an end, King Fahd's increasingly bad health necessitated his turning over a large part of day-to-day government operations to Prince Abdallah, the heir apparent. As king, Abdallah will establish his own personal style of government, but based on precedent, Saudi domestic and foreign policies will likely continue emphasizing economic development and social welfare within the framework of Islam and pan-Arabism.

THE LAND AND PEOPLE

Traditionally, land borders were relatively meaningless to Saudi rulers, who looked on sovereignty more in terms of tribal allegiance. Tribal areas were huge and only vaguely demarcated, as the tribes themselves followed the rains from water hole to water hole and wandered over broad areas. Later, when oil became so important in the region, fixed borders were to acquire much more importance.

Because of Saudi Arabia's predominantly desert terrain, a shortage of water is one of its main resource problems. In the interior are nonrenewable aquifers, which are being tapped at an unprecedented rate, particularly as urbanization and population growth expand and as irrigated agricultural development projects have been created in the interior. To augment water supplies, the kingdom has created a massive desalination system.

Although nearly all of Saudi Arabia is arid, only a part of it consists of real sand desert. There are three such deserts in the kingdom: the Great Nafud, located in the north (*nafud* is one of several Arabic words meaning desert); the Rub'al-Khali (literally, "the Empty Quarter"), stretching along the entire southern frontier; and the Dahna, a narrow strip that forms a great arc from the Nafud westward and then south to the Rub'al-Khali. The sand in all three bears iron oxide, giving it a pink color that can turn to deep red in the setting sun.

Excluding the Empty Quarter, the kingdom is divided into four geographical regions: central, western, eastern, and northern. Central Arabia, or Najd, is both the geographical and the political heartland of the country. Najd, Arabic for "highlands," is predominantly an arid plateau interspersed with oases.

Many cities and towns are scattered throughout Najd, the largest being the national capital, al-Riyadh. The name means "gardens": The city was so named for the number of vegetable gardens and date groves located there. From a small oasis town of about 7,500 in 1900, it grew to a major metropolis with a population over 3.5 million a century later. One of the world's fastest-growing cities, it is expected to approach 4.4 million by 2006. Riyadh remained generally closed to Westerners until the 1970s, when the Saudis opened it up to Western development. Between 1969 and 1975, the number of Western expatriates living in the capital rose from fewer than three hundred to hundreds of thousands.

Western Saudi Arabia is divided into two areas, the Hijaz in the north and Asir in the south. The Hijaz extends from the Jordanian border to just south of Jiddah, the kingdom's second largest city. The economic and social life of the Hijaz has traditionally revolved around the annual Hajj, or "great pilgrimage" to Makkah. With so much attention given to Saudi oil and Middle East politics, few Westerners are aware that to the Muslim world—one-fifth of the world's population—the kingdom is even more important as the location of the two holiest cities in Islam, Makkah and al-Madinah. Performing the Hajj once in their lifetimes is an obligation for all Muslims who are physically and financially able. Observed each year by roughly 2 million of the faithful, the Hajj is not only one of the world's greatest religious celebrations but also one of the greatest exercises in public administration. The Saudi government seeks to ensure that all those who attend do so without serious injury and with a minimum of discomfort.

Asir was quasi-independent until the Saudi conquest in the 1920s and 1930s, and it remained relatively isolated until modern roads were built in the 1970s. Its main cities are Jizan, a modest city on the coast; Abha, the provincial capital, atop the escarpment; and Najran, inland on the Saudi-Yemeni border.

Eastern Saudi Arabia is a mixture of old and new. Now called the Eastern Province, it includes al-Hasa, the largest oasis in the world, and al-Qatif Oasis on the coast. The primary significance of the region is that underneath it lies the bulk of Saudi Arabia's huge oil reserves. The Ghawar field, which stretches for over 200 kilometers north to south, is the largest single field in the world. The economy of the Eastern Province is predominantly based on oil, and even recent efforts to diversify focus on petrochemical industries.

The capital and principal city of the province is Dammam, just south of al-Qatif. Once a small pearling and privateering port, it is now a bustling metropolis. South of Dammam is Dhahran, whose name is far more familiar in the West. It is actually not a city but the location of Saudi Aramco headquarters, King Faysal University, the US Consulate General, and Dhahran International Airport.

The area extending along the kingdom's northern frontiers with Jordan and Iraq is physically isolated from the rest of the country by the Great Nafud. It is geographically a part of the Syrian Desert, and tribesmen in the area claim kinship with fellow tribesmen in neighboring Jordan, Iraq, and Syria as well as Saudi Arabia, occasionally possessing passports from all four countries. This area was the traditional caravan route for traders from the Fertile Crescent traveling to central and eastern Arabia.

Saudi Arabia has an estimated population of 20 million, of which roughly 5 million are expatriates. Though the country's population is relatively small in comparison to its great wealth, it has experienced a population explosion in the past quarter century that has radically changed the demography. With a median age of around eighteen years and a rapidly expanding life expectancy due to vastly improved health care, the kingdom still faces major socioeconomic problems far into the twenty-first century. Every year more and more young Saudis compete for a finite number of jobs and more and more of the aged must be supported by their children, both groups increasingly living off their families' income.

The indigenous Saudi population is among the most homogeneous in the entire Middle East. Virtually all Saudis are Arab and Muslim. Bloodlines, not geography, determine nationality, and being born in Saudi Arabia does not automatically entitle a person to citizenship. The importance of bloodlines is a manifestation of the basically tribal nature of Saudi society. The extended family is the most important social institution in Saudi Arabia. If put to the test, loyalty to one's family would probably exceed loyalty to the state. The state has been in existence for a few decades, but most Saudis trace their families back for centuries.

With genealogy so important, there is relatively little social mobility in Saudi Arabia. Najd is not only the center of Saudi political power; its tribal affiliations are among the most aristocratic in the Arabian Peninsula. Members of the leading tribal families of Najd are at the top of the social order, and nontribal families are near the bottom.

The Hijazi population is far more cosmopolitan than that of Najd because of centuries of immigration connected with the Hajj. The leading families constituted a merchant class that grew up in the Hijaz to serve the Hajj. The Eastern Province, with its concentration of the oil industry, also has a polyglot population.

The Eastern Province is the home of the only significant minority in the kingdom, the Shi'a community, which numbers between 500,000 and 600,000. The Shi'a live mainly in al-Qatif and Hasa Oases. Unlike much of the rest of the population, the Shi'a are willing to work with their hands and over the years have become the backbone of the skilled and semiskilled oil workforce.

A few families of non-Arabian origin have also become Saudi nationals. Most of them are found in the Hijaz and are descended from Hajjis who never returned to their homelands after the pilgrimage. Some of these families have lived in Jiddah and Makkah for centuries and have attained stature in society and high rank in government, mainly associated with the Hajj.

A group of non-Arabs that have become Saudi nationals more recently are the Central Asian community, locally often collectively called "Tashkandis," "Turkistanis," or "Bukharis," after areas and cities in former Soviet Central Asia. They are descendants of a group of political refugees who escaped overland from the Soviet Union in the 1920s. Fiercely anti-Communist and devoutly Muslim, members of the community took refuge in several countries before finally ending up in Saudi Arabia. Because of their faith, loyalty, and lack of interest in inter-Arab politics, many of them were accepted into the Saudi military services.

The distinction between "foreigners" and "natives" breaks down somewhat when one looks at neighboring states. Many of the old Sunni families of Kuwait and Bahrain migrated from Najd some 300 years ago. Northern Saudis have close tribal ties in Jordan, Syria, and Iraq. Gulf ties are reflected during the Hajj, when members of the Gulf Cooperation Council (GCC) states are not required to obtain Saudi visas. No matter how long a person's family has resided in the country, however, he is still identified by his family's original place of origin.

The foreign community constitutes about one-fourth of the total population. Before the 1970s, most foreigners were concentrated in the Eastern Province where, before Saudization, Aramco employed thousands of foreigners. Most of the rest of them were traditionally located in the Hijaz, drawn there by the Hajj. The original function of foreign diplomats was to look after Hajjis from their home countries.

In the 1970s, the oil boom spurred unprecedented economic development throughout the kingdom, and Najd was opened up to Westerners for the first time in a major way. A new diplomatic enclave, separate from the rest of the city, was created in Riyadh by the Saudi government, and many foreign and local businesses moved their headquarters to Riyadh as well. Thus, the capital is not only the largest city in the kingdom, it now probably contains most of the kingdom's foreigners.

Although the status of foreign workers varies from skilled and menial laborers to highly paid executives, all are generally in Saudi Arabia for one primary thing—to make as much money as possible and return to their homelands. That, plus the closed nature of Saudi society, has greatly limited social intercourse between Saudi nationals and the foreign communities. Thus, despite the huge number of foreigners, their social impact on Saudi society has been relatively slight.

ECONOMIC CONDITIONS

The backbone of the economy is oil, accounting for 75 percent of revenues and 90 percent of export earnings. Saudi Arabia has 26 percent of the world's proved oil reserves, the largest reserves in the world. When one looks at Saudi Arabia's huge oil wealth, it is difficult to imagine that prior to World War II, the country was one of the poorest on earth. Following the incorporation of the Hijaz into the Saudi realm in the 1920s, revenues generated from the Hajj became the major source of foreign exchange. When the world economic depression and political disorders greatly reduced the number of Hajjis in the 1930s, the Saudi economy was badly hit, and although oil had been discovered, revenues were insufficient to fill the gap.

Oil was first discovered in 1935 and discovered in commercial quantities in 1938, but international political and economic conditions prevented its being sold in significant quantities until after the war. In 1936, Socal invited Texaco to help market Saudi oil by becoming a joint owner in its new Saudi production company, which ultimately became Aramco. In 1948, Mobil and Exxon also became Aramco partners. By that time, oil revenues were rapidly transforming the kingdom into a major oil state. For almost three decades, Aramco dominated Saudi oil production and set prices. The Organization of Petroleum Exporting Countries (OPEC) was established in the 1960s to try to exert pressure on the companies to maintain higher prices, but OPEC had little influence. In the 1970s, however, due to a major oil shortage, the oil-producing countries, including Saudi Arabia, were able to wrest control of pricing from the companies, and ultimately to get ownership of the oil itself.

Oil revenues skyrocketed in the 1970s, further accelerated by the Saudi-led Arab oil embargo of 1973–1974. The embargo actually ran counter to Saudi economic interests in maintaining stable, reasonable oil prices to maximize its long-term revenues. King Faysal initiated the embargo for political, not economic, reasons, in large part because he felt he had been betrayed by President Richard Nixon in the 1973 Arab-Israeli war. Having personally promised Faysal that the United States would remain evenhanded in the war, Nixon announced that it would extend $2.2 billion in military aid to Israel.

The high revenues of the 1970s led to a spending spree in Saudi Arabia, as the Saudis accelerated all their economic and social welfare programs. However, high oil prices also led to increased worldwide energy efficiency and a drop in per capita demand, and in 1980 the market entered a glut from which it had not yet fully recovered twenty years later. The recent economic history of Saudi Arabia is one of seeking to adjust to reduced (though still sizable) revenues.

No one foresaw that the oil glut would last so long or that the large Saudi foreign reserve holdings amassed in the 1970s would be drawn down so quickly. No one foresaw either that not even a fraction of the billions of dollars loaned by Gulf Cooperation Council countries to Iraq to shore up its economy during the Iran-Iraq war would be repaid, or that Iraq would turn on its former benefactors by invading Kuwait, precipitating the Gulf War, which cost the Saudis another $55 billion in payment to the United States. In addition, the continuing post–Gulf War military threats of Iran and Iraq prompted a higher level of Saudi defense spending.

Much external concern has been expressed about the linkage between Saudi deficit spending and political instability. There is certainly linkage between economics and politics, but Saudi political stability is not overly dependent on government welfare. The kingdom will not be so dependent as the West on a social security system so long as Saudi extended families, the main source of social stability, do not allow their members to be destitute when the families have the means to help them.

Even when the oil glut ends, however, it will be crucial for the kingdom to carry through its economic reforms. With oil exports dominating the Saudi economy for the foreseeable future and the cyclical nature of world oil prices, reforms are vital if the kingdom is to avoid future economic instability. With a median age of about 18 years, there are more young people entering the job market each year than there are acceptable jobs available, and with life expectancy increasing with improved health care, there will be more nonproductive aged to care for.

In sum, although economic conditions do affect political stability in Saudi Arabia, the kingdom's tight-knit, family-based society is still strong insurance against the kind of political unrest found in many developing countries. But with the demographic problems the kingdom faces and inherent fluctuations in world oil prices, the end of the latest oil glut is no cause for complacency.

SAUDI POLITICAL DYNAMICS

Three areas are particularly important to Saudi political dynamics: the country's political culture, its political ideology, and the Saudi decisionmaking process.

Saudi Political Culture

Saudi culture is overwhelmingly Islamic. More than a religion, Islam is a totally self-contained, cosmic system. In assessing the influence of Islam on Saudi political culture, one must emphasize cultural values rather than religious piety. There are several characteristics of Saudi culture that are basic to Saudi politics. Among the most salient is a heightened sense of inevitability, based on the Islamic emphasis on God's will, often expressed in the Arabic phrase *Insha'allah,* or "God willing." Nothing can happen unless God wills it. Thus, Saudis (and other Muslims) tend to accept situations as inevitable far more quickly than people from Western cultures. Conversely, if they are convinced that a situation is not God's will, they will persevere against it long after Westerners would give up.

One other cultural characteristic, not directly associated with Islam, is the high degree of ethnocentricity in Saudi Arabia, derived in large part from its historical isolation and geographical insularity. Saudis, particularly Najdis, tend to see themselves as the center of their universe. Personal status is conferred more by bloodlines than by money or achievement, and nearly all Saudis claim a proud Arabian ancestry. Having never been under European colonial rule, Saudis have not developed a national inferiority complex as have many colonialized peoples. They see themselves not merely as equals of the West but in fact believe their culture is vastly superior to secular Western culture. Close personal relationships aside, they tend to look on outsiders as people to be tolerated as long as they have something to contribute.

Saudi Political Ideology

For the past 250 years, the Islamic teachings of Muhammad ibn Abd al-Wahhab have constituted the political ideology of Saudi Arabia. Those teachings have provided the Saudi regime an egalitarian, universal, and moral base that has served to bind the rulers and ruled together through many crises and troubles and has been a major factor in the survival of the Saudi state throughout its often turbulent history. One must use care, however, in looking at Abd al-Wahhab's revival movement as a political ideology. It has no ideology independent of Islam.

Saudi Decisionmaking

Islamic cultural traits have often made the Saudi political decisionmaking process appear highly arbitrary and capricious to the untrained eye. There is a systemic logic to the process, however. The creation of formal political institutions over the past sixty years has made government operations a great deal more orderly, but it has not fundamentally changed the system.

At the heart of the system are two fundamental concepts, *ijma'* (consensus) and *shura* (consultation). Consensus has been used to legitimize collective action in the Arab world for millennia and has been incorporated into Islam. Even the Saudi king, despite all the powers concentrated in him, cannot act without consensus. Thus, the chief task of the king is to create a consensus for action and then to implement it. Consensus is derived through *shura,* and those consulted actively participate in the decisionmaking process.

In the oil age, the consultation-consensus system is under heavy pressure. Government operations are too large and too complicated for this traditional, personalized process always to work effectively or fairly. Nevertheless, for any sustained increase in political participation, it seems necessary for some form of the consultation-consensus process to be present.

POLITICAL INSTITUTIONS

Saudi Arabia has always been ruled under Islamic law, the most recent reaffirmation being Article 1 of the Basic Law of Government, issued by King Fahd on March 1, 1992. It states, "The Saudi Arabian Kingdom is a sovereign Arab Islamic state with Islam as its religion; God's book and the Sunna [which together form the sources of Islamic law] are its constitution; Arabic is its language; and Riyadh is its capital."[1]

Islamic law, or *Shari'a* (literally, "the Pathway"), is much more complex than Islamic theology and is the primary area of specialization of Islamic scholars. Despite theological differences among the various branches of Islam (for example, between Sunni and Shi'a), Islamic law is universally respected by all Muslims. The sources of the law are the Quran and the Sunna ("Traditions" of the Prophet, Muhammad). The Sunna is composed of Hadiths, or sayings of the Prophet, which are considered divinely inspired.

Islamic law is supreme in Saudi Arabia, even over the king. Thus, despite there being no formal separation of powers or democratically elected representatives of the people, Saudi Arabia is not an absolute monarchy in the historic European sense; the doctrine of "divine right of kings" would be considered heresy.

Since Islamic law is a self-contained system, there is no place for statutory law in the Western sense. To meet the need for modern legislation, royal decrees (called *nizams*) have been promulgated over the years. Thus, although there is no secular criminal, civil, or commercial code in Saudi Arabia, the *nizams* provide a basis for regulating commercial transactions. In addition, special administrative tribunals have been created to adjudicate labor and commercial disputes.

Other than the Islamic legal system, Saudi rulers had almost no formal political institutions until the capture of the Hijaz in 1925. Najd was ruled by Abd al-Aziz in a highly personalized way through *shura* (consultation) with leading members of the royal court. The Hijaz, in contrast, had a much more formal system of government, including cabinet ministers. When Abd al-Aziz conquered the Hijaz, he left its political institutions intact. The early development of Saudi national political institutions, therefore, can be seen as a process by which political institutions, initially found only in the Hijaz, were slowly and with little planning adapted and expanded to meet the political and bureaucratic needs of the whole country. Saudi government structure, therefore, can best be described as a work in progress, evolving over the past three quarters of a century from a loosely structured, paternalistic, and personalized rule under King Abd al-Aziz to a more institutionalized structure required of a major oil-producing country.

The most important political institution created recently is the Majlis al-Shura, or consultative council, decreed by King Fahd on March 1, 1992. A number of Western observers have assessed the Saudi Majlis al-Shura as an embryonic parliament in the Western sense and a possible precursor to democratic representative government. Whether or not such a democratic institution ever evolves in the kingdom, the Majlis was not modeled on a parliamentary concept. King Fahd undoubtedly saw the need to expand public participation in the political process, but he publicly rejected a Western-style, democratic parliamentary system. Instead, he was drawing on the formal Islamic institution of *shura* to institutionalize what had been the informal means of political participation for centuries—consulting "people of knowledge and expertise and specialists" to come up with a consensus legitimizing public policy. With rapid modernization acquired with oil revenues, it was increasingly obvious that the informal system was no longer adequate to create a true consensus.

The Majlis al-Shura was inaugurated by King Fahd in December 1993. Originally made up of sixty members, it was expanded to ninety in 1997. The Majlis is charged with suggesting new decrees (regulatory law) and reviewing and evaluating foreign and domestic policies. Among the members are businessmen, technocrats, diplomats, journalists, Islamic scholars, and professional soldiers, representing all regions of the country. Breaking with tradition, most members are young by Saudi leadership standards—in their forties and fifties. Many have doctorates from the United States, Europe, or the Middle East. Similarly, the Islamic scholars are younger men with outside exposure, not the older generation of Islamic leaders. The real test for the Majlis will be the degree to which its members actually participate in the consultative process *(shura)*, or whether they devolve into a mere sounding board or rubber stamp for government policies. Whatever the future of the Majlis, it reflects remarkable vision as an adaptation of a classical Islamic concept to modern government.

FOREIGN AND NATIONAL SECURITY POLICIES

Saudi foreign and national security policies revolve around three major goals: preservation of an Islamic way of life at home and abroad, protection of the territorial integrity and economic welfare of the country, and the survival of the regime. How these are translated into relations with other states is largely a product of the Saudi view of the world. The Saudi worldview is influenced by two strong, though seemingly contradictory, themes. The first is an extraordinary cultural self-assurance based on a sense of Islamic heritage and tribe-based self-identity and on having never been under European colonial domination; the second is an "encirclement syndrome," a heightened sense of insecurity based on the historical experience of an insular people eternally surrounded by enemies.

Without the psychological baggage of a colonial past, Saudis never developed the same degree of anti-Western xenophobia as other Arab states and have consequently been far less reluctant to enter into close relations with the Western powers. The "rebirth" of secular Arab nationalism in the 1960s was largely a reaction to 200 years of Western political domination. The Saudis, who equate Arabness with the tribes of the Arabian Peninsula, had never lost their sense of Arab identity.

Likewise, pan-Islam is a relatively recent movement, originating in the nineteenth century as a spiritual and philosophical counter to Western secularism. The Saudi Islamic revival of Muhammad ibn Abd al-Wahhab emerged a full century earlier, and the Saudi worldview, uncluttered by Western perceptions, still conforms to the more classical bipolar Islamic view, which contrasts believers (monotheists) with unbelievers (atheists and polytheists). The believers (which also include Christians, Jews, and Zoroastrians) inhabit Dar al-Islam, the Abode of Islam, and the unbelievers inhabit Dar al-Harb, the Abode of War.

The Saudi sense of their responsibility for the preservation of the Islamic way of life was substantially strengthened in the 1920s when Abd al-Aziz occupied the Hijaz, where the holy cities of Makkah and al-Madinah are. As guardians of these holy sites, the Saudis assumed the responsibility of defenders of the Islamic way of life throughout the Muslim world.

In the 1960s, secular Arab nationalism swept the Arab world. Radical Arab nationalists, personified by Egypt's President Gamal Abd al-Nasser, castigated both Israel and the West as enemies. The Saudis shared the Arab world's sense of injustice over the creation of Israel, but they did not share the secular socialist concept of Arabism. More importantly, the Saudis saw atheistic communism as an even greater threat to the Muslim way of life than Zionism and looked to the West as the last defense of the Muslim world. Though stridently anti-Zionist, particularly after Israel seized East Jerusalem and the Aqsa Mosque, the third-holiest site in Sunni Islam, Saudi Arabia maintained a low profile in Arab politics. During most of the decade, Faysal and Nasser engaged in a political confrontation that took on a military dimension in the Yemeni civil war (1962–1970), in which the Saudis supported the royalists against the republican government, which was propped up by 80,000 Egyptian troops.

Radical Arab nationalism declined in the 1970s, and the Saudis, enriched by the energy crisis, began to take a more active role both in regional politics and in international economic and petroleum affairs. Saudi Arabia also assumed an active role in the Arab-Israeli dispute. During the 1973 Arab-Israeli war, King Faysal led the Arab oil boycott against the United States and the Netherlands.

The Camp David accords and the subsequent Egypt-Israel Peace Treaty of 1979 were considered a disaster by the Saudis. They believed that President Anwar Sadat not only had broken Arab consensus but also had been seduced into a separate peace for nothing more concrete than vague promises of Palestinian autonomy. The subsequent breakdown of the autonomy talks seemed to justify their fears. In 1981, Prince Fahd, who was then Saudi heir apparent, sought to restart the peace process outside the moribund Camp David formula by announcing an eight-point plan for a comprehensive peace. The "Fahd Plan" broke new ground by tacitly recognizing Israel through the affirmation of all states in the area to live in peace. The original plan was rejected by the Arabs at a foreign ministers' conference in 1981 but was adopted in modified form the following year at an Arab summit in Morocco. The opportunity to exploit Arab consensus was spurned by the United States and Israel, however, and the plan went nowhere. Thereafter, the Saudis disengaged from active participation in the peace process.

In the 1980s and 1990s, Saudi foreign policy was driven to a great degree by security concerns. The overthrow of the shah of Iran in 1979 led to a radical Islamic regime in Tehran, soon followed by the Iran-Iraq war, which lasted for most of the 1980s. For Saudi Arabia, Iran's revolutionary "Islamic" foreign policies represent a major security threat, only one part of which is military.

Previously, the major security threat came from left-wing Arab states and underground groups. Now, the kingdom is threatened from the revolutionary religious right, not only directly by Iranian subversive activities, but also indirectly by Iran's support of Islamist subversive groups throughout the Muslim world.

Iran aspires to be the leader of the Islamic world and sees Saudi Arabia as a major competitor. Tehran has made a special effort to undermine Saudi claims to Islamic leadership, seeking to embarrass the regime each year by sending in provocateurs to disrupt the Hajj. One of the most egregious provocations occurred at the 1987 Hajj when Iran incited bloody riots in which over 400 Hajjis were killed. To the Saudis, the riots were not only a political provocation but also a religious desecration.

The Iraqi invasion of Kuwait in 1990 also revived Saudi concern over the Iraqi threat, leading to unprecedented cooperation with the United States and other coalition partners during Desert Storm and, politically, to closer political cooperation with the Arab Gulf states in the Gulf Cooperation Council. Saudi Arabia has long depended on the United States as its last line of defense in case of conventional military attack. Because of what the Saudis consider overweening US support for Israel, however, they have always wanted to keep US forces "over the horizon," and not stationed in the kingdom. However, Desert Storm convinced them of the need for closer cooperation with the United States, as well as the GCC and other allied Arab states, as long as Iran and Iraq remain potential military threats.

The greatest challenge of the twenty-first century is likely to be adapting to the new global economy and the revolution in communications and information technology. Information can no longer be distributed on a "need to know basis," and policymaking can no longer be restricted to respected elders whose council and consensus is solicited. With a growing public demand for more transparency in government, neither foreign nor domestic policy decisionmaking can continue exclusively in quiet consultation. To avoid revolutionary change, the Saudi political system will have to continue to adapt to rapid but unstoppable economic and technological change.

CHAPTER 16

FISSURES IN THE FAÇADE
OF AMITY BETWEEN THE UNITED
STATES AND SAUDI ARABIA

Thomas W. Lippman

The 9/11 attacks on the United States were masterminded by Osama bin Laden, who is a Saudi, as were fifteen of the nineteen suicide hijackers. In the aftermath of 9/11, then, many Americans and Saudis reexamined the relationship between their two countries. Americans saw with new eyes an authoritarian regime that seemed to harbor or even support militant Islamists and that tried to blame Israel for the 9/11 attacks. Saudis saw an America that reacted to 9/11 with a "war on terror" that seemed to target Muslims indiscriminately while hypocritically ignoring Israel's bloody oppression of Palestinians.

Religious zealotry is strongly established in Saudi Arabia. Yet, despite their own adherence to the strict Islam of Wahhabism, Saudi rulers find religious extremism a serious threat to their national security. That is why the Saudis supported US military action in Afghanistan against the Taliban regime, which was sheltering bin Laden and his al-Qaeda fighters. It is also why the Saudis remain concerned about the Shiite theocracy in Iran.

The Saudis also perceive Iraq as a danger. They sought to contain Saddam Hussein's expansionist grab of Kuwait and allowed the stationing of US combat air units in Saudi Arabia to enforce the subsequent United Nations sanctions against Iraq. Hosting foreign troops so near Mecca and Medina, the holiest sites of Islam, has made the Saudi government a target for al-Qaeda terrorists. Ironically, the removal of the menace of Saddam Hussein in 2003 could present Saudi Arabia with the new challenge of a nearby democratic society in Iraq that could bring the pressures of liberalization to bear on the rigid politics and society of Saudi Arabia.

(Crown Prince Abdullah, prominent in the following chapter, became King Abdullah in August 2005.)

A former Washington Post *Middle East bureau chief,* **Thomas W. Lippman** *is a member of the Middle East Institute and the Council on Foreign Relations. He is the author of* Understanding Islam: An Introduction to the Muslim World *and* Inside the Mirage: America's Fragile Partnership with Saudi Arabia, *from which this excerpt is taken.*

My DINNER COMPANION was an amiable, well-spoken Saudi Aramco executive, fluent in English and comfortable with Americans, among whom he had worked most of his professional life. We were in an elegant seafood restaurant in al-Khobar that featured plump fish from the Gulf waiting to be grilled at the diner's selection.

It was a congenial and peaceful setting, and yet something was wrong. My companion was agitated, and angry at the United States and at Americans who, he said, were being unfair to Saudi Arabia. The American media were slandering Islam, he said, and the United States government was alienating its best friends in the Arab world by its actions. It was October 2002, thirteen months after the terrorist attacks that destroyed New York's World Trade Center and blew a lethal hole in the Pentagon. Deep fissures had appeared in the façade of amity between the United States and Saudi Arabia.

The fact that fifteen of the nineteen September 11 hijackers were Saudis by birth and took their orders from the renegade Saudi Osama bin Laden enraged Americans and shredded the protective cocoon that American business interests and diplomats had built around Saudi Arabia for decades. All the least palatable aspects of Saudi society—the tolerance for and even encouragement of extremism, the repressive political system, the anti-intellectualism of its schools, the corruption—were suddenly on glaring display. After years of looking the other way, Americans subjected Saudi Arabia to intense scrutiny, and they did not like much of what they saw. It seemed that everyone with access to the Internet was suddenly aware that Saudi Arabia's schoolbooks were replete with lessons in hatred, that its mosques resonated with fiery sermons calling for jihad against Jews and other infidels, and that the government in the past had done little to counter this inflammatory rhetoric.

The events of September 11 and the American response to them shocked the Saudis, too, for different reasons.

Many Saudis, including radical preachers and otherwise sensible newspaper columnists, simply refused to believe that Osama bin Laden and his al-Qaeda network were responsible for the attacks. Good Muslims would not do such a thing, some Saudis said. A lone Arab hiding in a cave in Afghanistan could not possibly have orchestrated such a strike against all-powerful America, others argued. And who benefited from an act of mass murder that drove a wedge between Saudi Arabia and the United States? The Jews, some Saudis said. Therefore Zionists must have been behind it—the evidence being the report that Jews employed at the World Trade Center were warned in advance and stayed home on the fateful day. This preposterous tale gained instant and widespread credence in Saudi Arabia and elsewhere in the Arab world. The degree of Saudi denial, and the willingness of many Saudis to spread and believe the most absurd theories about the terror attacks, presented a whole new perspective on the Kingdom's perpetual tug-of-war between modernism and medievalism, between progress and reaction.

In some ways, Saudi Arabia today functions at the highest levels of modernity and technical sophistication. As I was traveling around the country in the fall of 2002, conjoined twins from Malaysia were sent to Saudi Arabia for surgery to separate them. The successful operation was performed by Saudi doctors, of which there were none before the 1970s. A bank began offering a new service on its automated teller machines: payment of traffic fines. A newspaper presented detailed instructions to computer geeks about how to download the Linux operating system. New Internet providers went on line. Design work began on a new Ralph Lauren fashion store. This was the "Riyadh is just like Phoenix" phenomenon, as many American residents have described it.

Intellectually and politically, however, large contingents of the Saudi population live in a netherworld of xenophobia and conspiracy theories. Fearful that their culture and religious purity are being eroded by materialism and Western ideas, these Saudis are often unable to distinguish fact from fiction, especially about the United States and about Jews, and are susceptible to the reactionary ravings of isolationist, anti-American firebrands in the mosques.

Among this element of the Saudi population, the American response to the September 11 attacks confirmed their most negative feelings about the United States. When Washington imposed visa restrictions on Saudi travelers, froze the assets of various Islamic charities, and incarcerated hundreds of Muslim men— all while supporting Israel in its efforts to suppress the Palestinian uprising with bloody attacks that Saudis watched every night on television—it provided an opening for the most anti-American elements among Saudis to say, in effect, "We told you so" to their pro-Western compatriots.

Who were the Americans to criticize Saudi Arabia's human rights record or its Islamic justice system? a newspaper columnist demanded. What about human rights for the Palestinians? "Americans have played a shameful and conspiratorial role whose main objective for more than fifty years has been to provide political, financial and military cover enabling the Jews to maintain a brutal occupation of Palestinian land. All American presidents, as well as its extreme right politicians who are financed by the Zionists, are party to this," she wrote. "Where was [a critic of Saudi human rights policies] when the Palestinians were butchered and their homes demolished in Jenin refugee camp in front of the television cameras? Where was she when five million Palestinians were forcibly driven out of their land, 260,000 killed, and 350,000 maimed? Where was she when people were buried alive every day under the rubble of their homes? When women gave birth at military checkpoints and then watched their babies die while Israeli soldiers looked on indifferently? Where was the woman who claims to defend women's rights when Palestinian women trying to visit their imprisoned husbands were stripped naked by Israeli soldiers who subjected them to humiliating searches?" And what about America's treatment of Muslims in Afghanistan and Somalia, this columnist wanted to know. She referred to the incarceration of Muslim men at Guantanamo Bay, Cuba, as "America's shame," and declared that Muslims in America, like all nonwhite Americans, are at best second-class citizens.[1]

These were not ravings from the lunatic fringe. The columnist's comments reflect the thinking of many Saudis and other Arabs. The Saudis seemed unable to comprehend the ferocity of American outrage over what had happened on September 11. Everywhere I went I met Saudis who complained that the United States was overreacting, throwing out the good with the bad, alienating its best friends in Saudi Arabia, inflicting suffering on Afghan civilians in its indiscriminate attacks aimed at al-Qaeda, providing ammunition to the extremists at the expense of the moderates. Add to that the American support of Israel's suppression of the Palestinians and the suffering inflicted on Iraqi children by US insistence on maintaining an international economic boycott and the result was a wave of anti-American sentiment. Of course, the terrorist attacks were deplorable, the Saudis would say, but those fifteen hijackers were not representative of Saudi society—they were brainwashed by bin Laden's people, and anyway, they lived in Germany. Why are you blaming all Saudis? You Americans are at least as much responsible for this as we are, they would argue, because it was the United States that financed and equipped the jihad in Afghanistan, where bin Laden and his team got their start.

For months American diplomats, journalists, and congressional delegations who visited the Kingdom brought back reports of similar conversations. We all heard over and over again from Saudis who had invested their economic and personal lives in the United States and now felt betrayed and exposed.

Saudis seemed especially rankled by their sudden difficulty in obtaining visas for travel to the United States. Before September 11, Saudis could obtain visas virtually on demand; now they faced waits of many weeks. Saudi Aramco, which every year selects about three hundred of the country's best and brightest high school students and sends them to college in the United States, diverted all those chosen in 2002 to other countries because they could not obtain American visas. This was not good for either Saudi Arabia or the United States, said Yusof Rafie, the oil company's senior vice president for industrial relations. "These are the future leaders of our country," he told me. "I don't want to lose the American heritage. I want a Western mentality, with freedom of thinking and flexibility. I want open thinking and an open corporate culture."

"We refuse to see US-Saudi relations take such a turn that an entire people are blamed for a crime committed by a few," Ali al-Mousa wrote in an open letter to US ambassador Robert Jordan published by the newspaper *al-Watan*:

> Mr. Ambassador, over the past decades more than two million Saudis have visited your country and around a million studied at your colleges. . . . All of them according to your testimony have been good ambassadors for their country, religion and nation. Why, then, put them on the spot and refuse even to look at their applications, thus making them the victims of stalling and procrastination? Last summer nearly 150,000 Saudi tourists entered your country and spent $600 million in your hotels and shops, more than the amount spent by any other group of tourists visiting your country. They came back with a clean record without arousing the slightest suspicion. . . . Mr. Ambassador, thousands of our people have invested heavily in educating their children in your country. . . . Today, many of them find themselves standing in long queues outside your office hoping to return to their colleges but without receiving an answer. By so doing you are putting your country in the list of losers and jeopardizing historic relations that are nearing the breaking point. All this by generalizing things and leveling accusations at the innocent.[2]

"Angry, hurt, bewildered—those are the right words," said Usamah al-Kurdi, a prominent member of the Consultative Assembly. "People are asking, What is it we are not doing that we should be doing, there must be something wrong." He said that many Westernized Saudis felt "betrayed and disappointed," but there was a larger group in provincial cities whose attitude was, "Who cares?" In such cities as Tabuk, Buraida, and Khamis Mushayt, he said, ordinary Saudis reckoned that a breach with the United States would have no negative impact on their lives and might even be beneficial.

One prominent Saudi scholar invited me to his home, served me tea and cookies and, in a gesture of hospitality, invited his daughters to join our conversation. His complaint was that the US Department of Health and Human Services had just announced a $500,000 grant under President Bush's "faith-based initiative" to a group called Operation Blessing. The founder of Operation Blessing was the evangelist Pat Robertson, a serial reviler of Islam and of the Prophet Muhammad, whom Robertson denounced as "an absolute wild-eyed fanatic . . . a robber and a brigand." My host could not understand why the US government would support the activities of such a person.

Several Saudis voiced outrage over a briefing given to the Pentagon's Defense Advisory Board by a mysterious policy analyst named Laurent Murawiec. He told the group that Saudi Arabia was the "kernel of evil" in the Arab world and that its government supported and financed terrorism. If it continued to do so, Murawiec said, the United States should invade Saudi Arabia and seize the oil fields. Because the briefing was conducted under the auspices of the Rand Corporation, a respected think tank, and because the Defense Advisory Board was headed by the prominent Republican security strategist Richard Perle, many Saudis took his presentation to be a statement of American policy, even though it was repudiated by Defense Secretary Donald Rumsfeld.[3] A commentary in the Saudi newspaper *Okaz* said that news of the briefing revealed "the domination of the US administration by hard-line Jewish thinking" and showed hostility to the Kingdom prevalent in American think tanks, "which are backed by the Jewish lobby."[4]

Another irritant cited by several prominent Saudis was a mass lawsuit against the Kingdom and some of the most senior princes seeking $116 trillion in damages on behalf of the September 11 victims and their families. Seventeen American law firms joined forces to file this case in United States District Court in Washington. The named defendants included Prince Sultan, the defense minister and second in line to the throne; his brother Prince Salman, the governor of Riyadh; and nearly two hundred other Saudi Arabian individuals and institutions. They were described in the complaint as "those who promoted, financed, sponsored, or otherwise materially supported the acts of barbarism and terror inflicted on September 11, 2001." Whatever the legal and factual merits of this case, the Saudis who complained to me about it simply could not understand how such a lawsuit could be allowed to proceed in the US federal court system. It was a massive insult to Saudi Arabia by its very nature, they said.[5]

At the time I was traveling around Saudi Arabia, the United States was beginning serious preparations for war against Iraq. To many Saudis, this was another source of anxiety about their relationship with the United States, not because they supported Saddam Hussein but because of what they feared would follow the war. In their scenario, the United States would make a liberated Iraq the new foundation of its Middle East oil interests, to the detriment of Saudi Arabia. This was absurd, for many reasons, but many Saudis believed it. They had all read news stories about how American oil companies were looking for new frontiers, in Russia or off the coast of Africa or wherever, the Saudis said. Iraq would be easier than Russia. It made sense to them.

These were uncomfortable conversations for me. One reason was that I agreed with some of the Saudi complaints. I thought Israel's tactics in its conflict with Palestinian militants were at best counterproductive, and I did not attempt to justify them. Giving US taxpayers' money to a Pat Robertson organization was an insult to all Muslims; and a crackpot like Murawiec—a former disciple of Lyndon Larouche, the tax-dodging king of conspiracy theorists—should not have been invited to brief at the Pentagon. The larger reason for my discomfort was my sense that many Saudis I talked to seemed to be using these complaints about the United States to avoid coming to grips with the critical problems in their own society. If they could believe that Osama bin Laden and the fifteen Saudi hijackers were as much an aberration in Saudi Arabia as the Oklahoma City bomber Timothy McVeigh was in the United States—as many Saudis told me—they could avoid confronting the unpleasant realities that were all too visible to Americans.

In spite of all these rationalizations and denials, however, the events of September 11 and their aftermath did bring about a period of uncharacteristic introspection and self-criticism in Saudi Arabia, and a recognition that some serious reforms were necessary. Lively and quite public discussions broke out about what children are taught in Saudi schools, about the role of Saudi-based Islamic charities in funding terrorism, about the need for economic restructuring to reduce unemployment among young people, and about the fundamental question of whether true Islam requires hostility to non-Muslims. Saudis began to acknowledge the consequences of all the concessions to religious extremists that had been made in previous years.

"Though few would publicly admit it," the newspaper columnist Sulaiman al-Hattlan wrote, "Saudis have become hostages of the backward agenda of a small minority of bin Laden supporters who in effect have hijacked our society. . . . Because of the dominance of Wahhabism, Saudi society has been exposed to only one school of thought, one that teaches hatred of Jews, Christians and certain Muslims, like Shiites and liberal and moderate Sunnis. But we Saudis must acknowledge that our real enemy is religious fanaticism. We have to stop talking about the need for reform and actually start it, particularly in education."[6]

Sulaiman al-Hattlan was among the guests at a luncheon I attended in the Riyadh home of Prince Abdullah bin Faisal bin Turki. The prince argued that September 11 had had a positive effect on Saudi Arabia because "it woke everyone up." No longer, he said, could rich Saudis contribute funds without restriction to organizations linked to terrorism. The government, he said, recognized that Saudi Arabian money, some of it laundered through legitimate business and charities, was sustaining al-Qaeda and other extremist groups, and it was cracking down. His two dozen Saudi guests agreed, but they mostly wanted to talk about how their government's response to terrorism was being received in the United States. How could they make Americans understand, they wanted to know, that most citizens of Saudi Arabia are not bomb-building fanatics? They agreed that the answer did not lie in the expensive, multi-page advertisements promoting the Kingdom that had appeared in the *New York Times* and the *Economist*, but where did it lie?

I heard the same question from two prominent newspaper editors who asked me to meet with them in Riyadh. What could they do, they wondered, to narrow the breach between Saudi Arabia and the United States that had developed since September 11? How could they counter the negative images of Saudi Arabia and Islam that Americans were seeing? They agreed that there is a need for a credible, authoritative voice of mainstream Islam in the United States that could speak on behalf of the faith—perhaps a serious Islamic university, a Muslim Notre Dame, whose rector would be a scholar of unquestionable nonviolent probity. Yet they acknowledged that the real problem lies not in the United States but in their own country. So closed-minded are the religious zealots in Saudi Arabia, they said, that they spurn even Muslims from other societies, such as Morocco and Indonesia, however devout they may be, because their practice of the faith is different from Wahhabism.

As the US-led investigation of the September 11 attacks and interrogations of suspected terrorists captured in Afghanistan and elsewhere made clear the extent to which cash from Saudi Arabia was financing terrorism, the Saudis announced a crackdown. The years of willful negligence in which the Saudi authorities chose not to confront religious institutions that were preaching hatred and organizations that were financing violence were declared over. The government put in place new regulations on banks, charities, and money changers aimed at cutting off the flow of money to terrorist groups, froze assets of some individuals and institutions, and created a Financial Intelligence Unit to monitor contributions to charities, although American experts disagreed on the efficacy and completeness of these measures. Hundreds of the most radical preachers were removed from their positions.

Yet as usual in Saudi Arabia, the sincerity of the Kingdom's commitment to crack down on terrorists, their religious mentors, and their financiers was tempered by equivocation; some respected analysts in the United States said the Saudi government's antiterrorism rhetoric was simply not backed up by action. After Adel al-Jubeir told journalists in Washington that some of the radical imams were fired because they "preached hatred and intolerance," the deputy minister of religious affairs, Tawfeeq al-Sudairi, denied it, saying it was entirely an administrative decision. Al-Jubeir himself refused to repudiate Hamas, the organization behind the suicide bombings in Israel, because Saudi government aid to Palestinians, including the families of suicide bombers, was justified by conditions in the occupied territories: "We give money to Palestinian families in need," he said. "Are some of those families, families who have had a suicide bomber? Yes. But do we give the money because their son or daughter was a suicide bomber? No. Is that money an incentive for them to commit acts of terrorism? No."[7]

This kind of rhetorical maneuvering is probably inevitable, given the political situation in Saudi Arabia. Having built the state and its own power on an alliance with a narrow-minded, xenophobic strain of Islam, the House of Saud cannot simply repudiate it without undermining itself.

As the first anniversary of the September 11 attacks approached, Crown Prince Abdullah sent a message of sympathy and solidarity to the American people. "It was the perverted hope of the perpetrators of this heinous crime that they could bring humiliation to and terrorize the American nation," it said. "But the brave people of the United States of America, whose greatness lies in the strength of its brave sons and daughters in facing adversity, and which is enriched by their remarkable achievements, all of this will make them ever stronger than the designs of the evildoers. Instead of being terrorized by this catastrophe, they became more steadfast and determined." He denounced the attacks as "pure evil, condemned and abhorred by all religions and cultures."

He explicitly acknowledged that Saudi citizens were among the perpetrators. "We in Saudi Arabia felt an especially great pain at the realization that a number of young Saudi citizens had been enticed and deluded and their reasoning subverted to the degree of denying the tolerance that their religion embraced, and turning their backs on their homeland, which always stood for understanding and moderation." He vowed that terrorists would not be allowed to damage the "historic and strong" relationship between his country and the United States, and pledged "our continued will and determination to do our utmost to combat this malignant evil and uproot it from the world."[8]

It is tempting to snicker at Abdullah's assertion that Saudi Arabia, where only Islam is permitted and apostasy is punishable by beheading, has "always stood for understanding and moderation," but the crown prince had a point. Saudi Arabia has never since unification been a violent society. Intolerant and reactionary, perhaps, but not violent. The excesses committed in the name of Islam in such countries as Algeria and Sudan are alien to modern Saudi Arab culture and history. This is what made Osama bin Laden an aberrational figure in his homeland. Abdullah and his fellow princes understand that they are bin Laden's true target. That is why they supported US military action in Afghanistan against the Taliban militia, who were sheltering bin Laden and his al-Qaeda fighters. Saudi leaders may have been slow to grasp the extent to which bin Laden's ideas had taken root in Saudi Arabia and the extent to which Saudi citizens were financing al-Qaeda, but they are by no means complicit in al-Qaeda's campaign. It took some courage for Abdullah to proclaim solidarity with the American people when that very solidarity is the weapon used most effectively against the House of Saud by its most committed opponents.

Abdullah's anniversary statement was reciprocated by US Ambassador Robert Jordan, who published an article in the Saudi press acknowledging that the attacks had strained the relationship. "In both countries, for some segments of the population, rational thought has been replaced by emotion fed by ignorance, fear and misinformation and, sometimes, outright lies," he wrote. "This has led many to a state of anger that is harmful to both countries. This must not be permitted to continue. We cannot allow demagogues to define our relationship. . . . Nor can we allow perverters of religion to separate the world and provoke a clash of civilizations."[9]

At this official level, in commerce and in the military training missions, the bilateral relationship forged on undeterred by the September 11 attacks and their aftermath. Yet within three months of the attacks, reports began to appear in major American newspapers that the United States was contemplating the withdrawal of its remaining combat troops from Saudi Arabia and the Saudis were not asking them to stay. The problem was that pulling out the troops would be seen all over the world as capitulation to Osama bin Laden. The war on Iraq in the spring of 2003 changed the equation.

Leading an international coalition into war against Iraq for the second time in twelve years, US forces rolled northward from Kuwait against surprisingly weak resistance and seized Baghdad on April 9, 2003. The regime of Saddam Hussein collapsed, and with it the rationale for stationing US combat air units in Saudi Arabia to enforce United Nations sanctions against Iraq. It was now possible to withdraw the troops without appearing to be doing so to placate the terrorists, and the announcement was not long in coming. On April 29, Defense Secretary Donald H. Rumsfeld and his Saudi counterpart, Prince Sultan, announced at a joint news conference that the troops would be redeployed outside Saudi Arabia by midsummer. The only US military personnel remaining in the Kingdom would be those of the Military Training Mission and the National Guard team, fewer than five hundred troops.

This development eliminated al-Qaeda's biggest complaint against the Saudi government, but hope that the terrorist organization would be placated was quickly dispelled. On the night of May 12, suicide truck bombers attacked three Riyadh housing compounds after overpowering gate guards. At least thirty people were killed, including eight Americans. Some Saudis were also among those killed. This meant that the attackers had not only committed mass murder, they had deliberately killed Muslims, and they had done so in the royal capital of the House of Saud. The blasts shattered the illusion of safety that had comforted Western families in Saudi Arabia for nearly seventy years, and some headed for the exits. This could not be shrugged off or explained away.

In a message to friends back in the States, John Qualls described it as "a wake-up call to the Saudis that lets them know that they are in a fight to the finish with the terrorists who threaten their society—just as 9/11 was our wake-up call in the US. . . . I get the real feeling that they recognize, perhaps for the first time, that we are all in this together."[10]

The passionate and enraged response of Crown Prince Abdullah seemed to confirm Qualls's assessment. "There can be no acceptance or justification for terrorism. Nor is there a place for any ideology which promotes it, or beliefs which condone it. We specifically warn anyone who tries to justify these crimes in the name of religion. And we say that anyone who tried to so will be considered a full partner to the terrorists and will share their fate." Citing Koranic passages that prohibit killing Muslims, Abdullah said, "These messages, which do not require any interpretation, provide clear evidence that the fate of these murderers is damnation on earth and fury of Hell in the hereafter."[11]

Abdullah's statement was certainly unequivocal, and it put the extremists on notice. If, as Gregory Dowling speculated, the terrorists struck out of desperation because their message was not gaining traction with the Saudi populace; and if Abdullah and his government are now fully energized in the struggle against terrorism; and if the withdrawal of the US troops quells popular resentment, it is possible that the atmosphere will stabilize and the threat will recede. Nevertheless, these early years of the twenty-first century are a time of profound uncertainty for the House of Saud and all of Saudi Arabia.

Externally, the future of Iraq remains to be determined. The menace of Saddam Hussein has been removed, along with the threat of invasion, but the emergence of a liberal, democratic government in Iraq could present Saudi Arabia with a new challenge—the challenge of ideas. If an important Arab neighbor were to become an open society, with a free press, liberated women, and a vigorous intellectual class, the retrograde nature of the Saudi political system would stand exposed. Conversely, the emergence of a Shiite theocracy in Iraq could threaten Saudi Arabia from the right instead of the left.

Across the Gulf in Iran, the theocratic regime's apparent determination to acquire nuclear weapons is causing concern in Riyadh. Saudi Arabia and the Iranian mullahs have largely reached a political modus vivendi since the open hostility of the 1980s, but an Iran with nuclear weapons could prompt Saudi Arabia to reconsider its own 1988 decision to forswear the nuclear option, especially if the Saudis were no longer confident that Uncle Sam would protect them.

Saudi Arabia's near-term future is also unsettled internally, even assuming that the threat of terrorism is contained. The incapacitated King Fahd's designated successor, Crown Prince Abdullah, reached the age of eighty in 2003 and the next in line, Prince Sultan, is only a year younger. The line of succession after that is undetermined, and a power struggle that splits the Kingdom, while unlikely, cannot be ruled out. Whoever comes after Abdullah and Sultan will preside over a fractious country in which the population is growing far faster than jobs are being created and the standard of living is declining because oil revenue has stagnated.

As for the future of Saudi Arabia itself, it would be foolish to make predictions. The tension inherent in a society that is fully modernized in a physical sense and is part of the larger world, yet clings to cherished norms and traditions rooted in ancient ways, is readily apparent. It is the task of the Saudi monarch to manage that tension. Whether Fahd's successors will do so is an open question.

CHAPTER 17

EGYPT UNDER MUBARAK

Arthur Goldschmidt Jr.

Anwar Sadat was assassinated in 1981 by Muslim militants who opposed Sadat's backing of the exiled Shah of Iran and Egypt's 1979 peace with Israel. In the opinion of the militants, the treaty with Israel freed the Israeli government from the fear of Egyptian reprisals, allowing it to bomb guerrillas (and civilians) in Lebanon, conduct an air strike against an Iraqi nuclear reactor, increase Jewish settlements on the West Bank, and continue to oppress the Palestinians.

Sadat's successor, Husni Mubarak, has been in power ever since Sadat's death. Under Mubarak, Egypt has relied greatly on weapons and support from the United States. In turn, in the wake of Iraq's invasion of Kuwait in 1990, Egypt supported the US-led coalition of forces to protect Saudi Arabia and liberate Kuwait.

Yet Egypt under Mubarak has also resumed the ties with other Arab countries that had attenuated under Sadat, and it has not progressed toward the complete peace with Israel that Sadat had envisioned. Egyptians can identify themselves at various times as Egyptians, Arabs, or Muslims. Egypt's Arab identity is reviving, fueled in part by resentment against Israel for its repression of the Palestinians and (as Egyptians see it) its manipulation of US foreign policy. But Egypt's Islamic sentiment has also increased since the 1979 Iranian Revolution, enhancing the appeal of Islamic revolutionary groups among the Egyptian population. Deteriorating economic and social conditions also foster the attraction of Islamist groups, as does the coerciveness of the United States in Iraq and elsewhere, and the US backing of Israel against the Palestinians.

Arthur Goldschmidt Jr. is professor emeritus of Middle East history at the Pennsylvania State University. He is the author of the Biographical Dictionary of Modern Egypt *and* Modern Egypt: The Formation of a Nation State, *from which this chapter derives. He is the recipient of the Amoco Foundation Award for Outstanding Teaching and of the 2000 Middle East Studies Association Mentoring Award.*

WHEN HUSNI MUBARAK, SADAT'S VICE PRESIDENT, succeeded the slain leader, he pledged in a public speech before the People's Assembly to address Egypt's domestic and foreign problems. Mubarak has a less flamboyant leadership style than either Nasir or Sadat, but he has made few significant policy changes. At the time of this writing, he has held power for more than twenty-three years, making him Egypt's longest-serving head of state since Mehmet Ali. He has no vice president. If he were to resign his office or die suddenly, no one can be sure who would succeed him. Mubarak's own succession was orderly in a dangerous time in Egypt's history, a sign of the country's political maturity. Egypt seems to have become one of the most stable countries in the Middle East.

But is this true? There is reason to wonder whether in fact the government enjoys legitimacy in the eyes of the Egyptian people. Mubarak's leadership has not been charismatic, and at times it has been downright dictatorial. Egyptians have become apathetic about politics. Growing numbers do not even vote. A large number (no one knows the percentage) of Egyptians now endorse political Islam and believe that their country's laws should be based on the Shari'ah. Some would favor the reestablishment of the Islamic caliphate. In a prolonged political or economic crisis, the advocates of political Islam have enough supporters and indeed the financial means to seize control of the government.

In international relations, Egypt remains formally nonaligned. In practical terms, the government's weapons and support come mainly from the United States. It is still committed to achieving a comprehensive peace settlement with Israel along the lines laid down at the 1978 Camp David Summit and in the 1979 Egyptian-Israeli Peace Treaty, but under Mubarak it resumed its ties with the other Arab countries and did not progress toward the complete peace with Israel that Sadat had envisioned. Many Israelis believe that Egypt has reverted to its old posture of opposition to Jews, Zionism, and Israel; the Egyptians feel that their separate peace treaty freed Israel to annex the Golan Heights in 1981, invade Lebanon in 1982, crush the Palestinian Intifada in 1987–1991, and block Clinton's efforts to broker a peace settlement between 1995 and 2001. Although Egypt's government still sides with the United States in its war against terrorism, the public has in recent years strongly opposed the American attacks, sanctions, and invasion of Iraq and US support for Israel against the Palestinians. Four of the nineteen Arab men who hijacked the passenger planes and flew them into the World Trade Center and the Pentagon on 11 September 2001 were Egyptians.

More reserved than Sadat, Mubarak was an unknown quantity when he became president. His earliest acts were to refocus the attention of the People's

Assembly on Egypt's socio-economic problems and to free most of the 1,539 political and religious leaders whom Sadat had jailed in September 1981. Most Egyptians were relieved that Sadat's assassination did not lead to a prolonged rebellion against the government, but the government did suppress an Islamist uprising in Asyut and many fundamentalists were imprisoned or put under house arrest, their magazines banned, and their assets impounded. Students were especially suspect: males were forbidden to grow beards or to wear gallabiyyas and women had to remove their head coverings to enter university campuses.

EGYPT, THE MIDDLE EAST, AND THE SUPERPOWERS

Needless to say, a sensitive issue for Mubarak was the peace process with Israel, which in December 1981 annexed the Golan Heights. Israel's retrocession of the remaining areas of the Sinai to Egypt on 25 April 1982 seemed to remove that constraint on the Egyptian government, but the Israeli invasion of southern Lebanon deeply angered almost all Egyptians. In fact, though, Egypt's inability to fight Israel was matched by the weakness of almost all the other Arab governments. Syria and the Palestine Liberation Organization did intervene, but could not halt the Israeli advance. Egypt did withdraw its ambassador from Tel Aviv and suspended the Palestinian autonomy talks mandated by its peace treaty with Israel; it never ruptured diplomatic relations with the Jewish state. Mubarak mended Egypt's fences with PLO chairman Arafat, who had denounced that treaty, but only after Arafat had been driven from Lebanon by a dissident Palestinian faction. More telling was the action by most Arab governments to restore diplomatic relations with Egypt, even though Mubarak never renounced Sadat's peace policy and even sent back his envoy to Tel Aviv in 1986. Jordan, Saudi Arabia, some of the Persian Gulf States, and even Iraq were reconciled with Egypt, implicitly validating its peace policies.

Sadat's assassination opened the way for Cairo's reconciliation with Moscow, which agreed to reschedule Egypt's massive debt to the USSR, and the two countries resumed exchanging ambassadors in 1984. However, the US government remained Egypt's main benefactor, providing $1–3 billion annually in military and economic aid, essentially the price Washington paid for ensuring Egyptian-Israeli peace. Most of this money paid for the importation of American arms, capital goods, and food, but projects in the 1980s included expanding the water and sewer system of greater Cairo, upgrading the telephone network, building new schools, introducing better varieties of wheat and rice, and the extension of family planning services. Military aid involved training and the provision of fighter jet planes, modern artillery, tanks (now assembled in Egypt), and armored personnel vehicles, but its showpiece was Operation Bright Star, joint Egyptian–American military operations begun in 1981 and repeated in odd-numbered years. They have continued, but with less publicity and more involvement by other countries' armed forces.

Due in part to these close ties between Cairo and Washington, the United States managed to enlist the help of Egypt and most of the other Arab states in the campaign against Iraq's occupation of Kuwait. Mubarak had attempted during July 1990 to mediate the quarrels between these two countries, which centered on Iraq's repayment to Kuwait of debts incurred during the Iran–Iraq War, claims to an oilfield that lay athwart their territorial border, and Iraq's desire for greater access to the Persian Gulf. The surprise attack on 2 August violated commitments that Mubarak had received from Iraqi president Saddam Husayn, and Egypt spearheaded efforts by the other Arab heads of state to persuade him to pull his troops out of Kuwait. When Arab diplomacy failed, Mubarak was one of the Arab leaders who agreed to join the allied coalition to protect Saudi Arabia and eventually to liberate Kuwait; 40,000 Egyptian troops took part in "Operation Desert Storm."

POLITICAL CHANGES IN EGYPT

Since 1979 Egypt has had a multiparty system, but in practice the National Democratic Party remains the dominant legal participatory movement with Mubarak as its leader, even if his methods have been less dictatorial and less dramatic than those of his predecessor. Although regime politicians rarely speak critically of earlier leaders, Sadat's passing no longer is a cause for public grieving. Egyptians often criticize him in private and express some nostalgia for the now rather hazy years of Gamal Abd al-Nasir. The role of the People's Assembly did not become as important as Sadat may have envisioned early in his presidency, and on many foreign and defense policy issues it has no role at all. Mubarak is far more likely to initiate new laws than the parliamentarians, and even their committees are little more than sounding boards for the ministers. Egypt has a large and highly articulated court system, with an independent judiciary that has criticized and at times nullified the acts of Mubarak's administration and even supervised the 2000 elections, but it remains vulnerable to pressure from the executive—especially the justice and interior ministries. In recent years many high-profile criminal cases have been tried in the military courts.

Human rights constitute a major issue for Egypt. Although close ties with the United States may seem to foster more respect for individual liberties than was evident during the period of the monarchy or the dictatorship of Gamal Abd al-Nasir, this is illusory. Censorship of books, periodicals, and films continues, although the intrusive habits of Nasir's censors, who routinely opened letters and taped telephone calls, have not been resumed under Mubarak. Individuals and groups often censor themselves to avert future trouble, though, knowing that they can be pressured by Islamists as well as by the Egyptian government.

The government's censorship and repression is applied against Communists, obstreperous groups and individuals, and Islamists, usually in the name of "fighting terrorism." Using its emergency laws, the Mubarak regime has banned certain newspapers and magazines, placed its foes under house arrest or preventive detention without charges or trial, tortured suspects in police stations and prisons, broken up meetings, and restricted political rallies and demonstrations. In fact, when demonstrations do occur, as in March 2003 against the American attack on Iraq, outside observers can be certain that they convey a message from Mubarak's government, which like its citizens opposed the George W. Bush administration's policies.

ECONOMIC POLICY

In economic matters, the Egyptian government still pursues a policy that combines state planning and ownership of basic industries with private enterprise, both domestic and foreign. The trend, however, has been toward privatization of most businesses. Mubarak seems more dedicated to solving Egypt's economic problems than Sadat ever was. It is not clear, however, whether some of them can ever be solved. The country's population, 74 million in 2003, increases by another million every ten months; at the same time, the amount of arable land has actually declined, owing in part to the demand for housing but also to a legacy of ill-conceived agricultural policies that make it more profitable for some peasants to turn their soil into bricks than to raise the three crops per year made possible by perennial irrigation. Although the Aswan High Dam initially increased the amount of cropped land and now generates more electricity than Egypt can use, it has deprived the land of the silt that formerly came down with the annual flood and, hence, has increased Egypt's need for artificial fertilizers. The High Dam has also raised the water table, making it harder to flush away salt accumulations that reduce soil productivity. By 1980 Egypt imported more than half the grain consumed by its inhabitants, an ironic fate for a land that was the breadbasket of many ancient and medieval empires, but this dependency has lessened during the last two decades.

There have been some hopeful agricultural trends. The percentage of Egyptians who actually work as farmers has gradually diminished, while their use of farm machinery, modern techniques of cultivation and irrigation, and their technical knowledge have all increased. Egyptian cotton remains an important export crop, but it uses a much smaller share of the country's agricultural land, while wheat, corn, rice, and sugar have taken up the slack. The diversion of some of the waters that have backed up behind the Aswan High Dam for the Toshka Project, inaugurated in January 1997, will eventually create a second Nile Valley in Egypt's Western Desert, possibly raising the share of Egypt's land that is cultivated from 5 to 20 percent. Much of the new land will be used to raise cash crops, for it is generally understood that the future success of Egyptian agriculture will depend on the development of products that can be sold to Europeans and to other Arabs, such as fruit, vegetables, beet and cane sugar, honey, poultry, eggs, cut flowers, and decorative plants. But will many Egyptians agree to move to this new and remote region? And will the second Nile draw away water that is still needed by the original River Nile?

Egypt has industrialized less well than most Asian countries. The showcase heavy industries that Nasir set up all lost money. Sadat retained most of them to avoid antagonizing workers in the public sector factories. Mubarak's government has sold them off or entered into partnerships that allow the government and private investors to share in their ownership and management. Unemployment has become a problem for secondary school and university graduates, running to between 15 and 20 percent during the 1990s. By contrast, in many skilled trades, even some agricultural ones, the labor supply has been inadequate. The main reason for this scarcity was that 4 million Egyptians were lured to the oil-exporting Arab countries by wages ten times the amount that they could earn at home. However, the decline in oil prices in the 1980s and 1990s severely reduced employment opportunities abroad. Because of the 1991 Gulf War, many expatriate Egyptians lost their jobs in Iraq and returned home.

Falling oil revenues in the 1980s and 1990s also reduced the flow of Arab tourism to Egypt and reversed the trend of rising Arab investment in Egyptian real estate and industrial enterprises. Egypt's own oil production and prices have tended to parallel those of the larger oil exporters. Although it has not joined the Organization of Petroleum Exporting Countries, Egypt sets its level of production and prices in tandem with that group. Although Egypt has lost foreign exchange from falling oil sales abroad, its growing production of natural gas has made up for this.

Income disparities remain large. Although this was the case before the 1952 Revolution, the egalitarian propaganda of the Nasir era has made Egyptians less willing to accept vast differences between rich and poor, and of course they now know far better how the other half lives. Near-universal primary education may get higher marks for quantity than for quality, but it certainly has added to the public's awareness of the difference between the reality with which they are contending and the ideals of either capitalism or socialism. The value of the Egyptian pound has dropped from US$2.80 in 1952 to 15 cents in 2003. A weak currency helps to promote exports but makes it harder for businesses to import capital equipment and for individuals to buy foreign-made consumer goods. Annual double-digit price inflation has usually ensued, and morale has suffered among the people.

The Egyptian government narrowly avoided a crisis in repaying its foreign debts in 1987, when it opened extensive negotiations with the World Bank, the International Monetary Fund, and Western governments to reschedule its payments. In May 1991 the negotiating parties signed the Economic Reform and Structural Adjustment Program (or "ERSAP"), which called for macroeconomic policy adjustments (higher taxes relative to government expenditures), removal of government subsidies on consumer goods, elimination of price controls, foreign trade liberalization (elimination of quotas and protective tariffs), reform of labor legislation, and privatization of state-owned enterprises. Mubarak's government did implement these reforms in the 1990s, temporarily strengthening the Egyptian pound yet reducing the trade deficit. Overall national income rose, but some economists believe that the rich benefited at the expense of the poor.

NATIONAL IDENTITY

Egypt is both a nation (an object of loyalty) and a state (a political and legal system). The concept of the nation-state grew up in early modern times in Western Europe and North America. It did not necessarily apply either to the traditional loyalties of most Middle Eastern peoples or to the behavior patterns of their rulers. Faith and family remained the foci of popular identification. French and British imperialism (and schooling) did spread the spirit of nationalism, but mainly among a small stratum of the educated elite. Except in the sense of resistance to non-Muslim rulers, nationalism was slow to appear and spread in the Middle East. It developed in both intensity and extent in Egypt during the twentieth century, especially under Nasir and his successors, because of expanding public education, radio and television broadcasting, and almost universal male military service.

Egyptians tend to meander among their Egyptian, Arab, and Muslim identities, responding to current political conditions. Egypt's Arab identity went into eclipse after 1973, but it is now reviving, for the ties of language and culture with other Arabs are strong, as is resentment against Israel for what Egyptians view as its repression of the Palestinians and its manipulation of American foreign policy.

Egyptian feeling, deep-seated though it may be, does not exclude other loyalties. Islamic sentiment has increased ever since the June 1967 War and the 1979 Iranian Revolution. Sadat's assassins, or at any rate those whom the government managed to capture, belonged to a relatively new secret society called al-Jihad ("Struggle"). Their feat has actually increased the appeal to the Egyptian people of Islamic revolutionary groups, although they are strictly outlawed. Allied with the Jihadists in killing Sadat was al-Jama'a al-Islamiyya ("Islamic Group"), which grew out of the student Muslim groups formed in Egypt's universities during the Sadat era, and the two groups set up a consultative council led by Shaykh Umar Abd al-Rahman, who later escaped to Afghanistan, the Sudan, and finally the United States, where he was arrested, tried, and convicted for the 1993 bombing of the World Trade Center in New York. Egyptians of both groups went to Afghanistan and aided the Muslim rebels against the Soviet military occupation of that country. Those who returned home in the early 1990s, often called "Afghans," became leading terrorists against the Egyptian government, secularist writers, foreign tourists, and Copts between 1992 and 1997. One of the Egyptian Afghans was Dr. Ayman al-Zawahiri, a physician who allied himself with Usama Bin Laden and helped to form the network of terrorist groups, based in Afghanistan and many other Muslim countries, known as al-Qa'ida ("The Base"), now the focus for the American-led "War on Terrorism."

Although most educated Egyptians still adhere to the ideals of secular nationalism and would not welcome an Iranian-style "Islamic Republic" in their country, they have moved away from Sadat's "liberal socialism." Some, however, are attracted to the extremist groups, and more will join them if economic and social conditions continue to deteriorate. The Muslim extremists do not accord any legitimacy to the present regime and look to Libya and other radical states to help them deliver Egypt from its state of *Jahiliyya* (pre-Islamic ignorance). This term, applied by the Islamist writer Sayyid Qutb to secularized governments and westernized societies, has strong resonance for observant Muslims, who condemn rampant consumerism and immorality. These are evident not only in films and television shows imported from the West, but also in the behavior of Gulf Arabs who take vacations from their own governments' restrictions against extramarital sex, gambling, and drinking, all readily available to foreigners but not Egyptians in their country's luxury hotels.

It was easy for the extremists to exploit the bitter anger among the thousands of young men who served in the "Security Police" at a monthly wage of six Egyptian pounds—so easy that they exploded into mass demonstrations that destroyed three tourist hotels near the Giza Pyramids in February 1986. Their shouted slogan was "They eat meat, we eat bread." The Islamists organized campus demonstrations against Egypt's participation in the 1991 Gulf War. They also provided textbooks, lecture notes, Islamic clothing, and transportation to campus for Muslim students. After the severe earthquake of October 1992, Islamist organizations provided faster and more effective health services and reconstruction aid than did the Egyptian government agencies to its injured and homeless victims. Their protests against American missile attacks on Iraq in 1993 and 1998 expressed the sentiments of most of the Egyptian people and presaged their popularly supported opposition to the American war on Iraq in 2003. Rather more ominously, many Muslims (in Egypt and elsewhere) applauded when Egyptian and Saudi terrorists hijacked American passenger jets on 11 September 2001 and flew them into the World Trade Center and the Pentagon. Egypt's government was appalled, but the reaction of the Arab street was that the United States deserved what it got.

PAST, PRESENT, AND FUTURE

The Islamists' slogan, "Islam is the solution," expresses the basic loyalty of many Egyptians, but one wonders how applying the Shari'ah or restoring the caliphate could solve the problems of an urbanized society living in the twenty-first century. Islamist groups resorted to violence to weaken the hold of the Egyptian government over its citizens during the 1990s, but their terrorism actually antagonized the people as it threatened Egypt's economy, dependent as it is on tourism and foreign trade. Egyptians are also proud of what they call "national unity," or the mutual tolerance between Muslims and Copts, and faulted the Islamists for stirring up intercommunal tensions. The traditional subordination of women to men, often ascribed to Islam even by Muslims, is no longer functional in a society where women's earnings outside the home have become necessary to support most families, urban or rural. Both sexes need all the training and education they can get to ensure their ability to make a living and to live a better life.

Mubarak's regime will be judged by the degree to which it succeeds in alleviating (if not solving) Egypt's economic problems. Relations with other Arab and Muslim peoples, while certainly better than they were in Sadat's time, are secondary in importance. When will Egypt have its next revolution? Egyptians rebel less often than most other Arabic-speaking peoples; their patience is legendary. They defer to autocratic rulers and bureaucrats to a degree that astonishes Syrians and Palestinians. Centuries of dependence on a strong ruler to ensure equitable distribution of Nile waters and protection from foreign invasion have created a political culture that glorifies order, tranquility, and forbearance. Modernization has sapped this ethos, however, and the danger of a new popular uprising, even against so honest and self-effacing a leader as Husni Mubarak, is never remote.

The United States since 1979 has spent about $2 billion a year to support the Egyptian government, more than the amount given to any other country except Israel. US aid policy in 2003 is geared more to politics than to need. In the case of Egypt, US aid helps to pay for the subsidies that keep down the prices of bread, rice, cooking oil, and butane gas, thus staving off a popular uprising and the spread of terrorism. Egyptians comprehend this reasoning behind Washington's policy, and the degree of their gratitude depends on how much they want the present regime to last. Some complain that American aid is hard to see amid the continuing problems of congestion, unemployment, and low wages. The best projects are the ones that enable Egyptians to solve their own problems, but the main fault of US aid lies in its administration: Washington insists on a degree of supervision far stricter than that imposed on, say, Israel—a stance viewed by the Egyptians as an insult to their competence. The growing coerciveness of US policy in Iraq and elsewhere in the Middle East fuels resentment against Americans.

CHAPTER 18

EGYPT

The Community of Muslims

Mark Huband

Though Egyptian Islamist groups have been largely silenced in formal politics today, their influence nevertheless remains evident. Early Egyptian Islamists sought to harness political power from the struggle against British colonialism. The Muslim Brotherhood, for example, which was founded in 1928 and which at one time claimed to have half a million active members, allied with nationalist, anti-monarchist, and anti-British elements within the officer corps of the Egyptian army during World War II.

Egyptians have vacillated about whether their Arab or their Muslim identity is primary. The Muslim Brotherhood established a clear link between Arab and Muslim identities by decrying the non-Arab leadership of Islam as a cause of the decline of the religion in the face of European colonialism. It also identified Zionism as an enemy of the Arabs in 1947, called for jihad to save Palestine from partition, and sent troops to fight in the 1948 war in Palestine.

The Muslim Brotherhood was dissolved by the Egyptian government in 1948 and its founder, Hassan al-Banna, was assassinated by the government in 1949. The group was in disarray and had lost any real political influence by the time of the nationalist revolution of 1952, which deposed King Farouq, established Egyptian independence, and set the stage for Gamal Abdel Nasser's rise to power. Yet the Muslim Brotherhood survives, in large part because of the lack of credible alternatives in Egypt's moribund political life. If regimes such as Egypt's are too weak to eradicate Islamist organizations, the Islamists themselves are too weak and divided to seize political power, resulting in a persistent stalemate that ensures a political instability too typical of the Muslim world.

Mark Huband *is security correspondent for the* Financial Times *(London). He is the author of* Brutal Truths, Fragile Myths: Power Politics and Western Adventurism in the Arab World, *as well as* Warriors of the Prophet: The Struggle for Islam, *from which this chapter is excerpted.*

MAMOUN AL-HODEIBI PACED INTO THE WAITING ROOM in his socks. An assistant brought his shoes from the prayer room. His welcome was warm. He tied his shoelaces while talking animatedly, defying the signs of his advanced age with a reservoir of youthful energy and the dignity unique to those who have survived a lifetime of struggle into old age. For the spokesman of the Ikhwan al-Muslimin, the Muslim Brotherhood, the battle had straddled the latter half of the twentieth century. For the movement, it had been punctuated by violence, assassination, prison sentences, and torture. The old men, and some younger ones in the room next door, who walked past us as we talked, were the intellectual guardians of a rich history, the keepers of an Islamist tradition, the descendants of a distinguished line of religious thinkers whose claim to represent the will of the people has left them condemned to a rubble-strewn Cairo backstreet beside the river.

"People believe in Islam. But the government has not become more Islamic. Even so, what people want will be achieved," al-Hodeibi said. In 1928, Hassan al-Banna, the founder of the Muslim Brotherhood, rallied his followers with a call to create an "Islamic homeland." In 1946 the Muslim Brotherhood claimed to have 500,000 active members and 500,000 sympathizers organized in 5,000 branches throughout the country. Now it is banned in Egypt. Many of its followers are in jail and its leaders are silenced and barred from organizing their undoubtedly still significant constituency in any meaningful way.

The cultural and religious elements of the Arab identity, which for a century the Islamists have sought to bring to the fore in their bid to confront the formidable influence of Europe, have been channeled into the strategies of the modernizing regimes that have led Egypt since independence in 1952. The Egyptian Islamists have alternately been courted, ridiculed, tortured, and finally silenced by the passing regimes. But at no point has a more credible political philosophy succeeded in supplanting the Islamists' influence, despite their lack of a party political machine through which to apply their program.

Egyptian Islamists sought to harness growing anticolonialism into a formidable political movement from the beginning. The "Arab civilization" that was the Islamists' raw material was both exalted for its qualities and recognized as having been diminished during many centuries of decline. This decline, both in terms of the internal decay of the religion and its weakness in the face of colonialism, was obvious. But there had traditionally been differences over whether Arabism or Islam was the essential element of that identity. "We are Arabs before being Muslims, and Muhammad is an Arab before being a prophet,"[1] said Faisal, son of Sharif Hussain of Mecca, the ruler of Hejaz. Five decades later, at his trial for sedition in 1966, the Egyptian writer Sayyid Qutb appeared to refute the call to ethnicity and nation when he told the Egyptian court that was later to sentence him to death: "The bonds of ideology and belief are sturdier than those of patriotism based upon region, and this false distinction among Muslims on a regional basis is but one expression of crusading and Zionist imperialism, which must be eradicated."[2]

While some argued that Arabism should be viewed as an essential part of the Muslim identity by virtue of the Arabs' role as the guarantors of Islam's survival over the centuries, Qutb and the line of Islamist scholars of which he was a key part argued that the religion was itself the core of the Muslim identity. In Egypt, the weakness of the Arabs in the face of Muslim Ottoman rule and the British occupation of 1882 was accompanied by the decay of the religion, for which Cairo had been a major center of scholarship for eleven centuries. While the rituals of religious observance were well known, they were not necessarily widely practiced in nineteenth-century Cairo. The failure of Muslims to practice their religion as was required of them emerged as a central tenet of the Islamists' own agenda. Strict observance and the return to orthodoxy have been the hallmark of the Islamists' message in the twentieth century.

THE MUSLIM BROTHERHOOD

The Islamist path in Egypt, where the most influential Islamist thinkers continued to gather and emerge, was led by Hassan al-Banna (1906–1949), a schoolteacher from the Nile delta. In 1928, having qualified as an Arabic teacher, al-Banna was appointed to a state primary school in Isma'iliyya. There, he was as active in promoting discussions about Islam, politics, and the condition of the Arab world as he had been in Cairo. That year he founded the Society of the Muslim Brothers, also known as the Muslim Brotherhood, apparently in response to a demand by a group of British-employed laborers for the creation of an organization that would ameliorate their sense of servitude and that would allow them to follow al-Banna's leadership. In 1932, al-Banna transferred to another teaching job in Cairo, establishing a branch of the organization in the city and setting up its headquarters there.

It was in Cairo that the founding principles of the Muslim Brotherhood, formulated in the prevailing atmosphere of political ferment and religious debate, were set forth. The brotherhood established a clear link between the Arab world and Islam, citing examples of the leadership of the religion by non-Arabs—Umayyads, Abbasids, Turks—as a cause of the religion's decline, owing in part to these nationalities' inability to fully understand the language of Islam, which was Arabic. But it also particularly targeted Cairo's Al-Azhar Islamic University and the religious authority of the Grand Sheikh Al-Azhar, the supreme authority in Sunni Islam on matters of jurisprudence. The brotherhood condemned this revered thousand-year-old institution and its head for what it regarded as its failure to stem Islam's decay and to resist encroachment by foreign ideas.

The organization evolved at a time when other religious groups were also active. Throughout the 1930s it developed its ideas as its presence in the mosques, coffeehouses, and homes of Cairo continued to widen. World War II allowed the brotherhood to expand its political role, in the face of increasingly authoritarian demands by the British intended to thwart the activities of anti-colonialist and antimonarchist Egyptians who had established channels of communication with Nazi Germany. Al-Banna established close ties with politically active nationalist elements within the Egyptian army, from whose ranks a virulent stirring of anticolonial feeling was then emerging; the army's liaison with the brotherhood was conducted by Anwar al-Sadat, later president of Egypt.

The end of the war saw the stature and credentials of the principal Egyptian nationalist party, the Wafd, undermined by its corruption, elitism, and affirmation of loyalty to the British against Germany during the war. By 1945 the Muslim Brotherhood was the most formidable opponent to the Wafd on the Egyptian political scene and had positioned itself as the most important rightist political organization, sharing common cause with other movements opposed to communism and accepting the monarchist system despite King Farouq's playboy image and pro-British views.

Al-Banna's links with the royal palace during the late 1940s, facilitated by al-Sadat, allowed the Muslim Brotherhood the greatest period of political freedom it had known since its foundation. The organization was allowed access to cheap publishing facilities, cheap land upon which to build mosques, and army camps in which to train the uniformed activist *jawalla* or "rovers," who after 1937 made up what became known as the brotherhood's *kata'ib* or "battalions." Their role was the propagation of the organization's message and the defense of its structure.

The brotherhood was viewed by the elite surrounding King Farouq as a weapon against the Wafd party, which quickly identified itself after the war as the mouthpiece of Egyptian nationalism. Post–1945 maneuvering in Egyptian politics revolved around the progress of negotiations for Egyptian independence from Great Britain and the growing likelihood that the United Nations would seek to solve the growing violence in the British colony of Palestine by partition and the foundation of a Jewish state there.

For the brotherhood, the application of the Islamic order, in which the *sharia* was the heart of the legal system as well as the embodiment of principles governing all aspects of social and cultural life, was the challenge for Muslims in the twentieth century. But the aim was to apply it to modern life rather than to simply turn back the clock. These principles could be applied without overthrowing the political order, as long as the Islamic *sharia* was applied by the existing order.

As its importance grew, the brotherhood became increasingly fractious. Al-Banna's use of arbitrary power, as well as his use of a "secret apparatus" of informers, loyalists, and the *jawalla,* which also had the support of an armed element, had resulted in a powerful militant core within the broader organization. In 1947 al-Banna decreed that the Muslim Brotherhood's branches should prepare for jihad to "save" Palestine from partition. In doing so he launched what has since become the key rallying call of Middle Eastern Muslims, identifying Zionism as the enemy of the Arabs, identifying the West as having betrayed the Arab world by supporting Israel, and driving a wedge between Western "modernity" and Islamic reformism. The Arab League organized arms supplies and training for volunteers, and when Arab forces began fighting the army of the new state of Israel in May 1948, the Muslim Brotherhood dispatched both combatants and auxiliaries to ferry supplies to the various front lines.

The war in Palestine, coupled with an increasingly violent struggle between the Muslim Brotherhood and the Wafd, unleashed turmoil in Egypt, which only came to an end in 1952 when the nationalist element of the army seized power. The amassing of arms to fight the war in Palestine had essentially legitimized the creation of an armed Muslim Brotherhood, trained and equipped on Egyptian soil, at a time when those militants brandishing weapons could not be relied upon to use them solely for the defense of Palestine. They could just as easily turn their weapons upon their domestic opponents. The Egyptian government became aware of the brotherhood's "secret apparatus" and in November 1948 carried out a series of arrests after discovering documentary evidence linking the brotherhood to bomb attacks against political opponents.

On 8 December 1948, the brotherhood was dissolved by a governmental decree, accused of terrorism and of planning an armed insurrection aimed at seizing power. Upon the dissolution of the brotherhood, the "secret apparatus" fell apart. On 12 February 1949, Hassan al-Banna was assassinated by the Egyptian political police on a Cairo street.

DEATH, DEFIANCE, AND THE CALL TO JIHAD

After al-Banna's death, the brotherhood was in disarray, hounded by the government, deprived of its leader, and confronted by the failure of the Arab states to defend the Palestinians. Divergence within the organization developed into pronounced factionalism, resulting in the emergence of vastly different strategies. Political activism had brought conflict with the Egyptian authorities, who imprisoned, tortured, and, in some cases, executed those they considered enemies of the state.

At the same time, the consolidation of Israeli power in the midst of the Arab world convinced millions of Muslims of the treachery of the West and undermined the call by some Islamic modernists for the reform of the religion to follow a process of adapting to Western institutions along Islamic lines. In the 1950s and 1960s, following the nationalist revolution of 1952, the overthrow of King Farouq, and the rise to power of Gamal Abdel Nasser, the brotherhood's real influence over Egypt's political direction weakened. While the group's moderates urged social work as a means of retaining its relevance and profile, the radicals forged a new agenda of resistance to increasing state repression. Activism, originally rooted in the theory of religious revival, evolved in response to repression. Torture and imprisonment created a new momentum. Jihad was declared as the only means by which the Islamic civilization and way of life, the *din*, could be revitalized. Leading this call was Sayyid Qutb (1906–1966).

Born in the Egyptian town of Asyut, Qutb joined the Muslim Brotherhood in 1951. His profound knowledge of the Koran, the entirety of which he had memorized as a child, injected a dynamism into the Islamist lexicon that encapsulated the position of humanity within the complicated political-religious web within which the Islamists found themselves in the Egypt of the 1950s and 1960s. The social pressures to which the Muslim Brotherhood found themselves subjected played a major part in Qutb's interpretation of the Koran. The relationship between the ruler and the ruled, between the ruler and God, and the equality of races—these are the key issues to which Qutb says Muslims, in their struggle to achieve the *din,* must address themselves.

Qutb identifies "the overall conditions prevalent in society"[3] as the obstacle to the free expression of religious belief. By implication, society for him was entirely devoid of Islamic characteristics, whereas belief in the Islamic system, the *din,* is the ultimate freedom for which humanity as a whole is striving. Force, in the form of jihad, is a consequence of a particular situation in which freedom has not been achieved. Jihad is itself the process of purification of the world in pursuit of the *din;* it was not meant as a defensive measure in the face of aggression from those opposed to Islam but as a vital process in which Muslims should take the initiative. The struggle, which has emerged in the politics of the twentieth century, is a process that has adopted its own rules. Its success will lead to the freedom from which peace will emerge, and the harsh practice of jihad will then be replaced by the cohesion and justice that lie at the heart of the *sharia.* But first the world must be cleansed by struggle.

THE STATE OF ISLAM

The place occupied by Islamism in the Egyptian political scene of the 1990s reflects the victory of repression over idealism. The regime of President Hosni Mubarak (1981–), though more open than its predecessors, remains reliant upon the military and security apparatus, has no substantial ideological credibility, and has no proven popular appeal.

In July 1954, Sayyid Qutb was arrested along with an estimated 50,000 other members of the Muslim Brotherhood. A year later Qutb was sentenced to fifteen years in prison with hard labor, accused of planning the overthrow of the government. He was released a decade later, but rearrested within a year. In 1966 he was tried and found guilty by a military court of planning the assassination of President Nasser. On 29 August 1966, he was hanged.

Qutb's legacy has been profound. He projected jihad to center stage. Qutb's doubts about the relevance of the traditions of Islam—essentially the practices passed down through time in the words of Islamic jurists, whose rulings had developed into the body of Islamic jurisprudence—stemmed from his assertion of the Koran as the sole source of law: man-made law was innately partisan and lacked the pure justice of the Islamic *sharia.*

The introduction of the *sharia* as the sole source of law remains the goal of all Islamist movements, necessitating their control of political power. The

Islamists are not interested in reworking interpretations of the past; rather, they seek to Islamize all the contemporary institutions that are associated with the wielding of political power. They are essentially modern, though variations exist as to whether the political power they are seeking should be held by authoritarian theocrats, influential imams making firm but diplomatic suggestions to open-minded secularists, or Muslim democrats relying on a parliamentary system to Islamize society.

At heart, the brotherhood, which now stands in the shadows of Egyptian politics—more of a dinosaur than the dynamic force its intellectual, social, and historical significance warrants—draws its continued sense of purpose from the depth of popular religious faith. This strength is coupled with the failure of successive regimes to adequately address or ameliorate pitiful social and economic conditions. The society of which it is an integral part now lies in a state of intellectual repression; Egyptian political life is moribund and its leaders more concerned about halting political evolution than risking a looser power structure in the search for a valid national identity. Within this void, the Muslim Brotherhood has proved durable, extending its role as a provider of welfare and as a social movement with broader roots than any other Egyptian political organization.

Relative influence has now, in the twilight of the twentieth century, exposed political strength and weakness without allowing political Islam—*Islamism*—to enjoy its new golden age. Islamism, according to [Olivier] Roy, has largely been replaced by neofundamentalism. Far from striving to realize the political aims of the Koran as the all-embracing concept promoted and envisaged by Qutb and his predecessors, Roy claims that the Islamic movements of the late 1990s lack an intellectual vision and instead promote a form of "popular Islam," which involves ensuring the right to practice Islam in areas where Muslims are present. This goal marks a profound departure from the quest to restore the *umma* [community of Islam].

Roy's broad assertion encompasses hundreds of organizations and thousands of activists. Their variety, internal conflicts, and troubled relations with the states in which they operate are the major political issues facing an Islamic world out of which a plethora of radical movements has emerged. The simplicity of the colonial foe has been replaced by the complexity of Islam's internal conflicts. The Islamists have found their opponents among monarchists, nationalists, communists, and capitalists. The relatively straightforward opposition to colonial occupation has been replaced with the far more profound issue of whether Muslims should be permitted to declare jihad against fellow Muslims.

The profusion of Islamist organizations has created the shadow in which the Muslim world's entire political agenda now operates. The relative simplicity of independence from colonialism, with all the promises of liberation that such a significant and rare historical turning point was supposed to bring, has been followed by political experiments whose consequences have been the social and economic conditions out of which mass support for the late-twentieth-century Islamist movements emerged. But with the regimes they are confronting apparently too weak to thwart them, and the Islamists themselves too weak to seize political power, stalemate has ensured the Muslim world of instability for some time to come.

CHAPTER 19

ISLAMIST PERCEPTIONS OF US POLICY IN THE MIDDLE EAST

Yvonne Haddad

Just as Americans have created a stereotype of Islamic fundamentalists, so, too, have Islamists created a parallel stereotype of a "crusader-Zionist conspiracy" bent on subjugating Muslims and eradicating Islam.

Islamists and secular Muslims alike generally agree that US foreign policy has been skewed in favor of Israel since the 1967 Arab-Israeli war, when Israel gained control over the West Bank and Gaza Strip. As Yvonne Haddad conveys forcefully in the following essay, Islamism is a reaction to Zionism, which is perceived as Israeli aggression aimed at subjugating Palestinians and defying United Nations resolutions, with the aid of US intervention at the United Nations. Islamists see that the West maintains a clear double standard that supports Jews in having a Jewish state but demonizes Muslims who want an Islamic state, and that immediately and forcefully punishes Iraq for its trespasses while silently ignoring Israel's transgressions over the nearly forty years since the 1967 war.

Over fifteen Arab nations for a time established some sort of relationship with Israel after the 1993 Oslo agreement, Haddad points out, but this only led to increased arrogance on the part of the Israeli government, which continues to flout the many UN resolutions on the Palestinian-Israeli issue, including especially the one that stipulates the existence of a Palestinian state. Islamists conclude that Israel doesn't want peace but only pacification of Palestinians and legalization of its territorial acquisitions.

So convinced are Islamists that US policy is shaped by those with Jewish interests at heart that even President George W. Bush's war on terrorism in response to the 9/11 attacks on US soil is perceived, despite assurances to the contrary, as a war on Islam—in effect continuing a "thousand-year" crusade of Christian fanaticism and Western imperialism against Muslims.

> **Yvonne Haddad** *is professor of the history of Islam and Christian-Muslim relations at the Center for Muslim-Christian Understanding, Georgetown University. She is the author of* A Vanishing Minority: Christians in the Middle East, *and the coeditor of numerous volumes, including* Islamic Law and Modernity *(with Barbara Stowasser).*

FOR MORE THAN FIVE DECADES, the umbrella ideology of Islamism has cast an increasingly large shadow as Islamist groups strove to create a unified ethos in order to enhance their own sense of empowerment in facing repressive regimes and what they view as Western and Zionist hegemonic policies in the Muslim world. Designed as an alternative to liberal humanism and socialism, as well as to fundamentalist secularism and Marxism, Islamism has left itself vulnerable to attacks from various quarters, including the regimes of some Arab countries, secularists, Zionists, humanists, socialists, feminists, and most recently the government of the United States, which has since 9/11 dubbed them as evil. During the past twenty years, the US press as well as some people in the US academy and government have created a consummate stereotype, commonly identified as "Islamic fundamentalism" or "Islamic extremism." Individuals and groups who fall into this category tend more and more to be demonized by those who oppose or fear them.

Currently, a profound sense of victimization on the part of Islamists has led to the development of a parallel stereotype: the alliance between Israel and the United States, which is generally depicted as "the crusader-Zionist conspiracy," the Western demon bent on the eradication of Islam. This perception has its roots in the worldview of the Muslim Brotherhood, "the mother of all Islamist movements" in Egypt. Hasan al-Banna, who founded the Muslim Brotherhood in 1928, identified a comprehensive venue of operations for his organization in order to realize his futuristic vision of a vibrant Muslim nation (the *'umma*). The focus was to be on the development of a new Muslim human being brought about through moral and spiritual rearmament, a new society actualized through economic development and social justice, and a new vibrant nation free of foreign domination. He perceived the Muslim nation to be in mortal danger as a consequence of the abolition of the office of the caliphate (the generally acknowledged leader of the Islamist community dating to the initial successor of the Prophet Muhammad) in 1924 by Mustafa Kemal Ataturk in Turkey. The caliph had provided a sense of Islamic unity maintained by commitment to Islamic values in societies governed by Islamic law. From his vantage point, foreign interests, at the time mainly British, appeared to work diligently to divide the Muslim world into nation-states to facilitate their subjugation and to insist on implementing the Balfour Declaration of 1917, which had promised a national homeland for European Jews in Palestine. For al-Banna, the Balfour Declaration was not only a means of maintaining colonial interests in the area but was a continuation of European crusader designs on the holy lands.

Although all Islamists appear to agree on an agenda of bringing about the kinds of changes that provide empowerment and well-being for Muslim society, they differ on the means of actualizing change and on issues of political and religious pluralism in an Islamic state. Meanwhile, there is general agreement among Islamists and secularists that US foreign policy in the Middle East has been skewed in favor of Israel since the 1967 Arab-Israeli war (also known as the Six Day War, or June War). This perception has left an indelible mark on Islamist identity and its worldview. This chapter will analyze these perceptions and the Islamist response. It is based on Islamist literature, which is polemical and generally hostile as to Israel and US foreign policy as well as the Palestinian self-rule question.

ISLAMISM:
A REACTION TO DISEMPOWERMENT

Islamism is not a reactionary movement; it does not want to replicate the Islamic community of the Prophet Muhammad in the seventh century. Rather, it seeks control of the present and future of Muslim destiny. From its inception it has been reactive, responding to direct and imagined challenges posed by internal conditions as well as its violent encounter, during the last two centuries, with a dominant West. Its ideologues operate with a heightened sense of awareness of the importance of monitoring events in the world, particularly those that affect their lives, and responding to them. They see themselves as manning a defensive operation, the responsibility of which is to safeguard society from total disintegration.

Islamism was initially a reaction to the internal sense of decay in Muslim society. A central theme in most Islamist literature is a response to the deep awareness of the backwardness of Muslims, a critical assessment of what went wrong historically, and an effort to rectify the situation in order to bring about a vibrant future. Revival is seen by its advocates as a crucial means of infusing life into a community that is bogged down in centuries-old ideas and traditions that have led to the ossification of Islamic society, restricting its ability to adapt to the fast-changing reality of the modern world.

Islamism is a reaction against disempowerment and what is seen as the irrelevance of the nation-states created in the region as a result of the Sykes-Picot Agreement constructed during World War I, through which the British and the French artificially divided much of the Middle East into spheres of influence that were later sanctioned via postwar agreements into the mandate system comprised of state units that had hitherto not existed. There is general consensus in Islamist literature that the dominant world order that has prevailed since the nation-states in the area were carved out has not allowed for the inclusion of Arabs as full citizens of the world. Arab nations and peoples have continued to be subservient to foreign domination, which Islamists describe as a continuing predatory relationship.

Islamism is also a reaction to a profound feeling on the part of Muslims that they have been victimized over the centuries at the hands of Western Christians. The litany of perceived outrages includes European treatment of Muslims during the crusades. They cite the fact that Eastern Christians, Jews, and Muslims in Jerusalem were massacred by the Western invaders during the First Crusade whereas Salah al-Din (Saladin) treated the crusaders magnanimously by giving them assurance of safe passage after he led the Muslim recapture of the city eighty-eight years later in 1187. It includes the *reconquista* in Spain during which a ruthless de-Islamization policy gave Muslims the options of conversion, expulsion, or execution. It includes the colonialist movements of the nineteenth and twentieth centuries, along with the activities of Christian missionaries. It also includes the reality that in the Soviet Union Muslims living under Communist hegemony were not allowed to practice their faith or study the tenets of their religion. And it includes the perception that for five decades Zionism has been one more element of the long and continuous effort supported by Christians to eradicate Islam and Muslims from the holy places. Bosnia and Kosovo are seen as further manifestations of European efforts to eradicate the indigenous European Muslim population.

Islamism is a reaction to the demonization of Islam. Muslims are offended and angered at the way in which Islam has been defamed in inflammatory political statements, such as former US Vice President Dan Quayle's comparison of Islamic fundamentalism to Nazism and communism.[1] Islamists are very aware that since the late 1970s there has been a dramatic increase in the number of articles in the US press dedicated to Muslim-bashing. These tend to depict Muslims as irrational and vengeful and motivated by religious zeal and fanaticism that arise out of an innate hatred of the West, its Judeo-Christian heritage, and its secularist values. Such distorted presentations of Islam are seen by Muslims as conscious efforts at revisionist history, inspired by contempt for Islam or motivated by political considerations in an attempt to maintain unwavering US support for the state of Israel. They tend to validate for Islamists their perceptions that the West has a double standard by which it measures events in the area.

Islamism is a reaction to Zionism. Israel's 1967 preemptive strike, which resulted in a devastating defeat of Jordan, Egypt, and Syria, is generally referred to as aggression. Zionism's policies are perceived as Judaizing and aimed at disempowering, dispossessing, and displacing the Palestinians in an effort to destroy their identity. What is perceived as its persistent rejection of United Nations (UN) resolutions and violation of the Geneva Convention have fostered, nursed, and inflamed the Islamic response. It is enhanced by what is seen to be US intervention at the United Nations in support of these policies, which has made the international community ineffective in implementing resolutions that would uphold justice.

On another level Islamism can be said to be a kind of mirror image of Zionism. It may be seen as an attempt to emulate what is perceived as a winning Israeli formula in which religious zeal, divine justification, scriptural proof-texting, and victimization are employed to mobilize Jewish as well as Euro-American Christian support for the state. For some Muslim observers, the essence of the issue is that the state of Israel is a Jewish state. The question thus remains: Why is it acceptable for Jews to have a Jewish state and not for Muslims to form an Islamic state?

ISLAMISM AND THE "DOUBLE STANDARD"

Islamism is a reaction to what is perceived as the double standard (al-izdiwajiyya) that is used by the West in its foreign policy in the Middle East. For example, in demonizing the Islamists, Westerners claim that there is no room for religion in the modern nation-state. Islamists consider this not only to be hypocritical in light of Western support for Israel and enduring and prominent symbols of religiosity in the West, but in a very profound way the proof of the double standard. Hence they believe that the West is not against religion per se but against Islam. "Pakistan and Israel," says one writer, "are two countries created solely on the basis of religion and faith. But you may read in the Western press that Pakistan is backward and reactionary because it has emerged in the name of religion. Nothing whatsoever of this nature is said about Israel."[2]

There is a growing perception among Islamists that Jews and Christians, driven by religious fanaticism, triumphalism, and imperialism, have been engaged

in a "thousand-year war" with Muslims. Major events in the area have contributed to this perception, such as the success of the Iranian revolution, which
validated for the faithful the Qur'anic teaching that God will give victory to
those who believe, and Operations Desert Shield and Desert Storm, which
were widely seen as a continuation of the crusader-Zionist efforts to destroy
Islam.

Muslims have been intrigued by the fact that Israel and its supporters boast
that it is the only democracy in the area. They note that it functions as a democracy "for Jews" while denying religious minorities—both Christian and Muslim—equal access to resources such as water, housing, health, education, jobs,
and the ability to purchase land.

Islamists and the Gulf War

To Islamists, Western hypocrisy and duplicity were manifest in the Gulf war. The
real motive was never to defend international law, enforcement of which varies
from case to case and depends on whether the aggressor is a Western country or
a Third World country. The objective of that campaign was to "control the oil
resources, protect Israel, and achieve U.S. hegemony over the West [Europe]
itself."[3]

Operations Desert Shield and Desert Storm tapped into a reservoir of
Islamist distrust of Western policies in the Middle East that have long been
depicted as hypocritical, duplicitous, and racist. Islamists initially condemned
the Iraqi aggression against Kuwait. However, when the United States assumed
the leadership in redressing the aggression and did not allow for a negotiated settlement, the majority saw US intervention as a continuation of colonial policies
designed to rob Arabs and Muslims of their wealth, to foster the dismemberment
of the Muslim peoples by maintaining their divisions into nation-states, and to
destroy Arab power in order to maintain Israel's supremacy in the area.

Islamists ask why Iraq's aggression was immediately redressed while that of
Israel has been relegated to diplomacy and negotiations that have been protracted over thirty-five years. They heard the George H. W. Bush administration
affirm there could be no room for negotiation or delay in regard to the Iraqi
invasion of Kuwait. They ask why Saddam Hussein had to implement the UN
resolutions immediately and completely, given that Israel has been allowed to cir-
cumvent all UN resolutions except the one recognizing it as a state, with which
it has only partially complied, since the resolution also stipulates the existence of

a Palestinian state and the repatriation or compensation of the refugees. The following statement typifies the Arab feeling toward what is perceived to be a double standard:

> Everybody in congress stated accurately that Iraq stood in violation of the United Nations Charter and United Nations resolutions. But no one congressman or congresswoman mentioned the potential relevance of the fact that in the 23 years before Iraq started violating the United Nations Charter, Israel had been violating it every month and every week and every day. No one mentioned the 42 United Nations Resolutions on the subject. So while they were invoking the legitimacy of the United Nations, none in congress had enough honor, enough self respect, enough integrity even to acknowledge that there was another country besides Iraq in the Middle East which at that moment stood in violation of the United Nations Charter.[4]

The Bush administration accused Saddam Hussein of not respecting the international boundaries set by Britain. Islamists have questioned why, after nearly half a century, the United States has not restricted Israel to the boundaries delineated for it by the United Nations and why it has been allowed to continue occupying territories designated for Palestinian residence as well as parts of Syria and Lebanon.

The Bush administration justified the military operation against Iraq by depicting Iraq's invasion of Kuwait as a violation of Kuwait's right to self-determination. Islamists ask why the United States acquiesces in Israeli occupation and annexation of Palestinian territory and refuses to recognize the Palestinian right to self-determination.

ISLAMISTS AND THE ZIONIST LOBBY

The Islamist literature depicts the West as dominated by the Zionist lobby. This image has had several mutations as Zionist influence is perceived to have gained control of the inner circles of policymakers who determine the destiny of the region. Interviews I conducted with Islamists in Egypt in 1985 made clear that they resented the double standard with which they were treated. One leader talked about the "evenhanded" policy, which was then the buzzword used by the administration to describe the habit of the West "to stroke Israel with the palm of their hand and whack us with the back." That same year, the joke in Jordan was, Why doesn't Israel want to become the 51st state of the United States? The answer: It would then have to be satisfied with being represented by two senators whereas now it has 100.

In interviews I conducted in 1989, the image of Zionist control of the US government became even more dominant. One Islamist depicted the United States as a colony of Israel (a view that is shared by Arab secularists). He compared the state of affairs in the United States with the former British rule over Egypt, noting that there were three specific areas in which British power manifested itself. In the first place, Egyptians were not allowed to have an independent foreign policy but had to defer to Britain for direction. In the second place, there were foreign British residents in Cairo who made sure that Egyptian policy was in accord with the interests of Britain. In the third place, Egyptian tax revenues were sent to Britain to sustain its power. He drew the parallels by concluding, "What you have in the United States is a government that is unable to formulate an independent foreign policy without first asking how will Israel react. Secondly, the Congress is accountable to the Israeli lobby, which functions as a foreign agent placing the welfare of Israel above that of the United States. In the third place, the lobby assures the flow of billions of U.S. tax dollars to Israel."

US Foreign Policy and the Clinton Administration

For Islamists, the Clinton administration assumed authority at a critical time in history. Due to the collapse of the Soviet empire, the US administration was not only able to implement its policies unimpeded by considerations of balance of power, it also chose to shed its cooperative arrangements with old "allies," such as Pakistan and the Afghan Resistance Movement, and to rearrange its priorities. Clinton began what was perceived as a tilt toward India at the expense of Pakistan, the latter an ally during the cold war who had for years supported the policies of the United States and had allowed operations against the Soviet Union to be launched through its territory into Afghanistan. The dumping of Pakistan and the abandonment of Afghanistan were perceived as part of US duplicity and a sign of its increasing control by Zionist interests. The United States would feign friendship only when it needed to use nations for its own interests.

Despite their struggle for empowerment during this century, Islamists feel, it has been determined that Arabs should be maintained in weakness, mediocrity, and subservience. For many in the Islamist movement, the actions of the

Clinton administration and its pronouncements confirmed the perception of many Muslims that it is Tel Aviv that dictates policy in the area. The fact that over two dozen former employees of the Israeli lobby were directing administration policy in the Middle East led Muhammad Husayn Fadlallah of Lebanon to write: "The current American administration has become almost completely Jewish, if not in origin then in its clear and infamous political affiliation."[5]

An address by Martin Indyk (former assistant secretary of state for the Near East and North Africa) on May 18, 1993, raised further concern about the future of the region. Indyk outlined a Manichaean vision, one where the world is portrayed as a potential nightmare should the nationalists or Islamists realize their dream and form a united front. The alternative vision that he promoted was one of harmony and bliss in which Israel would attain its "normalization" in the region. Indyk stated that the United States is not an impartial arbiter of the peace process; rather he affirmed that "the President and the Secretary of State made it clear that our approach in the negotiations will involve working with Israel, not against it. We are committed to deepening our strategic partnership with Israel in the pursuit of peace and security."[6] This affirmation did not bode well for permanent peace in the area and in fact probably assured further growth of the Islamist movement. Furthermore, it served to undermine the very regimes (Egypt and the Gulf nations) the United States wishes to support. Those regimes were put in the position of seeming to collude in the empowerment of Israel at the expense of the Arab population.

In his speech to the Jordanian parliament in 1994, President Clinton appeared to be reiterating Indyk's vision of a Manichaean worldview. He portrayed the Middle East as "an arena of struggle between the forces of tyranny and freedom, terror and security, bigotry and tolerance, isolation and openness." In the process, he spelled out for Islamists the choices between good and evil in the area, with the good being assured when they associate with Israel. Meanwhile, administration policy appears to depict Islam in a similar fashion: At one end of the spectrum is Islam, represented by the faith that is confined to personal belief and ritual practices, on the other are extremist groups that insist on the political dimension of Islam and therefore are dubbed violent and terrorist. Although this policy affirms a respect for the religion of Islam, it is a disemboweled Islam that has no input into human, social, economic, and political values, which some Islamists have dubbed "American Islam."

Since 1967, the issue of Palestine has been adopted increasingly as part of the Islamic agenda. It seems all too clear that an unjust peace that thwarts all hopes will only intensify the anger at what is seen as long-standing injustice and will fuel the flames of Islamist reaction. After the 1967 Arab-Israeli war, one American administration after another has invited the Arabs to trust American even-handedness and come to the peace table and reap the benefits. And they have come. Over fifteen Arab nations for a time established some sort of relationship with Israel after the signing of the Oslo agreement. The consequences were perceived to be the increased arrogance on the part of the Israeli government. Many in the area feel that the Islamists were vindicated, that Israel does not want peace but pacification and the legalization of its acquisition of the rest of the land of the Palestinians with the indigenous population relegated to isolated Bantustans, while Yasser Arafat, the president of the Palestinian Authority, is seen as the enforcer for Israeli security interests. As one Islamist put it, "The Peace Process turned out to be the process by which Israel acquires Palestinian land piece by piece by piece."

The peace process engaged in by the Clinton administration was suspect from the beginning because the diplomats charged with shepherding it through were from the Israeli lobby and were working in support of Israel's interest. Not one had an Arab background; hence there was an underestimation of what the Palestinians, Arabs, and Muslims would find acceptable. At issue was the fact that the Arabs believed that they had given up all they could at Madrid. They had accepted Israel within its 1967 borders, relinquishing 78 percent of original Palestine for the Jewish state. But Israel wanted more land. It wanted to maintain settlements established on confiscated land in the West Bank and Jerusalem, a policy which is in violation of international law as set by the Geneva Convention and reiterated by a variety of UN resolutions. This was justified as necessary because of its security needs, that it was the dream of generations of Jews who had suffered during the Holocaust, and that Israel had won the war. To the Islamists, such demands were seen not only as excessive greed but in a very profound way as an unjust solution to the problem.

Arabs argue that it is unjust to expect the Palestinian Christians and Muslims to relinquish their rights to their lands and homes in order to satisfy Israel's expansionist security needs. That would reward Israel for what the Arabs call its War of Aggression (of 1967). If the argument is that Israel had won it by war, that in the final analysis might makes right, they say then the Arabs should wait until a new generation is able to rise and become strong enough to take it back. If Israel's acquisition of land is based on religious justification that 16 million Jews consider Jerusalem as the religious center of their life, they question why the sentiments of 1.3 billion Muslims about Jerusalem are not being taken into consideration. They question why Judaism is being privileged. If the argument is that God had promised the land in the Hebrew scriptures, they question why the Qur'an, the final revelation of God, which sees that the Jews will be dispersed throughout the world, is not taken into consideration.

US FOREIGN POLICY AND THE GEORGE W. BUSH ADMINISTRATION

Muslims expected a more equitable policy from the George W. Bush administration. During the presidential debates, he had questioned the use of racial profiling legislated by the Clinton administration that had targeted Arab-Americans. Furthermore, in the estimation of Arab- and Muslim-Americans, a change in administration would remove the Israeli lobby from the center of policymaking because the lobby was instrumental in defeating his father's bid for reelection (because it did not forgive his policy of demanding a halt to the construction and expansion of settlements on the West Bank). Consequently, George W. received the endorsement of the major Muslim and Arab organizations, and a large number of Arabs and Muslims in the United States registered and voted for the first time, accounting for 2 percent of the votes that the Bush-Cheney ticket received. Muslims believe that their votes were the decisive margin in Florida. They had not paid attention to the promises he had made to the Zionist lobby.

From the beginning, President Bush wanted to keep his hands off the Arab-Israeli conflict. In the process, he allowed the Israeli authorities to continue to grind down the Palestinian resistance to the occupation. His public and highly publicized refusal to meet with Yasser Arafat, while repeatedly welcoming Prime Minister Sharon to the White House, sent an important message to Islamists demonstrating that he was in total support of Israel and its policies. Whenever the Palestinians reacted to Israeli aggression, Bush blamed Arafat and the Palestinians. Such open support of Sharon infuriated Muslims and Arabs overseas since Sharon is particularly reviled because he is implicated in three massacres perpetrated against the Palestinians.

Then there was the 9/11 attack on the World Trade Center in New York and the Pentagon in Virginia, and Americans asked "Why do they hate us?" Osama bin Laden's statement provided an answer that few US policymakers wanted to hear. He identified our foreign policy vis-à-vis the Arab-Israeli conflict, our containment of Iraq that has degraded the life of the Iraqi people and led to their suffering, and the presence of US troops in the Gulf that maintains American hegemony in the area and supports autocratic regimes. His message was blunted by a parade of former US policymakers, diplomats, and army brass who appeared on American television stations around the clock to assure the American public that they hate us because of our "democracy," our "culture," and our "values." And as Raghida Dergham of the Lebanese daily *al-Hayat* has said, not one dared tell the American people that "It is the policy, stupid."

Since 9/11, the Bush administration has been engaged in rooting out terrorists in the world. To his credit, President Bush has reached out to the Arab- and Muslim-American communities and has assured them that the war the United States is waging is not against Islam but is against terrorism. He has called on the American people not to take out their anger and frustration on American Muslims. At the same time, his administration has incarcerated more than 5,000 Arabs and Muslims using the hastily legislated Patriot Act. Racial profiling of Arabs abounds. Meanwhile, there has been very little movement in adjusting US foreign policy to demonstrate more evenhandedness and justice. The Bush administration is caught in a double bind: If it alters its policies, it could be perceived as giving the terrorists a victory; at the same time, the constant blaming of Arafat for the bloodshed in Israel/Palestine and the daily saber-rattling about removing Saddam Hussein from Iraq have raised questions about US sincerity. The majority of Muslims overseas believe that the United States has declared war on Islam. Many question whether current policies are raising a new generation of Islamists who will seek to avenge what they perceive to be a war on Islam despite the assurances by the Bush administration to the contrary. They continue to await justice for the Palestinians.

CHAPTER 20

AMERICAN POWER AND THE MIDDLE EAST

Mark Huband

In this chapter, journalist Mark Huband contends that, instead of a policy committed to partnerships in the Middle East, the United States has pursued a policy of unilateral actions in the region, notably with regard to Iraq and the Israeli-Palestinian issue. As a result, whatever rapport the United States has developed with selected Arab leaderships (as in Egypt, Saudi Arabia, and Kuwait) is increasingly vulnerable to deep popular antagonisms felt toward US influence and the US-Israeli alliance.

It is important to understand, says Huband, that the primary aim of US conservatives has not been to create the conditions for Arab-Israeli peace but rather to sustain Israel as a pro-US island in the Middle East, thus subordinating the interests of the region to those of the United States. Though US policy is usually couched in terms of increased "freedom" and "democracy," a truer freedom of the press in the region would probably mean the expression of even more strident popular resentment of the United States, and truer democracy would likely make Islamists a major power bloc in key countries.

With regard to Iraq, the links between Saddam Hussein and al-Qaeda and other terrorists had been greatly exaggerated to begin with, meaning that the benefits of conducting the 2003 Iraq war as part of a global war on terror have fallen far short of assurances. But the war was not really about Iraq in any case, but about Saudi Arabia. The attacks of 9/11 opened American eyes to the deep-rooted loathing of the United States in the Saudi kingdom, and the financial support available there for al-Qaeda. Seizing Iraq and its oil was a rational US strategy to reduce American dependence on Saudi Arabian reserves.

On the Israel-Palestine issue, there can be no expectation of success in US-led diplomacy while the United States plays both arbiter and one-sided ally. On the one hand, the United States has historically sought the role of mediator between Israelis and Palestinians but on the other it has provided billions of dollars in loans underwriting Israel's illegal settlement building, and it never votes against Israel in the United Nations.

Mark Huband *is security correspondent for the* Financial Times *(London). He is the author of* Warriors of the Prophet: The Struggle for Islam *as well as* Brutal Truths, Fragile Myths: Western Adventurism in the Arab World, *from which this chapter derives.*

BETWEEN THE LAUNCH OF THE WAR AGAINST AL-QAEDA in October 2001 and that against Iraq eighteen months later, the rise to prominence of ideologues capable only of speaking the language of conflict with the Arab world allowed the Bush administration to construct a matrix of excuses in place of a Middle East policy. In an article entitled "Forget the 'Arab Street,'" Reuel Marc Gerecht of the alarming and sinister American Enterprise Institute think tank in Washington—from which the administration of George W. Bush has seconded some twenty advisers to work in various government departments—wrote in April 2002:

> The administration that has done so much to reverse the image of American weakness in the Muslim Middle East—weakness that is the jet fuel behind the appeal of bin Ladenism in the Arab world—may well deal, quite unintentionally, a severe blow to America's *hayba*, the majesty and magnetism that inhere in unchallengeable power. Without this mystique, there is no guarantee of peace and security for us and our friends in the region.

> If this happens in the next few months, it will be a very good idea for Bush and company to march to Baghdad as quickly as possible. They'll need to do something stunning to reverse America's fortunes and keep the suicide bombers from our gates.[1]

Today, America's "friends in the region" can be counted on only one finger: Israel. With every other country in the Arab world still awaiting the long-term consequences of the invasion of Iraq, even relatively long-term allies like Egypt, Jordan, and Kuwait are aware that the inconsistencies in their relations with the United States cannot be obscured forever. The unraveling will emerge from the contradictions inherent in the exercise of American power in the region. While the United States sought partners in the region—in pursuit of oil, peace between the Palestinians and Israelis, trade development, and the longer-term goals of fostering religious harmony in a region whose resonance is global—it was possible for the military, diplomatic, and economic power it invested to bolster its Arab interlocutors to act as a counterweight to the deep popular resistance to American goals. Now, the United States has only one partner in the region, as the "peace process" in which it was able to engage the region as a catalyst has collapsed, and the rapport it had developed with selected Arab leaderships is increasingly vulnerable to the deep popular antagonism felt toward US influence and the US–Israeli alliance.

The awful success of the September 11, 2001, terrorist attacks in New York and Washington was in part the success of American power being challenged. America's weakness and failure were exposed for all to see. The Bush administration's response was to construct a wholly self-serving security policy, requiring all the countries of the world to wrap themselves in the straitjacket of US interests. Many regimes—not least in the Arab world—saw some advantage to themselves in doing so, attacking dissident groups and silencing dissent under cover of the "war on terror," free from the accusation that they were engaged in human rights abuses by the fact of their once biggest critic—the United States—having become the most enthusiastic supporter of their robust actions. But just as the US alliance with the soldier-kings and potentates of the region has long been fraught with dangerous contradictions, the new alliance can only be temporary, as interests diverge and the social currents of the Arab world divorce the United States from what is really taking place beneath the surface.

The primary aim of US conservatives is not to create the conditions for Arab–Israeli peace but to build a pro-US island in the Middle East. All countries seek allies around the world. The United States is not exceptional in wanting a genuine ally in the Middle East, as opposed to relations with Arab states like Saudi Arabia that are based purely on the need for oil and the expansion of the market for US and UK arms manufacturers. But in seeking to build up Israel so that it may "transcend" the Arab–Israeli conflict, US conservatives have created in their minds ambitions that have replaced the interests of the region with those of the United States.

The ambitions harbored by US conservatives and the interests of Israel itself are not easy bedfellows, do not guarantee Israel's long-term future, and ignore altogether the fact that the US tendency to see the entire Middle East through the prism of the Palestinian–Israeli conflict has created a warped and superficial attitude toward the Arab world, its complexity, and its diversity. The fellows of the American Enterprise Institute—to whom President George W. Bush has paid regular homage—today provide clear signs of the myopia now stalking official thinking. The new lease on life given to the American Right by the September

11 terrorist attacks has given them carte blanche to accuse any opponent of Israeli strategy of being a terrorist.

The relevance of Arab public opinion is meanwhile a major challenge facing American foreign policy professionals seeking to influence administration strategy on the Middle East. State control of the media in much of the Arab world—either through ownership or less direct influence—is cited as a reason for arguing that ordinary Arabs would be less opposed to Israel if they had the "freedom" to think for themselves and enjoyed Western-style democracy and press freedom. In fact the opposite is probably true; the Arab press generally reflects the Arab view of Israel, whether it be the views of governments or "the street." In Egypt, for example, popular anti-Israeli opinion is probably far more strident than that expressed in state-owned media that occasionally fall little short of being anti-Semitic. If there were democracy in the Arab world, it is likely that Islamists would become the major power bloc in key countries, making the prospect of Israel's acceptance in the region even less likely.

On the other side, it is an important part of the Israeli and pro-Israel propaganda machine to identify all Arabs—governments and peoples—as roughly similar, and in particular to daub them all as either actual or potential terrorists. In its June 9, 2003, "Middle East Report," the American Israel Public Affairs Committee—known by its acronym AIPAC—which leads Israel's lobbying efforts in the United States, reported the following: "Arab countries have demonstrated an unwillingness to truly combat the suicide bombings and other attacks against Israeli citizens."[2] In view of the fact that the demise of Saddam Hussein in Iraq two months earlier was supposed to have removed the vital conduit for Palestinian terrorist backing, the apparently ongoing support from other "Arab countries" is baffling; Israel has yet to provide any evidence that Palestinian suicide bombers are continuing—if they ever did—to receive assistance from other Arab countries. Moreover, the sweeping generalization failed to identify whether, in the absence of Saddam Hussein, it was now Jordan, Egypt, Morocco, Qatar, Oman, or others—countries that had sought to improve their ties with Israel when Israel had appeared ready to make peace—that were now providing assistance to terrorists bent on destroying Israel. The paper did not say, leaving the impression that all Arabs are the same.

The role of AIPAC as a lobbyist has focused on demonizing the Arabs. It presents a version of history intended to minimize understanding within the United States of the motivation behind Arab actions and responses to Israeli actions. Its chronological account of Arab–Israeli relations[3] is intended to show

Israel as the party ready for peace and the Palestinians as embarked on inexplicable acts of violence. It is blunt in its assessment that "peace is not possible without firm American backing for Israel. Israel's potential peace partners must know that the bond between the U.S. and Israel is unbreakable, even if there are occasional disagreements. . . . Israel must negotiate from a position of strength backed up by U.S. aid."[4] The view is reciprocal; at a March 2003 AIPAC conference, Condoleeza Rice, the U.S. national security adviser, stated:

> AIPAC is an important advocate for strong friendship between the United States and Israel and is, thus, a great asset to our country because we share so much with Israel, but most importantly we share values. You can have lots of friends, but friends who share your values are the ones who are most steadfast and most important, and I want to thank you for your support of our good friend, Israel.[5]

In the same speech to AIPAC, Rice drew clear linkages between the fate of Israel and the war in Iraq, which by then had been advancing for ten days, telling her audience:

> We will help Iraqis build institutions that are democratic that protect the rights of all Iraqi citizens. . . . A free Iraq can, after all, add momentum to reform throughout the Middle East. . . . We should join hands with those in the Middle East who want to build a different future for the Middle East. . . . We see signs that this new thinking also extends to a new generation of Palestinian leaders and it is one of the reasons that President Bush is very hopeful that success in Iraq can set a new stage for Middle Eastern peace.[6]

In fact the Bush administration's focus on the Israeli–Palestinian issue as a part of the post–Iraq war framework—which suffered from the same chaos and ineptitude as all aspects of the postwar planning for Iraq itself—emerged largely at the insistence of UK Prime Minister Tony Blair. Blair's government did not regard the overthrow of Saddam Hussein as having created a Middle East "peace dividend" similar to that which prevailed at the end of the Cold War and out of which the Madrid conference on the Palestinian–Israeli conflict emerged. Instead, officials in London knew that to retain credibility in the eyes of regional governments, from their new interlocutors like Syria, Libya, and Iran to established allies in Egypt and Jordan, they had to seek ways of diluting deep popular distrust of the West in the region, by accelerating improvements in the lot of the Palestinians.

The problem for the Bush administration in creating the link as it did—between Iraq, Palestine, Israel, and international terrorism—was that these were connections it needed to conjure up to justify launching the war that overthrew Saddam Hussein. But as has emerged since, the links were spurious: Saddam's role as a backer of terrorism was not of such importance that his overthrow has removed a major impediment to Israeli–Palestinian peace, as his financial gifts to the families of Palestinian suicide bombers are far from proven to have inspired more attacks on Israelis; nor did he have links to al-Qaeda. Saddam was a limited threat within the region, and no real threat to the United States at all. The true extent of his threat to Israel is also likely to remain potential, though it is probable that he would have turned the potential into reality if he had had the means. But he did not.

The United States thus has far less capital to draw upon from its "victory" in Iraq than its prewar positions suggested. The reason for this is simple: The war was not really about Iraq at all, but about Saudi Arabia. When the US Congress on July 25, 2003, issued its 858-page report on the intelligence failures that had permitted the nineteen hijackers to launch the September 11, 2001, attacks, twenty-eight pages mostly referring to Saudi Arabia were deleted from the public version and have remained secret.[7] Clearly there is a great deal the US government wishes to hide about the extent to which its relations with the kingdom have collapsed. The fact that fifteen of the hijackers were Saudis was a thunderbolt striking US attitudes toward Saudi Arabia. While Saddam Hussein was an irritation in the region, the imposition of no-fly zones over parts of Iraq, the strict embargoes imposed on the regime in the wake of the 1991 Gulf war, and deep distrust of Saddam and his henchmen felt by Arabs across the region had reduced the threat to one of potentialities rather than realities. In the wake of the September 11 attacks, however, Saudi Arabia emerged as a much greater threat—the extent of financial support for al-Qaeda emanating from within the kingdom, and the deep-rooted loathing there of the United States, having become clear. The September 11 attacks transformed Saudi financial power, oil reserves, and facilities for key US military installations in the region from features of a US–Saudi alliance into potential weapons of war. The subsequent US strategy has been nothing but rational from the perspective of US national interests: reducing its reliance upon Saudi Arabia by greatly diminishing its military presence there, relocating its facilities, and—most important—seizing Iraq and its oil resources to reduce reliance on Saudi reserves.

US in Iraq to get off Saudi oil + bases?

RED LINES

For most Arab states, the US agenda is not based on responding to regional needs but on determining those needs, as President Bush made clear on June 24, 2002, when he firmly placed all aspects of the Palestinian response to Israel's aggression into the category of "terror," which now strikes such a powerful chord with the American public. In demanding that Palestinians replace Yasser Arafat, Bush sought to blackmail the Palestinians into ending their resistance to Israeli aggression, and made only a feeble request that Israel halt the settlement building that lies behind so much of the anger among Palestinians. Bush effectively demanded the capitulation of the Palestinians to US and Israeli demands if they ever wanted to secure their own state, portraying the Palestinians as the cause of the violence that had raged since September 28, 2000, when Ariel Sharon found a way to promote antagonism by visiting the Muslim holy site *Haram al-Sharif* [Temple Mount], making clear that it would never become part of a Palestinian state.

Much of what Rice and Bush have said about how to resolve the Israeli–Palestinian issue has been said before; the main distinction has been in exploiting the post–September 11 atmosphere as a means of levering Yasser Arafat out of the way, to engineer the installation of a Palestinian leadership that will be less "obstructive" and will therefore make even more concessions to Israel than Arafat was prepared to do. But instead of creating new conditions for peace, such a strategy can only create the conditions in which bad deals may be signed under duress, inevitably creating the conditions for further conflict, as has been seen in the rise of Hamas [a militant Palestinian organization].

The reasons for the failure of previous agreements must be forensically examined and frankly recognized, if the most recent proposal—the "road map" presented by the "Quartet" of the United States, the European Union, the United Nations, and Russia on April 30, 2003—is to be rescued from collapse. Bush, in his June 24, 2002, speech, said: "A Palestinian state will never be created by terror. It will be built through reform. And reform must be more than cosmetic change or a veiled attempt to preserve the status quo."[8] Bush clearly held the incumbent Palestinian Authority responsible for the failure to build a state, and in so doing exposed how deeply partisan the United States is, and how deeply attached it remains to the game plan first put in place by the Netanyahu government in 1996.

In an effort to flesh out his charade of seeking "peace with security," Netanyahu was forced to go through the motions of negotiations when he met Arafat at Wye Plantation in Maryland in October 1998. The agreement, signed

on October 23, was intended to address two key issues: Israeli anxiety over security and the need of the Palestinians to secure enough territory on which to create a viable state. The agreement provided for Israel to withdraw from 13 percent of the West Bank and bound the two sides to negotiate further withdrawals
at final status talks scheduled to be held by May 4, 1999. In return, the Palestinian Authority would combat terrorist organizations, prevent illegal weapons distribution, and amend articles in the Palestinian National Charter that
Netanyahu viewed as threatening aggression toward Israel. The accord was in
effect part of the piecemeal series of interim agreements begun after Oslo,
intended to build up to the final status negotiations, which would deal with
Jerusalem, water arrangements, and the return of Palestinian refugees.

Even if fully implemented, the Wye accord would have meant that Israel
retained control of 82 percent of the West Bank, while 400,000 Israeli settlers
would have maintained their presence on 180 illegal settlements in the Occupied
Territories. It was not surprising that the agreement was widely criticized: Palestinians said the land from which Israeli troops would withdraw was regarded as
grossly inadequate, and would anyway remain subject to Israeli security control.
On the Israeli side, half of Netanyahu's cabinet opposed Wye. These pressures
meant it was doomed to fail. In December 1998, as his government was beginning its head-long plunge toward electoral defeat, Netanyahu canceled all Israeli
troop withdrawals after accusing the Palestinian Authority of failing to register
or confiscate illegal weapons or outlaw the "support structure" of terrorist organizations, despite the US administration's recognition that it had taken action
against terrorist activity.

Five months later, Netanyahu had fallen from power, replaced by the former
army chief of staff and Israel's most decorated soldier, Ehud Barak, who secured 56
percent of the votes. "The new government of Israel has clear guidelines. We are
not going to build new settlements and we are not going to dismantle ones,"[9] Barak
told the gathering of skeptical reporters—myself among them—in Alexandria,
while President Mubarak of Egypt stood beside him listening intently to see if the
man who had ousted Netanyahu would deliver on the promises his predecessor
never saw as his responsibility to keep. In fact, new homes for twenty-two thousand settlers were built in the Occupied Territories during the Barak premiership.
Barak asserted that he would implement the Wye accord signed and then canceled
by Netanyahu, on the basis that "Israel abides by international agreements."[10]
However, he remained vague about how he would pursue this commitment, and
did not commit the new government to halting the expansion of existing settlements. Moreover, he made clear that there were "red lines" that Israel would not

cross, the key one being that Israel would not withdraw to its 1967 border, that "Greater Jerusalem, the eternal capital of Israel, will remain united and complete under the sovereignty of Israel,"[11] and that Jewish settlements would remain in "Judea, Samaria and Gaza."[12] Thus, Barak made clear that UN resolutions would be ignored, and that the foundation of the dialogue with the Palestinians was doomed to fail from the start, as the right to build a real state in the West Bank and Gaza was clearly not going to be the result.

Opponents of the peace process throughout the 1990s have clearly sought to undermine it by using violence, as in the case of the Palestinian suicide bombers or Israeli extremists such as [Prime Minister Yitzhak] Rabin's assassin, Yigal Amir, or the murderer of Palestinian worshippers, Baruch Goldstein, at the Hebron mosque. The horrifying violence has shaken—as it is intended to do—both sides, as actions and reprisals spiral and confidence is lost. The readiness or not to keep an eye on the bigger picture has varied according to the agendas of successive political players in the awful drama. Netanyahu demanded rigid Palestinian Authority adherence to every letter of every agreement—while ignoring Israel's own obligations—largely to slow the process. In a crisp assessment of both sides' strategies for the interim period between Oslo and the planned final status negotiations, Robert Malley, President Clinton's special assistant for Arab–Israeli affairs, and Hussein Agha of Oxford University wrote in 2002:

> Lacking a clear and distinct vision of where they were heading, both sides treated the interim period not as a time to prepare for an ultimate agreement but as a mere warm-up to the final negotiations; not as a chance to build trust, but as an opportunity to optimize their bargaining positions. As a result, each side was determined to hold on to its assets until the endgame. Palestinians were loath to confiscate weapons or clamp down on radical groups; Israelis were reluctant to return territory or halt settlement construction. Grudging behavior by one side fueled grudging behavior by the other, leading to a vicious cycle of skirted obligations, clear-cut violations, and mutual recriminations.

> By multiplying the number of obligations each side agreed to, the successive interim accords increased the potential for missteps and missed deadlines. Each interim agreement became the focal point for the next dispute and a microcosm for the overall conflict. . . . Yet another interim agreement could not cure ills that are inherent in the culture of interim agreements. . . . As all

these factors suggest, the current confrontation is not an argument in favor of acting small, but rather a call to start thinking big.[13]

CAMP DAVID 2000

After just over a year in power, Ehud Barak sat down with Yasser Arafat and President Clinton at Camp David in Maryland on July 11, 2000, for what the Israeli leader described as "the moment of truth."[14] Fifteen days later, President Clinton emerged from the marathon negotiating sessions to announce: "I have concluded with regret that they will not be able to reach an agreement at this time."[15]

The process of peacemaking during the Clinton years is seen by some as having had as its central premise US power—pax Americana—rather than a durable peace between the parties. As Stephen Zunes of San Francisco University, a former executive director of the Institute for a New Middle East Policy, wrote during the Netanyahu premiership:

As long as Am is looking out for the rus no peace

> Most observers believe true peace requires a comprehensive settlement to the Arab–Israeli conflict, a dramatic reduction in military expenditure, and support for democratization and human rights. US policy in the 1990s worked contrary to these goals—that is, with American economic and strategic interests in the region taking precedent—which means that a comprehensive peace which allows the region to form its own terms was impossible.[16]

Zunes identifies the Clinton administration as being "the first in US history to see the West Bank and Gaza as disputed territories, insinuating that the Israelis and Palestinians had equal claim to the land, rather than the view of the UN and others in the international community which continued to recognize East Jerusalem and other lands gained during the Israeli advances in 1967 as territory under foreign military occupation."[17] As a result, wrote Zunes, more than a year before the failure of the July 2000 Camp David talks:

> It was inevitable that a Clinton Administration-directed peace process would not lead to a settlement meeting legitimate Palestinian demands for self-determination. Rather, the goal seemed to be the establishment of economic and political structures that would severely limit the [Palestinian

Authority] *vis-à-vis* Israel and thus lead to virtual continuation of Israeli control.[18]

The failure at Camp David was the clearest evidence that the foundation of discussion had to change fundamentally if negotiation was to bring a solution to the conflict. It was a major blow to the longer-term negotiating process that Barak and Clinton insisted on holding Arafat solely responsible for the collapse of the talks, by blaming him for his failure to accept Israeli proposals that he— and they—knew he could not sell to the Palestinians. The trust that some had thought had replaced the suspicion prevailing throughout the Netanyahu years disintegrated, as Israel and the United States in concert took to blaming the Palestinians for apparently being "not ripe for peace."[19]

From the Palestinian perspective, the inadequacy of the Israeli proposals was as pronounced as the readiness of the Palestinians to make concessions. As the official Palestinian assessment of what was offered makes clear, "Israel's Camp David proposal presented a 're-packaging' of military occupation, not an end to military occupation."[20] On the key issue of Jerusalem—the issue specified by Barak as the cause of the talks collapsing—the Palestinian position was that the Israeli proposals "would create Palestinian ghettos in the heart of Jerusalem,"[21] which "would remain separated not only from each other but also from the rest of the Palestinian state."[22] Meanwhile, the Palestinian state envisaged by Barak was to have been divided into five noncontiguous areas, four in the West Bank split from each other by access roads leading to Israeli settlements, and the fifth covering the area of the Gaza Strip. The movement of people and economic activity between them would be under Israeli control, and "such a Palestinian state would have had less sovereignty and viability than the Bantustans created by the South African apartheid regime," the PLO [Palestine Liberation Organization] argued.[23]

Finally, on the question of the return of Palestinian refugees—and their descendants—forced out of the area when Israel was created, the Palestinian view was that the issue was never seriously discussed at Camp David because Barak "declared that Israel bore no responsibility for the refugee problem or its solution." But the Palestinian view remained clear that any settlement must include an agreement on the rights of the refugees, which would include addressing Israeli concerns that any right of return would be negotiated, and that Palestinian refugees might claim land and property seized from them by Israel in 1948. Instead, the issue was sidestepped.

MYTHS AND MAPS

Clinton's failure at Camp David was just that: a failure of US diplomacy. There can be no expectation of success in US-led diplomacy in the Israeli–Palestinian conflict while the US plays both arbiter and one-sided ally. It was Clinton's own failure—and that of the United States as a world power capable of wielding influence in a manner that drew upon what it knew of the world rather than what it would like to see serving its own interests—that was at the heart of the problem. The reasons for the failure at Camp David have subsequently been subject to the most outrageous manipulation by those involved, adding vast amounts of fuel to an already raging fire; by blaming Arafat, both Clinton and Barak further undermined the Palestinian leader and lent huge credibility to the incoming government of Ariel Sharon in its subsequently near successful campaign to force Arafat out of the picture altogether. There is something vengeful about the way Clinton and Barak—both of whom have applauded each other's roles in the discussions—have misrepresented Arafat's approach during the talks as a way of concealing the true extent to which US bias toward Israel has failed both Palestinians and Israelis by failing to play a genuine role as arbiter.

The presidency of George W. Bush has seen the myths of the Israeli–Palestinian conflict take on far more importance than the realities. President Bush clarified his administration's approach in a June 24, 2002, speech. The speech laid blame for the failure to achieve peace squarely on the structure of the Palestinian administration, and thus on Arafat, the embattled Palestinian leader who had watched Israeli tanks blast all but a few rooms of his Ramallah headquarters to dust while he was inside. Israel was blameless, according to Bush, and Palestinian suffering was something that the president said he understood as being the result of their having "been treated as pawns in the Middle East conflict. Your interests have been held hostage to a comprehensive peace agreement that never seems to come," he said. Clearly, in Bush's view all the Arab states that had ever involved themselves in Palestinian affairs were to blame for the Palestinian predicament, while the one country whose ambitions had forced Palestinians off their land had played no part in creating the suffering that had brought with it anger and violence.

Bush's warped perspective and unlimited bias against the Palestinians mean that the US role in the search for peace between Israelis and Palestinians will hinder rather than help. With this in mind, the "road map" agreed to in October 2002, the sidelining of Arafat, and the installation of Mahmoud Abbas as a short-lived Israeli- and US-approved Palestinian prime minister are elements riddled with familiar shortcomings. The determination of the Bush administration to identify the Palestinian character as being the main fault line—rather than as being the consequence of the crisis—is a major weakness in the process. Pressuring the Abbas administration to tailor its functions to Israeli requirements will edge the underlying reality of the Palestinians' plight further outside the negotiating process.

Despite the United States' ability to remain active, convene meetings, and appear involved, its efforts have failed at most stages, if considered in their own terms. All US administrations have sought to portray their initiatives as historic, when in fact they have ended up being part of a painfully slow and incremental process of building ties between the opposing sides. The US role has been dominated by words rather than deeds and by a search for a US place in history that distinguishes it from all other nations on the basis of its intellectual weight rather than merely its financial and military resources. But the United States has often been responsible for undermining its capacity to achieve this status. On the one hand, it has sought the role of "sponsor" and arbiter, but on the other it has provided the loan guarantees for illegal settlement building—$9 billion more of which were agreed to with Israel on August 20, 2003—and does nothing to discourage American Jews from going to live illegally in the Occupied Territories; it provides the military equipment Israel routinely unleashes on Palestinians; and it never votes against Israel at the United Nations.

The Palestinian Authority has had no choice but to accept a US role, despite Washington's bias against it, for the simple reason that no other body has presented itself as a viable alternative as mediator. However, US credibility should not be seen as invincible. Foreign policy failure has been the hallmark of the Bush administration since its election. Compensating for that failure is what lies behind the launch of the "Global War on Terror" or GWOT, as well as the creation of the entirely spurious "Axis of Evil" and the plan to lead the political transformation of the entire Middle East. But circumstance rather than vision has lain behind the Bush project since September 11, 2001, the administration's image being that of a militaristic roller coaster that is out of control rather than a political force equipped with credible and durable plans for global betterment.

The consequences of diplomatic failures to which the United States has been integral have brought a growing need to widen the scope of discussions and bring more players into the equation in more than the symbolic roles the United States allots to the "Quartet." The initial isolationism that the Bush administration has been forced to dilute in pursuit of its own security interests has been a key element in this shift. The "war against terror" has brought the most vehement Middle Eastern enemies of Islamism into the open as potential allies of the United States, among them Libya and Syria. Both, from the Islamists' perspective, are regimes that are vulnerable to criticism as human rights abusers. President Bush's "you're either with us or you're with the terrorists" choice was foisted on Arab regimes, who for a very short time hoped for leverage over US policy in return for their commitment. But even America's long-term allies—Egypt, Jordan, and Morocco—have secured no additional leverage, particularly on the vital issue that concerns them all: the Israeli–Palestinian conflict. The regimes have now been left empty-handed, a fact from which their domestic political opponents will draw invaluable political capital.

This scenario is a familiar one to the Arab world, the history of Arab relations with Europe and the United States being littered with similar episodes of Western opportunism. It is the core reason why bin Laden and others like him will cement division with the West, on the basis that it is duplicitous and cannot be trusted. If the United States were evenhanded in its treatment of the Israeli–Palestinian conflict and went further, for example, than calling the killing by Israeli aerial bombardment of fourteen Palestinians—among them nine children—in Gaza in July 2002 merely "heavy-handed," if the war in Iraq had been portrayed as being in Arab as well as US, UK, and Israeli interests, then the waves from the Middle Eastern epicenter of the al-Qaeda network would have less global resonance and bin Laden's task would be more difficult. Instead, distrust of US motives has escalated, with the fault lines appearing both *within* the West and beyond, intensifying debate within the United States over whether the superpower knows what to do with its power.

CHAPTER 21

THE CONTEMPORARY
MIDDLE EAST

Some Questions, Some Answers

Shibley Telhami

In this question-and-answer essay, Shibley Telhami addresses many issues facing both the United States and the nations of the Middle East. He points out, for example, that the US occupation of Iraq has had the unintended consequence of turning Iraq into a breeding ground for al-Qaeda and other terrorist groups. The fight against al-Qaeda is not, or at least should not be, primarily a military concern; it should be instead a political struggle to ally the United States with the majority of Muslims who, while they may dislike the United States, nonetheless do not support al-Qaeda. Sectarian issues in Iraq, notably the possibility of a strengthened relationship between Iraq's Shiite Arabs with Shiite Iran, contribute to Iraq's uncertain future. Iran is in the unusual position of having an interest both in supporting the new Shiite-dominated regime in Iraq and in supporting the Sunni insurgency against that US-supported regime. Controversially, perhaps, Telhami endorses announcing a relatively short timetable for withdrawing US troops from Iraq.

US advocacy of democracy in the Middle East needs to be supported by an open and consistent promotion of human rights, balanced pragmatically with ongoing American strategic interests. With regard to the Palestinian issue, the United States can help most by providing economic and political aid to the Palestinian Authority, and by assuring Palestinians about a final-status resolution that addresses the issues of Palestinian state boundaries, the fate of Jewish settlements on the West Bank, the rights of Palestinian refugees, Israeli security concerns, and the distribution of scarce water resources. It remains to be seen if negotiations that appeal to their nationalist and political goals can successfully dissuade Hamas and Hezbollah from continued violence so that they might assume peaceful roles in open elections.

Shibley Telhami *is Anwar Sadat Professor for Peace and Development at the* *University of Maryland, a Non-Resident Senior Fellow at the Saban Center at the* *Brookings Institution, and a member of the Council on Foreign Relations. A frequent* *radio, television, and newspaper commentator on the Middle East, he is the author of* Reflections of Hearts and Minds: Media, Opinion, *and* Identity in the Arab World *and* The Stakes: America in the Middle East: The Consequences of Power and the Choice for Peace.

How has the Iraq war affected the political landscape of the Middle East and America's standing therein?

To begin with, no one in Washington would have imagined that with all the human and financial costs of the war, the United States would find itself supporting a government headed by an Islamist, Prime Minister Ibrahim al-Jaafari, whose power depends on the blessing of a Grand Ayatollah, Ali al-Sistani, who has close ties to Iran and who would sign a military agreement with Tehran for the training of Iraqi forces, even as over 130,000 US troops remained on Iraqi soil.

Certainly much of this is the outcome of the surprising insurgency, which remains mostly Iraqi. (Of the 1,700 hundred suspected insurgents recently detained by American forces, only 51 were foreigners.) But it is also clear that al-Qaeda and its killer allies have established themselves in a land where they had no roots before. Anarchy and instability in Iraq have turned the country into what many hoped the war would prevent: a new breeding ground for al-Qaeda and those who share its aims and methods.

But there are other surprises. Although some of the war supporters believed that the war would result in a sustained US presence in Iraq that would turn Iraq into a key US ally in the Persian Gulf and diminish the strategic importance of Saudi Arabia, there is now more realism that the American presence may, in fact, be short-lived. In part, this is the consequence of the surprising strength of the insurgency and of the American public's diminishing support for continued occupation without a clear end in sight. These factors have created another unintended consequence of the war: the perception in the Middle East and in many parts of the world that the United States is weaker in the short term than it was before the war.

Although some in Washington had argued that the United States would emerge empowered by the war in a way that would translate into leverage with other states, the assessment that the United States is now stretched too thin in Iraq has led states like Iran and North Korea to conclude that the United States is not likely to wage war against them any time soon, and thus to accelerate their nuclear programs. The difficulties in Iraq have also meant that the United States is learning that it must rely on others in the international community more than it had previously realized. In relations with European governments as well as countries in the Middle East such as Saudi Arabia and Egypt that the US is trying to influence, the tone of US foreign policy has lately been far more cooperative and multilateral than the unilateralism expressed before the war.

HOW SERIOUS IS THE THREAT OF AL-QAEDA TODAY?

Al-Qaeda and its allies remain a major threat. Whatever the original causes for its existence, al-Qaeda's objective is to destroy the existing order in the Arab and Muslim world and to create a puritanical Islamist state. It sees the United States as the anchor of the order it seeks to overthrow. While it cares about Islamic issues such as the Palestinian-Israeli conflict and Iraq, it is hard to imagine that any realistic and fair outcome on these issues would satisfy its aspirations. In that sense the conflict with this group is zero-sum and that makes it very dangerous. I have little doubt that this group will use any method available to it, including weapons of mass destruction. While its members may be relatively few in number, it is clearly still strong and capable of carrying out attacks, and the new training grounds in Iraq provide it with additional capabilities. So it is not unreasonable to conclude that al-Qaeda remains one of the most serious threats to US security.

But the mistake made in the approach to terrorism is not in characterizing al-Qaeda. It is in not realizing that the fight against al-Qaeda requires a strategy toward the majority of Muslims and others who are not allies of al-Qaeda but who have come to dislike the United States even more than they fear al-Qaeda. One can see in the public opinion surveys I have been conducting (with Zogby International) in six Arab countries (Saudi Arabia, Egypt, Morocco, Jordan, the United Arab Emirates, and Lebanon) that, while anti-Americanism is high in many parts of the world, it is certainly highest in Arab and Muslim countries. More troubling, however, is the public's view of American intentions. Few believe the stated objectives of the Iraq war, and the vast majorities believe that two of the primary American motives are controlling oil and helping Israel. This itself is not new. But what is distressing is that majorities now add to oil and

Israel the belief that the US intention is "to weaken the Muslim world." This may be in part responsible for the rise of what I call "Islamic nationalism." In 2004, "Islamic identity" trumped "Arab identity" and identification with the state in four of the six countries I surveyed. This does not appear to be as much a rise in puritanical religious belief as it is in Islamic nationalism. For example, when asked if they supported women's working outside the house, majorities in every single country stated that they supported women's working either always or when economically needed. When asked whom among world leaders they admired most, none of the religious fundamentalists made the top three. In fact, the top two vote getters were the late pan-Arab Egyptian leader Gamal Abd el-Nasser and the current French president, Jacques Chirac, most probably because of their perceived defiance of the United States.

But unfortunately, Osama bin Laden still has his supporters and appears on the list of top five in several countries. The real danger, however, lies not only in bin Laden's ability to recruit but also in failing to reduce the incentive for others to join the fight against him. If the war on bin Laden is perceived primarily as a war between the United States and al-Qaeda, even those who reject al-Qaeda's ways may not be rooting for the United States.

Is there a danger of larger regional conflict along Shiite-Sunni lines?

There is a sectarian problem in Iraq and the Gulf region, and it has in the past played into Saddam Hussein's hands during the Iran-Iraq war. We have to be clear, however, that the sectarian issue and its implications for Gulf states such as Saudi Arabia and Bahrain that have significant Shiite communities are only one part of the story. The other part is a genuine strategic concern in the Arab Gulf states about Iranian power, in realpolitik terms. Many in the Gulf have traditionally envisioned Iraq as the only state in the region capable in the long term of balancing Iranian dominance in the region. Today, however, they face a problem. Iraqi Sunnis, who had been the ruling minority under Saddam Hussein, have boycotted the recent Iraqi elections. But even if its new government were Sunni, Iraq is not capable of balancing Iran or anyone else in the near future. That alone is an issue of concern, even if the American military presence in the Gulf mitigates the problem in the short term. But the fear of many is that strategic worries may be exacerbated by the sectarian issue: that a Shiite-dominated government in Iraq may be inclined to become Iran's friend or, even worse, client state, leaving Iraq politically dependent on Iran. Many of these concerns are exaggerated: Iraqi Shia are Iraqi and Arab as much as Shiite, and so are not automatic allies with Iran. Nevertheless, there is much strategic uncertainty as well as confusion in the Gulf region about the best policies to pursue in this environment.

WHAT ROLES ARE IRAQ'S NEIGHBORS PLAYING IN THE IRAQ WAR?

The vast majority (more than 90 percent) of the insurgents are Iraqis. Most of the suspected insurgents killed or taken into custody are Iraqis. There is no lack of skill in the methods of war in Iraq after the dismantling of its large army whose soldiers have known nothing but war and conflict over the past two and a half decades. And we know that there are sufficient munitions that have gone missing from Iraqi stockpiles to last the insurgency for many years to come. So the primary threat to the US presence in Iraq today is local, not international, even if it is also true that al-Qaeda terrorists have also taken root there.

There is no question that it has become easier for groups to infiltrate into Iraq since the war. By far the most important reason for this is the collapse of the Iraqi army, the state of anarchy, and the insufficient number of US and international troops immediately after the war to police the borders. Undoubtedly, many have infiltrated from Syria, Saudi Arabia, Iran, and Jordan—Iraq's neighbors. Even Jordan, which has fully cooperated with the United States, allowing US special forces to operate as needed from its soil, has not been able to prevent such infiltration, or for that matter, the participation of its own citizens in the insurgency.

Saudi Arabia, Syria, and Iran have played different roles. Saudi Arabia had made a strategic decision to collaborate with the United States even as it was worried about its own popular opinion among its populace, and it has increasingly waged a campaign against al-Qaeda within its own boundaries. It is hard to know exactly how much priority it has given to policing the borders, or how much capacity it has, but it is clear that many of its citizens must be sympathetic with the insurgency in Iraq. It would be surprising if nongovernmental entities within the Saudi kingdom did not provide assistance to the insurgency. It is also easy to believe that even within the armed forces in Saudi Arabia many people are sympathetic with the insurgency, regardless of their government's official position.

In the case of Syria, which had opposed the Iraq war, even though it had been the Arab world's biggest enemy of Saddam Hussein (even siding against him in the Iran-Iraq war), there is probably much rooting for the insurgency at the public and official levels. Whether or not the Syrian government deliberately assisted the insurgents is hard to know, but it is evident that they did not mount a major effort immediately after the war to prevent movement into Iraq. Even if the governmental position increasingly shifted in the direction of limiting the movement of insurgents across the border with Iraq, that position was probably not fully enforced.

Iran's role is unique. One the one hand, Tehran cannot be unhappy with the shape of the current Iraqi government. In some ways, Tehran was a tacit ally of the United States in enabling the Iraqi elections of early 2005, knowing full well that Shiite empowerment would be the outcome. But on the other hand, it is also clear that Iran has benefited from the insurgency that brazenly challenges the current government. That insurgency has pushed the United States to accept the sort of government it would probably have rejected otherwise. More important, the insurgency has resulted in an entanglement of American forces, thus reducing the prospect of an immediate military action against Iran, which the United States has previously labeled a member of the "axis of evil," suspected of sponsoring terrorists and developing a rogue nuclear-weapons program. How Iran has balanced those interests—deciding to support either the new Shiite regime or the insurgents that challenge the regime—is not fully clear, but there is little doubt that Iran has had the capacity to employ many intelligence and operative assets in Iraq to enable it to affect the course of events in the future.

SHOULD THE UNITED STATES WITHDRAW FROM IRAQ?

In the United States, division over withdrawal from Iraq is not limited to the liberal community; even some neoconservatives now believe withdrawal may be prudent, and certainly conservatives are divided. I find myself torn between the fear that rapid American withdrawal could bring about further anarchy and civil war and the worry that a continued American presence will reduce the incentives of the local parties to move toward a lasting arrangement. Above all, I think the region and many around the world who opposed the war are torn between hoping Iraq will emerge as a stable, unified country and hoping that the United States will fail. For example, al-Qaeda is now capitalizing on the anti-American mood in Iraq and on a genuine Iraqi insurgency, but could have far fewer allies in Iraq if the United States were to remove itself from the equation there.

To my mind the best course of action is an American challenge to the Iraqi government and to the Sunni population: if a constitutional deal is struck that attracts the majority of Sunni leadership, and if elections are held in which majorities of all major communities participate, the United States would announce a timetable for withdrawal of forces and would commit significant foreign aid directly to the Iraqi government over a period of ten years. The key to success in Iraq is a national pact that incorporates the Sunnis.

In any case, I am now of the opinion that announcing a reasonable timetable (within 18 months) for the beginning of American withdrawal is more good than bad. If Iraqi forces are not significantly enhanced by then, and if the insurgency is not sufficiently weakened to allow for partial American withdrawal, the American public will surely demand an even more hasty withdrawal that could have an even higher cost. Some may argue that an announcement of a timetable for withdrawal could "embolden" the insurgents, but frankly it does not appear that the insurgents need any more incentive than the continued American presence.

DO RECENT DEVELOPMENTS SUPPORT DEMOCRACY IN THE MIDDLE EAST?

It is important to differentiate between, first, the impact of the Iraq war itself on the issue of political reform in the region and, second, the advocacy of democracy as a priority in American foreign policy, along with its actual consequences for political reform in the region. I would argue that the consequence of the Iraq war has been largely negative on the issue of reform in the Middle East in the short term, and that the consequence of the advocacy of democracy has been more positive than negative on reform in the Middle East. Let me give you examples of what I mean and how the region sees it.

In my most recent survey of Arab public opinion, I asked Arabs one year after the Iraq war if they believed that the spread of democracy was one of the American motives for invading Iraq. Large majorities in every country studied rejected this notion. Asked if they believed Iraqis were better or worse off than before the war, most said they were worse off.

One may ascribe these attitudes to the fact that most Arabs opposed the war and are therefore less inclined to see any good coming out of it. But there is also something objective that Arabs are responding to in what they saw transpire just before the war, during the war, and immediately after the war. In a situation in which 90 percent of the Arab public passionately opposed the Iraq war, believing that it went against Arab interests, Arab governments nonetheless had to make a strategic decision whether to support the United States or not—and they generally decided to support the United States. In the process they became far more insecure: they preempted political organizations, they arrested opposition leaders, and they limited the freedom of speech. In the case of Egypt, the rule of emergency law was suddenly extended on the eve of the Iraq war. That is what the public sees, and that is what the public is reacting to. In general, then, the war has clearly had a negative impact on reform, at least in the short term.

In contrast, the advocacy of democracy has had a more positive impact. The Bush administration's advocacy of democracy since the end of the war has been consequential at home and abroad, though not entirely as expected. At home, it surely served to provide a popular motive among the citizenry that helped divert attention from the administration's originally stated goal for the war: to neutralize Saddam's weapons of mass destruction—weapons that were never found. But even here at home it had another unanticipated impact. Where a clash-of-civilization thesis had dominated some of the discourse before the war, postulating a fundamental incompatibility between Islamic and Western worldviews and values, Arabs were now portrayed as a freedom-loving, democracy-yearning people like others around the world. The new and implicit argument became that, if we were simply to get rid of bad governments, the democratic impulses of the Arab people would be freed to find full expression.

In the Middle East, the advocacy of democracy has had some good effect. Because the Bush administration gave democracy such a high profile, all those seeking good relations with the United States had to offer the administration something, if only for political reasons. These governments probably don't believe that the Bush administration is advocating democracy as an end in itself. They believe instead that the Bush administration is using the issue of democracy to get strategic cooperation from them on such matters as Iraq, the war on al-Qaeda, and the Palestinian-Israeli conflict, and also to claim political credit at home. What each of them has done is give the Bush administration enough to claim political credit. The problem for the Bush administration will be that once they have moved a country from the negative ledger to the positive ledger, their hands are tied. It's politically very hard to move a newly "promoted" country back into the negative ledger.

WHAT POLICIES SHOULD THE UNITED STATES PURSUE TO PROMOTE DEMOCRACY IN THE MIDDLE EAST?

Human rights should be at the top of the priorities in advocating democracy. It is an issue over which there is a body of literature and international agreements and rulings, not just an American preference for what we happen to think is right or wrong.

There is probably room for maneuvering on human rights even with governments whose help the United States absolutely needs, including those outside the Middle East. For example, Pakistan, where the United States depends on General Pervez Musharraf in the war on al-Qaeda, is clearly an American strategic interest. There is a balance to be maintained in Pakistan between ongoing security concerns and human-rights issues. That kind of tradeoff between national-security interests and human-rights or democracy issues will always be there for US foreign policy, but I think the public in the region understands those tradeoffs at some level. If we were more open and honest about them, it would probably be better than not.

I consider credibility a fundamental issue as well. If you measure public opinion over the past several years on the question, "What has been the most important transformation in public opinion in the Arab and Muslim countries toward the United States?" you will not find a dramatic increase in the number of people who hold an unfavorable view of American foreign policy. In fact, in the 1980s and 1990s, most people in the Arab world had an unfavorable view of American foreign policy. Perhaps that sentiment is more intense now, but it is a matter of degree and not a profound change.

The real change has been a collapse of confidence, the collapse of American credibility, and we can quantify that. In the spring of 2000, a State Department survey in Saudi Arabia and the United Arab Emirates asked people whether they "had confidence in the United States of America"—not whether they liked American foreign policy or not, but whether they had confidence in it. At the time, the finding was that over 60 percent of the public expressed confidence in the United States of America. Right now, though, that measure is in the single digits.

The difference here is very important. People may agree or disagree on issues, but if they believe or understand what they are both doing, they can often learn to deal with each other. They can find a way to have a relationship, to bargain, to negotiate, to take things into account. When people believe that American policy in the Gulf is mostly motivated by oil, they don't necessarily like it but it is something they understood, and they can negotiate and bargain with that perception in mind. However, when people started believing that the United States is aiming to weaken the Muslim world, which our opinion surveys recorded at the top of recent attitudes, they can't negotiate that. What we have to keep in mind here is that confidence and credibility in the end are very important to the effectiveness of American foreign policy, and confidence and credibility start with honesty about what the United States can and cannot do.

WHAT IS THE ROLE OF THE MEDIA IN SHAPING ARAB OPINION?

In the public-opinion polling that I've conducted, there is no statistically significant relationship between what people watch on television and their attitudes toward the United States: attitudes toward the United States are not a function of the media.

People have what I call a "core identity," which might be informally defined as a set of predispositions based on a whole host of issues related to policy, awareness of historical trends, and sense of self. When people watch the media, they generally go to the media that reflect their opinions on those core issues. The media may affect you on matters that you don't care much about or that you don't know much about, but in general, if you have preformed views on issues that are related to your core identity, you will tend to watch the media that reflect your view.

For example, in the heat of battle in an American election, when you watch a television story that is a negative for the Democrats, and if you're a Democrat, you probably don't respond by announcing that you are going to vote for the Republicans—you say instead that the station is biased, the facts are incomplete, or whatever. And that happens on every issue that people care about in general, so I think there is a huge exaggeration of the relationship between the media and public opinion in the Middle East, particularly on attitudes toward the United States. Too often that exaggeration is an excuse for poor policy, and we should not allow it to detract from appreciative considerations of popular opinion in the Middle East.

Second, I think there's a misunderstanding about where the media do have an impact as a phenomenon. Different from 10 years ago, the Middle East news media today are market driven—not financially driven, but viewership driven. The media are therefore putting out what people want to see far more than before, because in a competitive news market people now have choices and will turn to news outlets that give them what they want. When the media show things that we consider militant, like their reporting of bloodshed in the West Bank and Gaza, which we think is inciting the public, that is instead simply a function of the state of affairs that is taking place. The fact is that the public is not responding to the media, they are responding to the event, whether it's positive or negative.

The al-Jazeera television channel is often accused of being part of the anti-American machine, but we forget that it's sponsored by Qatar, one of the most pro-American governments in the region, which hosts American forces on its soil. We also forget that in the late 1990s, al-Jazeera was accused by Arabs of being an agent for America and Israel because it was seen to be normalizing the idea of Israel in the Arab world. It was the first station to feature the Israel issue prominently by having an al-Jazeera representative in the West Bank and the Knesset (the Israeli parliament) and by covering Israel in a "normal" fashion—it was getting criticism from Arabs for that coverage.

The fact that the news media cover the Abu Ghraib prison scandal is not what is troubling; what is troubling is that the Abu Ghraib scandal takes place at all. Frankly, when something like that does happen, as a citizen I want to see news coverage of it. In the same vein, there has been criticism of the media coverage of bloodshed in the war. I endorse that coverage because I don't think wars should be rendered so sterile in our news. The hard truth is that wars are horrible, they are painful, they are troubling. As a citizen, I want to see the reality of war covered adequately and I want to know about it; I don't want to be systematically separated from it. That stance is perhaps arguable, but I do think the news media are blamed unnecessarily for states of affairs that are already in place for other reasons.

HAS THE ELECTION OF MAHMOUD ABBAS CREATED A NEW OPPORTUNITY FOR A PEACE SETTLEMENT BETWEEN ISRAEL AND PALESTINE?

The election of Mahmoud Abbas as president of the Palestinian Authority in 2005—he is also the current chairman of the Palestine Liberation Organization—has been a positive development that has improved the atmosphere for negotiations if only because of the decided opposition of the United States and Israel to his predecessor, Yasser Arafat. But this improvement in the atmosphere may be hiding a large gap between the expectations of Israelis and Palestinians, which could lead to a confrontation after the recently announced Israeli withdrawal from Gaza. The current Israeli withdrawal plan is not part of a negotiated agreement but remains a unilateral plan that is part of the Israeli mood to create further "separation" from the Palestinians. The Palestinians are now cooperating with the expectation that this will be a step toward a more comprehensive peace.

If Israeli prime minister Ariel Sharon succeeds in getting out of Gaza, building the separation barrier that his public has supported, in reducing the violence—all while maintaining the support of the United States—he will be even more popular in Israel. The mood of the Israeli public will not be to move quickly past incremental interim agreements to final-status negotiations. The Palestinians will inevitably be impatient, as they expect rapid movement. The Bush administration will be caught between the international demands for meeting its commitment to the establishment of a Palestinian state on the one hand, and, on the other hand, the domestic environment, in which the president is far weaker than he was during his first term. The outcome is likely to be a coordinated US-Israeli plan for a provisional Palestinian state without addressing final-status issues—something most Palestinians say they reject.

Given what has transpired in the past five years (the bloodshed on both sides, the collapse of trust—even the loss of faith in a two-state solution among some), and given the asymmetry of power on the ground, it is unlikely that the parties can move to a final settlement without US help. And no American diplomacy can succeed on this issue unless it is elevated to the top of presidential priorities.

WHAT COULD THE ROLE OF THE UNITED STATES BE IN RESOLVING THE PALESTINIAN ISSUE?

From the point of view of the United States, two things in resolving the Israel-Palestine issue are extremely important. One is helping the Palestinian Authority in the short term, both economically and politically, to reform and stabilize both the security arena and the economic arena. That can only be done if the president of the United States makes such aid a priority issue. We have already seen—when the president offered significant aid to the Palestinian Authority—that some important members of Congress raised questions about it. To push aid of this kind through, the president can only succeed if he makes it a priority issue, because it is going to come with some political expense.

Second, the role of the United States is perhaps chiefly indispensable in assuring the Palestinians about a final-status resolution that would determine the exact boundaries of the Palestinian state and the fate of Jewish settlements on the West Bank, and settle difficult issues such as the rights of Palestinian refugees, Israeli security concerns, and the sharing of scarce water resources. It is clear that the Israelis at this point do not feel obligated to provide further details about their notion of a final status for Palestine, and so at this stage they are essentially implementing a unilateral withdrawal plan that is supported by the United States, and which the United States hopes will be one step toward implementing the "road map" and reviving the peace negotiations. Given that the president gave assurances to the Israelis about some parameters for final settlement prior to the 2004 US election, it is extremely important for him also to assure the Palestinians about what the American notion of the final status should be. The biggest worry for the Palestinians is, in fact, the final-status arrangement, particularly if that arrangement is likely to be postponed, which is what the Israelis want to do. If there is a conventional wisdom in Israel, it is "let's get through this, find some security, and then and only then begin negotiations." Many Israelis are very comfortable delaying the final settlement to the next generation. I don't think that is the Palestinian position, and, clearly, this is where the United States can step in in a potentially helpful fashion.

WHAT IS THE ROLE OF HEZBOLLAH AND HAMAS IN PALESTINE?

Any deliberate targeting of civilians by any group is terrorism, regardless of the objectives of the groups. When Hamas blows up a bus of innocent civilians, that is terrorism, and must be rejected. It is the right policy to seek an end to terrorism of all kinds.

The problem is this: "What is a terrorist group?" A group cannot be defined simply by the methods it employs, abhorrent though those means may be. For most groups, terrorism is not an ideology, not an end in itself. Terrorism is instead one of a range of available instruments. In that regard, one has to differentiate among groups based on their objectives—while also recognizing that these objectives do not legitimize unacceptable means. The debate should thus shift to what the groups seek, and not focus only on what means they employ.

There is a difference, for example, between the al-Qaeda of Abu Musaab al-Zarqaui (who apparently heads the insurgency in Iraq) and the Hezbollah of Hassan Nasrallah (who has on occasion negotiated with Israel). With al-Qaeda, there is no reasonable or achievable way to dissuade it from continued violence, and one therefore has to treat it as if its violence were an end in itself. With Hezbollah and Hamas, in contrast, their aims are primarily nationalistic and political. To achieve those aims, then, the question becomes whether Hezbollah and Hamas can be engaged in good-faith negotiation and dissuaded from employing terrorist means—or, even if not, whether the constituencies whose support they seek would stop supporting them if nationalist aspirations were otherwise being met. It is evident, for example, that the support for Hamas in the Palestinian areas has been a function of two related things: the performance of the Palestinian Authority and the prospect of peace. The support of Palestinians for Hamas was lowest in the mid-1990s when it looked like the Oslo agreements were likely to result in a Palestinian state. Now, with the waning of the Oslo momentum, both Hezbollah and Hamas have demonstrated significant public support in open elections. No policy can ignore this public sentiment. Parallel to the rightful rejection of terrorism, there must be an avenue of engagement to test for possible change, to see whether the objectives of these groups are reconcilable with the interests of the United States.

SELECT BIBLIOGRAPHY

William L. Cleveland

This section is intended primarily as an introductory bibliography of works in English to guide readers to the basic books on various aspects of modern Middle Eastern history. Each of the works listed here contains its own bibliography that readers seeking more specialized references may want to consult.

Reference Works and Periodicals

The Encyclopaedia of Islam, new ed. (Leiden, 1960–ongoing), with a changing editorial committee, has now reached eleven volumes. This major scholarly undertaking concentrates on terms, important figures, and concepts of classical and medieval Islam, but also pays some attention to modern developments. Philip Mattar ed., *The Encyclopedia of the Modern Middle East,* 2nd ed., 4 vols. (Woodbridge, CT, 2005), is intended for the student and the educated layperson and contains entries on a variety of fields (politics, history, the arts) covering the area from Morocco through Afghanistan.

The *International Journal of Middle East Studies* (New York) is the scholarly journal of the Middle East Studies Association. It is comprehensive and multidisciplinary, publishing articles that embrace the full chronological scope of Middle Eastern studies from the rise of Islam to the present. The *British Journal of Middle Eastern Studies* often carries thoughtful interpretive essays. The *Middle East Journal* (Washington, D.C.) treats contemporary affairs and foreign policy matters and contains useful chronological and bibliographical sections. *Middle Eastern Studies* (London) concentrates on modern history. *Middle East Report* (New York) offers a critical, left-of-center approach to a broad range of current events. The periodical's challenging and sometimes controversial coverage offers a perspective often at odds with official Washington policy. In addition to the journals that provide regional treatment, various scholarly organizations publish periodicals on almost every country in the Middle East. Many of these are excellent.

For anyone seeking to follow current events in a systematic fashion, the World Wide Web provides access to such essential newspapers as the *New York Times,* the *Washington Post,* and the *Guardian Weekly* as well as English-language editions of several daily and weekly publications originating in the Middle East.

General Works on Islam and Middle Eastern History

Three outstanding overviews of Arab and Islamic history are now available. Marshall G. S. Hodgson, *The Venture of Islam: Conscience and History in a World Civilization,* 3 vols. (Chicago, 1974), places Islam in a global context and is one of the most stimulating and challenging explorations of Islamic history yet written. Ira M. Lapidus, *A History of Islamic Societies,* 2nd ed. (Cambridge, 2002), explores the shaping of Islamic civilization in all Islamic regions from the time of the Prophet to the twentieth century. Albert Hourani's masterful synthesis, *A History of the Arab Peoples* (Cambridge, Mass., 1991), treats the entire Arab world, emphasizing the development of social patterns and institutions. An additional survey of all the Islamic regions, John Obert Voll's *Islam: Continuity and Change in the Modern World* (Syracuse, 1994), concentrates on the period after 1800. Two excellent overviews are Francis Robinson, ed., *The Cambridge Illustrated History of the Islamic World* (Cambridge, 1996), and John Esposito, ed., *The Oxford History of Islam* (Oxford, 1999). Both works offer a combination of chronological and topical treatment in contributions from leading specialists; both are also handsomely illustrated and contain very fine bibliographical essays.

The Quran is the essential foundation for an understanding of Islam. The translation used in this book [that is, William Cleveland, *A History of the Modern Middle East,* 3rd ed.] is A. J. Arberry, *The Koran: Interpreted* (New York, 1955). Introductions to the faith and institutions of Islam include Malise Ruthven, *Islam in the World,* 2nd ed. (Oxford, 2000), a refreshing book that examines the impact of Islamic doctrines on Muslim patterns of living. H. A. R. Gibb, *Mohammedanism,* 2nd ed. (New York, 1970), despite its inappropriate title, remains useful. English-language surveys by Muslim writers include Fazlur Rahman, *Islam,* 2nd ed. (Chicago, 1979), and Seyyed Hossein Nasr, *Ideals and Realities of Islam* (Chicago, 2000). A most helpful study of Shi'ism is Moojan Momen, *An Introduction to Shi'i Islam: The History and Doctrines of Twelver Shi'ism* (New Haven, 1985).

Any list of historical surveys must still include Bernard Lewis, *The Arabs in History,* rev. ed. (Oxford, 1993), a graceful and accessible synthesis. Marilyn R. Waldman presents a stimulating reappraisal of the periodization of Islamic history in her contribution, "The Islamic World," *New Encyclopaedia Britannica,* 15th ed. (Chicago, 1990), pp. 102–133. In a similar vein is Richard M. Eaton's *Islamic History as Global History* (Washington, D.C., 1990), a historiographical essay in the American Historical Association's series of studies on world and comparative history; Eaton's essay should be required reading for all who seek to understand the global significance of the consolidation of an Islamic civilization.

General Works on Political, Social, and Economic History in the Modern Era

An important analysis of recent social and economic trends is Alan Richards and John Waterbury, *A Political Economy of the Middle East: State, Class, and Economic Development* (Boulder, 1996). Roger Owen and Şevket Pamuk, *A History of Middle East Economies in the Twentieth Century* (London, 1998), is a very good introductory survey with both a country-specific and regional focus.

Roger Owen, *State, Power and Politics in the Making of the Modern Middle East,* 2nd ed. (London, 2004), employs a combination of narrative and thematic approaches to produce a sophisticated introductory political study of the region from World War I to the present. A masterful synthesis of the post-Ottoman period to the present and a work I highly recommend is Avi Shlaim, *War and Peace in the Middle East: A Concise History,* rev. ed. (New York, 1995). For studies of elites and politics, see Michael C. Hudson, *Arab Politics: The Search for Legitimacy* (New Haven, 1977), which, in addition to its analysis of contemporary regimes, provides sound historical background on the formation of the modern Arab states. At the opposite end of the economic spectrum are the ordinary people whose lives are the subject of Edmund Burke III, ed., *Struggle and Survival in the Modern Middle East* (Berkeley, 1993). Augustus Richard Norton, ed., *Civil Society in the Middle East*, 2 vols. (Leiden, 1995 and 1996), is an enormous undertaking that seeks to examine most of the countries of the Middle East and North Africa within the analytical framework of civil society, a concept on which the contributors do not have a shared definition but one that has nonetheless enabled them to produce some very important case studies of specific countries in the contemporary era.

A rich collection of essays dealing with such themes as religion and gender, state and family, and the emergence of women's movements is Margaret Meriwether and Judith Tucker, eds., *Social History of Women in the Modern Middle East* (Boulder, 1999). The book contains extensive bibliographical entries. A major reference guide for works on women's history written since 1990 is Nikki Keddie, "Women in the Limelight: Some Recent Books on Middle Eastern Women's History," *International Journal of Middle East Studies,* vol. 34 (August 2002), pp. 553–573.

Palestine and Israel

In recent years, a lively and occasionally acrimonious debate has swept through Israeli scholarly circles as a result of the work of a group of so-called new historians who have challenged some of the long-accepted historical assumptions about Zionism and the early years of the Israeli state. Their work and that of other like-minded revisionist scholars may be sampled in Michael N. Barnett, ed., *Israel in Comparative Perspective: Challenging the Conventional Wisdom* (Albany, 1996). Two critical reappraisals of Israel's role in the events surrounding the war of 1948 by leading representatives of the new history are Avi Shlaim, *Collusion Across the Jordan: King Abdullah, the Zionist Movement, and the Partition of Palestine* (New York, 1988), and Ilan Pappé, *The Making of the Arab-Israeli Conflict, 1947–1951* (London, 1992). The contributors to Eugene Rogan and Avi Shlaim, eds., *The War for Palestine: Rewriting the History of 1948* (Cambridge, 2001), examine the role of the states participating in the conflict with the objective of distinguishing various national myths from historical reality. A revisionist interpretation of Israel's policy toward the Arab world from 1948 to 1998 is Avi Shlaim, *The Iron Wall: Israel and the Arab World* (New York, 2001). A spirited refutation of the new historians' methods, evidence, and motives is found in Efraim Karsh, *Fabricating Israeli History: The "New Historians"* (London, 1997).

In addition to Noah Lucas, *The Modern History of Israel* (London, 1974), Israeli political, social, and religious institutions are treated in Yossi Beilin, *Israel: A Concise Political History* (New York, 1992); Nadav Safran, *Israel, the Embattled Ally* (Cambridge, Mass., 1981), a domestic history that nevertheless also emphasizes the development of the US-Israeli relationship; Alan Dowty, *The Jewish State: A Century Later* (Berkeley, 1998), a combination thematic and chronological analysis of the challenges facing the evolving Israeli democracy from the mandate to the 1990s; and Clive Jones and Emma C. Murphy, *Israel: Challenges to Identity, Democracy and the State* (London, 2002) a concise topical analysis with emphasis on the issue of Israeli identity. A good introduction to the workings of the Israeli electoral and political systems is Gregory S. Mahler, *Israel: Government and Politics in a Maturing State* (San Diego, 1990). A more critical approach to the US-Israeli relationship than Safran's is Cheryl A. Rubenberg, *Israel and the American National Interest: A Critical Examination* (Urbana, 1986). For the Palestinian community within Israel, see Ian S. Lustick, *Arabs in the Jewish State:*

Israel's Control of a National Minority (Austin, 1980), which examines the system of controls Israel used to maintain the quiescence of its Arab citizens. Lustick has also examined the rise of militant Jewish settler groups with special emphasis on Gush Emunim in *For the Land and the Lord: Jewish Fundamentalism in Israel* (New York, 1988). Ilan Peleg, *Begin's Foreign Policy, 1977–1983: Israel's Move to the Right* (New York, 1987), is a critical interpretation of the role of the Right in influencing the Begin government's policies. Taking 1967 as their starting point, Dan Horowitz and Moshe Lissak examine twenty years of changes in *Israel in Trouble in Utopia: The Overburdened Polity of Israel* (Albany, 1989).

The reasons for the Palestinian exodus are carefully documented by Benny Morris, one of the new historians, in *The Birth of the Palestinian Refugee Problem, Revisted* (Cambridge, 2004), which successfully refutes earlier explanations. The outstanding study of the PLO is Yezid Sayigh, *Armed Struggle and the Search for a State: The Palestinian National Movement, 1949–1993* (Oxford, 1997). Also valuable is Helena Cobban, *The Palestinian Liberation Organisation: People, Power, and Politics* (Cambridge, 1984) and Emile Sahliyeh, *In Search of Leadership: West Bank Politics Since 1967* (Washington, D.C., 1988). For the impact of the continued Israeli occupation on Gaza, see Sarah Roy, *The Gaza Strip: The Political Economy of De-Development* (Washington, D.C., 1995). On the Palestinian presence in Lebanon, see Rex Brynen, *Sanctuary and Survival: The PLO in Lebanon* (Boulder, 1990). An important study of politics and gender within the Palestinian community in Lebanon during the period 1968–1982 is Julie M. Peteet, *Gender in Crisis: Women and the Palestinian Resistance Movement* (New York, 1991).

A thorough study of the first *intifada* is F. Robert Hunter, *The Palestinian Uprising: A War by Other Means*, 2nd ed. (Berkeley, 1993), a work that is enhanced by the author's interviews with Palestinians during the early phase of the uprising. Joost R. Hiltermann, *Behind the Intifada: Labor and Women's Movements in the Occupied Territories* (Princeton, 1991) focuses on how the formation of trade unions and women's committees among Palestinians in the occupied territories contributed to the struggle for national liberation. Glenn E. Robinson, *Building a Palestinian State: The Incomplete Revolution* (Bloomington, 1997), connects the rise of a new Palestinian elite during the *intifada* with Arafat's oppressive policies as head of the PA after 1994. Robinson's work also includes an excellent analysis of Hamas. A more recent account is Nathan J. Brown, *Palestinian Politics After the Oslo Accord: Resuming Palestine* (Berkeley and Los Angeles, 2003), which discusses the challenges of institution building in the occupied territories. Studies of Palestinian Islamic activist organizations include Ziad Abu-Amr, *Islamic Fundamentalism in the West Bank and Gaza: Muslim Brotherhood and Islamic Jihad* (Bloomington, 1994), and Shaul Mishal and Avraham Sela, *The Palestinian Hamas* (New York, 2000), which stresses the pragmatic nature of the organization.

A useful reference work for the period after Oslo I is Lawrence Joffe, *Keesing's Guide to the Mid-East Peace Process* (London, 1996), which reproduces the major documents, provides capsule biographies of the main participants, and offers an analysis of the peace process itself to mid-1996. Of the several studies that present the Oslo accords as a potential disaster for the Palestinians, Farsoun Samih and Christina Zacharia's *Palestine and the Palestinians* (Boulder, 1997) is recommended, as is Baruch Kimmerling and Joel S. Migdal, *The Palestinian People: A History* (Cambridge, Mass., 2003), an updated version of an earlier work that now contains a lengthy section on the Oslo peace process. A recent penetrating critique of the accords is Cheryl A. Rubenberg, *The Palestinians: In Search of a Just Peace* (Boulder, 2003). An account of the effects of the Oslo accords on the individual states of the region is Robert O. Freedman, ed., *The Middle East and the Peace Process: The Impact of the Oslo Accords* (Gainesville, Fla., 1998). For an understanding of US policy during the rise and fall of the Oslo peace process, the chapters on the Clinton presidency in William B. Quandt, *Peace Process: American Diplomacy and the Arab-Israeli Conflict Since 1967*, rev. ed. (Washington, D.C., and Berkeley, 2001), are "must reads."

Iraq

The best historical survey of Iraq is the very fine work by Charles Tripp, *A History of Iraq* (Cambridge, 2000). See also Phebe Marr, *The Modern History of Iraq*, 2nd ed. (Boulder, 2004). One of the most significant historical studies of any modern Middle Eastern state is Hanna Batatu, *The Old Social Classes and the Revolutionary Movements of Iraq: A Study of Iraq's Old Landed and Commercial Classes and of Its Communists, Ba'thists, and Free Officers* (Princeton, 1982). Batatu's book is not for the beginner. Yitzhak Nakash, *The Shi'is of Iraq* (Princeton, 1994), is a comprehensive and revisionist study of the subject from the mid-eighteenth century to 1958. Edith Penrose and E. F. Penrose, *Iraq: International Relations and National Development* (London, 1978), deals with the mandate through the revolutionary era and is especially strong on economics and the petroleum industry. Of the three books on Iraq by Majid Khadduri, the first, which examines the period from formal independence to the overthrow of the monarchy, is the best; it is *Independent Iraq, 1932–1958: A Study in Iraqi Politics*, 2nd ed. (London, 1960). The process of setting up a nationalist-oriented educational system is discussed in Reeva S. Simon, *Iraq Between the Two World Wars: Creation and Implementation of a Nationalist Ideology* (New York, 1986).

A detailed political history treating the period from the revolution to the 1990s, with considerable attention paid to the Saddam Husayn regime, is Marion Farouk-Sluglett and Peter Sluglett, *Iraq Since 1958: From Revolution to Dictatorship*, 3rd rev. ed. (London, 2001). A very important and effectively illustrated study of the Ba'thist regime and its attempts to use the pre-Islamic past to create a unifying secular culture is Amatzia Baram, *Culture, History, and Ideology in the Formation of Ba'thist Iraq, 1968–1989* (New York, 1989). Samir al-Khalil, *Republic of Fear: Saddam's Iraq* (Berkeley, 1989), gained wide acclaim during the 1991 Gulf War, in large measure because it portrayed the Iraqi regime the way the US public and administration wanted to see it. The most satisfactory work on the Iran-Iraq War is Dilip Hiro, *The Longest War: The Iran-Iraq Military Conflict*, updated ed. (London, 1990).

For the moment, the best accounts of Iraq's invasion of Kuwait and the resulting Gulf War are Lawrence Freedman and Efraim Karsh, *The Gulf Conflict, 1990–1991: Diplomacy and War in the New World Order* (Princeton, 1993); and Dilip Hiro, *Desert Shield to Desert Storm: The Second Gulf War* (New York, 1992). The coverage in *Middle East Report* offers a stimulating alternative view to the explanations released by the Bush administration. Two excellent studies of the border disputes between Iraq and Kuwait are David H. Finnie, *Shifting Lines in the Sand: Kuwait's Elusive Frontier with Iraq* (Cambridge, Mass., 1992), and Richard Schofield, *Kuwait and Iraq: Historical Claims and Territorial Disputes*, 2nd ed. (London, 1993).

Iran

A very good introduction to all of Iranian history, with an emphasis on the modern period, is Elton L. Daniel, *The History of Iran* (Westport, Conn., 2001). Nikki R. Keddie's stimulating

Modern Iran: Roots and Results of Revolution (New Haven, 2003) includes three updated chapters covering events from 1979 to the late 1990s. One of the most lucid and perceptive studies of any transforming Middle Eastern society is Ervand Abrahamian's *Iran Between Two Revolutions* (Princeton, 1982).

The Iranian revolution of 1978–1979 and its aftermath have been the subjects of numerous studies, and the list continues to grow. Only a sampling can be noted here. The best political and social analysis of the revolutionary regime from 1979 to the mid-1980s is Shaul Bakhash, *The Reign of the Ayatollahs: Iran and the Islamic Revolution* (New York, 1990). See also Nikki Keddie and Eric Hooglund, eds., *The Iranian Revolution and the Islamic Republic*, 2nd ed. (Syracuse, 1986); Mohsen M. Milani, *The Making of Iran's Islamic Revolution: From Monarchy to Islamic Republic*, 2nd ed. (Boulder, 1994); Said Amir Arjomand, *The Turban for the Crown: The Islamic Revolution in Iran* (New York, 1988); and Ervand Abrahamian, *Khomeinism: Essays on the Islamic Republic* (Berkeley, 1993), a stimulating work that situates Khomeini and his ideas in the realm of populism rather than rigid fundamentalism. Parvin Paidar's *Women in the Political Process in Twentieth Century Iran* (Cambridge, 1995) is a challenging analysis of the links between gender and political process, with excellent sections on the Khomeini period. Eric Hooglund, ed., *Twenty Years of Islamic Revolution: Political and Social Transition in Iran Since 1979* (Syracuse, 2002), is a solid collection of essays on domestic and foreign policy issues. One of the best studies of domestic politics and foreign policy since the death of Khomeini is David Menashri, *Post-Revolutionary Politics in Iran: Religion, Society and Power* (London, 2001). An outstanding and readily comprehensible study of contemporary Shi'a Islam is found in Roy Mottahedeh's evocative work, *The Mantle of the Prophet: Religion and Politics in Iran* (New York, 1985). For a collection of the writings of Khomeini, see the work translated and annotated by Hamid Algar, *Islam and Revolution: Writings and Declarations of Imam Khomeini* (Berkeley, 1981). The early foreign policy of the Islamic Republic is examined in Rouhollah K. Ramazani, *Revolutionary Iran: Challenge and Response in the Middle East* (Baltimore, 1986). Critical assessments of US policy toward Iran are presented in James A. Bill, *The Eagle and the Lion: The Tragedy of American-Iranian Relations* (New Haven, 1988), and Richard W. Cottam, *Iran and the United States: A Cold War Case Study* (Pittsburgh, 1988).

Saudi Arabia

A solid study of the history of the Saudi state from its formation to the year 2000 is Madawi al-Rasheed, *A History of Saudi Arabia* (Cambridge, 2001). The ruling family is closely studied in David Holden and Richard Johns, *The House of Saud: The Rise and Rule of the Most Powerful Dynasty in the Arab World* (London, 1981). Nadav Safran, *Saudi Arabia: The Ceaseless Quest for Security* (Ithaca, 1988), concentrates on developments since 1970. Mordechai Abir, *Saudi Arabia in the Oil Era: Regime and Elites, Conflict and Collaboration* (Boulder, 1988), offers an important analysis of the new administrative elite and the tensions created by their continued exclusion from decisionmaking; Abir's sequel, *Saudi Arabia: Government, Society, and the Gulf Crisis* (New York, 1993), is an equally significant contribution. The excellent work by F. Gregory Gause III, *Oil Monarchies: Domestic and Security Challenges in the Arab Gulf States* (New York, 1994), offers a comparative reinterpretation of the bases of politics in the six Gulf monarchies during the period immediately before and after the Iraqi invasion of Kuwait.

Egypt

The most comprehensive and up-to-date treatment of modern Egypt is M. W. Daly, ed., *The Cambridge History of Egypt:* vol. 2, *Modern Egypt, from 1517 to the End of the Twentieth Century* (Cambridge, 1998), which incorporates recent historical interpretations in a series of chronologically ordered chapters by leading experts. A skillful combination of synthesis and substance makes James Jankowski, *Egypt: A Short History* (Oxford, 2000), an excellent introductory survey. Although not without its biases, P. J. Vatikiotis, *The History of Modern Egypt: From Muhammad Ali to Mubarak*, 4th ed. (Baltimore, 1991), remains an important survey.

A good introductory overview is Derek Hopwood, *Egypt: Politics and Society, 1945–1984*, 3rd ed. (New York, 1991). Among the many attempts to explain the Nasser era by studying the life of its dominant personality, P. J. Vatikiotis, *Nasser and His Generation* (New York, 1978); Jean Lacouture, *Nasser: A Biography* (New York, 1973); and Robert Stephens, *Nasser* (London, 1971), may be recommended. There are several good books on foreign policy matters. Egypt's relations with other Arab states are treated in A. I. Dawisha, *Egypt and the Arab World: The Elements of Foreign Policy* (New York, 1976), and Malcolm H. Kerr, *The Arab Cold War: Gamal Abd al-Nasir and His Rivals, 1958–1970*, 3rd ed. (London, 1971). The Egyptian-Soviet relationship is examined in Karen Dawisha, *Soviet Foreign Policy Towards Egypt* (New York, 1979), and Alvin Rubinstein, *Red Star on the Nile: The Soviet-Egyptian Influence Relationship Since the June War* (Princeton, 1977). The Suez crisis has received extensive treatment, and the following works are but a sampling of the material available: Kennett Love, *Suez—The Twice-Fought War: A History* (New York, 1969); Keith Kyle, *Suez: Britain's End of Empire in the Middle East*, new ed. (London, 2003); and Wm. Roger Louis and Roger Owen, eds., *Suez 1956: The Crisis and Its Consequences* (Oxford, 1989), which is a reassessment based on new documentary evidence. The 1967 war is analyzed in Nadav Safran, *From War to War: The Arab-Israeli Confrontation, 1948–1967* (New York, 1969). The best analysis of the circumstances leading up to the 1967 war is Richard B. Parker, *The Politics of Miscalculation in the Middle East* (Bloomington, 1993). The same author's edited collection, *The Six Day War: A Retrospective* (Gainesville, 1996), offers new perspectives on the policies and motivations of the belligerents and the major outside powers.

A thorough and critical assessment of state policies for three decades after 1952 is found in John Waterbury, *The Egypt of Nasser and Sadat: The Political Economy of Two Regimes* (Princeton, 1983). See also Kirk J. Beattie, *Egypt During the Nasser Years: Ideology, Politics, and Civil Society* (Boulder, 1994). Sadat is the subject of a scathing biography by Irene Beeson and David Hirst, *Sadat* (London, 1981); a more sympathetic approach is taken in the detailed political study by Kirk J. Beattie, *Egypt During the Sadat Years* (New York, 2000). Sadat staked his own claim to a place in history in a self-serving autobiography, *In Search of Identity* (New York, 1978). William B. Quandt, *Camp David: Peacemaking and Politics* (Washington, D.C., 1986), is a thorough discussion of the intricacies involved in securing the Camp David Accords. A good discussion of a variety of the issues faced by the Sadat regime is John Waterbury, *Egypt: Burdens of the Past, Options for the Future* (Bloomington, 1978). The politicization of students under Nasser and Sadat is discussed in Ahmed Abdalla, *The Student Movement and National Politics in Egypt* (London, 1985). An excellent account of the Islamic opposition is Gilles Kepel, *The Prophet and Pharaoh: Muslim Extremism in Egypt*, trans. Jon Rothschild (London, 1985). An important study that portrays the Islamist revival of the 1990s as permanent and moderate is Geneive Abdo, *No God But God: Egypt and the Triumph of Islam* (Oxford, 2000).

Robert Springborg, *Mubarak's Egypt: Fragmentation of the Political Order* (Boulder, 1989), examines the relationship between political authority and economic change during the first six years of Mubarak's presidency.

International Politics During and After the Cold War Era

In addition to the country-specific studies listed above, a number of important works examine the interaction of external powers with the region as a whole. A very good introductory survey of US policy toward the Arab Middle East from the late 1940s to the early 1990s is Burton I. Kaufman, The *Arab Middle East and the United States: Inter-Arab Rivalry and Superpower Diplomacy* (New York, 1996). L. Carl Brown, ed., *Diplomacy in the Middle East: The International Relations of Regional and Outside Powers* (New York, 2003), examines the foundations of foreign policymaking among the core regional states as well as the Middle East policies of the United States, Britain, France, and Russia. The involvement of the United States and the USSR with various regional states is the subject of Fawaz A. Gerges, *The Superpowers and the Middle East: Regional and International Politics, 1955–1967* (Boulder, 1994). See also Rahid Khalidi, *Resurrecting Empire: Western Footprints and America's Perilous Path in the Middle East* (Boston 2004). David W. Lesch, *1979: The Year That Shaped the Middle East* (Boulder, 2001), is a stimulating interpretation of the impact of three major domestic and international events of 1979 on the subsequent unfolding of Middle Eastern history. Of the several works that deal with the crises generated by the attacks of September 11, 2001, I recommend Shibley Telhami, *The Stakes: America and the Middle East: The Consequences of Power and the Choice for Peace* (Boulder, 2003).

GLOSSARY

Some alternate spellings of main entries appear in parentheses.

Abbasid Pertaining to a Muslim empire (750–1258) ruled from Baghdad by a family descended from Abbas, Muhammad's uncle.

administered territories. *See* occupied territories.

ahl al-kitab "People of the book"; Muslim term for Jews and Christians, and sometimes other peoples, whose religions are founded on sacred writings, or scriptures.

amir (emir) Muslim prince or ruler, with or without territorial jurisdiction.

Arab nationalism Movement based on the common interests of Arab peoples and nations, particularly against domination by non-Arabs. *See also* Pan-Arabism.

ayatollah Title of respect for eminent Shiite clergy.

Ba'ath (Ba'th, Baath) Arab nationalist party ruling Syria since the 1960s and Iraq from 1968 to 2003.

Babylonian Captivity (or Exile) The deportation and exile of Jews from the Kingdom of Judah to Babylon by King Nebuchadnezzar in the early sixth century BCE. On conquering Babylon, King Cyrus of Persia allowed the Jews to return home in 537 BCE.

Balfour Declaration Official statement in 1917 by the British foreign secretary, Arthur Balfour, supporting a Jewish national home in Palestine.

Bantustan Term of disparagement for a segregated territory that is assigned to an ethnic group but that is stripped of many aspects of authentic legal, economic, and political autonomy. The term was first applied to Bantu "homelands" established by the South African apartheid regime but is also used for various proposed resolutions of the Palestinian issue that stop short of creating a true Palestinian state.

caliph Successor to Muhammad as head of the universal community of Islam, the umma.

caliphate The political institution led by the caliph as the head of Islam. The Ottoman caliphate, representing the largest and most powerful independent Islamic political entity, was abolished in 1924.

Camp David accords (or agreements) Peace talks in 1978 between Menachem Begin of Israel, Anwar Sadat of Egypt, and Jimmy Carter of the United States that culminated in the 1979 Egypt-Israel peace treaty.

chador Head-to-toe covering for women.

Committee of Union and Progress (CUP) Turkish nationalist party that ruled the Ottoman Empire from 1908 to the end of World War I in 1918; also known as the Young Turks.

diaspora The usually forcible dispersion of a people from their traditional homeland. The term originally referred specifically to the scattering of Jews around the world that began with the Babylonian Captivity in the sixth century BCE and that continued through the destruction of the state of Judea by the Roman Empire in the second century CE. It has since been applied to any of several analogous cases, including the dispersal of Palestinians in the wake of the 1948 war following the founding of the state of Israel.

dual containment United States foreign policy aimed at isolating both Iran and Iraq, and preventing either from gaining too much power relative to the other, so that neither could prove to be a destabilizing force in the Persian Gulf.

European Union (EU) A supranational union of 25 European countries, established in 1992 to regulate (in varying degrees) matters of economic policy, foreign relations, and defense.

al-Fatah (Fateh) Palestinian guerrilla group founded in 1959 by Yasser Arafat.

fedayeen (feda'iyyin, fidaiyin, fidayyin) Literally "self-sacrificers"; usually applied to Palestinian guerrillas or militant Shiites.

Fertile Crescent The arc of territory extending north along the eastern Mediterranean coast and then east and south via Syria and Mesopotamia to the Persian Gulf, and which includes parts of the modern nations of Israel, Jordan, Lebanon, Syria, Turkey, and Iraq.

Gaza (Strip) A narrow section of southwest Palestine inhabited by Arabs; occupied by Israel after the 1967 Arab-Israeli war; in 1993 the Oslo Accords brought much of Gaza under the limited control of the Palestinian Authority. In 2005, Israel began withdrawing from Gaza.

Gulf Cooperation Council (GCC) A regional organization formed in 1981 that includes Saudi Arabia, Kuwait, Bahrain, the United Arab Emirates, Qatar, and Oman.

Gulf War The 1991 conflict between Iraq and a United Nations–sanctioned coalition of 34 nations, led by the United States. The war was triggered by Iraq's invasion of Kuwait in 1990. Iraq's quick defeat led to the imposition of economic sanctions as well as a program of United Nations weapons inspections, with which Iraq never fully complied.

***Hajj* (Hajj)** Muslim rite of pilgrimage to Mecca; one of the pillars of Islam.

Hamas Palestinian Islamist group, active in both intifadas.

Haram al-Sharif Site of the original Temple of Solomon (the First Temple) and the rebuilt Second Temple in Jerusalem, and thus also known as the Temple Mount; sacred to Jews and Christians. The site of two major Muslim shrines, the Dome of the Rock and Al-Aqsa Mosque (where tradition holds that Muhammad ascended to heaven), it is also the third-holiest site in Islam, after Mecca and Medina.

hegira (hejira, hijra, hijrah) Migration of Muhammad and his followers from Mecca to Medina in 622 CE (and marking year 1 of the Muslim calendar).

Hijaz (Hejaz) Western portion of Saudi Arabia containing Mecca and Medina.

Husayn-McMahon correspondence Letters exchanged 1915–1916 between Amir Husayn, sharif of Mecca, and Henry McMahon, Britain's high commissioner in Egypt, offering British support for Arab independence in exchange for an armed Arab revolt against the Ottoman Empire in World War I. Arab nationalists considered Britain's pledge of support for Arab independence to be violated by the subsequent Sykes-Picot Agreement (1916) and the Balfour Declaration (1917).

imam Muslim religious or political leader; among Shiites, one of a succession of leaders viewed as a legitimate through descent from Muhammad's son-in-law, Ali.

intifada (intifadah) Palestinian uprising against Israeli occupation (1987–1990); a "second intifada" followed Ariel Sharon's visit to the Temple Mount (or al-Haram al-Sharif) in 2000.

Iran-Contra Affair Reagan administration's secret sales of arms to Iran during the Iran-Iraq War while also secretly channeling the proceeds of those sales to the support of Contra insurgents battling the Sandinista government of Nicaragua.

Iran-Iraq War Protracted conflict between Iran and Iraq (1980–1988).

Islam Major religion practiced extensively in the Middle East as well as Asia and Africa, in which the will of God (Allah) is believed to have been revealed to a series of prophets, culminating with the revelation of the literal word of God to Muhammad in the form of the sacred text of the Quran.

Islamic Jihad (al-Jihad al-Islami) Militant Palestinian group.

Islamism Ideology advocating government according to religiously conservative Muslim principles.

Israel Defense Forces (IDF) Israel's armed forces, comprising the army, navy, and air force, formed after the 1948 founding of the nation of Israel.

jihad Struggle in defense of Islam, including inner struggle against temptation but also including "holy war" against non-Muslims.

King Crane Commission US committee named by President Wilson in 1919 that recommended against establishing a Jewish national home in Palestine.

Knesset Israel's parliament.

Kurd Member of a non-Arab ethnic group concentrated in southeastern Turkey, northern Iraq, northwestern Iran, and parts of Syria.

Likud Right-wing Israeli political party.

Magrib (Maghrib, Maghreb) Literally "west"; the Arab states west of Egypt in North Africa, specifically Morocco, Algeria, Tunisia, and sometimes Libya. Contrasted with the Mashriq (Mashreq), the Arabic-speaking countries east of Egypt.

mandate Commission awarded by the League of Nations after World War I to Western powers to prepare a former territory of Germany or the Ottoman Empire for eventual self-rule;

also, the polity so governed under this commission (Palestine, Transjordan, and Iraq by Britain; Syria and Lebanon by France).

Mecca (Makkah) Birthplace of the Prophet Muhammad, and therefore an Islamic holy site and pilgrimage center in what is now western Saudi Arabia.

Medina (al-Madinah) City in what is now northwestern Saudi Arabia to which Muhammad fled (from Mecca) in 622 CE.

Middle East Term currently used for the eastern Arab countries *(mashriq)*, Israel, Cyprus, Turkey, and Iran, but sometimes also including North Africa, Afghanistan, or Pakistan.

millet Non-Muslim religious community accorded a large degree of autonomy within the administration of the Ottoman Empire.

mullah *(mollah)* Member of the Islamic clergy.

Muslim Brotherhood (Muslim Brothers) Political group founded in Egypt in 1928 in opposition to British imperial rule and advocating an Islamic social and political system. Outlawed in 1954, the Muslim Brotherhood remains Egypt's most popular opposition group.

Najd (Nejd) Plateau of central Saudi Arabia and the location of the capital, Riyadh.

al-nakba **(Nakbah)** Literally, "the disaster or catastrophe"; the establishment of the state of Israel in 1948 and the subsequent displacement of Palestinian Arabs from their homeland.

Near East Term formerly used for what is currently called the Middle East.

9/11 (or September 11) An attack by Arab militants against the United States, in which hijacked airliners were flown into the twin towers of the World Trade Center in New York City and the Pentagon building in Washington, DC (a fourth plane crashed into the ground in Pennsylvania), killing over 2,700 people; so named for the date (September 11, 2001) of the attack.

North Africa Term commonly used for the western Arab countries *(magrib)* Morocco, Algeria, Tunisia, and Libya, and sometimes also including Egypt and Sudan.

occupied territories Territories seized by Israel in the 1967 war, including the Sinai Peninsula, the Gaza Strip, the West Bank (including East Jerusalem), and the Golan Heights. The Sinai was returned to Egypt by terms of the 1979 Egyptian-Israeli peace treaty. The Golan Heights were annexed by Israel in 1981, though Syria still claims them. Israel began withdrawal from Gaza in 2005. The West Bank remains disputed territory in ongoing negotiations between Israelis and Palestinians.

Operation Desert Shield US-led military buildup in 1990–1991 to protect Saudi Arabia from an Iraqi invasion and to prepare for the liberation of Kuwait from Iraq.

Operation Desert Storm US-led attack on Iraq in January–February 1991 that led to the liberation of Kuwait.

Operation Iraqi Freedom US-led invasion of Iraq in March 2003 leading to the overthrow of President Saddam Hussein.

Organization of Petroleum Exporting Countries (OPEC) Cartel of oil-producing countries whose purpose is to negotiate with oil companies the production and prices of petroleum; founded in 1960, its current members are Algeria, Indonesia, Iran, Iraq, Kuwait, Libya, Nigeria, Qatar, Saudi Arabia, the United Arab Emirates, and Venezuela.

Oslo Accords Agreement (also called the Declaration of Principles) signed between Israel and the PLO in 1993; also including a subsequent 1995 Israeli-PLO agreement.

Ottoman Empire Multinational Islamic state (1299–1923) that at its height included Anatolia, the Balkans of southeastern Europe, the coast of North Africa, and much of the Fertile Crescent.

Palestine The region between the Mediterranean Sea and the Jordan River; the former British mandate (1922–1948) that included what are now Israel, the West Bank, and the Gaza Strip; the lands now governed wholly or in part by the state of Israel, including territories occupied and/or claimed by Arab inhabitants.

Palestine Liberation Organization (PLO) Group formed in 1964 by Yasser Arafat that came to serve as an umbrella organization for Palestinian aspirations; recognized by Israel in the Oslo Accords as the legitimate representative of Palestinians in negotiations over the future of Palestine.

Palestinian Inhabitant of Palestine, used especially of Arabs either living in Palestine or in diaspora from there.

Palestinian Authority (PA) Organization established in the Oslo Accords to administer areas relinquished by Israel to the Palestinians.

Palestinian National Council (PNC) Parliament in exile of the Palestinian people.

pan-Arabism Ideology or movement advocating the unification of Arabs into a single nation. *See also* Arab nationalism.

pan-Islam Ideology or movement advocating the unity of all Muslims.

Persia Name used for Iran till 1935.

political Islam Ideology or policy based on Islamic principles.

Prophet Person to whom God is believed by Jews, Christians, or Muslims to have vouchsafed a mesasage; (if capitalized) Muhammad (570–632).

al-Qaeda (al-Qa'ida) Literally "the base." An international network of militant Islam organizations that originated in the resistance to the Soviet occupation of Afghanistan in 1979. Led by Osama bin Laden, al-Qaeda was responsible for the 9/11 attacks on the World Trade Center in New York and the Pentagon in Washington, DC, in 2001.

Quran (al-Quran, Qur'an, Koran) Muslim holy scriptures, believed by Muslims to have been revealed by God to the Prophet Muhammad through the angel Gabriel.

"Road map" for peace Plan proposed in 2002 by the United States, Russia, the European Union, and the United Nations (but not accepted by Israel) for resolving the Israel-Palestine dispute. In his speech presenting the principles of the plan, President George W. Bush became the first US president to call explicitly for an independent Palestinian state alongside Israel.

Seljuk Turkish dynasty that occupied parts of the Middle East and Central Asia from the eleventh to the fourteenth centuries.

sharia (shari'ah) Literally "the pathway." The body of Islamic doctrine, law, and ritual derived from the Quran and the sunna (the sayings and actions of Mohammed).

sharif Term given to individuals claiming descent from Muhammad.

shaykh (sheik) Arab tribal leader; also, a learned Muslim.

Shiite Muslim who believes legitimate leadership of the Muslim community, the *umma*, passed from Muhammad to the descendents of his son-in-law, Ali. Sunni. (*Shi'a* or *Shia* is the noun; *Shi'i* or *Shii* is the adjective; Shiite serves as either noun or adjective.)

Sunni Muslim who accepts the legitimacy of the caliphs who succeeded Muhammad.

Sunni triangle Roughly triangular territory of Iraq, with corners near Baghdad, Tikrit and Ramadi, and heavily populated by the former ruling-minority Sunni Muslims.

Sykes-Picot Agreement Secret agreement (1916) between France and Britain for dividing the post–World War I Middle East into spheres of influence. The agreement's principal terms were ratified in the United Nations mandates established in 1922.

Taliban Islamist regime that ruled most of Afghanistan 1996–2001.

Umayyid (Umayyad, Omayyed) Arab Muslim dynasty that ruled in Damascus (661–750) and Spain (756–1030).

umma (ummah, 'umma) The universal political, social, and spiritual community of Islam.

United Nations Security Council Resolution 242 (1967) Resolution affirming the principle of land for peace, in which Israel was called upon to withdraw from territories occupied in the 1967 war in return for termination of "all states of belligerency" and for acknowledgment of the sovereignty of "all States in the area."

United Nations Security Council Resolution 338 (1973) Resolution calling on all participants in the 1973 Arab-Israeli war to cease fire in the positions they then occupied, and to implement Security Council Resolution 242 (1967).

velayat-e faqih (vilayet-I faqih) The exercise of governmental authority by an Islamic jurist; this principle was incorporated into the constitution of the Islamic Republic of Iran in 1979.

Wahhabism Puritanical Muslim doctrine, established by Muhammad ibn Abd al-Wahhab (1703–1792), now dominant in Saudi Arabia.

West Bank Area of Arab Palestine annexed by Jordan in 1948 and captured by Israel in 1967; partly governed by the Palestine Authority since 1996.

Zionism Movement to create a Jewish national state in Palestine and, since 1948, to maintain Israel as that state.

BRIEF BIOGRAPHICAL REGISTER

Some alternate spellings of main entries appear in parentheses.

Abbas, Mahmud Palestinian prime minister (2003) and president (2005–).

Abdullah King of Saudi Arabia (2005–).

Ahmadinejad, Mahmoud President of Iran (2005–).

Arafat, Yasser Palestinian Arab nationalist, founder of al-Fatah, PLO chairman, and Palestinian Authority president (1996–2004).

Ataturk, Mustafa Kemal Founder and first president (1923–1938) of the Republic of Turkey.

Banna, Hasan al- (Hassan al-Banna) Egyptian social and political reformer, and founder of the Muslim Brotherhood in 1928.

Barak, Ehud Prime minister of Israel (1999–2001).

Begin, Menachem Prime minister of Israel (1977–1983).

bin Laden, Osama (Usama bin Laden) Leader of al-Qaeda and presumed mastermind of the 9/11 (2001) attacks on the United States; originally from Saudi Arabia.

Chalabi, Ahmad Leader in exile of the Iraqi National Congress, who advocated the US invasion of Iraq (2003).

Fahd King of Saudi Arabia (1982–2005).

Faysal King of Saudi Arabia (1964–1975).

Hussein, Saddam (Saddam Husayn) President of Iraq (1979–2003).

ibn Sa'ud (Abd al-Aziz ibn Abd al-Rahman) Arab leader who conquered most of the Arabian peninsula between 1902 and 1930 and ruler of Saudi Arabia (1932–1953).

Khatami, Mohammad President of Iran (1997–2005).

Khomeini, Ayatollah Ruhollah Leader of the Islamic revolution in Iran (1978–1979) and supreme lawmaking authority (1979–1989).

Lawrence, T. E. British intelligence officer who aided the Arab revolt against the Ottomans (1916–1918), and advocate of Arab nationalism; also known as Lawrence of Arabia.

Mohammad Reza Shah Pahlavi Shah of Iran (1941–1979).

Mubarak, Husni (Hosni Mubarak) President of Egypt (1981–).

Muhammad Arab religious leader, born in Mecca and founder of the Islamic *umma*, viewed by Muslims as God's messenger, whose revelations were recorded in the Quran. (d. 632)

Muhammad ibn Abd al-Wahhab Founder of the strict Islamic Wahhabi movement in the eighteenth century.

Nasir, Gamal Abd al- (Gamal Abdel Nasser) Leader of the 1952 Egyptian revolution, later prime minister and then president of Egypt (1954–1970).

Netanyahu, Benjamin Prime minister of Israel (1996–1999).

Peres, Shimon Prime minister of Israel (1984–1986) and acting prime minister (1995–1996).

Rabin, Yitzhak Prime minister of Israel (1974–1977 and 1992–1995).

Sadat, Anwar (al-Sadat) President of Egypt (1970–1981).

Shamir, Yitzakh Prime minister of Israel (1983–1984 and (1986–1992).

Sharon, Ariel Prime minister of Israel (2001–).

Zarqawi, Abu Musab al- Leader of the insurgency against the United States and the Iraqi interim government following the US occupation of Iraq (2003–).

Chronology

All dates are Common Era.

  622 *Hegira* of Muhammad and his followers from Mecca to Medina.

  632 Death of Muhammad.

1096 The First Crusade begins.

1299–1923 Ottoman Empire.

1453 The Ottoman capture of Constantinople ends the Byzantine Empire.

1492 Expulsion of Jews and Muslims from Spain.

1897 World Zionist Organization formed.

1908 Young Turk revolution.

1913 Arab Congress (in Paris) demands equal rights and cultural autonomy for Arabs within the Ottoman Empire.

1914–1919 World War I.

1916 Sykes-Picot Agreement.

1917 Balfour Declaration.

1919 King-Crane Commission.

1920 San Remo agreement gives mandates to Britain in Palestine and Iraq, and to France in Syria and Lebanon.

1921 British name Faysal king of Iraq.

1923 Ottoman sultanate abolished, Turkish Republic declared.

1924 Caliphate abolished.

1932 Iraq becomes first state of the former Ottoman Empire to graduate from mandate status by achieving independence.

1936–1939 Palestinian revolt against British authorities.

1939–1945 World War II.

1941–1979 Reign of Mohammad Reza Shah Pahlavi in Iran.

1945 Arab League formed; United Nations formed.

1948 Israel declares independence as British troops quit Palestine; Arab armies attack but are defeated; most Palestinian Arabs flee.

1954–1970 Presidency of Gamal Abdel Nasser in Egypt.

1964–1975 Reign of King Faysal in Saudi Arabia.

1967 Arab-Israeli War (Six Day War, or June War); Israel occupies the Sinai, Jordan's West Bank, and Syria's Golan heights.

1969 Yasser Arafat elected PLO head.

1970–1971 Jordan crushes PLO rebellion.

1970–1981 Presidency of Anwar Sadat in Egypt.

1973 Arab-Israeli war (Yom Kippur War). Syria and Egypt coordinate a surprise attack against Israel; after an initial setback, Israel penetrates Syria and crosses the Suez Canal into Egypt.

1978 Israel invades southern Lebanon; Camp David accords negotiated by US president Jimmy Carter, Israeli prime minister Menachem Begin, and Egyptian president Anwar Sadat.

1979 Iranian revolution culminates; Shah Reza Pahlavi goes into exile; Ayatollah Khomeini returns to Iran and proclaims Islamic Republic; Iranian Revolutionary Guards storm the US embassy in Teheran and take 90 people hostage (52 Americans remain hostages for 444 days). Egypt and Israel sign peace treaty, causing other Arab states to break ties with Egypt. Saddam Hussein officially takes power in Iraq.

1980–1988 Iran-Iraq War.

1981 Anwar Sadat, president of Egypt, assassinated. Israel bombs Iraqi nuclear reactor, annexes Golan Heights. Saudi Arabia, Kuwait, Bahrain, Qatar, the United Arab Emirates, and Oman form the Gulf Cooperation Council (GCC).

1982 Israel returns Sinai to Egypt; invades Lebanon and drives back Syrian and PLO forces. PLO moves headquarters from Beirut to Tunis.

1986 Iran-Contra affair exposed.

1987 Palestinian *intifada* breaks out in Gaza and West Bank, protesting Israeli occupation.

1988 Palestine National Council declares independent state of Palestine; PLO formally renounces terrorism and recognizes Israel's right to exist.

1990 Iraq invades Kuwait.

1991 Gulf War: US-led coalition hastens Iraqi withdrawal from Kuwait; UN Security Council imposes economic sanctions on Iraq. Israel and Arab countries begin peace negotiations in Madrid.

1993 Oslo Accords implemented as PLO and Israeli representatives sign Declaration of Principles on White House lawn, offering autonomy to Palestinians in Gaza and Jericho and eventually to the rest of the West Bank following Israeli troop withdrawals.

1994 Jordanian-Israeli peace treaty.

1995 Oslo II: further Palestinian-Israeli agreements on phased Israeli troop withdrawals. Prime Minister Yitzakh Rabin of Israel assassinated.

1997 Mohammad Khatami elected president of Iran.

2000 Camp David II: Ehud Barak of Israel and Yasser Arafat of the PLO fail to reach final peace settlement. Ariel Sharon's visit to Temple Mount sparks a new Palestinian uprising, the Second Intifada (or al-Aqsa Intifada).

2001 9/11: Islamist militants hijack four American passenger jets and fly two of them into the World Trade Center and another into the Pentagon, killing over 2,700 people; United States leads coalition invading Afghanistan to overthrow the Taliban regime harboring Osama bin Laden, who evades capture.

2002 Pursuing his "war on terrorism" in the wake of 9/11, President George W. Bush identifies Iran, Iraq, and North Korea as an "axis of evil."

2003 United States and United Kingdom invade Iraq to overthrow Saddam Hussein but fail to find weapons of mass destruction (WMD) or credible Iraqi links to al-Qaeda; US troops capture Saddam Hussein. With support from the United Kingdom, European Union, and United Nations, President Bush announces a "road map" for resumption of Israeli-Palestinian negotiations.

2004 United States transfers "sovereignty" to Iraq's interim government. Arafat dies.

2005 Palestinians choose Mahmud Abbas to succeed Arafat. Sunnis boycott Iraqi elections; Shiites and Kurds form new Iraqi government. Mahmoud Ahmadinejad elected president of Iran; United States and European Union pressure Iran to end its nuclear power research program. King Fahd of Saudi Arabia dies and is succeeded by his half-brother Abdullah.

NOTES

Notes to Chapter 4

1. Saad Eddin Ibrahim, "Domestic Developments in Egypt," in *The Middle East: Ten Years After Camp David,* ed. William B. Quandt (Washington, D.C.: Brookings Institution, 1988), p. 60.

2. William B. Quandt, "Introduction," in *The Middle East: Ten Years After Camp David,* ed. William B. Quandt (Washington, D.C.: Brookings Institution, 1988), p. 5.

Note to Chapter 11

1. Gary Sick, "The United States in the Persian Gulf: From Twin Pillars to Dual Containment," in *The Middle East and the United States: A Historical and Political Reassessment,* 2nd edition, ed. David W. Lesch (Boulder: Westview Press, 1999), p. 282.

Notes to Chapter 13

1. US Army Third Infantry Division, After Action Report.

2. Colin Powell, interview, *New York Times,* March 29, 2003.

3. Suzanne Freeman, "Rebuilding Iraq: Who Decides?" *Scholastic News;* April 2003.

4. Mark Fineman, Warren Vieth, and Robin Wright, "Dissolving Iraqi Army Was Costly Choice," *Los Angeles Times,* August 24, 2003.

5. Ambassador L. Paul Bremer, interview, Department of Defense, July 24, 2003.

6. Briefing by Defense Secretary Donald H. Rumsfeld, US Department of Defense, September 5, 2003.

7. Cited in a briefing by Defense Secretary Donald H. Rumsfeld, US Department of Defense, August 21, 2003.

8. Briefing with Defense Secretary Donald H. Rumsfeld, US Department of Defense, July 24, 2003.

9. Briefing by General John Abizaid, US Department of Defense, August 21, 2003.

10. Deputy Secretary of Defense Paul Wolfowitz to the Senate Foreign Relations Committee, July 29, 2003.

11. Anonymous interview with the author on August 5, 2004.

12. Evan Thomas and Mark Hosenball, "The Rise and Fall of Chalabi: Bush's Mr. Wrong," *Newsweek,* May 31, 2004, 22.

13. Craig S. Smith, "Cleric in Iran Says Shiites Must Act," *New York Times,* April 26, 2003, A1.

14. Radio Free Europe/Radio Liberty, November 13, 2003.

15. Scott Wilson, "Bremer Adopts Firmer Tone," *Washington Post,* May 26, 2003, A13.

Note to Chapter 15

1. *The Basic Law of Government of the Kingdom of Saudi Arabia,* trans., Foreign Broadcast information Service (FBIS), London, March 1, 1992.

Notes to Chapter 16

1. This item appeared in the newspaper *al-Riyadh* in June 2002; a translation was posted on the Web site of the English-language *Arab News,* http://www.arabnews.com.

2. Translated by *Arab News,* posted at http://www.arabnews.com.

3. Jack Shafer, "The PowerPoint That Rocked the Pentagon," *Slate,* August 7, 2002, http://www.slate.msn.com.

4. Translated by the Foreign Broadcast Information Service, August 19, 2002.

5. For a useful explanation of the issues in this case, see Christopher H. Johnson, "Terrorism as Mass Tort: Responsibility for 9/11"; Johnson is a Washington lawyer who practiced in Saudi Arabia for several years. Available at http://www.arabialink.com/SAF/Newsletters/SAF_Essay_03.htm.

6. Sulaiman al-Hattlan, "Homegrown Fanatics," *New York Times,* May 15, 2003.

7. See the Reuters news agency account by Carol Giacomo, June 12, 2003.

8. Available at http://www.saudiembassy.net.

9. Robert Jordan, *Arab News* (Jeddah), September 11, 2002.

10. Qualls sent his report to the National Association for Business Economics, which posted it on the Internet at http://www.nabe.com/publib/qualls.html.

11. See http://www.saudiembassy.net/pressrelease/releases/03-pr–0513-abdullah-terrorism.htm.

Notes to Chapter 18

1. Faisal, quoted in Edward Mortimer, *Faith and Power: The Politics of Islam* (New York, Vintage Books, 1982), p. 232 n.

2. Sayyid Qutb, quoted in Fouad Ajami, "In the Pharaoh's Shadow: Religion and Authority in Egypt," in *Islam in the Political Process,* ed. James P. Piscatori (Cambridge: Cambridge University Press, 1983), p. 25.

3. Sayyid Qutb, *Milestones* (Indianapolis: American Trust Publications, 1990), p. 50. The same work, originally published in Arabic as *Maalim fil Tariq,* is sometimes referred to as "Signposts" or "Signposts on the Road."

Notes to Chapter 19

1. Graduation speech at the U.S. Naval Academy, Annapolis, Maryland, May 30, 1990.

2. Muhammad M. al-Fahham, "The Restoration of Jerusalem," in *The Fifth Conference of the Academy of Islamic Research* (Cairo: Government Printing Office, 1971), p. 53.

3. Rachid Ghannouchi, "Islam and the West: Realities and Prospects," *Inquiry* 2(7)

(March/April 1993), p. 45.

4. "The Great Betrayal," *Al-Mashriq* (January-February 1991), p. 9.

5. Muhammad Husayn Fadlallah, *Ru'a wa Mawaqif,* volume 3 (Beirut: al-Markaz al-Islami al-Thaqafi, 1997), p. 10.

6. Martin Indyk, "Address to the Soref Symposium, The Washington Institute, May 18, 1993," p. 3

Notes to Chapter 20

1. Reuel Marc Gerecht, "Forget the 'Arab Street,'" *Weekly Standard,* April 1, 2002, also available at www.aei.org/include/news/newsID15645/mews_detail.asp.

2. Available at www.aipac.org/documents/realner060903.html.

3. Available at http://www.aipac.org/timeline2.

4. "The US and Israel: Partners in Peace," available at www.aipac.org.

5. Condoleeza Rice, speech to AIPAC, March 31, 2003.

6. Ibid.

7. Available at http://www.fas.org/irp/congress/2002_rpt/911rept.pdf.

8. Bush, public statement, June 24, 2002.

9. Ehud Barak, press conference, Alexandria, Egypt, July 9, 1999.

10. Ibid.

11. Israeli government, "Basic Guidelines," July 1999.

12. Ibid. Judea and Samaria are the Israeli names for the occupied West Bank.

13. Robert Malley and Hussein Agha, "The Last Negotiation: How to End the Middle East Peace Process," *Foreign Affairs* (May/June 2002).

14. Ehud Barak, comments before leaving for the Camp David talks, July 10, 2000.

15. President Clinton, statement after the Camp David Talks, July 25, 2000.

16. Stephen Zunes, "Between the Arms Race and Political Lobbyists: How Pax Americana Threatens Middle East Peace," in *Structural Flaws in the Middle East Peace Process,* ed. J. W. Wright Jr. (Basingstoke, U.K.: Palgrave, 2002), 25.

17. Ibid., 27.

18. Ibid., 28.

19. Ehud Barak, statement after the Camp David talks, July 25, 2000.

20. Palestine Liberation Organization, Negotiation Affairs Department, "Camp David Peace Proposal of July 2000: Frequently Asked Questions," available at http://www.nadplo.org/eye/news38.html.

21. Ibid.

22. Ibid.

23. Ibid.

Credits and Acknowledgments

Chapter 1 Adapted from pages 1–4 of Chapter 1 ("Introduction") by David E. Long and Bernard Reich, in David E. Long and Bernard Reich, *The Government and Politics of the Middle East and North Africa*, Fourth Edition (2002, Westview Press). MAP 1.1 from Map 1–2 (page 9) of Colbert C. Held, *Middle East Patterns: Places, Peoples, and Politics*, Fourth Edition (2006, Westview Press).

Chapter 2 Adapted from pages 94–120 of Colbert C. Held, *Middle East Patterns: Places, Peoples, and Politics*, Fourth Edition (2006, Westview Press).

Chapter 3 Adapted from pages 203–221 of Arthur Goldschmidt Jr. and Lawrence Davidson, *A Concise History of the Middle East*, Eighth Edition (2006, Westview Press).

Chapter 4 Adapted from pages 82–92 of David W. Lesch, *1979: The Year that Shaped the Modern Middle East* (2001, Westview Press).

Chapter 5 Adapted from pages 315–339 of Chapter 12 ("The Palestinians") by Ann Mosely Lesch, in David E. Long and Bernard Reich, eds., *The Government and Politics of the Middle East and North Africa,* Fourth Edition (2002, Westview Press).

Chapter 6 Adapted from pages 233–251 of Chapter 14 ("The United States and Israel: The Nature of a Special Relationship") by Bernard Reich, in David W. Lesch, ed., *The Middle East and the United States: A Historical and Political Reassessment,* Third Edition (2003, Westview Press).

Chapter 7 Adapted from pages 499–517 of William L. Cleveland, *A History of the Modern Middle East*, Third Edition (2004, Westview Press).

Chapter 8 Adapted from pages 241–262 of Calvin Goldscheider, *Israel's Changing Society: Population, Ethnicity, and Development,* Second Edition (2002, Westview Press).

Chapter 9 Adapted from pages 297–317 of Samih K. Farsoun with Christina E. Zacharia, *Palestine and the Palestinians* (1997, Westview Press).

Chapter 10 Adapted from pages 8–19 of Phebe Marr, *The Modern History of Iraq*, Second Edition (2004, Westview Press).

Chapter 11 Adapted from pages 57–81 of David W. Lesch, *1979: The Year that Shaped the Modern Middle East* (2001, Westview Press).

Chapter 12 Adapted from pages 187–222 of Anthony Shadid, *Legacy of the Prophet: Despots, Democrats, and the New Politics of Islam* (2001, Westview Press).

Chapter 13 Adapted from pages 133–141 and 155–168 of David L. Phillips, *Losing Iraq: Inside the Postwar Reconstruction Fiasco* (2005, Westview Press).

Chapter 14 Adapted from pages 131–166 of Shibley Telhami, *The Stakes: America in the Middle East: The Consequences of Power and the Choice for Peace* (2002, Westview Press).

Chapter 15 Adapted from pages 72–101 of Chapter 4 ("Kingdom of Saudi Arabia") by David E. Long, in David E. Long and Bernard Reich, *The Government and Politics of the Middle East and North Africa*, Fourth Edition (2002, Westview Press).

Chapter 16 Adapted from pages 325–347 of Thomas W. Lippman, *Inside the Mirage: America's Fragile Partnership with Saudi Arabia* (2004, Westview Press).

Chapter 17 Adapted from pages 185–200 of Arthur Goldschmidt Jr., *Modern Egypt: The Formation of a Nation State*, Second Edition (2004, Westview Press).

Chapter 18 Adapted from pages 73–93 of Mark Huband, *Warriors of the Prophet: The Struggle for Islam* (1998, Westview Press).

Chapter 19 Adapted from pages 467–490 of Chapter 27 ("Islamist Perceptions of U.S. Policy in the Middle East") by Yvonne Yazbeck Haddad, in David W. Lesch, ed., *The Middle East and the United States: A Historical and Political Reassessment*, Third Edition (2003, Westview Press).

Chapter 20 Adapted from pages 247–287 of Mark Huband, *Brutal Truths, Fragile Myths: Power Politics and Western Adventurism in the Arab World* (2004, Westview Press).

Chapter 21 Portions of Chapter 21 appeared previously in modified form in "Unintended Consequences (excerpt)" by Shibley Telhami from the August 15, 2005 issue of *The Nation*. Reprinted with permission from the August 15, 2005 issue of *The Nation*. For subscription information, call 1-800-333-8536. Portions of each week's Nation magazine can be accessed at http://www.thenation.com.

Selected Bibliography Adapted from pages 555–578 of William L. Cleveland, *A History of the Modern Middle East*, Third Edition (2004, Westview Press).

INDEX